HQ
2039
U6
E93
1993

The Experts book of
hints, tips, &
everyday wisdom.

The Experts Book of
HINTS, TIPS & EVERYDAY WISDOM

From Leading Authorities . . .
More Than 1,000 Problem–Solving Secrets
for Easier, Healthier Living

Rodale Press, Emmaus, Pennsylvania

If you have any questions or comments concerning this book, please write:
Rodale Press
Book Readers' Service
33 East Minor Street
Emmaus, PA 18098

Library of Congress Cataloging-in-Publication Data

The Experts book of hints, tips, and everyday wisdom : from leading
    authorities...more than 1,000 problem-solving secrets for easier,
    healthier living / edited by Edward Claflin
            p.   cm.
    Includes index.
    ISBN 0–87596–150–9 : hardcover
    1. Life skills guides—United States.   I. Claflin, Edward.
HQ2039.U6E93   1993
646.7′9—dc20   92–23624
                                                              CIP

Distributed in the book trade by St. Martin's Press

2 4 6 8 10 9 7 5 3 1   hardcover

Our Mission

We publish books that empower people's lives.

RODALE BOOKS

CONTRIBUTORS

Editor: Edward Claflin
Executive Editor: Debora Tkac
Senior Editor: Alice Feinstein
Contributing Writers:
     Michael Castleman (Health)
     Terry Krautwurst (Yard and Garden)
     Jacquelyn Peake (Cleaning)
     David Schoonmaker (Car Care)
     Janet Groene and Gordon Groene (Home Maintenance and Repair)
     Judy Serra Lieberman (Kitchen and Cooking)
     Kathleen Martin Beans (Money Management)
     Eva Shaw (Beauty and Grooming)
     Michael Hofferber (Country Living)
     Joan Price (Exercise and Sports)
     Tina Cantelmi Bradford (Clothing)
     Sid Kirchheimer (Pets)
     Arjay Morgan (Personal Safety and Security)
     Joseph E. Brown (Traveling the U.S.A.)
     Bea Tusiani (Conservation and Recycling)
Research Chief: Ann Gossy
Research Staff:
     Christine Dreisbach
     Melissa Dunford
     Anne Imhoff
     Karen Lombardi
     Paris Mihely-Muchanic
     Debbie Pedron
     Bernadette Sukley
Production Editor: Jane Sherman
Book Designer: Rhoda Krammer, *Plus Graphics*
Cover Design and Illustration: Greg Imhoff
Illustrators: Sally Onopa and Susan Rosenberger
Copy Editor: Ellen Pahl
Office Staff:
     Roberta Mulliner
     Julie Kehs
     Mary Lou Stephen

Notice

The information in this book has been carefully researched, and all efforts have been made to ensure accuracy. Rodale Press, Inc., assumes no responsibility for any injuries suffered or damages or losses incurred during or as a result of following this information. All information should be carefully studied and clearly understood before taking any action based on the advice presented in this book.

Information related to health, exercise, and sports is intended for reference only, not for medical guidance. This is not a manual for self-treatment, nor a substitute for any treatment prescribed by your doctor. If you suspect that you have a medical problem, please seek competent medical care.

CONTENTS

Chapter 6 Kitchen and Cooking:
Skills and Tools for Tasty Cuisine   158

Chapter 7 Money Management:
What You Save Is What You Win   181

Chapter 8 Beauty and Grooming:
The Skinny on Skin, Nails, Hair,
and the Package That Says You   204

Chapter 13 Personal Safety and Security:
Take Steps to Protect Yourself 320

Chapter 14 Traveling the U.S.A.:
Better Bargains on Visits and Vistas 336

Chapter 15 Conservation and Recycling:
Doing Your Part to Save the Earth 365

PREFACE

A Fountain of Know-How

"There's *got* to be a better way."

Ever said that to yourself?

Chances are, you're right. Whether you're solving everyday problems around your home, kitchen, and garden; figuring out ways to be safer, happier, and healthier; caring for cars, pets, kids, and possessions; planning to save more, spend less, and prepare for the future; chances are you're *always* looking for ways to do things better. Trouble is, how do you find them? Where do you look them up? Who do you call? How do you get the information you need when you need it? Who *are* the experts, anyway?

Well, we've got good news...and more good news, because that incredibly helpful everyday knowledge is now at your fingertips. In fact, these pages are jam-packed with more than 1,000 snippets of the kind of practical advice that's likely to make your whole life easier. Yes, Grandpa and Grandma's best hints are here—and so are the newfangled tactics of fast-paced, microwave-age, silicon-chip-driven, recycle-centered living.

Not only that, this practical wisdom comes straight from the sources. We cast a wide net, calling on doctors, engineers, woodsmen, farmers, bankers, housekeepers, homemakers, gardeners, groundsmen, curators, collectors, professors, painters, plumbers, pilots, realtors, dog trainers, meteorologists, runners, mechanics, models, hairdressers, accountants, sheriffs, chefs, chemists, and many more, all across the nation, to find out what they know. And although we had many questions, they all boiled down to one: "Do *you* know a better way?"

The results? Well, pull up a chair, turn a few pages, and you'll soon find...

High-return tips on how to multiply your savings and cut your spending. Sure-fire hints on stress, stretching, and aerobics. The lowdown on pet care and pet-training tactics. Wise words on country living, from treating an ax handle to painting the side of a barn.

Look in chapter 8, "Beauty and Grooming," if you want free consultation from hairdressers and beauticians in the look-good capital of the world (Hollywood). Want to house a toad in your garden to control bugs and grubs? Turn to chapter 2, "Yard and Garden." Need to figure out a better way to store newspapers for recycling? In "Conservation and Recycling" (chapter 15), heed the advice of an expert architect who specializes in kitchen design. In chapter 5, "Home Maintenance and Repair," you'll find hints from technologists involved in new-product creation and from do-it-yourselfers with tried-

and-true methods. The president of Harry's Body and Fender in Asheville, North Carolina, tells the best ways to keep your car rust-free in "Car Care" (chapter 4). And if you want to save significant dollars on your next plane flight, just listen to the bargain-savvy experts in chapter 14, "Traveling the U.S.A."

There's a deputy sheriff in "Personal Safety and Security" (chapter 13) with some great advice on home security, as well as a leading meteorologist with a caution or two about lightning storms. From the people who make comforters, crystal, and silver, find out how to clean these treasured items in chapter 3, "Cleaning." Or turn to chapter 6, "Kitchen and Cooking" for valuable advice on dinner-party planning (from the former chef at the Waldorf-Astoria hotel) and the inside scoop on crisper crust (from the head of Peter Kump's New York Cooking School). Want to cure hiccups? Assess your stress? Beat the winter blues? Sleep more soundly? Just turn to chapter 1, "Health," which is full of advice on remedies, cures, and prevention, all suggested by leading medical authorities around the country.

So, whether you're faced with a knotty problem, feeling some aches and pains, scratching your head about what to do next, or just browsing for ideas to make tomorrow easier, here's a cornucopia of know-how to help you solve every problem.

In fact, if the house is burning down, and you have time to grab only one item, here's the sum of advice from our experts:

Save this book!

Edward Claflin
Editor

CHAPTER 1

Health

You're the Doc, Too!

The late comedian Sam Levinson once quipped, "One time I got so sick, I *almost* went to the doctor." Of course, we can't promise that this collection of practical, do-it-yourself health tips will keep you forever from darkening your doctor's door. But we're confident that it will save you a good deal of time, money, physical discomfort, and emotional aggravation.

Doctors and other health authorities get sick and injured just like the rest of us. Instead of sitting around waiting rooms, whenever possible they treat themselves using the self-care shortcuts they've learned through years of study and experience. We asked them to share their most useful self-care secrets, and they did—more than 100 effective self-treatment techniques. Of course, some health problems require prompt professional attention, so we've included a special section: "When to Consult a Doctor" starting on page 28.

You can also *prevent* many everyday health problems. Prevention is almost always faster, cheaper, and less trouble than treatment. And quite often, prevention begins with a simple phone call, self-exam, or screening test. In recent years, physicians have become increasingly committed to prevention and to the simple steps that can make a world of difference to your health and well-being. So we've also included the preventive health tips physicians consider most important.

Of course, a key part of medical self-care is understanding when you really *should* consult a physician. But many everyday health concerns can be prevented or handled effectively at home—*if* you have the latest practical information from the experts. And here it is!

Relief from Pains and Sprains

The Yoga Prescription for Back Pain

"Yoga doesn't cure every case of low back pain," says Mary Schatz, M.D., a pathologist at Centennial Medical Center in Nashville, Tennessee, and author of *Back Care Basics*, "but it helps a surprisingly large number of people."

Sixteen years ago, Dr. Schatz suffered terrible chronic back pain. She tried everything: bed rest, pain medication, physical therapy, you name it. She was considering back surgery when a friend suggested that she try yoga.

"It was amazingly therapeutic," she explains. "I can honestly say that yoga cured my back and changed my life."

If you want to try yoga, begin working one-on-one with an instructor trained in back care, or work through the program in Dr. Schatz's book *Back Care Basics*. From there you may want to take one of the many yoga classes that are available around the United States, or try an instructional home video.

RICE in a Trice

RICE is an acronym for rest, ice, compression, and elevation. "Forget the locker-room saying, 'No pain, no gain.' It's stupid," says Ben E. Benjamin, Ph.D., director of the Muscular Therapy Institute in Cambridge, Massachusetts. "If it hurts, stop doing whatever causes the pain."

RICE treatment should begin as quickly as possible after any joint injury, says exercise physiologist and physical therapist Scott Hasson, Ed.D., associate professor of physical therapy at Texas Women's University in Houston. "In addition to resting the injured part," he says, "wrap a few ice cubes in a clean cloth to make an ice pack and place the ice pack in a plastic bag to prevent dripping. Apply the ice pack for 20 minutes, remove it for 20 minutes, and repeat this for several hours. For compression, wrap the injured part in an elastic bandage. And elevate it above the level of the heart."

If the injury causes no skin discoloration, then use aspirin or ibuprofen because they relieve both pain and inflammation. However, if the injured area turns black and blue, that indicates bleeding under the skin surface.

"Don't use aspirin or ibuprofen," Dr. Hasson says, "because they can increase bleeding. Just take acetaminophen, which treats only pain."

"Don't treat joint injuries with heat," Dr. Hasson says. "Heat feels good at first, but it increases blood flow to the area, and that extra fluid causes additional pain."

Stretch, Don't Kvetch

"As quickly as possible after a joint injury, start moving the joint through as much of its range of motion as you comfortably can," Dr. Hasson says. Keep stretching it gently and frequently, but not to the point of pain.

Muscle-Sore No More

Put the Clamps on Muscle Cramps

To prevent muscle cramps, Dr. Scott Hasson, Ed.D., associate professor of physical therapy at Texas Women's University in Houston recommends "hydro-loading and electrolyte loading," meaning drink plenty of fluids high in electrolytes and eat balanced meals that include vegetables and fruits.

Cramping is usually the result of dehydration with a loss of certain minerals known as electrolytes, among them potassium. Drinking plenty of water before, during, and after workouts prevents the dehydration that causes cramping. And bananas are a rich source of potassium. "You might also drink athletic fluids—for example, Gatorade," Dr. Hasson says. "It has both water and electrolytes."

Cramping also suggests muscle overuse. "Decrease the intensity of your workouts and focus on conditioning the muscles prone to cramping," Dr. Hasson advises.

Sore No More the Day After

"You can prevent most delayed muscle soreness by taking one standard dose of ibuprofen before and after you exercise," Dr. Hasson says.

Muscle soreness the day after is very common among "weekend warriors," people who are inactive during the work week and overactive on weekends. Soreness is caused by microtrauma to unconditioned muscle tissue, leading to inflammation and fluid accumulation (edema), which cause the all-too-familiar soreness. Ibuprofen before exercise helps prevent the inflammation.

If you develop soreness the day after, Dr. Hasson suggests combining ibuprofen with rapid extension exercises. "If your calves feel sore," he says, "sit on a table so your feet don't touch the floor, and move your ankles up and down rapidly. If your arms feel sore, flex and extend them rapidly. The rapid movement decreases the edema—and the soreness."

Caution: Ibuprofen is not recommended if you have black-and-blue bruises, as it may increase bleeding in the bruised area.

A Pound of Prevention

Measure Your Pressure

"Everyone should have a blood pressure check at least annually," says Margo Denke, M.D., a member of the nutrition committee of the American Heart Association and assistant professor in the Department of Internal Medicine and Center for Human Nutrition at the University of Texas Southwestern Medical Center in Dallas.

Blood pressure is as important to health as oil pressure is to a car. High blood pressure (hypertension) is a key risk factor for both heart disease and stroke, which together account for almost half of all U.S. deaths.

These days you don't have to visit a doctor to have your blood pressure checked. Coin-operated units have appeared in malls and health clubs, and home blood pressure monitors are available for those who need close monitoring. If your diastolic blood pressure is 90 or above, or your systolic pressure is 140 or above, you may be diagnosed as having hypertension. So be sure to consult a doctor if your blood pressure reading is 140/90 or above.

When was the last time *you* had your pressure checked?

Be Heart Smart: Check Your Cholesterol

"If you don't know your total blood cholesterol level, get it checked," Dr. Denke advises.

Like blood pressure, cholesterol is another important risk factor for heart disease and some strokes.

"Cholesterol should be less than 200 mg/dl [milligrams per deciliter]," Dr. Denke says. "If it's below 200, simply have it checked every other year. If it's from 200 to 240, have it checked annually, and use lifestyle approaches to bring it down—a low-fat diet and regular moderate exercise. And if it's above 240, you may need cholesterol-lowering medication in addition to a low-fat diet and exercise."

For Women: A Cervical Smear Every Year

"Every sexually active woman or woman over 18 should have a Pap test annually to check for cervical cancer," says Dorothy Barbo, M.D., professor of obstetrics and gynecology and director of the Center for Women's Health at the University of New Mexico in Albuquerque. "Cervical health can change rapidly, so I tell all my patients to have this screening test every year."

Annual Pap tests became the standard recommendation shortly after George Papanicolau, for whom the test is named, developed it more than 30 years ago. But during the mid-1980s some medical organizations said women with normal Paps could have the test as infrequently as once every three years. This provoked an outcry from women's health advocates, and today annual Paps are once again recommended, especially for women who have had multiple sex partners.

"The more partners a woman has, the more likely she is to develop pre-cancerous cervical changes," Dr. Barbo explains.

Cervical cancer is usually curable—*if* it's diagnosed early.

Mammograms Are a Must!

"Every woman should have an annual professional breast exam and regular mammograms," says Daniel W. Nixon, M.D., American Cancer Society (ACS) vice president for detection and treatment.

The ACS says women should have a baseline mammogram sometime from age 35 to 40, a mammogram every other year from age 40 to 49, and an annual mammogram after age 50. Mammograms can detect breast tumors

---

YOUR PERSONAL MEDICAL HISTORY

"Compile a personal medical record and a family medical history," says University of California assistant clinical professor Anne Simons, M.D. "Update them regularly, for example, every January as a New Year's resolution. Then it will be up to date when you need it."

Your own medical history is one of most important clues to your health. Record and date all your immunizations, significant injuries and illnesses, hospitalizations, and medical treatments; and keep a list of the drugs you take. When you visit a physician, take your medical record with you.

Your family medical history can also have a major impact on your health. Many significant illnesses run in families—heart disease, high blood pressure, diabetes, several cancers, and some mental health problems. When you visit a physician, be sure to mention your family history. It might affect decisions about medical tests and examinations you should have.

too small to feel, allowing the earliest possible diagnosis and greatest success in treatment.

If a woman's mother or sister has had premenopausal breast cancer, however, she should mention her family history to her physician, who might advise earlier or more frequent mammograms.

Care for Your Colon

"Starting at age 40, men and women should have an annual digital rectal exam to check for colon cancer," Dr. Nixon says. "And after age 50, they should have a test for hidden—occult—blood in their stool yearly and sigmoidoscopy every three to five years."

Colorectal cancer screening is not exactly pleasant. The occult blood test involves using toilet paper or a wooden spatula to place a stool sample on a slide. And the digital rectal exam and sigmoidoscopy are internal exams. Are these tests worth it? You bet. Colorectal cancer is the nation's leading cancer killer among nonsmokers—more than 150,000 new diagnoses a year and 60,000 deaths. Colorectal cancer screening may not be fun, but it just might save your life.

A Self-Exam for Every Man

"Men from puberty onward should examine their testicles once a month to check for hard, painless lumps that might be testicular cancer," Dr. Nixon says. "In recent years there have been major strides in testicular cancer treatment—*if* it's caught early."

Testicular self-exam is not difficult. In the shower, simply roll each testicle in your fingers, squeezing it slightly. If you detect a small, hard lump or swelling, you should contact a urologist for a more thorough exam.

For more information, the ACS publishes a how-to pamphlet. Call the local office of the American Cancer Society to obtain a copy.

Take a Tour around Your Skin

"With the increasing rate of malignant melanoma [skin cancer], monthly skin self-exams are a very good idea," Dr. Nixon says, "especially for those with fair skin or a family history of this disease."

Malignant melanoma usually begins with a change in a mole. The mole might grow larger, bleed, or crust over. Get to know your moles as you examine yourself. That way you'll be in a better position to notice any changes.

If You Have Diabetes—Check Your Feet!

"If you have diabetes, examine your feet regularly for cuts, scrapes, blood, and loss of sensation—and make sure your doctor does, too," says

Daniel Lorber, M.D., an associate clinical professor of medicine at Albert Einstein College of Medicine in New York City, and medical director of the Diabetes Control Foundation in Flushing, New York. "If people with diabetes were more aware of their feet, they might be able to prevent the diabetic foot infections that sometimes necessitate amputation."

Diabetes is a serious disease that requires regular professional care. But Dr. Lorber says many physicians do not sufficiently encourage good diabetic foot care. Diabetes often damages the nerves of the feet, and people with diabetes lose the ability to sense foot pain from cuts, scrapes, and pebbles in their shoes. If the cuts become infected, the person often doesn't notice because there's no pain. But the unnoticed infection can spread and the foot may develop gangrene.

"Any infection in a diabetic foot is a limb-threatening—and possibly life-threatening—medical emergency," Dr. Lorber says. "It's not difficult for people with diabetes to check their feet. They should do it regularly and insist that their doctor check them at every visit."

Curing Constipation, Diarrhea, and Heartburn

Bulk Up

"A good way to prevent constipation," says James A. Duke, Ph.D., an economic botanist and medicinal plant expert with the U.S. Department of Agriculture (USDA) in Beltsville, Maryland, "is to eat a high-fiber diet." High-fiber foods include cooked pearl barley, dried pears, and many kinds of peas and beans including chickpeas, kidney beans, and refried beans.

Another bulk-up suggestion from Dr. Duke: "If you need some extra help, take a few tablespoons of psyllium seed every day."

If psyllium (SILL-*ee-um*) seed doesn't ring a bell, Metamucil might. Metamucil's main ingredient is this tiny seed. In the intestine, it absorbs water and swells, adding bulk to the stool—and for constipation sufferers, the bulkier the better. Compared with dense stools, the bulkier kind exert more pressure against the colon wall. This pressure helps trigger the wavelike muscle contractions (peristalsis) we experience as "the urge."

Psyllium seed is available at most health food stores. Metamucil is available at drugstores and many supermarkets.

Caution: When you take psyllium seed, be sure to drink plenty of water. Otherwise it won't swell up, and may in fact plug you up more. And be careful not to inhale the tiny seeds. That might trigger an allergic reaction, Dr. Duke warns.

FROM CONSTIPATION TO OTHER ANNOYANCES

Preventing constipation, one of the nation's leading medical annoyances, also helps prevent two others—hemorrhoids and flatulence. Anne B. Simons, M.D., an assistant clinical professor of family and community medicine at the University of California's San Francisco Medical Center, explains that straining to defecate, a common occurrence among those with chronic constipation, contributes to the formation of hemorrhoids. And the longer food remains backed up in the intestines, the more likely it is to ferment, causing gas.

Have a Java—Or Hot Water

"Some people find that a morning cup of coffee has a laxative effect," says gastroenterologist Kenneth Klein, M.D., a research associate professor of medicine at the University of North Carolina School of Medicine in Chapel Hill. "Perhaps it's the caffeine, in which case other caffeinated beverages might also help: tea, cocoa, and cola drinks. But maybe it's the heat. For some people, plain hot water works just as well."

To Halt the Runs

"At the first sign of diarrhea, start sipping an electrolyte-replacement fluid like Gatorade," says Anne B. Simons, M.D., a family practitioner and assistant clinical professor of family and community medicine at the University of California's San Francisco Medical Center.

Many diarrhea sufferers stop drinking fluids in the belief that they contribute to this watery problem. But increasing your fluid intake is very important. The major hazard of diarrhea is water loss (dehydration).

The body is mostly water. The function of the colon is to reabsorb 2 to 4 quarts of water a day from solid wastes. Diarrhea disrupts this process, resulting in excessive fluid loss in watery stools, and possibly dehydration, a particular problem for infants, children, and the elderly.

Diarrhea-related water loss also depletes the body of certain minerals (electrolytes). Gatorade contains these minerals in addition to water. Bouillon and other clear broths are also helpful.

"But don't give Gatorade to infants," Dr. Simons says. "Instead, give other electrolyte-rich—but less concentrated—fluids, sold under such brand names as Pedialyte, Infalyte, and Lytren. They're available at pharmacies."

BRAT May Help Diarrhea

"The BRAT diet—bananas, rice, applesauce, and toast—is binding and helps treat diarrhea," Dr. Simons says.

It's often difficult to pinpoint the cause of common everyday diarrhea. Many cases are viral, particularly in children. Sometimes combinations of foods, drugs, and stress precipitate it—for example, too much pizza and coffee the night before final exams. Sometimes it's related to travel—not a full-blown case of *turista*, but frequently when people travel, even within the United States, they react poorly to the local water supply.

If the BRAT diet and fluids don't resolve diarrhea within a few days, consult a physician, who can evaluate other possible causes: infections, intestinal parasites, drug side effects, or lactose intolerance, an inability to digest dairy products.

A New-Meal Approach to Heartburn

"You can often prevent heartburn by changing what you eat and how you eat it," says the University of North Carolina's Dr. Kenneth Klein.

Heartburn has nothing to do with the heart. It results when the muscular opening into the stomach (the lower esophageal sphincter or LES) does not close properly, and stomach acid washes up (refluxes) into the food tube (the esophagus).

Foods that may impair the LES include: high-fat items, alcohol, chocolate, and coffee—even decaf, Dr. Klein says. In addition, large meals are more likely to cause problems than smaller ones.

Dr. Klein also recommends making mealtime a time of relaxation, not rushing. And don't wolf your food, or eat on the run or shortly before bedtime. Eat more slowly, sitting down, and chew thoroughly.

Soothing Posterior Problems

Hazel to the Rescue

"For the itching, burning, and discomfort of hemorrhoids," Dr. Kenneth Klein, M.D., a gastroenterologist at the University of North Carolina, says, "it often helps to wipe with toilet tissue, a cotton ball, or a soft cloth dipped in witch hazel."

Witch hazel is an over-the-counter astringent that cools and comforts. It is sold at pharmacies and at some supermarkets. It's also a major ingredient in Tucks pads—but you can save money by simply buying witch hazel and cotton balls.

A Tip on TP

"For anal itching, this may sound crazy, but stop using toilet paper," says Laura-Mae Baldwin, M.D., an assistant professor of medicine at the University of Washington School of Medicine in Seattle.

People often think they itch because of poor personal hygiene, Dr. Baldwin says, so they wash and wipe more. In fact, the cause is often overzealous hygiene, too much washing and wiping, which irritates sensitive anal tissue.

"Wash the area gently with warm water and no soap," Dr. Baldwin says. "And instead of toilet paper, use cotton balls dipped in water. Then, of course, wash your hands."

Ending Ear-itations

Travelers' Tricks for "Airplane Ears"

You know the feeling: The plane takes off, and almost immediately your ears start hurting. What to do?

"Swallow, yawn, or chew gum from takeoff until the plane reaches cruising altitude," says Harvey Komet, M.D., an ear, nose, and throat specialist and associate clinical professor of otolaryngology at the University of Texas Health Sciences Center in San Antonio. "Or for more severe ear pain, pinch your nostrils closed and gently attempt to exhale through your nose, with your mouth closed."

The pain of "airplane ears" develops because aircraft cabins are pressurized to the altitude equivalent of 8,000 feet, where the air is considerably thinner than it is at sea level. This thinner air does not exert as much pressure on the eardrum as the denser air trapped behind the drum. The dense air pushes the eardrum outward, causing ear pain. All the techniques for dealing with airplane ears equalize the pressure on both sides of the eardrum by opening the tiny tube that allows air into the area behind the eardrum.

"If airplane ears are a real problem," Dr. Komet adds, "try taking an over-the-counter decongestant about a half hour before flying." Decongestants also help open the tube that equalizes air pressure in the ear.

Ginkgo for Ringing Ears

Do you sometimes hear a ringing or roaring sound in your ears? This could be tinnitus, the medical term for persistent ringing in the ears.

"I've recently seen effective relief with ginkgo," Dr. Komet says. The large, stately ginkgo tree adorns many streets and parks around the United States. In Europe, an extract of ginkgo leaves is also a potent medicine used to treat many conditions—among them, tinnitus.

But don't expect relief from a tea made with a few ginkgo leaves. Medicinal ginkgo is a concentrated extract that must be purchased at health food stores, herb outlets, or from herb catalogs. Dr. Komet recommends one 40-milligram tablet three times a day.

"Tinnitus is often quite difficult to treat," he explains. "But quite a few of my patients have experienced complete relief with ginkgo. Others report a certain amount of residual ringing, but considerably less than they had before taking ginkgo."

Something in Your Ear? Float It Out!

Never use hairpins, needles, matchsticks, or cotton swabs to dig an object out of the ear. "That might cause significant pain and injury," Dr. Komet says, "not to mention the distinct possibility of pushing the object in deeper."

Instead, irrigate the ear canal with tepid liquid and float the object out. "The liquid depends on the object," Dr. Komet says. "For bugs, I recommend baby oil. The oil drowns them and floats them out. For anything else, I recommend a solution of half hydrogen peroxide and half tepid water. The peroxide is an antiseptic, which reduces the risk of infection."

As for technique, Dr. Komet advises bending your head so the plugged ear tilts up, then using an eyedropper to squirt the liquid gently into the ear. A flow that's too forceful can be painful. Be persistent. It sometimes takes a while for hardened wax to soften and float out.

For Swimmer's Ear—The Eyedropper Stopper

For swimmer's ear, a painful bacterial infection of the ear canal, Dr. Komet recommends: "Mix up a solution of half white vinegar and half tepid water, and use an eyedropper to dribble it into the ear several times a day." The vinegar is acidic, and the acid kills the bacteria that cause the infection. (Dr. Komet notes that this remedy should not be used by people who have perforated eardrums.)

Another Remedy for Swimmer's Ear: Try Going Dry

What *causes* swimmer's ear? Frequent immersion reduces the amount of protective wax that lines the ear canal and allows bacteria to grow in the unprotected—and extremely sensitive—tissue that lines it.

"If you're prone to swimmer's ear," Dr. Komet says, "you may be able to prevent it by using earplugs or drying your ears thoroughly after immersion, using a blow dryer on low setting."

Just make certain you don't handle the blow dryer with wet hands or use it where there is any chance of it falling into the water. Electrocution is a danger.

Building a Brighter Outlook

For Depression, Don't Fret—Sweat!

When you're feeling blue, instead of moping around feeling sorry for yourself, get some exercise, advises Michael Freeman, M.D., an assistant clinical professor of psychiatry at the University of California's San Francisco Medical Center. Take a walk. Work in your garden. Go for a swim or bike ride. Take an aerobics class.

"Exercise is mood-elevating," Dr. Freeman says, "because it's pleasurable. It is also distracting, and the distraction helps take your mind off your troubles."

A Marx-Fest for Those Gray Days

Marx? Not Karl but Groucho and the other Marx brothers in any of their hilarious comedy films.

"Laughter is a powerful antidepressant," Dr. Freeman says. "Anything that helps you feel the joy in life is therapeutic for the blues."

Bright Lights, High Lux

"Using special high-intensity lighting, you can beat the winter blues," says Michael Terman, Ph.D., director of the Light Therapy Unit of the New York Psychiatric Institute at Columbia Presbyterian Medical Center in New York City.

Winter blues (Seasonal Affective Disorder, or SAD), caused by lack of sunlight, strikes millions of Americans who live in the northern half of the country from October through April. The farther north you live, the more likely you are to experience some winter depression.

The typical home is illuminated at a twilight level of 250 lux (the unit of light intensity). But daily half-hour exposure of 10,000 lux, the equivalent of the level of light 40 minutes after sunrise in summer, can help prevent winter depression for the entire day. Dr. Terman suggests using a fixture such as the new Ultra-Bright 10,000 or 10,000-plus lux lamp, which looks like an oversized desk lamp. "Place it on your kitchen table, and by the time you've read through the morning paper, you'll be protected for the whole day," he says.

You can order the Ultra-Bright lamp from Medic-Light, 34 Yacht Club Drive, Lake Hopatcong, NJ 07849; 1-800-LIGHT-25. Ask for prices.

Keys to Less Stress

Assess Your Stress

"In about an hour, you can get a comprehensive picture of both your stress problems and your coping strengths with StressMap," says Rod Libbey, a certified employee assistance professional and director of the employee assistance program at the Bank of America in San Francisco.

StressMap™ is more than another "rate your stress" self-test. Developed by a team of psychologists, its 21 question scales cover all aspects of life that might contribute to—or help cope with—stress. The ingenious scoring grid shows at a glance where you have the strongest coping abilities. It also shows where your personal challenges lie.

"We use StressMap in our program," Libbey says. "It's sophisticated, but easy to use, and often provides important insights."

For more information, contact Essi Systems, 126 South Park Avenue, San Francisco, CA 94107; (415) 541-4911.

Count Your Blessings

" 'Count your blessings' is an old-fashioned way of saying 'get some perspective on your life,' " explains David Sobel, M.D., northern California regional director for patient education for the Kaiser Permanente Health Maintenance Program in San Jose, California. "People who feel stressed often become preoccupied with their own problems. When you reach out to others and see that they have problems too—often worse problems than yours—you come to understand that maybe the stresses in your life aren't so bad after all."

If you have trouble counting your blessings, Dr. Sobel recommends volunteering at a social service agency that helps those less fortunate than you are. "Volunteering not only helps people count their blessings," Dr. Sobel says, "it also provides real help for the recipients. And making a difference in someone's life is stress-reducing for the volunteers because it gives them feelings of control and competence in the world. In other words, there are a lot of selfish reasons to be altruistic."

Call an Old Friend

"Quite often, just a few words from an old friend can make you feel calmer and better able to cope with the stresses you face," says Alan Elkin, Ph.D., director of the Stress Management and Counseling Center in New York City. "Old friends provide valuable emotional grounding. They have valuable perspectives on your life. They've seen you at your best, which really helps when you're feeling frazzled."

When was the last time you called your best friend from high school? College roommate? Old Army buddy? Favorite cousin? Or trusted co-worker who moved away? As the commercials say, "Reach out and touch someone." They'll touch you back.

New View on Eye Care

Beware the Glare of Computer Screens

"Computer screens should face away from windows. Make sure that incoming window light does not reflect from the screen into your eyes," says San Francisco ophthalmologist Wayne Fung, M.D., a consultant at the California Pacific Medical Center there. "In addition, use an incandescent desk lamp, not fluorescent. Fluorescent lamps are more likely to produce glare," Dr. Fung says.

Give Your Monitor a Lift

Another suggestion from Dr. Fung can give your eyes a break when you're working at the computer. "If you have overhead lighting, place a few old magazines under the back of your screen to tilt it slightly downward. That keeps the overhead light from reflecting off the screen and into your eyes."

Blink and Cry

Something in your eye? "Rapid blinking and a few tears usually wash out most irritating particles," Dr. Fung says.

What if you can't cry on demand? No problem. Just head for the kitchen and slice an onion, Dr. Fung says. The tears should quickly start flowing—and with them, the painful particle should soon be history.

A Quick Dunk for Eye Relief

"If blinking and crying don't do the trick," Dr. Fung says, "fill a basin with water, dunk your face in it, and open your eyes underwater as you would in a swimming pool. Immersion usually washes out the offending particle. Of course, if it doesn't wash out right away, come up for air and try again."

This tip is a variation on the standard recommendation to irrigate the eye, flooding it with water to wash out irritants. "But it can be quite a challenge to irrigate the eye," Dr. Fung says. "Most people find it easier simply to open their eyes underwater."

Stepping around Athlete's Foot

Shower in Shoes

"Wear thongs in public showers and locker rooms to keep your feet off the floor," says the University of California's Anne Simons, M.D., assistant clinical professor of family and community medicine.

Athlete's foot is caused by a fungus that lives in warm, damp places—like shower floors in locker rooms. If you walk on those floors in your bare feet, you can pick it up, and if you have athlete's foot, you can deposit it for others to catch. Wearing thongs in public locker rooms and showers prevents the direct contact that spreads this infection.

Heat Treatment

"From a distance of at least 2 feet, use a hair dryer on your feet after bathing," advises Laura-Mae Baldwin, M.D., assistant professor of medicine at the University of Washington.

Athlete's foot fungus needs moisture to survive. If it dries out, it dies. So dry your feet thoroughly, not just with a towel, which might still leave them slightly damp, but with hot air.

Get Air in There

"Whenever possible, go sockless," Dr. Simons says. "Wear sandals or ventilated shoes to keep your feet dry." Socks often trap moisture, promoting fungal growth.

First Aid Facts

First aid can be a real lifesaver. About 100,000 Americans are killed in accidents each year. Many of those lives could be saved if friends, family members, and passers-by knew first aid. Do you? These tips come from two experts: Paul S. Auerbach, M.D., professor and chief of the Division of Emergency Medicine at Stanford University, and author of *Medicine for the Outdoors*, and first aid authority Frank Carroll, manager of health and safety program development at American Red Cross headquarters in Washington, D.C.

When in Doubt, Don't Hang Up

When you call 911 or any other emergency number, be sure to *stay on the line*. "It doesn't do any good to cry 'Emergency!' and hang up," Dr. Auerbach

---

Wear It

"If you have a history of seizures, diabetes, anaphylactic reactions, or other significant medical problems that might cause loss of consciousness, get a MedicAlert bracelet," says Paul S. Auerbach, M.D., professor and chief of the Division of Emergency Medicine at Stanford University. (Anaphylactic reactions sometimes occur in people who have become hypersensitive to certain drugs, allergens, or insect stings.)

For a $30 lifetime membership fee, you receive a wrist bracelet or necklace which lists your illness and MedicAlert Foundation's 24-hour emergency telephone number. Call the number, and operators provide the name and phone number of your physician, and information about any medications you might require. Contact MedicAlert Foundation at 1-800-344-3226 or 1-800-432-5378 (ID-ALERT).

---

says. "The operator needs to get your address and possibly directions and additional information about your emergency."

The operator might also be able to talk you through the first aid required to deal with your emergency. "Ask if the operator knows first aid," Dr. Auerbach says, "and if so, follow his or her instructions."

Note: Many areas have the 911 number for emergencies, but some don't. If your area doesn't have 911, check the front of your phone book for police, fire, ambulance, and other emergency numbers. Keep those numbers in a prominent place near your phone.

Learn CPR...Just in Case

"We encourage everyone to learn CPR and first aid," the Red Cross's Carroll says. "It feels good to know that you can deal with emergencies because you never know when they might occur. But even more important, what we've found is that people typically use their CPR or first aid training to help a friend or relative, so getting trained is a good way to express caring for those you love. We have whole families getting trained together."

The American Red Cross has several First Aid and CPR courses offering essential lifesaving and safety information. Red Cross chapters throughout the country have course materials for the very young, the community, the workplace, and for professional rescuers. Courses vary in length from a few hours to 45 hours (for the professional rescuer courses).

For information (including costs) on CPR or first aid training, call your local American Red Cross office, listed in the white pages of your phone book.

Bleeding: How to Stop It

"Apply firm, direct, prolonged pressure," Carroll says. "Be patient. If necessary, strip off some clothing and press it into the wound."

Bleeding can involve injuries to either veins or arteries. Venous bleeding involves a steady flow of blood. Arterial bleeding involves spurts of blood. But the treatment is the same—firm, direct, persistent pressure.

Broken Bones: What to Do

"For suspected broken bones, don't move the person," Carroll advises. "Just keep the person warm, manage any bleeding, and reassure the person that help is on the way."

But if you're out in the wilderness, broken bones are another story. You may have to make a temporary splint before you transport the person to help. "Then the rule is 'splint 'em as you find 'em,' " Dr. Auerbach says. "Don't try to reset broken bones yourself. And don't try to push pieces of bone protruding through the skin back into place. Just clean an area of dirt and debris, cover it with a clean, moist cloth, splint the limb, and get the person to an emergency medical facility as quickly as possible."

Use anything handy for a splint, Dr. Auerbach says: a walking stick, branch, or backpack frame. "But don't tie splints too tightly," he warns. "The tissue around a broken bones swells, and splint ties often become tourniquets. First-aiders should *never* tie tourniquets. They can cut off circulation to the limb, causing limb loss. Check the splint ties as the limb swells and loosen them so they don't limit circulation in the limb."

Frostbite: Forget the Myths

Frostbite myths abound and include: Rub the affected part with snow, then massage it.

"Wrong," Dr. Auerbach says. "Never massage frostbitten tissue. Touch it as little as possible to minimize tissue damage. Rewarm the affected part as quickly as possible—unless there's a danger of refreezing, in which case leave it frozen. Refreezing is worse than keeping the part frozen.'"

Hypothermia: Into Shelter

In hypothermia, the body's core temperature becomes dangerously low—below 95°F. It doesn't have to be 20° below zero for someone to get a bad case of hypothermia. The elderly and children can develop hypothermia at temperatures above freezing—if they're wet and cold and exposed to blustery winds.

"Get the person to a warm shelter, strip off all wet clothing, wrap the person in blankets, and then call for emergency medical assistance," Stanford's Dr. Auerbach says.

"And never give alcohol," Dr. Auerbach advises. "It feels warming, but actually, it cools the body, a big mistake when treating hypothermia."

Overexposure to Sun and Heat

Overexposure problems come in two varieties: heat exhaustion and heatstroke. In the former, victims often look pale and feel warm and damp, with possible nausea, weakness, and light-headedness. In the latter, victims—typically the elderly—feel hot and dry, with rapid heartbeat, confusion, agitation or lethargy, and loss of consciousness. The treatment is the same."

Get the person out of the sun," Dr. Auerbach says. "Douse the person with cool or tepid water, or immerse them in a cool pool. Or place ice packs in their groin area, armpits, or around the neck. Then call for medical assistance."

MOTOR VEHICLE ACCIDENTS

What's the best first aid in case of a car accident? Here are tips from the experts.

Survey for safety. "While attempting to help others, never risk your own life," says first aid authority Frank Carroll of the American Red Cross. "If a car is burning or teetering on a cliff, don't approach it. Help as best you can from a safe distance."

Triage victims. "Help those you can help best," says Stanford professor Paul S. Auerbach, M.D.

It's not easy bypassing someone who is hurt and suffering, but in a multicar motor vehicle accident, many people may need assistance and you have only so much time, skill, and energy.

The ABCs of helping. "When helping an accident victim," Carroll says, "Remember ABC: airway, breathing, and circulation."

- Airway. Clear the airway of any debris so the person can breathe.
- Breathing. If the person isn't breathing, begin rescue breathing (taught in CPR classes).
- Circulation. Check for a pulse. If you can't find one, begin CPR.

Near-Drowning: Reach, Throw, Go

"If you see someone flailing in the water," says Red Cross authority Frank Carroll, "don't just attempt a rescue by jumping in. Follow the rescue sequence: reach, throw, go. A person who fears drowning panics, and if you get too close, you could get hurt."

Reach. Many near-drownings happen close to safety. First try to reach the person with an oar, paddle, branch, or your hand.

Throw. If you can't reach the person, throw a flotation device, a rescue ring, or anything that can help the person float and recover from panic. (If you're at a lake or beach, look for a rowboat that you can use to get closer.)

Go. Jump in only as a last resort, and ideally with something to throw the person so you don't have to approach too closely.

Poisoning: Dial for Directions

If people know anything about poisoning, they know ipecac. Every home medicine chest should contain ipecac, but most experts advise: *Don't give it unless a poison control center operator tells you to.*

Ipecac, also known as syrup of ipecac, induces vomiting, the standard treatment for some—*but not all*—poisons. If you suspect poisoning, first call your local poison control center, listed in the white pages of your phone book under "Poison." Tell the operator what you think the person swallowed, and then follow the operator's instructions. Of course, if the operator says, "Give ipecac," you must have some on hand. Do you?

Tooth Knocked Out? Retrieve It!

"Knocked-out teeth can often be successfully replanted in their sockets," Dr. Auerbach says, "if you act quickly and don't cause additional injury to the root tissue that remains attached to the tooth." Here's what he recommends.

1. Recover the tooth.
2. Don't touch the root part.
3. If it's clean, try to replace it in the socket and get to an emergency medical facility as quickly as possible.
4. If it's dirty, rinse it gently in water, but don't scrub. Scrubbing causes additional injury to the root tissue.

Instead of replacing the tooth, you can also drop it into a container of cool, whole milk, then get to an emergency room as quickly as possible. Don't use tap water, and don't wrap the tooth in paper or plastic—these injure the root tissue.

HOW TO GET INFO

Do you have medical questions you'd like to have answered?

Call 1-800-4-CANCER to reach the National Cancer Information Service, a free program of the National Cancer Institute. Operators can send you information packets about any type of cancer. And through a physician, you can request a state-of-the-art information packet that contains more technical information—which is often helpful in making treatment decisions.

For other medical conditions, information is available from prominent national organizations including the American Heart Association, the American Arthritis Association, and the American Diabetes Association.

What if you have a less well-publicized condition—scleroderma, bulimia, or porphyria? You can get important information about these conditions—and many more—by contacting the American Self-Help Clearinghouse (ASHC), which can put you in touch with an organization or support group. And if no organization or support group exists, the ASHC can help you start your own. The place to begin is with the organization's *Self-Help Sourcebook,* a directory of more than 600 information and support organizations. The directory is available for $10.00 from the American Self-Help Clearinghouse, St. Clares-Riverside Medical Center, Denville, NJ 07834.

Personalized medical research is also available. Do you have a medical question your doctor can't answer to your satisfaction? Would you like more information about a medical subject than your local library has available? Then try The Health Resource, a personalized medical research service whose information specialists use computers plugged into all the nation's health and medical databases. Founder Janice Guthrie was familiar with computer databases back in 1984 when she developed ovarian cancer and had to make some difficult treatment decisions. Her computer research helped a great deal, and when she recovered, she established The Health Resource to help others find the answers to their medical questions. Fees per search are based on the type of report requested, and reports vary in length from 50 to 150 pages. Contact The Health Resource at 209 Katharine Drive, Conway, AR 72032.

Headache and Nosebleed Remedies

To Head Off Headache—Feverfew Frequently

"If I had migraines," says Dr. James A. Duke, economic botanist at the U.S. Department of Agriculture, "I'd take feverfew before trying anything else."

Feverfew has never been shown to reduce fevers. The name is a corruption of the Middle English, *featherfew*, a reference to this perennial's feathery leaf borders. But recent studies have shown that chewing two medium-size fresh leaves a day, or taking 85 milligrams of powdered leaf, provides significant preventive benefits for many, though not all, migraine sufferers.

Feverfew can be purchased at health food stores or by mail from herb catalogs.

Or grow your own, either indoors or out. In addition to migraine prevention, feverfew produces attractive daisylike flowers.

Nosebleed-Stopping Know-How

What's a quick way to stop a nosebleed? "Press on one nostril, or pinch both together for 10 minutes," says the University of California's Dr. Anne B. Simons.

Nosebleeds are rarely serious, but they should be treated like other kinds of bleeding—with firm, direct, prolonged pressure.

"You've really got to pinch your nose for a full 10 minutes—sometimes longer," Dr. Simons says. "Most people stop before the pinching has stopped the bleeding."

Controlling Cholesterol

Garlic—A Natural Cholesterol Cutter

"Garlic reduces cholesterol about as well as oat bran," says James A. Duke, Ph.D., medicinal plant authority with the USDA, "and has a more interesting flavor."

And if you think garlic means just Italian food, think again. The pungent herb is used extensively in Middle Eastern, Indian, Southeast Asian, and Chinese cooking. Pick up a few new cookbooks, and delight your palate while saving your heart.

A Seedy Solution to Cholesterol

"If people have ever heard of psyllium seed, they probably recognize it as the major ingredient in Metamucil, the bulk-forming laxative," says Dr. Duke. "But psyllium also helps reduce cholesterol."

A study in the *Journal of the American Medical Association* of patients with elevated cholesterol showed that 1 teaspoon of psyllium three times a day for eight weeks cut their cholesterol levels an average of 5 percent.

Note: Psyllium also helps prevent constipation. If you take it for either regularity or cholesterol reduction, consult the caution on page 7 for information on psyllium safety.

Health Help: Improving Diet

Take Your Calculator to the Supermarket

Many cardiologists, cancer specialists, and clinical nutritionists agree that reducing fat in the diet should be a high priority for good health. Many studies have shown that excess fat raises serum cholesterol; it also increases the risk of heart attack, adult-onset diabetes, and several kinds of cancer. Not only that, but there's the obvious problem that excess fat makes people overweight—which leads to many other kinds of health problems.

So, how do you trim excess fat from your diet? Here's a way to calculate.

"Fat contains 9 calories per gram," says Anne B. Simons, M.D., family practitioner and assistant clinical professor of family and community medicine at the University of California's San Francisco Medical Center. "Look at a food item's nutritional label. Where the label says *fat*, multiply the number of grams per serving by 9 and divide that number by the total number of calories per serving. What you get is the percentage of calories from fat. Think twice before buying items with more than 30 percent of calories from fat."

Why no more than 30 percent? Because the American Heart Association recommends that Americans get no more than this amount.

Small Is Beautiful

"Eat three or more small meals throughout the day instead of one big one," says Margo Denke, M.D., assistant professor in the Department of Internal Medicine and Center for Human Nutrition at the University of Texas in Dallas.

People who eat one big meal during the day often become so ravenous, they lose control of their diet and eat high-calorie, high-fat foods they really shouldn't. Smaller meals help control the Cookie Monster inside each of us and provide more opportunity to eat the variety of foods that contribute to a well balanced diet.

Eat at Home

"It's usually easier to eat a healthy diet at home," Dr. Denke says. "Compared to eating out, home cooking is usually lower in fat and calories. And when you eat out, it's hard to know what you're eating. That grilled chicken breast sandwich may seem to be low in fat and calories, but if it's cooked in butter, it isn't."

Out of Sight, out of Mind

"Replace your cookie jar with a bowl of fresh fruit," Dr. Denke advises. That way, when a snack attack strikes, you'll be more likely to grab a banana than a cookie.

Many snack decisions, Dr. Denke says, are made impulsively. What you see is what you eat. So make sure that what you see is good for you.

"An occasional cookie is okay," she says, "but fruit is lower in fat and calories, and has more nutrients."

Pop Goes the Fat

When you crave a junk-type snack, munch the healthy one—popcorn.

"As long as it's not doused with butter, popcorn is a healthy snack," the University of California's Dr. Simons says. "It's high in carbohydrate and fiber, and low in fat. I buy light microwave popcorn and season it with a sprinkle of Parmesan cheese."

Beat the Eggs

"Egg substitutes can be a tasty alternative to eggs, but they contain no cholesterol," Dr. Denke says. "The American Heart Association urges Americans to eat no more than four eggs a week. Egg substitutes can help meet this guideline."

Egg substitutes—sold under such brand names as Egg Beaters—are available in supermarket frozen food cases.

Tips for Men

Impotence: Erection Detection

For impotence, it's essential to find out whether there's a physical problem that prevents having an erection. "A quick, easy way to assess erection problems involves the postage stamp test for nocturnal erection," advises Theresa Crenshaw, M.D., a San Diego sexual medicine specialist.

Get a roll of postage stamps. Lick a few and wrap them around your penis before you go to bed. If you have an erection at night, the stamps tear apart. If not, they remain connected. The ability to have erections at night but not during the day suggests that there's a psychological reason rather than a physical problem. No erections at night suggests that a physical checkup is needed to find the cause of the problem.

"For best results with the postage stamp test," Dr. Crenshaw says, "be sure to bend the perforations back and forth a few times before placing the stamps, and overlap one stamp at the end.

The postage stamp test is not definitive, Dr. Crenshaw says, but it provides an important clue to the nature of an erection problem.

Be Aware of the Sex Offenders

Sex offenders? They include...Alcohol. Sedatives. Tranquilizers. Some high blood pressure medications. And many other drugs with a label that says "may cause drowsiness," including over-the-counter antihistamines. What Dr. Crenshaw calls "sex offenders" are common drugs with largely unpublicized erection-deflating effects.

"If men with erection problems stopped using the sex offenders that are in their liquor cabinets and medicine chests," Dr. Crenshaw says, "many erection problems would improve and some would clear up."

So many prescription and over-the-counter medications have erection-impairing side effects that Dr. Crenshaw says *every* drug should be considered a sex offender until you're reassured otherwise.

"Never take a prescription drug without asking your physician or pharmacist whether it has sexual side effects," she advises. "And ask your pharmacist about over-the-counter preparations as well." (However, before going off a prescribed medication, be sure to check with your doctor.)

Cures for Minor Ills

Boils and Styes: Don't Pop Them!

Boils are bacterial infections of the skin. Styes are boils in the eyelid. Popping them can spread the infection to surrounding tissue, increasing the pain and making them more difficult to treat. Yet many people are tempted to "pop the pimple" when a whitehead forms on a boil or stye.

"Popping pimples can make things worse," according to the California Pacific Medical Center's Dr. Wayne Fung. "Instead of squeezing boils and styes, apply hot compresses as often as possible until a whitehead forms and the boil or stye ruptures and drains."

The heat of hot compresses opens up the blood vessels in the area, drawing more blood—and infection-fighting white blood cells—into the area. The white blood cells combat the infection, and as they gain the upper hand, a pimplelike whitehead forms. Eventually the whitehead ruptures and out drains the debris of the body's battle against the infection.

"Keep applying compresses as the boil or stye drains to draw out all the debris," Dr. Fung says. "Then wash the area thoroughly with soap and water and apply an antibacterial ointment."

Stop the Hiccups

Doctors aren't sure why we get hiccups, but everyone has an opinion on how to get rid of them. We've all heard that a loud noise or sudden scare will chase away hiccups, but there are more reliable ways. Dr. Anne B. Simons at the University of California suggests the following:

- Drink from the opposite edge of a glass. (You have to bend over to do this.)
- Swallow a teaspoon of granulated sugar.
- Swallow a tablespoon of peanut butter.
- Hold your breath for as long as you can.
- Inhale and exhale into a paper bag.

One way to cure hiccups: Fill a glass with water almost to the rim, bend over, and sip from the "wrong" side of the glass.

Soothe That Bruise

What if you have a bruise?

"Apply ice packs for 48 hours," says Dr. Paul S. Auerbach of Stanford University. But after 72 hours have gone by, he suggests, you should begin applying heat.

A bruise indicates bleeding under the skin. Ice packs help minimize bleeding, pain, and swelling. To make an ice pack, wrap a few ice cubes in a clean cloth and place the cloth in a plastic bag to prevent dripping. Hold it on the bruise for 20 minutes, then remove it for 20 minutes and repeat. Don't apply ice directly to the skin or leave an ice pack on longer than 20 minutes. If you do, you might cause tissue damage similar to frostbite.

By the third day, the bruise should have turned purple. Then apply hot compresses to help speed reabsorption of the blood trapped under the skin.

Balms for Burns

"Keep a potted *Aloe vera* in your kitchen, site of most household burns," says the University of California's Dr. Anne B. Simons. "Snip off a leaf, slit it open, scoop out the inner leaf gel, and apply it to the burn."

Aloe has been shown to speed the healing of all sorts of minor burns, from kitchen mishaps and sunburn to the burns associated with radiation therapy for cancer. Aloe gel can also be purchased at pharmacies and health food stores. Refrigerate it to preserve its potency.

Rescue from Colds and Flu

Prevention Is Possible

It's that time of year when *everybody* has a cold. So how do you avoid getting one?

"Keep your distance from cold sufferers," says cold researcher Elliott Dick, Ph.D., chief of the University of Wisconsin's Respiratory Virus Research Laboratory in Madison. "Quick visits don't often transmit colds, but if you're close to a cold sufferer for several hours, you run the risk of catching the cold."

Dr. Dick has proven what folklore has long held: Colds spread through the air. So keeping your distance from cold sufferers keeps you away from the virus-filled air that surrounds them as they cough, sneeze, and exhale.

"But cold sufferers aren't just contagious when they're coughing and sneezing in the late stages of a cold," Dr. Dick says. "They can also transmit the virus in the early stages when they just have a sore throat. So when people say they're just catching a cold, that's the time to start keeping away from them."

You Can Believe in C

"I was a vitamin C skeptic," Dr. Dick says, "until I ran some experiments on it. All three of my studies showed that compared with participants who took placebo tablets, those who took 2,000 milligrams a day of vitamin C caught fewer colds and had milder colds. Now I'm a vitamin C believer. I use it myself."

But if you're about to become a C believer, take note: a dosage as high as 2,000 milligrams is safe for only a few days when you feel a cold coming on. Extended use of high dosages can have side effects. (A safe dosage is about 500 milligrams a day—but check with your doctor before taking supplements.)

Think Zinc

"When I feel a cold coming on, I take a zinc lozenge and let it dissolve in the back of my mouth," says cold researcher William Halcomb, D.O., a family practitioner in Mesa, Arizona. (He is coauthor of a study showing that zinc gluconate lozenges can help stop a cold in the sore throat stage.) "I take two 23-milligram lozenges the first hour, then one every 2 hours after that. My symptoms are usually gone within 12 hours."

But Dr. Halcomb says you've got to use zinc gluconate, not other forms of zinc. Zinc gluconate lozenges are available at most health food stores and supplement outlets.

"The problem with zinc is that it doesn't taste very good," Dr. Halcomb says. "But personally, I'd rather endure zinc for 12 hours than have a cold for two weeks."

Consider Coneflower

Purple coneflower, a beautiful, 4-foot-tall, daisylike ornamental, is also known as echinacea (*eh-kin*-AY-*sha*). Herbal medicine experts revere its immune-stimulating properties.

"I take echinacea not only for colds and flu, but whenever I'm ill," says the USDA's Dr.James A. Duke. "It rarely hurts to stimulate your immune system."

Echinacea is safe for adults even in large doses. It is available in teas, pills, and tinctures (alcohol extracts) at health food stores, and by mail from herb catalogs.

Shortly after taking echinacea, you may feel some numbness or tingling of the tongue. Don't be alarmed. This is normal and harmless.

WHEN TO CONSULT A DOCTOR

It is expensive, time-consuming, and unnecessary to run to a doctor for every little thing. But many people don't consult physicians even when they really should. This can be a serious—possibly fatal—mistake. The following list contains a consensus of recommendations from Paul Auerbach, M.D., of Stanford University; Anne B. Simons, M.D., of the University of California; and Laura-Mae Baldwin, M.D., of the University of Washington. If you, or those you care about, develop any of the following symptoms, consult a physician promptly.

Injuries
- Any kind of injury that requires first aid. (Even if the person who received first aid seems fine, it's a good idea to consult a physician just to be sure.)

Possible Heart Problem
- Chest pain, especially if it extends up to the jaw, left shoulder, or arm.
- Shortness of breath from minor exertion.

Possible Stroke or Other Nervous System Emergencies
- Loss of consciousness.
- Disorientation, vomiting, or unusual behavior after a head injury.
- Seizure.
- Numbness or weakness in the arms or legs.
- Frequent or persistent dizziness or faintness.
- Unusually severe or persistent headache.
- Headache with slurred speech.
- Headache with fever and pain that increases when you bend your chin to your chest.
- Any headache that increases in severity over several hours or wakes you at night.
- Sudden or significant memory loss or disorientation.

Possible Cancer
- A firm, painless lump anywhere in the body, but particularly in the breasts, testicles, or collarbone area.
- Any mole that begins to bleed, ooze, grow, or change in any way.
- Sudden or unexplained weight loss unconnected to dieting.
- Persistent nipple discharge unrelated to pregnancy or breastfeeding.
- Blood in stool.

Fever, Infection
- Any fever during pregnancy.
- Fever higher than 103° in an adult, or 102° if over age 60, or 100° in children younger than three months, even if there are no symptoms accompanying it.
- Any fever that does not respond to home treatment after three days.
- Any fever that appears in association with cough or chest pain just as you think a cold or flu is on the mend.
- Any fever with other significant symptoms, such as rash; difficult breathing; painful urination; persistent cough or runny nose; red, swollen, or painful joints; pelvic or abdominal pain in women.

Respiratory Problems
- Shortness of breath while resting.
- Cough with shortness of breath.
- Cough that lasts more than two weeks despite home treatment.
- Cough that brings up brown or reddish mucus.
- Persistent wheezing or any difficulty breathing.

Circulation
- Painful swelling in one or both legs that doesn't go away after elevation.

Skin
- Any dizziness, agitation, hives, or difficulty breathing after an insect sting, or after taking a new medication.
- An animal bite, puncture wound, burn, or cut if you haven't had a tetanus shot within the last five years.
- A tick bite if you develop an unusual rash or any joint pains.
- Any cut, burn, or wound which, despite home treatment, becomes increasingly painful, red, tender, swollen, or oozing, or develops a red streak extending from the wound toward the trunk.
- Any burn that causes no pain, and any blistering burn of the hands, face, feet, or genitals.

Mental Health
- Any suicidal thoughts or persistent feelings of helplessness, hopelessness, or worthlessness.
- Unusual feelings of fear, anxiety, or panic.

(continued)

WHEN TO CONSULT A DOCTOR—*Continued*

Digestion
- Swallowing any suspected poison.
- Sudden or unexplained weight loss unconnected to dieting.
- Vomiting blood.
- Severe or persistent diarrhea, especially in an infant.
- Anal bleeding, black stool, or blood or mucus in stool.
- Intense or persistent abdominal pain or tenderness, especially with fever, vomiting, or other significant symptoms.

Eyes
- Severe or persistent eye pain or change in vision.

Ears
- Severe or persistent ear pain or change in hearing.

And...
- Any significant change in bowel or bladder habits.
- Unusually frequent urination, with sweet-smelling urine or increased thirst.
- Severe or persistent joint pain or swelling, particularly in combination with other symptoms.
- Vaginal bleeding unrelated to menstruation.
- When in doubt about the severity of any symptom or change in your health.

The Helpful Side of Caffeine

"Some people have problems with caffeine's stimulant action," says Dr. Duke, "but caffeine also has a decongestant effect. If you're all stuffed up from a cold, beverages that contain caffeine—coffee, tea, cocoa, and cola soft drinks—might help."

Caffeine also helps minimize the chest congestion of hay fever, Dr. Duke says.

Get That Flu Shot

"The annual flu shot is your best protection against influenza," says Steven Mostow, M.D., a professor of medicine at the University of Colorado in Denver and chairman of the influenza and pneumonia committee of the American Thoracic Society.

Most people call any bad cold "the flu." But flu is a much more severe illness. It hits you like a truck with fever, body aches, and general misery, which often keep you in bed for several days. And for those over 65 and anyone with a chronic illness, flu can also lead to pneumonia, which can be fatal.

"It's so easy to get a flu shot," Dr. Mostow says. "Physicians and city and state health departments make them available every October and November. Even if you're not at risk for flu-related pneumonia, you can get immunized. It takes only about an hour—and it can save you days of misery."

Help for Hay Fever

Morning Warning

"Pollen counts are highest in the early morning hours," says Allan Giannini, M.D., an associate clinical professor of allergy and immunology at the University of California's San Francisco Medical Center. "Limit physical outdoor activity, particularly in the morning. Also, keep air-conditioning on in your car and home. Shopping malls that are air-conditioned are also very helpful."

Manage Mites

"Dust mites, microscopic pests that live by the millions in our homes, are major allergy triggers," Dr. Giannini says. "To protect yourself, remove that cloth sofa; pull up your bedroom carpeting; vacuum rugs and upholstery weekly; wash all blankets, spreads, and sheets in hot water; and enclose your mattress in zippered plastic."

Down with Down

"Replace your feather pillows with foam or fiberfill," Dr. Giannini advises. "Compared with feathers, foam and fiberfill are much less likely to trigger allergy symptoms."

Toenail Treatments

Try a Soak Solution

"At the first sign of pain from an ingrown toenail, soak the toe to soften the nail," says the University of California's Dr. Anne Simons. "Then try to raise the nail with a clean tweezers and pack a small wad of cotton under the ingrowing corner to train the nail away from the skin. Repeat this procedure daily until the ingrowing nail comes free."

Ingrown toenails cause pain, redness, swelling—and sometimes infection. But if you begin this program as soon as toe pain develops, when the nail is only slightly ingrown, you can usually extract it from the skin before it becomes infected. If infection develops, consult a physician.

Nail Clip Tip

"To prevent ingrown toenails," Dr. Simons says, "cut your nails straight across, not curved with rounded edges. Short-cut rounded edges are the ones that become ingrown. The edges of nails that are cut straight across lie safely on top of toe skin and rarely become ingrown."

Beating Bug Bites

Scrape, Don't Squeeze

"For bee, wasp, hornet, and yellow jacket stings, don't grab stingers with your fingers or tweezers," Stanford's Dr. Paul Auerbach says. Fingers and tweezers often squeeze additional venom into the wound, adding to the pain. Instead, *scrape* stingers out of the skin with a clean, sharp knife. If a knife isn't available, you can use the edge of a credit card.

Then Apply Paste, Post Haste

"Once the stinger has been removed, apply a paste of meat tenderizer and water to the sting site," the University of California's Dr. Anne Simons says. "The meat tenderizer contains chemicals that help break down the venom."

Watch the Clock for Shock

"After an insect sting, watch the person carefully," says University of California's Dr. Allan Giannini. "If any anxiety, with difficult breathing, develops, or there are generalized hives, call for medical assistance and get the person to an emergency medical facility immediately." (A doctor or medic is likely to give the person a shot of adrenaline before anything else.)

Hives or breathing difficulty indicate anaphylaxis, the most severe—in fact, life-threatening—allergic reaction. Several hundred Americans die each year from anaphylactic reactions, not only to insect stings, but also to some drugs (penicillin), and certain foods. Emergency medical treatment involves administration of the hormone epinephrine (adrenaline), which restores normal breathing and blood flow.

"Anyone who's ever had an anaphylactic reaction should always carry a preloaded adrenaline injection kit such as EpiPen or Ana-Kit," Dr. Giannini advises. "If they develop another anaphylactic episode, they can inject themself, and quite possibly save their own life." Ask your family doctor for a prescription.

Taking the Itch Out of Poison Plants

Soda Salvation

Want some soothing relief for the rash caused by poison ivy, oak, or sumac?

"Apply a paste of baking soda and water to the rash," advises Dr. Anne Simons of the University of California. "That often helps relieve the itching."

To make the paste, pour a small amount of baking soda in a bowl and add just enough water to moisten. Spread over the itchy area; it washes off easily.

Poison ivy, oak, and sumac produce a resin which irritates the skin, producing a blistery rash that itches intensely, often for up to a week. The best defense against the itchy misery of a poison plant encounter is to know what these plants look like, and then avoid them like the plague they are.

Oatmeal Bath

"Another effective home treatment for itching is an oatmeal bath," Dr. Simons says. "Grind 2 cups of oatmeal in a coffee grinder and add it to your bath."

Grinding the oatmeal reduces it to a fine powder called colloidal oatmeal. Although colloidal oatmeals like Aveeno are available in pharmacies, you create the same product by grinding it yourself!

Sounder, Snore-Free Sleep

Stop All Stimulants

Sure, you know not to drink coffee after dinner, but what about other stimulants? In addition to drinking decaf, Michael Stevenson, Ph.D., clinical director of the North Valley Sleep Disorders Center in Mission Hills, California, says anyone with insomnia should cut out all sources of caffeine: tea, cocoa, chocolate, and most cola soft drinks.

"And always read the labels of any over-the-counter medicines you take," Dr. Stevenson says. "Some contain caffeine." And even if they *don't*, some common drugs can prevent sleep, notably the decongestants used in cold, flu, and allergy formulas.

Sweat before Sunset

Regular, moderate exercise helps many insomniacs get their ZZZZ's, but Dr. Stevenson says that for sleep promotion, the best time to work out is in the late afternoon. "Three to five o'clock or so," he recommends, "but not within 4 hours of retiring because exercise also has a short-term stimulating effect."

Set Your Alarm

One of the most important sleep promoters is getting up at the same time every day—including weekends. "Getting up at the same time every day sets your biological clock so that come late evening, you feel tired and ready to sleep," Dr. Stevenson says.

But weekends? *Must* you really forgo the joy of sleeping in? 'Fraid so, Dr. Stevenson says: "Sleeping in on Sunday morning may feel good after a late Saturday night, but it throws off your biological clock and in the long run, perpetuates insomnia."

Do Only 2 Things in Bed

Sleep and make love—nothing else. "Don't eat, drink, read, work, watch TV, or talk on the phone while in bed," Dr. Stevenson says. "Psychologically, if you associate time in bed with nonsleep activities, you contribute to insomnia."

But what about sex? Dr. Stevenson explains that sex may be exciting, but it's also relaxing and helps some people fall asleep. "Of course," he says, "if you think lovemaking in bed is contributing to your insomnia, you might try having sex somewhere else."

Get Up

If you eliminate all stimulants, hit the stairclimber at 3:00 P.M., and move the TV out of your bedroom, and you still can't fall asleep within 30 minutes of your bedtime, Dr. Stevenson advises getting up and reading, watching TV, or listening to music until you feel tired. Then retire and repeat the process of getting up if you don't fall asleep within 30 minutes. "This works for most people," Dr. Stevenson says, "although some find this program too stimulating. Experiment and see for yourself."

The Tennis Ball Cure for Snoring

Here's an off-the-court idea for stopping your spouse in midsnore: "Sew a tennis ball into a pocket on the back of the snorer's pajamas," Dr. Stevenson advises.

Sound ridiculous? It's not. People are most likely to snore when sleeping on their backs. That's why snorers' bedmates often resort to kicking them at night. A kick often gets the supine snorer to roll over, and the snoring stops. But why have your sleep disturbed at all? The tennis ball cure prevents snorers from sleeping on their backs—and often produces nights of blissful silence for their bedmates.

Women's Health

BSE for Breast Care

Remember this name: Mammacare. Recently, a study by Suzanne W. Fletcher, M.D., editor of Annals of Internal Medicine, showed it to be the best form of breast self-exam (BSE).

The American Cancer Society (ACS) recommends that women give themselves a once-a-month self-exam for possibly cancerous lumps. Yet most women say they have no confidence that they could find any suspicious lumps even if they were there. That's why the Mammacare method was developed—to give women BSE confidence. The Mammacare method includes an instructional video and lifelike breast models containing all sorts of lumps, including ones that feel like tumors.

Dr. Fletcher's independent study showed that, compared with women taught by the traditional method, Mammacare-trained women detected much smaller tumors much more consistently and confidently. In fact, the Mammacare group's tumor-detection ability rivaled that of trained physicians.

"Women should use the best BSE method available," Dr. Fletcher says. "As far as I'm concerned, Mammacare is it."

The Mammacare method, including models and a 45-minute VHS video, can be ordered from Mammatech Corporation, 1-800-MAM-CARE.

Try the Antacid Angle

"Women should try to get most of their calcium from their diet," says Dr. Dorothy M. Barbo, of the University of New Mexico. But for a little extra, pop a few Tums or Rolaids."

"Even though they're sold as antacids, Tums and Rolaids help prevent osteoporosis because they contain calcium carbonate, the richest source of supplemental calcium," Dr. Barbo points out.

Calcium carbonate is 40 percent calcium. Other calcium supplements contain less calcium, some as little as 10 percent.

Dr. Barbo says premenopausal women should consume 1,000 milligrams of calcium a day (pregnant and nursing women should get 1,500 milligrams). Postmenopausal women, who are at greatest risk for osteoporosis, should consume 1,500 milligrams of calcium a day. Unfortunately, Dr. Barbo says, most women consume only about 500 milligrams of calcium a day.

"Working Out" Menstrual Cramps

"In addition to either aspirin or ibuprofen, regular exercise often helps relieve menstrual cramps," Dr. Barbo says. Scientists aren't sure why this is so, but they believe cramp relief comes from endorphins, the body's own pain-relieving chemicals, which are released during physical activity.

Tea Tip, Too, for Cramps

Women bothered by painful cramps might also try raspberry leaf tea. The USDA's Dr. James A. Duke says it is reported to relax the uterus and may help relieve some cramping.

Raspberry leaf is available at health food stores, and through herb catalogs. Or grow your own. But if you decide to grow some, watch out! This thorny shrub grows like a weed: Plant a couple and they may take over your whole garden.

Berry Protection for Bladder Infection

Bothered by recurrent bladder infections? No matter what you call this ailment—cystitis, urinary tract infection, or UTI—it's no fun. For years, women have been trying to prevent bladder infections by drinking cranberry juice, but some chronic sufferers and even some doctors say that this bit of folklore may actually be folk wisdom.

"Cranberry juice acidifies the urine," says Dr. Barbo. "It's harder for bacteria to grow in acidic urine, so cranberry juice may help prevent this infection."

Dr. Barbo says the red juice won't treat bladder infections. "Once you're infected, you have to take antibiotics," she explains. "But we often encourage women taking antibiotics for UTIs to drink cranberry juice at the same time as a complementary treatment."

Tame the Yeast with a Yogurt Feast

If you suffer recurrent vaginal yeast infections, run right down to your supermarket or health food store and pick up some live-culture yogurt. Or buy acidophilus milk, which contains *Lactobacillus acidophilus* bacteria, and make your own.

In a study of women with this annoying problem, Eileen Hilton, M.D., an infectious disease specialist at Long Island Jewish Medical Center in New Hyde Park, New York, found that eating 1 cup of live-culture yogurt a day produced "a dramatic reduction in infection recurrences."

Better Climax with Kegels

"Better orgasms are only a few squeezes away, once you learn how to do Kegel exercises," says Louanne Cole, Ph.D., a San Francisco sex therapist. Kegel exercises, named for the physician who came up with them, strengthen the pubococcygeus (PC) muscle, which surrounds internal organs in the pubic area. The PC's contractions provide the sensation of orgasm. "Strengthening the PC adds intensity and enjoyment to orgasm," Dr. Cole says.

It's easy to strengthen the PC. First, identify it. The PC is the muscle you squeeze to interrupt urine flow. Once you've identified your PC, simply squeeze it when not urinating. Dr. Cole recommends several sets of five to ten squeezes a day. That's all there is to it!

Kegel exercises are quick and private, and you can practice them anywhere: at a desk, while stopped at red lights, or while watching TV.

But don't overdo them. In this case, more is not necessarily better. If you overdo it, especially the first time, you won't have more pleasure during sex. You'll probably have a sore muscle.

The Experts

Paul S. Auerbach, M.D., is professor and chief of the Division of Emergency Medicine at Stanford University in California. He is author of *Medicine for the Outdoors.*

Laura-Mae Baldwin, M.D., is assistant professor of medicine at the University of Washington School of Medicine in Seattle.

Dorothy M. Barbo, M.D., is professor of obstetrics and gynecology at the University of New Mexico in Albuquerque and director of the Center for Women's Health there.

Benjamin E. Benjamin, Ph.D., is director of the Muscular Therapy Institute, a sportsmedicine center in Cambridge, Massachusetts.

Frank Carroll is a first aid authority and manager of health and safety program development for the American Red Cross in Washington, D.C.

Louanne Cole, Ph.D., is a San Francisco sex therapist.

Theresa Crenshaw, M.D., is a San Diego sexual medicine specialist.

Margo Denke, M.D., is a member of the nutrition committee of the American Heart Association and assistant professor in the Department of Internal Medicine and Center for Human Nutrition at the University of Texas Southwestern Medical Center in Dallas.

Elliott Dick, Ph.D., is chief of the University of Wisconsin's Respiratory Virus Research Laboratory in Madison.

James A. Duke, Ph.D., is an authority on herbal medicine and medicinal plants who works as an economic botanist for the United States Department of Agriculture in Beltsville, Maryland.

Alan Elkin, Ph.D., is director of the Stress Management and Counseling Center in New York City.

Suzanne W. Fletcher, M.D., is the editor of *Annals of Internal Medicine*, a leading medical journal.

Michael Freeman, M.D., is assistant clinical professor of psychiatry at the University of California's San Francisco Medical Center.

Wayne Fung, M.D., is a San Francisco ophthalmologist and consultant at the California Pacific Medical Center in San Francisco.

Allan Giannini, M.D., is associate clinical professor of allergy and immunology at the University of California's San Francisco Medical Center.

William Halcomb, D.O., is a cold researcher and family practitioner in Mesa, Arizona.

Scott Hasson, Ed.D., is an exercise physiologist and associate professor of physical therapy at Texas Women's University in Houston.

Eileen Hilton, M.D., is an infectious disease specialist at Long Island Jewish Medical Center in New Hyde Park, New York.

Kenneth Klein, M.D., is a gastroenterologist and research associate professor of medicine at the University of North Carolina School of Medicine in Chapel Hill.

Harvey Komet, M.D., is a San Antonio ear, nose, and throat specialist and an associate clinical professor of otolaryngology at the University of Texas Health Sciences Center in San Antonio.

Rod Libbey, certified employee assistance professional, is the director of the employee assistance program at Bank of America in San Francisco.

Daniel Lorber, M.D., is an associate clinical professor of medicine at Albert Einstein College of Medicine at Yeshiva University in New York City, and medical director of the Diabetes Control Foundation in Flushing, New York.

Steven Mostow, M.D., is a professor of medicine at the University of Colorado in Denver, and chairman of the influenza and pneumonia committee of the American Thoracic Society.

Daniel W. Nixon, M.D., is the American Cancer Society vice president for detection and treatment.

Mary Schatz, M.D., is a pathologist at Centennial Medical Center in Nashville, Tennessee, and author of *Back Care Basics*.

Anne B. Simons, M.D., is a family practitioner and an assistant clinical professor of Family and Community Medicine at the University of California's San Francisco Medical Center.

David Sobel, M.D., is the northern California regional director for patient education for the Kaiser Permanente health maintenance program in San Jose, California.

Michael Stevenson, Ph.D., is clinical director of the North Valley Sleep Disorders Center in Mission Hills, California.

Michael Terman, Ph.D., is the director of the Light Therapy Unit of the New York Psychiatric Institute at Columbia Presbyterian Medical Center in New York City.

CHAPTER 2

Yard and Garden

Tricks to Try
in Your Own Backyard

Finding an easier, cheaper, simpler, or more enjoyable way to do things has been a preoccupation among gardeners since the dawn of horticulture, when some aboriginal ancestor first poked a seed into soil, hoping that it might grow. Chances are that the first gardeners on earth traded tips and shared their shortcuts. It's not hard to imagine the neighbor of that primeval First Farmer dropping by and mentioning in guttural oogs and boogahs that it's easier to poke a planting hole in the ground with a sharpened stick than with a finger. Soon enough, no doubt, someone else spread the word that you don't have to bend over so much if you use a long stick. And so began the kind of friendly hint-sharing that has filled the annals of gardening history.

This chapter, as you've already guessed, perpetuates that time-honored tradition of sharing newfound know-how. If you tend a yard or garden and are looking for some better ways to get things done, these pages are for you. You'll find advice here from landscapers and arborists, nursery owners and turfgrass science professors, truck farmers and garden writers, groundskeepers and orchard researchers.

What's the best sort of hoe for all-around garden work? You'll find out from an expert who buys the best—but also makes his own. Is your lawn plagued by moles? You'll learn how to trap the critters—and even catch them live—from a man who is both a professional mole trapper and a reverent admirer of the little mammals.

Are you interested in growing a green, healthy lawn without chemicals? Read how it's done from an organic "grass gardener" who manages 100 acres of college campus. Do crows steal your corn? Learn how to scare them away with plastic grocery bags.

Plus, you'll find tips on pest control, buying plants by mail order, growing better tomatoes and corn, mulching, recycling, raising fruit, staking trees, making your own seed tape—and a whole lot more.

Oh, and by the way: A long, sharpened stick *does* make a very good stand-up planting dibble. But if you take a 3- or 4-foot length of 1-inch PVC pipe instead and cut one end at a steep angle, you can jab the pointed end into the ground to make a hole, drop a seed down the pipe's hollow center, and, presto, a dibble your ancestors would never have dreamed of!

Garden-Guardin' Tactics

Not Tonight, Deer

"One of the traditional methods for repelling deer is to spray eggs around your garden," says commercial grower Sylvia Ehrhardt, co-proprietor of Ehrhardt Organic Farm in Knoxville, Maryland. "When the stuff turns rotten, it smells bad and keeps the animals away."

Alternative? Wettable sulfur, a common natural fungicide that exudes a distinct rotten-egg odor. When Ehrhardt sprinkled the sulfur around her potato plants, she found that the deer left those potatoes alone. "I think they either smell the sulfur or take a taste and don't like it," she says. Wettable sulfur is available at most farm and orchard supply stores.

Use Soap to Bar Bambi

Deer dearly love to nibble at tender branch tips and buds. In a short time, a few deer can seriously damage young trees in an orchard. A good, tall fence is a generally reliable solution. "But we've found a cheaper cure," says Pat Williams of Gravel Switch, Kentucky, who with her husband, Greg, writes and publishes *HortIdeas*, a monthly digest of reports on gardening and agricultural research and techniques. "We hang pieces of deodorant soap in our fruit trees."

- Make soap pouches by cutting up panty hose or using old plastic-mesh onion bags. ("Any material that's basically porous will do," says Williams.)

- Put about a quarter of a bar of deodorant soap into each pouch.
- Tie one or two of the bags to a tree's branches or to a stake next to the tree.

Plain soap such as Ivory, by the way, *isn't* effective. "I don't know what's in deodorant soap, but it keeps deer away better than any other deer repellent we know of—except a large fence," Williams reports. "Our orchard used to be a favorite winter browsing spot. But the soap really helps keep the deer away."

Techno-Tip

LIFEBUOY TO THE RESCUE

A study conducted at the Smithsonian Institution's National Zoological Park in Front Royal, Virginia, produced eye-opening results in the field of deer-repellent technology. In individual trials lasting up to six days, researchers left apples and apple shoots on stakes specifically to attract Bambi and pals. Some of these yummies were accompanied by "deer repellents" and some weren't. The candidates tested included baby powder fragrance, perfume, hot sauce, several commercial chemical deer repellents...and deodorant soap (chips of Lifebuoy placed in cheesecloth bags). Of all these deer-away substances, only the soap had a significant effect for the entire six days.

Fence Out Diggers and Hoppers

A simple 3-foot-high fence made of chicken wire should keep rabbits out of your garden, but burrowing animals like groundhogs will just tunnel their way to vegetable heaven. How can you keep out the diggers and the leapers? With a fence like the one surrounding Pat and Greg Williams's garden in Gravel Switch, Kentucky. "We live in the middle of the woods, basically," says Pat Williams, "so we had to come up with a fence that would keep out all sorts of animals." Their garden fence has three lines of defense to prevent animals from climbing over, burrowing under, or just strolling in.

Here's pest control, the Williamses' way.

- Dig a trench about 6 inches deep and 1 foot wide around the perimeter of your garden, and set fence posts on the inside (the garden side) of the trench.

- Install 48-inch welded-wire fencing. Before attaching it to the posts, bend the bottom 12 inches outward at a right angle, so that it lines the trench bottom.
- Backfill the trench. Add a single strand of electric fencing a few inches above the top of the welded-wire fence. "That takes care of just about everything that tries to get under or over," says Williams. "Either way, they don't have much luck."

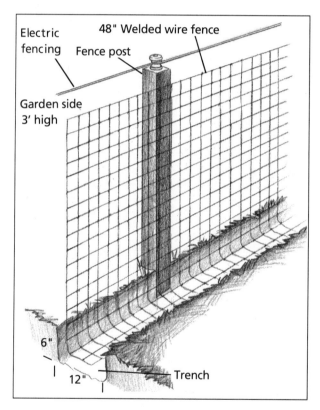

To keep out garden bandits, install a "trenched fence" that's partially buried. Backfill the trench and add a single strand of electric fencing on top.

Gaudy Duds Draw Garden Bugs

If you wear bright-colored clothing in the garden, you may be inviting a passel of pests to come with you, according to Larry Hollar, a consulting horticulturist from Hendersonville, North Carolina, who is horticulture instructor at Blue Ridge Community College as well as editor and publisher of *Landscape* IPM *Updates*, a newsletter on safe pest management for landscape professionals. Hollar notes that growers trap whiteflies with sticky yellow-colored boards, and thrips are drawn to the color blue. "So if you're wearing yellow or blue clothes, you may actually be attracting those pests and spreading them around from one planting to another," says Hollar.

An alternative?

You can't beat basic khaki, always in style in garden circles.

Debugging Plants? Sock It to 'Em!

Rotenone and Bt are effective bug chasers that don't hurt the environment. But how should you apply them?

"I've discovered the absolute best way to get the job done," says Susan Sides, a garden writer from Fairview, North Carolina, and former head gardener at *Mother Earth News* research gardens. "Put rotenone or Bt powder in an old cotton sock. In the early morning, shake the sock over and between the plants you want to cover. At that time of day, every leaf is covered top and bottom with dew. The powder that comes through the sock is very fine; it slowly floats down and sticks to the dewdrops, even underneath the leaves."

Sides says she usually shakes the sock over the tops of the plants first, then goes back between rows, dusting some more.

Scare the Crows and Spare the Greens

In spring, just-sprouted corn and tender young seedlings offer a tasty feast to winged marauders. The traditional rag-draped, straw-hatted scarecrow adds charm to a garden but unfortunately doesn't always do his job. Now, along comes Sylvia Ehrhardt's Appalachian born-and-bred neighbor with a plan for air-bag-style "scarecrows" that really *do* keep the crows away. The ingredients: plastic grocery bags, a few rubber bands, and some lung power.

To make an air-bag scarecrow:

- Blow into a plastic grocery bag until it's filled with air.
- Twist the end shut, secure it with a rubber band, and tie the bag closed.
- Attach it to the top of a 3- or 4-foot stake.
- Place the stakes strategically every 30 feet or so along each row.

According to Ehrhardt, the bags sway and rustle in the wind—and that's enough disturbance to keep crows away.

Be Kind to Your Web-Spinning Friends

To keep your crops free of serious insect damage, simply invite spiders to your garden.How? Spread a hay or dried-grass mulch between rows of vegetables when you plant them in the spring, suggests Susan Riechert, Ph.D., professor of zoology at the University of Tennessee in Knoxville.

In controlled studies conducted over a two-year period, Dr. Riechert found that insect damage to spinach, cabbage, brussels sprouts, potatoes, beans, and tomatoes was 60 to 80 percent less in hay-mulched plots than in identical bare-ground plots. And in the hay mulch, spider populations were 10 to 30 times higher.

To confirm that the spiders had indeed made the difference, Dr. Riechert removed the arachnids from mulched plots—and discovered that insect damage soared.

Techno-Tip

WHY ARACHNIDS HAVE A YEN FOR MULCH

Why do spiders like hay-mulch habitats? "A spider moves from place to place by a process called ballooning," explains University of Tennessee zoology professor Susan Riechert, Ph.D. "It lets some silk threads go in the air. When the air currents catch the threads, the spider lets go of its perch and off it goes. If it lands where conditions are unfavorable, it will take off again. And a new, bare-soil garden is probably one of the most unfavorable landing places possible.

"Peak spider migration occurs early in the growing season—April and May—when most gardens have just been planted and are still fairly bare," says Dr. Riechert. "That's why it's important to get the mulch down right away in the spring, so the spiders will stay."

Toe-See-Toe to Trap a Mole

Want to catch a live mole to liberate *outside* your garden? The method comes from professional mole trapper Tom Schmidt of Cincinnati, Ohio.

To locate deep tunnels, probe the soil in likely places with a metal rod, spading fork, or hand cultivator. To determine which of the exploratory surface tunnels a mole may be working in, use your heel to crush down a 6-inch section in each of the tunnels. Then come back later in the day, or the next day, to see which one the animal reopens.

Once you've identified the fresh tunnel, you may be able to catch the mole without a trap. "When I come back to a yard to check for new digging," says Tom, "I don't just walk in. I'll stand back 10 or 15 feet from the area. Then, if I see a fresh tunnel that wasn't there a few hours earlier, I find the point where it intersects with another single tunnel."

At the intersection point, crush the spot with your heel. Then go to the end of the new digging and start walking back on the tunnel. Tap your foot as you go, lightly squashing down the tunnel. Keep your eyes on the spot you pushed down first. If you see the topsoil move, step down hard about 6 inches *behind* the movement. With the tunnel squashed down firmly in front of and behind the mole, you'll have the animal trapped. Then get a shovel and pop the live animal out of the ground.

And what do you do with the critter? "Well, that's up to you," says Schmidt. "Moles are fascinating, likable creatures—and not a problem at all in their natural habitat, in woodland or pasture. When I catch one live, I often put it in a coffee can, punch a few holes in the top, and drive it out to the woods somewhere."

Techno-Tip

THE WAYS (AND BYWAYS) OF MOLEDOM

Pest-control experts agree that the *only* certain technique for getting rid of moles is to trap or remove them. Otherwise, you may succeed in chasing moles away temporarily, but it's nearly certain they'll be back. And then they'll probably dig a deeper, more extensive tunnel system under your property.

But how do you find the rascals in the first place?

Look for places where worms hang out, suggests Tom Schmidt, a professional mole trapper from Cincinnati, Ohio, where he's known as The MoleMan. "Eighty to 90 percent of a mole's diet is earthworms. If you find the worms, you'll find the mole."

Worms go for any place that's moist and cool, such as a mulched flower bed or a place where leaves collect. Another wormy area is the strip along a fence where grass grows a little higher.

"Moles also often follow around the foundation of a house," says Schmidt, "because there's more moisture and more food there." The edge of a flower bed, where water collects, is another prime feeding ground. "A mole will lay a good tunnel there, where it can always pick up a few worms, and then it will branch out in search of new food."

Slug Out with Cabbages!

To keep slugs away from your crops, just set a "cabbage trap." Bill Bricker, president of Bricker's Organic Farm in Augusta, Georgia, says. "I started noticing that most of the slugs in a mixed planting would attack the cabbage but not the flowers. So now I put cabbages and other ornamental cole crops among my other plantings specifically to trap slugs. One time I found 67 slugs in a single cabbage plant!"

A Slippery Scheme for Ant Attacks

Bricker has also discovered a way to foil ants. At his home in Georgia, he found that a layer of petroleum jelly would keep ants out of hummingbird feeders. "So I tried spreading the stuff on the stems of my okra plants to keep ants off the flowers and fruit," he says. And..."It works!"

Past Performance

INSECT SPRAY THE "GOOD" OLD WAY?

There were relatively few commercial chemical pesticides on the market at the turn of the twentieth century. But that doesn't mean Great-Grandpa's farming methods were entirely organic.

Arsenate of lead, for example, was considered "the best insecticide for chewing insects." The recommended solution strength: 2 pounds for every 50 gallons of water. Considering the mega-risks of lead poisoning, it's amazing Great-Grandpa survived his own garden!

Bisulphide of carbon, a liquid sold at pharmacies, was the weapon of choice against pea and bean weevils. "When exposed to the air," explains an old farming magazine, "it quickly vaporizes into a poisonous and explosive gas which is heavier than air and which will destroy all insect life. (Caution—Do not inhale the vapor, and allow no lights near.)"

Those were the days...when a tiptoe through the tulips was playing with fire.

A Castle Fit for a Toad

Don't underestimate the power of the homely "hoptoad." Studies show that during the summer, a single toad gobbles up 110 grubs, slugs, cutworms, caterpillars, and other plant-maulers *every day*. That's just under 10,000 during the hoptoad's busy season—June, July, and August. Although toads do consume some beneficial species such as earthworms and honeybees, research shows that most of their diet consists of pests.

To welcome toads to your garden, just provide a cool, sheltered place in which to hide and raise a family. "My mother taught me *that* years ago," says organic gardener Bricker. "She'd never throw a broken ceramic pot away. Instead she'd put it upside down in the garden for the toads. Mama toad crawls in there where it's dark and cool and wet, and lays her eggs. You get a real good crop of toads in the fields."

You can make a toad house out of a plastic bucket or large plastic container. Turn the container upside down, and cut a toad-size archway at the base. Put the shelter in a moist place out of the sun, and throw a little soil up around the side to keep it anchored. Then wait for the toads to come and set up housekeeping.

More Produce per Plot

Cool Your Iceberg with White Mulch

After a few too many warm, dry days, lettuce bolts to seed and becomes disagreeably bitter. But Steve White, an Asheville, North Carolina, commercial organic market grower who specializes in growing certified organic produce, has found a way to delay bolting: He covers his lettuce beds with plastic mulch painted white. The material reflects sunlight and helps the soil keep its springtime cool.

As an experiment, White planted 1,200 lettuce plants *with* plastic mulch and another 1,200 *without*. "The lettuce on the unmulched side bolted, but the white-mulched lettuce didn't," observes White.

To install White's white mulch in your garden, you can paint ordinary black plastic mulch with a roller and latex paint. Prepare your lettuce bed and lay the mulch on top. (Anchor it along the sides with soil or rocks if necessary.) Then poke a hole through the mulch wherever you want to put a seedling.

Batten Down the Carrots!

Carrot seeds need to stay moist to germinate. But in moist soil, weed seeds sprout way ahead of the carrots and crowd out the tiny seedlings.

The solution?

Lumber.

"After I plant carrot seeds," says *Hort Ideas'* Pat Williams, "I put old boards right on top of the bed. It keeps the soil moist. Weeds don't have much chance to get started, but the carrots come up really well. Just be sure to take the boards off as soon as the seeds germinate, so the plants can get some sun."

Williams suggests the same trick for other moisture-loving, slow-to-germinate seeds, too, such as parsley.

Pinch Your Peas and Beans

Here's a way to shorten the trip from the plant to the pot.

"When you're picking beans or edible-podded peas, don't yank the whole pod off," says Susan Sides, a garden writer from Fairfield, North Carolina. "If you do that, you'll still have to cut the stem ends off all those pods back in the kitchen before you can cook them. Instead, grab each pod just below the stem end between your thumbnail and forefinger. Then *pinch* it off the plant. That way, you'll leave the calyx behind."

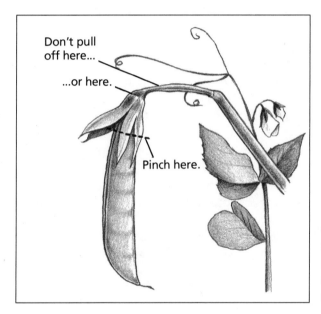

Don't pull off here...

...or here.

Pinch here.

A hint for picking beans or edible-podded peas: Pinch off the pea or bean as shown, leaving the calyx behind.

Stake Your Squash

Have you ever tried to find the main stem of a fully grown squash, pumpkin, or melon?

You know it's in that thick, tangled mass of leaves *somewhere*—but how do you track it down to check for vine borers or to give the plant's central roots a good dose of fertilizer?

"It's aways good to know where home base is on viney plants," says North Carolina garden writer Susan Sides. "So I make sure to mark them when I plant them, before it gets to be a jungle out there."

Any marker will do, as long as it's tall. Just put a 2- or 3-foot stake in the ground near the roots when the vine begins growing, and you'll have no problem finding the source.

EASY-DOES-IT GARDENING TIPS

If you love to garden, you know it *can* be hard work—especially if you have arthritis or if you're given to aches and pains. Arty Schronce, information director for the H. G. Hastings Seed Company in Atlanta, Georgia, offers these suggestions for anyone who would like to make garden chores a little less laborsome.

- To reduce bending and kneeling, mound the soil into high raised beds or terraces. With walkways between the beds, you can reach without stretching.
- Wear foam rubber knee pads for kneeling. Many garden and sporting goods stores sell them.
- Reduce lifting. Use a lightweight wheelbarrow or garden cart to move tools and supplies.
- Attach foam rubber pads to tool handles to make them more comfortable.
- Wear a carpenter's apron (with pockets) to keep seed packets and small tools handy.
- Stiff fingers? Instead of handling tiny seeds, buy young plants from a nursery, or use prepackaged seed tapes, available from most seed companies.
- In spring, put soaker hoses or sprinklers in your garden and leave them in place through the season. That way, you won't have to drag around hoses or tote a watering can.
- Worried about emergencies, like a bad fall? Wear a whistle around your neck...just in case.
- Wear heavy cotton or canvas gloves to cushion sensitive joints and protect your hands from blisters. Or buy oversized gloves and put foam padding in them.
- When buying large bags of fertilizer, compost, or mulch, ask someone at the garden center to pour the materials into smaller, more manageable bags.
- Pace yourself. Move slowly and easily. And quit working *before* you get tired.

A Guide to Your Veggies

"If you grow different varieties of the same crop and want to keep track of which ones you like best, write down their locations on a piece of paper," advises Sides. "Don't depend on little tags or row markers: They just don't stay put!"

The map doesn't need to be detailed. Just draw an outline, then note the relative locations of look-alike crops.

"If you start seeds in flats, make a map of those plantings, too," says Sides. "I guarantee if you start five different seed varieties in the same flat and mark them with tags, the tags will disappear."

Let the Good Seeds Roll

Ready-to-plant seed tapes are convenient but often expensive. With creative use of toilet paper, however, you can make your own seed tapes, using your favorite varieties of seed.

Pat Patterson, editor of the *Lane County Master Gardener Newsletter* and program assistant at Lane County Extension Service in Eugene, Oregon, suggests:

- Place seeds at their recommended spacing along the centerline of a length of ordinary toilet paper.
- Fold the paper lengthwise in thirds and dampen it slightly so the tissue sticks together.
- Let the paper dry.
- When planting conditions are right, lay the "TP tapes" in the garden and cover the row with moist soil.

And here's a bonus tip for TP plants: If you want to give your seeds a little extra boost, mix some gelatin in water and dribble it over the seeds before folding and wetting the paper. The gelatin will provide seedlings with a shot of nitrogen.

Float a Cover for Better Crops

Breathable, "floating" row covers made from superlight textiles are great insect screens and season extenders. Just drape the fabric over your plants. One such product is Reemay, a spunbonded polyester that's similar to (though heavier and more durable than) the inner liner of a disposable diaper. Sylvia and Walter Ehrhardt, who grow organic produce in Maryland for 60 families, use Reemay to reflect heat from tender crops. "It won't work in the dead of summer, but in late spring Reemay does a super job of keeping crops like radicchio and bok choi from bolting in hot weather," says Sylvia Ehrhardt.

Reemay and products like it come in 5- to 6-foot-wide rolls, in varying lengths, and are available at most garden centers. Just lay the fabric directly on top of a row (or bed) of plants. Most instructions say to anchor the edges with boards or soil, but Ehrhardt suggests using bricks spaced every 4 feet along each side. "When you want to feed or weed your plants, it's easy to move a few bricks and lift the Reemay."

A Shady Deal for Summer Lettuce

There's nothing like a good, crisp summer salad brimming with fresh leaf lettuce—but woe to the gardener who tries to raise lettuce under the blaze of the mid-July sun. Lettuce is strictly a *cool*-weather crop—unless, that is, you resort to the sort of trickery practiced by Knoxville, Maryland's cooperative market gardener Sylvia Ehrhardt.

"I tried everything to keep my lettuce growing all summer," says Ehrhardt, "but nothing worked well until I discovered shade cloth."

Shade cloth, a durable fabric screen sold by commercial farm suppliers and some garden mail-order houses, is available in a variety of lengths and widths. It comes in several light-reducing grades expressed as percentages: 50 percent shade cloth, for example, reduces the sun's intensity by half. For lettuce? "We use 63 percent grade shade cloth," says Ehrhardt.

To install:
1. Put 2- or 3-foot stakes at each corner of the bed.
2. Pair off a number of stakes to hold up the middle.
3. Stretch wire between stakes, and drape the shade cloth on top.
4. Use the clips that come with the shade cloth to hold the fabric in place (so the wind doesn't blow it off).

It's also essential to choose heat-tolerant lettuce varieties, Ehrhardt adds. "We've had good luck with Red Sails and Oak Leaf," she says, "and also with a head lettuce called Hanson."

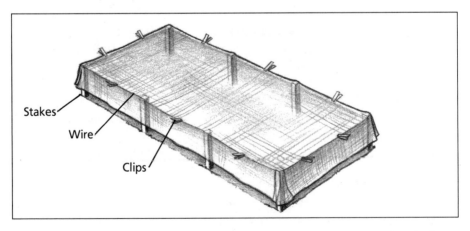

Stakes

Wire

Clips

A longer growing season for lettuce: Grow heat-tolerant varieties under shade cloth stretched between staked wires and fastened with clips.

A Trim for Summer Lettuce

Another way to keep leaf lettuce growing all season long, says Ehrhardt, is to *keep the leaves trimmed*. Most growers snip lettuce at the base, but that's no way to get all-season results.

"Let your lettuce grow until it's about 4 inches high," the Maryland grower advises, "then cut it just above the growing tip, about an inch higher than the crown. You get nice, crisp leaves, and the plants keep right on growing without wilting. You can come back every two or three weeks and cut it again. Last year we kept our lettuce growing right up until our first hard frost!"

A Feast of Soybean Meal

Organic fertilizers are now available at most garden supply centers. "Trouble is, organic bagged fertilizers are expensive, especially for us commercial growers," says Steve White, who raises organic lettuce, bell peppers, squash, broccoli, and several other crops on 2 acres in North Carolina. But White has discovered that soybean meal is an economical substitute. A natural by-product of soybean oil processing, available at feed stores, soybean meal is easy to apply.

"It's granular and passes easily through a fertilizer spreader," says White. "It gives you about 6 to 8 percent nitrogen (plus 2 to 3 percent each of phosphorus and potassium) for around $7 a bag. By comparison, commercial organic mixes run about twice as much for 5 percent nitrogen."

Stone Your Garden

Like most bedding plants, small annuals need to be mulched to prevent weeds from taking over. You can always use leaves, pine straw, or wood chips, but why not something more permanent?

"Use flat stones," says *HortIdeas* publisher Pat Williams. "Just arrange them around the plants and lay them close together, so there are only small cracks in between. The stones keep most of the weeds out and stabilize the soil temperature, too."

Try Some Tomato Inversion

Bedding-plant producer Walenty Szlosek has come up with an inverted way to grow better tomatoes. Szlosek, who works at the Tall Pine Greenhouses in Southbridge, Massachusetts, hangs his tomato plants upside down in containers and lets gravity go to work.

Why do so many of his customers like the results—and why might you consider raising your own topsy-turvy tomatoes? Walenty offers up several convincing reasons.

- Upside-down tomatoes need no staking.
- They can be moved indoors when frost threatens.
- The fruit is easy to pick.
- Soilborne diseases are virtually eliminated.
- Yields are generally higher than from conventionally grown tomato plants. Besides, the hanging vines are attractive—and a whole lot of fun to grow.

  Like to give it a try?

1. Drill or cut a hole in the bottom of a 3- or 4-gallon container. The hole should be just barely large enough for the roots of a four- to six-week-old tomato plant to fit through.
2. Wet the roots.
3. Slip the roots carefully through the hole; then gently spread them flat so they won't fall out.
4. Add about 4 inches of growing mix. (Szlosek recommends regular potting soil combined with about 2 cups of composted cow manure.)
5. Hang the inverted plants well above the ground, usually about 7 feet up. "It doesn't hurt if the full-grown plants touch the ground a little bit," Szlosek says.
6. Water the plants regularly, and layer-feed them as you would regular tomatoes.

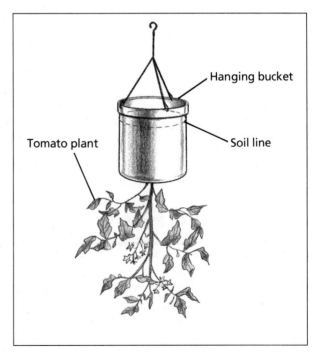

Hanging bucket

Soil line

Tomato plant

Container for an upside-down tomato plant.

What's layer-feeding? Szoslek explains: "Don't fill the whole container with soil right away. Start off with 4 inches. Every two to three weeks, add another 3 or 4 inches of potting soil mixed with composted manure. The reason is, every time you water the plant, calcium and other soilborne minerals leach downward." By adding growing medium in layers as the plant grows, you avoid the leaching, and you give the roots fresh new soil to reach into.

After the container is full to the top, Szoslek suggests scraping off the top layer of soil every three weeks or so, replacing it with a couple of inches of new soil. "Layer-feeding the plant like that keeps it greener and healthier longer, and it sets a lot more fruit.'

Don't Slip Up! Save Those Banana Peels!

Banana peels are an excellent source of potassium and phosphorus for fertilizing plants, says Andrew Plasz, Ph.D., a chemist and hobby rose grower who writes regularly for *American Rose* magazine. Here's the Plasz method of using peels for fertilizer.

1. Let the banana peels air dry until they're crisp.
2. Crumble them up and store the pieces at room temperature in sealed envelopes. ("I use about three crumbled-up peels for a large plant, and one small peel for a miniature rose," says Dr. Plasz.)
3. When you want to fertilize something, just pick the appropriate envelope and add the pieces of peel to the planting hole or potting soil.

Dr. Plasz uses the peels primarily for roses, but they can also give a boost to vegetables and houseplants.

Wash Your Produce and Soak Your Soil

To conserve water, wash off harvested garden vegetables outdoors on top of an old window screen, suggests Tennessee gardener John Meyer. "I just keep a couple of old folding chairs and an aluminum window screen at one corner of the garden. I put the chairs in a thirsty garden patch, lay the screen between them, and hose off the vegetables on the screen. The veggies get washed, and the dry patch gets the water it needs!"

Pinch Basil

The easiest way to harvest basil (and most other herbs) is to pinch back the leaves several times throughout the season. That keeps the plants growing and also keeps them compact. "Pinch out the flower buds and one or more pairs of leaves below them," says Libby J. Goldstein, food and garden writer for the *Philadelphia Daily News* and president of Philadephia's Food and Agriculture Task Force. The right place to pinch is just above the *next* set of leaves.

Pinch off
new leaves
here.

*Harvest hint for basil
and other herbs: Pinch
the new leaves.*

A Place to Pop Your Basil Pinchin's

Two or more basil plants should give you enough pinchings for pesto, basil oil, and basil vinegar, according to Goldstein. To make herb-flavored condiments, she simply keeps canning jars of olive oil and vinegar on her kitchen counter, and drops in any pinched-off leaves that she can't use fresh. "If the herbs in a jar start looking sort of pickled after a while," says Goldstein, "I just pour the liquid through a coffee filter, toss the old leaves out, and add new ones. When the oil or vinegar smells and tastes about right to me, I pour it through a filter one last time and bottle it up in a nice-looking container."

For Peas on Earth...Use Christmas Trees!

"There are lots of ways to put old Christmas trees to good use in the garden," says Goldstein. After the holidays, when neighbors drop their trees at the curbs for pickup, be ready with the pruners. There are garden supplies galore in all those trees.

- If you grow peas or pole beans and don't have a permanent trellis, "carry home a few of the trunks," suggests Goldstein. Drive a few trunks upside down in your garden and crisscross string between them to create a perfect trellis.
- "The branches with needles make great green winter mulch," she adds. "Just lay them down flat. That's how I mulch my raspberry bed."

- "In the spring, when all the needles have fallen off, take the branches off and stick some of them upright in the soil to support plants. Grow peas up them."
- If you have perennials that flop over because they don't get enough sun, or because the flowers are top-heavy, use Christmas tree branches to prop them up.

At the end of the season, just gather up all the old twigs and branches and use them for kindling. "And then you can put the wood ashes back into the garden," Goldstein suggests.

Compost the Bed You Grow On

Sure, we all like the idea of making compost from organic leftovers—but what if you don't have the patience to tend a compost pile? Try this technique suggested by Goldstein.

1. Throw organic material into the pathways between raised beds. (Compost material can include wood chips, grass clippings, rye straw, tree needles, and folded newspaper.)
2. Go about your gardening chores as always. Walk on the paths, and add more material as you get it. ("Everything I put down gets rained on and trampled on and watered on and walked across, over and over," says Goldstein.)
3. The following season, scrape the dry top layer off the paths. Underneath is wonderful, composted humus!
4. Then...pitch all that compost up onto the beds, and start the process all over again.

Each year, you'll lower the paths by digging up the trod-upon compost—and you'll raise the beds with an extra layer of organic matter, adding nutrients in the bargain.

Tuck In Your Cukes

Cucumber vines have a cumbersome habit of reaching into neighboring rows. How can you rein them in without reducing production? Paul Ledig, a retired wholesale manager who worked at Petoseed in Saticoy, California, recommends a simple technique used by professional growers. It's called vine tucking.

"When the vines start to take over another row," says Ledig, "just take the ends of the vines and tuck them back under the mass of foliage. It sounds too easy to be effective, but the trick works like a million bucks. The plant stays compact and keeps right on producing."

Vine tucking, says Ledig, also keeps row-hungry watermelons and cantaloupes under control.

Tassel Hassles? Give Corn a Helping Hand

The essence of disappointment: You peel back the husk of an ear of homegrown sweet corn and find...lots of cob and precious few kernels. The problem? Your corn wasn't pollinated sufficiently.

To avoid such disappointment, BackHome magazine's garden editor Pat Stone, of Fairview, North Carolina, says to watch the tassels on your corn carefully and wait for the spikes to open. "When the anthers hang down from the tassels and are covered with a fine, deep yellow powder—the pollen—it's time to get into the act," he says.

In the morning, after the dew has dried, go into your corn patch and, plant by plant, gently bend each tassel over and shake it just above the silk on a young ear. "You have to be careful, or you'll break a tassel off," cautions Stone, who is also publisher of the literary gardening journal Green Prints. "Take your time. Try to get pollen on every strand of silk. And pay extra attention to the plants along the outside edges of the corn patch, where pollen is most likely to blow away."

Secrets Revealed

A PRIMER ON POLLEN

How come some corn is well-pollinated, and some isn't? Here's a quick recap of the action in springtime.

Corn pollen forms on the tassel at the top of the plant, and that pollen has to reach the female flowers (each one a potential kernel) deep inside the young ears. The "pipeline" between the tassel and the kernel-to-be is the silk at the top of the ears.

Each silk is connected to two female flowers inside. Under ideal conditions, wind and insects spread enough pollen from tassel to silk to do the job thoroughly. But in a well-sheltered home garden, there may not be enough action from insects or wind. So the corn pollen doesn't always get where you want it to go. Result: Many flowers aren't fertilized. So you get skimpy, all-but-empty ears instead of plump, juicy corn.

"Sometimes nature just needs a helping hand," says Pat Stone of Fairview, North Carolina, garden editor for BackHome magazine and publisher of the literary gardening journal Green Prints. "If you really want to make absolutely, positively sure you'll get good sweet corn, you've got to put the pollen on the silk yourself. It's a little bit of a bother—but hey, we're talking sweet corn here. It's worth the trouble!"

Repeat the procedure the next morning and every subsequent morning for about a week or until the tassels stop producing pollen. With patience and luck, you'll be the proud parent of the plumpest, sweetest sweet corn ever.

Who Needs a Two-Legged Carrot?

Almost every gardener has run into this common carrot malady: forked carrots. To the carrot-grower's dismay, Bugs Bunny's favorites end up looking like nature's notion of an underground ballerina.

"Carrots usually fork when there's too much nitrogen in the soil," says Tarheel grower Susan Sides. "They do better if they follow a heavy-feeding crop, such as corn. And don't give them any extra nitrogen fertilizer."

A Cure for Green-Shouldered Carrots

If your carrots come out of the ground looking green around the tops, there's an easy cure.

"The culprit is sunshine," says Sides. "Just make sure to hill dirt up around the carrot roots when you're thinning them early in the season. If there's plenty of soil over each plant, you won't have the problem."

Make a "Covered Wagon" Cold Frame

Garden editor Pat Stone sows spinach, kale, and hardy types of lettuce such as oak leaf and Black-seeded Simpson in late summer or early fall. As a result, he looks forward to fresh greens way after most people have put their gardens to bed for the winter.

But how?

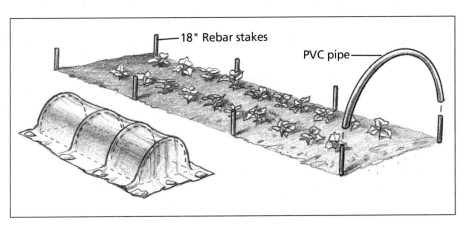

To make a covered wagon–style cold frame, bend PVC pipe over rebar stakes to form the frame, then cover the hoops with polyethylene.

"I protect my greens with a quicky, covered wagon cold frame," says Stone. To make one:

1. Drive an 18-inch length of steel rebar into the ground at each corner of the growing bed. (Rebar, steel reinforcement bar used in construction, is available at home-building supply stores.)
2. Drive in more rebar stakes opposite each other every 5 feet along each side of the bed.
3. Slide PVC pipe over the stakes opposite each other, to form the "hoops" of the "wagon."
4. Cover the hoops with a wide sheet of polyethylene, anchored at the sides with rocks or firewood.

"I can put a cold frame over a 4 × 20-foot bed in just 20 minutes this way," says Stone, "and there's no *easier* way to extend the growing season."

Tool Tips

A Study in Scarlet: Paint Your Tools

Is there a gardener anywhere who hasn't inadvertently left a tool in the garden overnight...or over winter? Wooden tool handles have a way of mellowing to a nice, earthy brown, just about the same color as garden soil. That's why Sides suggests painting your tool handles bright red—or some other color that will shout "Here I am!"

Plant a Mailbox and Hide a Tool

Tired of lugging all your tools and supplies back and forth from the garden? Set up a mailbox, suggests Michigan grower Eva Bordner. A regulation U.S. mailbox is rainproof, animalproof, and roomy enough to hold plenty of gear—gloves, stakes and twine, a trowel or hand cultivator, seed packets, shears, you name it. Plant the box near a hedge or tree to make it look right at home in your garden—or decorate it as you wish.

And by the way, adds Bordner, that box can do double duty as a bandit-chaser. "When the corn's ripe, I put a transistor radio in the box and leave it on a rock station all night," says Bordner. "*That* keeps the raccoons away!"

Half a Hoe Blade Is Better Than One

Many of the new hoe designs on the market today are clearly superior to the old traditional styles, according to Phil Colson, Garden Center manager at Highland Hardware in Atlanta, Georgia, and past president of the Georgia Perennial Plant Association. "Ergonomically, anything that works by pushing and pulling has a distinct advantage over the *old* hoe design." Unfortunately, the new-design hoes also tend to be expensive, and some are difficult to find. "But you can always modify a conventional hoe," Colson observes.

To produce a light, efficient hoe from a common store-bought model, try this.

1. Cut the hoe's blade in half, horizontally, with a hacksaw.
2. File the half blade, beveling the outside edge to match the bevel on the original blade.
3. With a hammer, bend the blade inward slightly to slant it better for chopping weeds.

The result? "You'll have a hoe that's a lot easier to use and that does a much better job of cultivating and weeding," says Colson.

Care with Handle

"When I buy a new wooden-handled tool, I sand the whole thing smooth," says Colson. "Then I close my eyes and start feeling the surface. If I feel any sharp edges, I take a rasp and round them off. When the handle feels just right, I give the whole thing a final sanding, and rub tung oil into the wood."

Why tung oil instead of traditional linseed oil?

Linseed oil, observes Colson, requires repeated applications. "Tung oil penetrates and sets up overnight. It seals the wood and keeps moisture out right from the start."

Past Performance

WHEELBARROW PLANTING MARKER

Gardeners have always sought an easy way to keep their rows neat and to space their plants perfectly. Here is one method devised by an Indiana farmer 80 years ago.

Take an old leather strap and tack ½-inch squares of wood to it, spacing the squares the same distance apart that you want to sow seeds or place plants. Then wrap the leather strap around the wheel of a wheelbarrow and fasten the ends together. As you walk a straight line, pushing the wheelbarrow in front of you, the leather strap turns with the wheel, and the blocks make regular indentations in the soil. All you have to do is go back and place a seed or seedling wherever there's an indentation— and your plants will be perfectly spaced!

Lessons in Lawn Care

Think of Your Lawn as a "Grass Garden"

That's how Irvin Brawley treats 100 acres of campus lawn and athletic fields at Davidson College in Davidson, North Carolina. As associate director of buildings and grounds at the college, Brawley grows grass the way some people tend their gardens.

"If you take the time to find out the plant's needs and provide favorable conditions, you'll get a good, healthy crop, and you won't need to use a lot of chemicals," he observes.

Picking Grass? Consider pH

Choose the right grass variety for your climate and conditions, suggests Brawley. Ask any experienced garden center dealer for advice. When you're selecting a variety, find out its cultural requirements, such as soil pH. (That's a measurement of the soil's acidity, expressed as a number.)

Check the Soil

Take a soil sample and have it analyzed. "Some seed stores will test it for free if you buy your seed and fertilizer there," says Brawley, "or you can have it analyzed by your state's extension service." Once you get the results, ask the garden center or extension service how much fertilizer to add. (Brawley uses composted turkey litter.)

It's a Lawn—Not a Skinhead!

Never cut more than one-third off the height of your grass. "Most people cut their grass too short and too often," says Brawley. "Somewhere around 3 inches is the right height for most cool-season grasses." (The cool season grasses include Kentucky bluegrass, bent grass, and fescue that grow in the northern United States.)

Cool-Season Grasses: Feed in Fall

Fertilize cool-season grasses in early fall. According to Brawley, that encourages deeper root growth: The plant builds reserves to take it through the winter and give it a good start the following year. (Late spring and summer are the best times to fertilize warm-season grasses like zoysia, Bermuda, and St. Augustine grass.)

Let the Clippings Lie

Leave grass clippings on the lawn instead of raking them up, says Brawley. If you mow so that you never remove more than one-third of the height at a time, you'll never see the clippings. They'll decompose and return nutrients to the soil.

Easy Does It

Don't try to force grass in shade. "If you have an area under a shade tree that you're having trouble getting grass to grow in," Brawley suggests, "why keep on trying? Either cut some limbs to let more sunshine reach the ground, or put in a shade-tolerant ground cover, and don't worry about it."

Get Along with Weeds

Learn to accept a less-than-perfect lawn. "If you want to reduce or eliminate chemical use, you'll have to live with a few weeds—crabgrass, plantain, dandelion, and clover," says Brawley. "But by and large, if you take good care of your grass, weeds won't do well. They grow in poor soil and don't tolerate mowing."

Past Performance

NOW, *THAT'S* A LOW-MAINTENANCE LAWN

There was a time when tidying up the yard didn't mean pushing a mower around. Instead, all you needed was a broom.

"The swept yard was quite common, particularly in the South, throughout the eighteenth and nineteeth centuries and to some extent even into the twentieth century," says Peter Hatch, a horticulturist who spent three years restoring the historic gardens in Old Salem, North Carolina, before taking the post of director of gardens and grounds at Monticello, Thomas Jefferson's historic home outside Charlottesville, Virginia.

The swept yard was simply bare earth. "But it was kept very well groomed, by sweeping it with a broom once a day," explains Hatch. "It was really sort of an auxiliary room of the house, where the children played and the wood was split."

Grass, in fact, was considered an undesirable invader in Thomas Jefferson's well-swept yard. "The idea of walking and playing on grass was totally foreign," says Hatch. "People were afraid vegetation, and especially grass, would catch on fire and spread to the house. And there was fear of snakes, too. They wanted to keep the area around their homes clean and tidy. So they just didn't have grass."

Anyone for bringing the swept yard concept back to the future?

Respect Your Grassroots Movement

For years the standard advice for watering lawns has been to soak the soil thoroughly but infrequently—once every week or two—to encourage a deep root system. That may be a good idea in the spring and fall, says Martin Petrovic, Ph.D., associate professor of turfgrass science at Cornell University in Ithaca, New York, but in the summer you may be wasting water if you soak the lawn. Not only that, you may be imposing unnecessary stress on your grass.

"Cool-season turfgrasses such as Kentucky bluegrass and fescue produce 70 percent of their roots in April and May and the other 30 percent in the fall," says Dr. Petrovic. "In June, July, and August, the roots naturally die back."

Just how *should* you water your lawn then? Cornell's turfgrass expert says lawns need about 1½ to 2 inches of water a week in midsummer. If rain doesn't fill that need, water three or four times a week to make up the difference. Research shows that the *best* time to water your lawn is between 3:00 A.M. and 8:00 A.M., but any time before noon is acceptable.

Growing Trees That Thrive

Tree Stakes? Make 'Em Rare!

Staking newly planted trees used to be common practice. Today, most horticulturists agree that tree staking should be rare.

Why? Because rigidly staked trees that aren't allowed to sway in the breeze become leggy, and their weak, slender trunks are susceptible to wind damage. They grow taller faster, but at the expense of outward growth. "If you *don't* stake a tree it grows more tissue at the ground line, because that's where the most stress is," says Ronald L. Perry, Ph.D., associate professor of horticulture at Michigan State University in East Lansing. "So the trunk develops a wide base and tapers upward." The result is a shorter, more compact tree with a strong, flexible trunk.

On very windy sites, however, extra support might be called for. In those cases, stake a tree low and loosely, so it can sway a good 6 inches in any direction. And remove the stake after a year.

Get Your Saplings Shipshape

Buying trees by mail can be convenient, and you have many varieties to choose from. On the other hand, purchasing anything sight unseen carries some risks. Horticulturist David Creech, Ph.D., director of the Stephen F. Austin State University Arboretum in Nacogdoches, Texas, says you should consider the climate where you live and where the nursery is. Most companies ship only during the spring and fall. If you live in the South and want an early spring planting, it's probably best *not* to order from a nursery far north of you. Since winter lasts longer there, the northern nursery will likely ship later than a southern one.

Bargain Arbor

Many nurseries—both local and mail-order—offer substantially lower, wholesale prices for bulk orders. If you're buying a large number of plants, look for a grower that offers a quantity discount. Watch for end-of-the-season specials, too.

Be Ready for a Tree's Arrival

If there are days when you are usually not at home, call the nursery and work out a suitable arrival date for your order, suggests Dr. Creech. Be ready to take immediate care of your order when it's delivered. With "bare root" plants, don't let the roots freeze or dry out. If you need to hold them longer than a few days, "heel them in" by placing them in a shallow trench and covering the roots with earth. Keep the soil moist as long as the trees are heeled in; but be sure you don't flood the shallow trench by overwatering. Another method is to pot them in shallow containers.

Note: Good mail-order nurseries will replace stock that doesn't survive or give you a refund or a credit on your next order. Most companies do have a cutoff period for reporting problems, however, so it's important to act promptly.

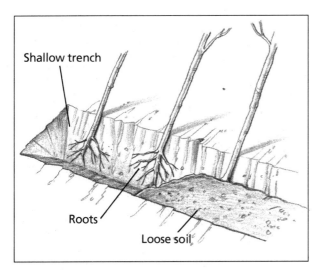

To "heel in" bare-rooted saplings, place the saplings at an angle in a shallow trench, with the roots covered by soil.

The Handspan Plan for Bigger Apples

If you love apples, you may be delighted to see your apple tree heavy-laden with developing fruit in the spring. But too heavy a crop can result in small apples of poor quality. It's better to thin the young fruit to allow the remaining apples to grow full and plump.

How much should you thin? "Open up your hand so your thumb and pinky are spread wide," says Sam Benowitz, owner of Raintree Nursery in Morton, Washington. "That's the distance you should leave between apples when you're thinning."

Sunny Side Up for Apples

You can help apples (and other fruit) ripen more quickly and evenly by pruning your trees so that the leaves don't shade the fruit, suggests Benowitz. "Don't go overboard, though," he warns. "Leaves are necessary to keep a tree in production. An apple tree needs about 30 leaves to photosynthesize sufficiently to produce one apple."

Frost Biting Fruit Blossoms?

Fool the trees, suggests Benowitz.

In sunny but cold climates, fruit trees tend to flower too early, leaving them susceptible to frost. You can fool them into flowering later by planting them on a shady, colder site near the north face of a building. The colder ground and reduced sunlight are enough to delay blooming for at least several days. "But you do have to site the planting carefully," Benowitz cautions. "The tree needs to be shaded in winter but get plenty of sun in the summer, so fruit will ripen. You have to account for the sun's angle throughout the seasons."

Fruit Trees: Between a Rock and a Cold Place

In regions where mild springs cause blossoms to open early, a little extra heat can save those blossoms from a killing nighttime frost. "Put light-colored rock around a tree's base to reflect light and absorb heat," suggests Benowitz. "Or plant your trees near a stone or brick wall. The thermal mass stores heat during the day and releases it at night."

A Push-Up Test for Pear Picking

Knowing when to pick pears can be tricky; you can't wait until the fruit actually ripens on the tree. Most types turn mushy or mealy when they tree-ripen; others take too long—sometimes as late as December. "Harvest pears before they're ready to eat and let them ripen indoors," says Benowitz.

How do you find out the perfect picking time? "Just cup your hand underneath a pear and push up," says Benowitz. "If the fruit breaks off at the stem, it's ready to pick."

Past Performance

COLONIAL PEACH PIG-OUTS

Back in the eighteenth century peaches were a prized crop, largely because peach brandy was widely popular. To ensure a healthy harvest, colonists would enlist the services of readily available local labor: hogs.

"They'd let the hogs into the orchards when the trees started bearing," explains Monticello's gardens and grounds director Peter Hatch. "The animals would manure and cultivate the ground and keep the grass back. And they'd also eat any dropped and mummified fruit, which helped control pests."

Another peach-pest-prevention technique was popularized by one of Thomas Jefferson's neighbors, says Hatch. In order to discourage peach tree borers, which are still a major problem for modern orchardists, the colonial grower would wrap moistened tobacco leaves around the trunks of his trees. "It was a very effective control method," Hatch states. Imagine that: a *good* use for tobacco leaves.

The Experts

Sam Benowitz, the owner of Raintree Nursery in Morton, Washington, has extensive experience with fruit tree cultivation in the Northwest.

Irvin Brawley is associate director of buildings and grounds at Davidson College in Davidson, North Carolina.

Bill Bricker is president of Bricker's Organic Farm, makers of organic compost, topsoil, and Kricket Krap recyclers, in Augusta, Georgia.

Phil Colson is the Garden Center manager at Highland Hardware in Atlanta, Georgia, and the past president of the Georgia Perennial Plant Association. He has gardened for 20 years.

David Creech, Ph.D., is a horticulturist and director of the Austin State University Arboretum in Nacogdoches, Texas.

Sylvia and Walter Ehrhardt, proprietors of Ehrhardt Organic Farm in Knoxville, Maryland, are cooperative market gardeners who conduct nationally known organic gardening workshops each spring.

Libby J. Goldstein, a food and garden writer for the *Philadelphia Daily News* in Philadelphia, Pennsylvania, is president of the Food and Agriculture Task Force there.

Peter Hatch is director of gardens and grounds at Monticello, Thomas Jefferson's historic home outside Charlottesville, Virginia.

Larry Hollar, a consulting horticulturist in Hendersonville, North Carolina, is horticulture instructor at Blue Ridge Community College and the editor and publisher of *Landscape* IPM *Updates*.

Paul Ledig is the former wholesale manager (now retired) at Petoseed in Saticoy, California.

Pat Patterson, editor of *Lane County Master Gardener Newsletter*, is program assistant at Lane County Extension Service in Eugene, Oregon.

Ronald L. Perry, Ph.D., is associate professor of horticulture at Michigan State University in East Lansing, Michigan.

Martin Petrovic, Ph.D., is associate professor of turfgrass science at Cornell University in Ithaca, New York.

Andrew Plasz, Ph.D., of Waukegan, Illinois, is a chemist at Abbott Laboratories and contributor to *American Rose* magazine.

Susan Riechert, Ph.D., is a professor of zoology at the University of Tennessee in Knoxville.

Tom Schmidt, who operates a business as "The MoleMan," is a professional mole trapper in Cincinnati, Ohio.

Arty Schronce is information director at H. G. Hastings Seed Company in Atlanta, Georgia.

Susan Sides, a garden writer from Fairview, North Carolina, is former head gardener at *Mother Earth News* research gardens.

Pat Stone, the garden editor of *BackHome* magazine and the editor and publisher of *GreenPrints*, lives in Fairview, North Carolina.

Walenty Szlosek is a commercial bedding-plant producer at Tall Pine Greenhouses in Southbridge, Massachusetts.

Steve White, an Asheville, North Carolina, commercial organic market grower, specializes in growing certified organic produce.

Pat Williams, of Gravel Switch, Kentucky, and her husband, Greg, write and publish *HortIdeas*, a monthly digest of reports on gardening and agricultural research and techniques.

CHAPTER 3

Cleaning

Shortcuts to Shine
and Sparkle

S crub and sweep, wipe and dust, polish, shine, and...step back to admire your handiwork. Just make sure you enjoy that squeaky clean look while it lasts.

It's the nature of housecleaning that you no sooner get it all done than you have to start all over again. That's the bad news. For the good news, read on: If you put *these* handy household hints to work for you the next time you clean house, things may go a little easier and a lot faster. Not only that, but by taking expert care of your prized possessions, you may be adding longer life as well as luster.

In this chapter we've gathered the wisdom of cleaning wizards from all walks of life, from representatives of companies with worldwide reputations to women who hold 8-to-5 jobs and don't have all day for the at-home cleaning that always needs doing. There's no right way for everyone, but there sure are tried-and-true shortcuts—and this candid advice from experts will give you a lot to choose from.

Of course, we've recommended cleaning methods that are in line with today's emphasis on being environmentally safe. Why have caustics and poisons on hand if you don't have to use them? Today, there are dozens of mixtures and methods that we've found to replace the problem pollutants: Read labels, choose carefully—and here's some know-how to lend a hand.

Sprucing Up Walls

Washing Wallpaper? Check Your Files

On the back of every roll of wallcovering is information from the manufacturer about how to clean it, notes Jeanne Byington, director of public relations for the Wallcovering Information Bureau (WIB) in New York City. "Scrubbable" means you can rub the surface briskly with a damp cloth and any nonabrasive cleaner. "Washable," means you can wash the surface gently with a mild cleaner.

Here's what the folks at the WIB suggest: At the time the paper is installed, snip a piece and file it in a household notebook. When you're ready to clean that grubby patch of wallpaper around the light switch in Junior's room, you'll know exactly how to safely remove the grime.

Save Your Dough—And Use Some!

Old wallpaper? Nothing on file to say whether it's washable or not? Don't take a chance—use some dough, says Byington. The WIB suggests buying a dough-type cleaner at any large wallcovering store. Just roll this dough back and forth on the paper, much as you would a rolling pin on pie dough. The material will pick up dust and most grime. Reshape the dough, with the clean side out, to pick up more grime. (If you can't find this product, try using slices of plain white bread.)

A Vinyl Sin

Be careful with vinyl-coated wallpapers, says Bruce Barden, technical director of GenCorp Polymer Products in Columbus, Mississippi, where wallcoverings are manufactured. "Never use any kind of abrasive cleaner, even the soft-scrub types, on vinyl-coated papers," he says. "And don't use a cleaner such as Formula 409 that contains solvents, either. It can dissolve the ink on the paper. Instead, just wash the wall with a mild dishwashing detergent and water."

Cleanser, Cleanser, on the Wall...

...What's the safest one of all?

The key to cleaning painted walls is a light touch, according to John Kolb, national accounts administrator for the Sherwin-Williams Company in Cleveland, Ohio. "On interior walls, we recommend washing off ordinary soil with a mild dishwashing detergent such as Ivory or Dawn. It will clean both flat and gloss paints, as well as those finished with polyurethane," he says.

Before You Curse Crayola...

Resistant stains, such as crayon marks, can usually be removed with a mildly abrasive cleanser such as Soft Scrub on a soft cloth, says Kolb. "Don't use too much pressure, though," he warns. "You might damage the paint."

A Solvent Solution to Stains

Tough stains on painted walls demand tough measures. Real disasters, such as a splash of motor oil, can probably be removed only with a solvent such as paint thinner, says Kolb. "On enameled surfaces in good condition you can usually get such stains off," he says. "But some residual stains would probably remain on flat paints."

The Art of Cleaning Artwork

Art Enemies in the Air

Not many of us have a painting by Rembrandt or Cassatt hanging in the living room. "But even if that painting on the wall is an 'original' by Grandmother, we want to take good care of it," observes Betsy Court, chief conservator of the Balboa Art Conservation Center in San Diego. Court suggests preventive maintenance as the first line of defense in keeping your paintings beautiful. "The main thing," she says, "is *don't smoke!*" Airborne pollution (especially cigarette smoke) is a great enemy of artwork.

Brush Up on Your Painting

Examine paintings regularly for cracks or loose paint, using a strong light directed from one side, suggests Court. If you're examining an oil painting and you find cracks, you'll do best to leave the painting alone and take it to a professional conservator. You could easily damage it by cleaning.

If the paint is sound, though, dust it every few months with a small, flat brush 2 to 3 inches wide, the kind sold in camera shops. Brush off the painting from top to bottom with light, short, downward strokes.

Swab the Canvas, Mate

If the picture is an oil painting, you can usually remove superficial grime safely with cotton swabs and distilled water, says Court. The watchword, though, is *go slowly*. Slightly dampen (do not soak) the swab in the distilled water and test it on a tiny area of each color first. (Water can be dangerous, even to oil paintings, especially if there are cracks.) If the paint appears to be solid, work gently and evenly over the surface with damp swabs, changing them often.

Some Art Won't Wash

Watercolor, tempera, acrylic, pastels, and many other media *shouldn't* be washed with water. Unless you know the painting is an oil, you should avoid using any kind of cleaning liquid, according to Court. Just dust them.

Pampering Furniture

For Lacquer, Try Naphtha

Painted designs on furniture deserve special care when it comes to cleaning.

"Never use any polish or cleaning solvent that has a petroleum base on painted furniture," warns Darrell Stegenga, a finisher at La Barge Mirrors in Holland, Michigan, a manufacturer of fine furniture. "Over time, the petroleum will soften the lacquer and make it gummy and sticky. In extreme cases, the paint becomes so soft that anyone leaning against it can actually leave the imprint of their clothing on the furniture."

Instead, Stegenga recommends cleaning painted furniture with a soft cloth dampened with plain water.

What if it's a substance like lipstick that won't disappear with water? "Just wipe it quickly with a cloth barely dampened with naphtha," he advises. "The naphtha will evaporate almost immediately and won't harm the finish."

Outfox Light Rings

Someone put down a damp glass, goshdarnitawmighty, and now there's an unsightly white ring on the finish of your wood tabletop. Wait—*act* before you *gripe*!

Because moisture from the glass hasn't penetrated the furniture's finish, white rings are actually easy to remove, says Roy Carpenter, owner of Carpenter Furniture Refinishing in Bremerton, Washington. Rub the ring with a rag or sponge dampened with denatured alcohol or mineral spirits. "That will usually remove the ring right away," says Carpenter. "Then all you have to do is polish or wax the area to restore the shine."

Suntan for Dark Rings

If you find *dark* rings on wooden furniture, it means moisture has penetrated the finish to the wood itself.

Secrets Revealed

BRUSHING UP ON MATTRESS MANAGEMENT

Most of us make the beds we lie in, but how often do we *clean* them? A mattress that has become a home to dust mites can invite allergies—and every bed benefits from occasional airing. So, what does a bedding expert recommend?

- Cover *both* the mattress and box springs with fitted pads to keep out household dust. "Use the type that is quilted on the sides as well as on top to give protection from soiling," says Todd O'Neill, manager of Arnold's Home Furnishings in Bremerton, Washington.
- Give mattresses an occasional airing. "Open the room windows and place the mattress and box springs (with bedding removed) on their long sides," says O'Neill. "The air will pass through, ventilating and freshening them."
- For surface soil, O'Neill suggests using a special fabric cleaning agent such as Fabri-Kleen, available at many furniture stores. (If the product comes in the form of coarse granules, it must first be mixed with tap water.)
- "Put the liquid in a spray bottle and spray on the stain or spot," recommends O'Neill. "Rinse quickly with a damp sponge." You want a cleaner that has no soapy sudsing agent, so it doesn't leave a residue on the mattress to attract more dirt.
- Give mattresses a deep-down deodorizing. Sprinkle a layer of carpet deodorizer (a floral scent is especially nice) onto the mattress's surface, wait 15 minutes, then vacuum off using the upholstery attachment—leaving the whole bed with the aroma of spring.

To remove dark rings, you first need to remove the finish in the area of the ring. Here's the method recommended by Carpenter: "Mix oxalic acid with water to make a paste. Dab that onto the rings, and put the furniture out in the sun if possible. That speeds up the chemical action of the oxalic acid. It may take two or three applications to remove the ring. Then go over the entire piece with a diluted mixture of oxalic acid and water to even out the color. Sand it lightly, and refinish."

Oxalic acid comes in powdered form and is available at hardware stores.

Leather: Go with the Grain

According to Charlie Coffey, who does research and development for the Classic Leather Company of Hickory, North Carolina, many kinds of leather upholstery have a faint "grain." That's the direction the hair originally grew on the hide. You need to pay attention to the grain when you clean the leather.

"Always wipe in the direction of the grain if the leather has one," cautions Coffey.

Soap Your Hide

The best leather cleaner, according to Coffey, is a gentle soap. "The main thing to be concerned with is simply removing surface dirt," he says. "A non-acid-based soap such as Neutrogena is the best cleaner to use. It won't leave spots and rings as most other soaps (even saddle soap) can do."

Coffey suggests making up a very mild solution of liquid Neutrogena and warm water and gently wiping the leather. "And don't spot-clean; work in sections such as an arm or an entire cushion," he advises. Once the leather is clean, go back and wipe it (again, *with* the grain if it has one), using a cloth dampened with clear, warm water.

Leather Eats Oil

An oil stain on leather upholstery requires immediate attention.

"Blot up as much of the oil as you can with soft cloths or tissue," Coffey says, "then let nature take over. In most cases, the stain will dissipate as the leather gradually absorbs the remaining oil."

Water Is Wicked on Wicker

Thinking of washing your wicker furniture?

Think again. "Water will impair the finish of wicker, just as it will rattan," warns Katherine McGuire, showroom manager for the McGuire Furniture Company in San Francisco. Her advice? "Just wipe it regularly with a dry cloth, and use the dusting attachment on your vacuum to remove dust that accumulates deep within the woven fibers."

Give Coated Brass a Window Treatment

Lacquer-coated brass won't actually tarnish, but it can accumulate surface soil, says Doris Loven, a consumer affairs consultant formerly with the Henredon Furniture Company, in Morgantown, North Carolina. She suggests cleaning lacquer-coated brass with a product such as Windex. "But *don't* use just an ammonia/water mixture," she says. "Ammonia can damage that lacquer finish."

Boffo Brass Buffer

Uncoated brass *will* tarnish, notes Loven, and she recommends a commercial product such as Brasso for the buff-up job. "It will do an excellent job of polishing away the grime and tarnish," she observes. "Just follow the package directions."

Keep a Tip-Top Marble Top

Ordinary household dust can obscure the natural luster of marble, but there are quick remedies, according to Shawn Norton, project manager/estimator for Northwest Marble and Terrazzo Company in Seattle, Washington.

"First wet the marble thoroughly, then wash it with a mild detergent and soft brush. Never use an abrasive cleaner," warns Norton. "Wipe it dry with a soft cloth. Then polish the dry marble with a good quality, nonyellowing paste wax, or brush on a penetrating sealer to forestall future soil." He suggests washing marble twice a year.

To Make Marble Gleam Brighter...

And if you want a brighter gleam to that marble surface, here's a swift way to polish it recommended by Pet Niebergall, restoration manager for the Marble Refinishing and Restoration Company in Seattle, Washington. Wet the marble surface with clear water and sprinkle on marble-polishing powder (available at marble dealers, lapidary stores, and some hardware stores). Rub the powder onto the marble with a damp cloth or by using a buffing pad with a low-speed power drill. Continue buffing until the marble shines.

FYI

CALL TO CLARIFY

Ever find that you're uncertain about how to clean or care for a certain appliance or household item, yet you've misplaced the booklet that came with the item? What if you can't find anyone locally who can answer your questions?

In that case, just call 1-800-555-1212 (directory assistance for toll-free 800 numbers) and ask if the manufacturer of your item is listed. Almost all major companies today have customer service departments to answer questions, and many of them can be reached by simply dialing a toll-free 800 number.

Secrets Revealed

A PENETRATING POULTICE FOR MESSY MARBLE

Exceptionally dirty marble can be cleaned by using a poultice technique, according to Pet Niebergall, restoration manager for the Marble Refinishing and Restoration Company in Seattle, Washington. Niebergall suggests the following method for cleaning and restoring heavily soiled or stained marble.

1. Mix household bleach or 6 percent hydrogen peroxide with enough white flour to make a paste the consistency of cake icing. (Figure about 1 pound of paste per square foot of surface.)
2. Wet the marble with the bleach or peroxide.
3. Using a wood or plastic spatula, spread the mixture over the marble to a thickness of ½ inch, making sure the paste extends past the dirty area.
4. Tape plastic sheeting over the poulticed area to retain moisture, and allow the poultice to set for 48 hours.
5. After two days, dampen the poultice with clean, cool water, then remove it with a wood or plastic spatula.
6. Rinse the cleaned area thoroughly with clean water, blot or wipe off excess water, and allow the marble to dry.

Tableware Care

Dishwasher Drying: A Bull in the China Shop

One reason antique china is still beautiful after a hundred-plus years is that it had careful treatment: It was washed and dried by hand. Even though dishwashers have become fixtures in most homes, "fine bone china should be washed by hand," says Una Ciardella, customer service manager for The Royal China and Porcelain Companies, in Moorestown, New Jersey. "However," she adds, "it *can* be washed in a dishwasher if you use a very mild dishwashing detergent."

But she cautions: Do *not* let it go through the drying cycle. "The heat can damage the finish," says Ciardella. "So stop the dishwasher before it reaches that cycle."

Hand Wash the Gold

"Gold-trimmed china that's used frequently should *not* be washed in the dishwasher, even if you avoid the drying cycle," says Ciardella. The gold is fragile and will wear away with this treatment. "If the china is used only occasionally, say once a month, then it could be washed in a dishwasher."

Best policy: Gently hand wash using a mild detergent.

Painless Stainless Washing

"Stainless flatware is dishwasher-safe," advises David Gymburch, account executive for the Oneida Silver Company in Oneida, New York, manufacturers of both stainless and silver-plated flatware. "But," he cautions, "you should try to remove it after the last rinse cycle and dry it by hand to avoid discoloration from hot-air drying."

He also recommends that stainless owners avoid using harsh dishwashing detergents. "Try to wash your stainless separately from aluminum, sterling, or silver-plated items," says Gymburch.

For Stainless: Remove the Dark Marks

High mineral content in the water, undissolved particles of certain detergents, or food with a high salt content can cause stainless steel flatware to develop unsightly dark marks. To remove these discolorations, use a quality stainless polish, suggests Gymburch.

But..."follow the instructions closely," he cautions, "especially in rinsing. Many cleaners contain strong chemicals that can damage flatware if they're not removed immediately."

Silver Plate Needs TLC

"Although silver plate has been tested as dishwasher safe, we recommend washing it by hand for the best results," advises Gymburch. He suggests hand washing the flatware in hot water with a mild dishwashing liquid. It should then be rinsed in hot, clear water, and dried promptly with a soft cloth to prevent water spotting.

Never soak it, even in plain water.

Silver: Dos and Dips

Any spots or tarnished areas on silver tableware can be easily removed with a good brand of gentle silver polish, says Gymburch. After polishing the flatware, wash and rinse it, then dry with a soft cloth.

"Be cautious," he warns, "of using tarnish and stain-removing silver 'dips.' " They can damage or remove the attractive dark accents on silver tableware. (And be careful with sterling silver, too: Dip can damage it.)

Polish Your Sterling Daily...The Easy Way

Sterling used regularly almost *never* needs polishing. But like silver plate, it shouldn't be put in the dishwasher. "Some of the automatic dishwashing detergents contain chemicals that can darken sterling silver," explains Delores Chandler, owner of Designs by Delores, a custom jewelry and silver shop in Port Orchard, Washington.

"Simply wash after every use with a mild dishwashing detergent, then dry with a soft cloth. That will keep it beautiful," she says. (If your sterling already has that dark stain, start by polishing with a cream polish such as Gorham, Wrights, or Haggerty.)

The Toothpaste Backup for Silver

Chandler recommends using a cream polish to keep sterling gleaming brightly. But what if you're all out of polish?

"In an emergency you can even use toothpaste to polish sterling," says Chandler. "It contains similar ingredients to silver polish and rinses off easily with plain water."

Worst-Case Cure for Silver

If you've tried using cream polish on badly tarnished silver and it just doesn't work, you may have to take semidrastic action.

For silver so badly tarnished that even polish won't restore the gleam, Chandler recommends sprinkling the piece with salt, then rubbing it gently and quickly with a sponge that's been dampened with vinegar. "The chemical reaction of the salt and vinegar will take the tarnish right off," she says.

But this is a last resort effort, she warns. Only use "the salt cure" on silver in the worst condition.

Hot on Crystal? Try Lukewarm

Carlene Weachock, marketing communications assistant for Waterford Crystal, in Wall, New Jersey, warns against using hot water with fine crystal. Tests have shown that repeated washing in very hot water with detergents can damage the surface polish of the finest crystal.

So Weachock recommends washing one piece of crystal at a time in warm water, using mild soap flakes. Also, rinse in warm water, then dry and polish the glass with a nonfluffy and lint-free cloth. This will keep the glass crystal-clear and sparkling.

Washing Crystal—Do a Rice Job

Small-necked crystal decanters and vases are tough to clean. But you can get to the bottom of the situation by pouring in a handful of rice with warm, soapy water. Swish the water and rice around gently, says Weachock, then rinse with clean, warm water and dry immediately.

Note: This works with any glassware.

Vinegar Power

Vinegar works nicely to remove the lime deposit that hard water leaves on crystal vases, says Weachock. Wipe the stains with a cloth that's been soaked in vinegar and wrung out. Then rinse and dry the crystal.

Rub Out Candle Drips

You don't have to scrape old wax from glass, sterling, or brass candle holders: Just give them the hot water treatment, says Judy Anderson, manager of Wicks and Sticks candle shop in Silverdale, Washington. "Just place the candle holder in very hot water until the wax softens. Then you can easily rub it off with a paper towel."

The Chip-Off Technique

To get the wax off *wooden* candle holders, put them in the refrigerator until the wax hardens. Then chip it off, says Anderson.

A Drip off the Old Cloth

The candles dripped on your linen tablecloth! Don't worry, that wax will come off, according to Anderson. With a blunt knife, scrape as much wax as you can off the tablecloth. "Then place a thick pad of paper towels under and over the remaining wax. Set an iron on 'hot' and apply heat to the pad of paper towels. The heat will melt the wax, and the towels will absorb it."

Repeat the procedure if some wax remains.

Kitchen Cleanup

Tight Squeeze Is a Breeze

To clean those tight places behind and under the refrigerator, Jim Fowler, franchise service manager of the Merry Maids cleaning service in Omaha, Nebraska, suggests that you extend your reach by a yard. Dampen a small towel with water or vinegar and wrap it around a yardstick. Slide your yardstick cleaner into the narrow space and whisk it back and forth to pick up lint and grime. As the towel collects dirt, rinse if off, wrap it around the stick, and repeat until the crevice is clean.

You can use the same technique to clean between the stove and cabinets, or in other hard-to-reach places.

Stop Sink Stain...Before It Happens

Enamel kitchen sinks do stain—but they will stay beautiful for years with just a bit of care.

To remove stains: Never use any harsh abrasives on the enamel surface, advises Nancy Depotolla, manager of public relations at Kohler Company, makers of kitchen and bathroom fixtures, in Kohler, Wisconsin. Use only mild household cleaners for daily use, and on occasion, a very *mild* abrasive cleaner to eliminate stains.

Stainless steel sinks? Some of them do stain (depending on the grade of steel). But you may be able to rub out the stain with vinegar, Soft Scrub, an automobile rubbing compound, or chrome cleaner.

To *prevent* sink stains:

1. Never leave dishes or pans soaking for any length of time.
2. Don't put coffee grounds or tea bags into the sink.

Secrets Revealed

HOW TO COUNTER STAINED COUNTERS

What's the best way to get stains out of laminated countertops? It all depends—on the laminate surface and the type of stain. Matte-finish and high-gloss laminates should be cleaned with a nonabrasive, damp cotton cloth and mild liquid detergent or gentle household cleaner, says Brenda Cave-Grevious, manager of consumer relations at Formica Corporation in Cincinnati, Ohio. Any residual smears or streaks may be removed with a mild glass cleaner on a cotton cloth.

For stains left by hair dyes and rinses, laundry bluing, and iodine, blot the stained area for no longer than 1 minute with a clean, soft cloth dampened sparingly with household-strength chlorine bleach, says Cave-Grevious. Rinse quickly with water to remove any residual bleach.

Other products that can cause permanent staining on laminates include wood stains, indelible inks, marking pens, cash register ink, newsprint, and food pricing and label inks. To remove such stains, or at least lighten them, apply full-strength Pine-Sol liquid cleaner or a mild household spray cleaner, says Cave-Grevious. Give the cleaner time to draw out the stain. Then blot it away with a damp cloth and rinse. (If a stain remains after this treatment, try sponging it with denatured alcohol.)

A few kinds of stains will usually disappear after repeated daily cleaning. They are fruit juices, coffee, tea, glass rings, and water marks.

Your Teflon Resident

Teflon pans must be treated gently to preserve their coating. "Just wipe the Teflon surface with an oily cloth, then put it in the dishwasher," advises William H. Samenfink, an instructor of hotel and restaurant management at Washington State University in Pullman, Washington. "You can scour the bottom with Ajax or Comet, but never the cooking surface."

Pan Handling—The Recommended Way

The best way to clean brass- or copper-bottom pans is with a commercial polish, says Samenfink.

For heavy aluminum pans?

"Use a strong cleanser such as Comet or Ajax and a scouring pad to clean them," he says. "Just scrub, then rinse. That's all they need."

Eliminate Lime

Your dishwasher puts in a lot of time scrubbing and cleaning. But the time comes when the dishwasher itself needs cleaning.

"If you have hard water in your area, you'll probably get a lime buildup on the inside of your dishwasher," says Christine Brosnan, consumer assistance representative for KitchenAid Dishwashers located in Benton Harbor, Michigan. She recommends dissolving this film with Lime-Away, a product available in any grocery store. "You can also use citric acid crystals if you prefer," she adds. "Most grocery stores carry them."

A Dressing for Dishwashers

The Vinegar Institute in Atlanta, Georgia, has another solution to the problem of hard-water film; cleaning the dishwasher every week with vinegar.

Just place a cup of vinegar in the bottom of the machine and run it through its cycle, advises Sandra Davenport, administrative assistant for the institute. Since no one wants to waste water these days, do some glassware at the same time: The vinegar rinse will leave them gleaming, too.

Spiffy Floors and Carpets

Raise the Pile to Scour the Soil

Everyday dirt and grit are the greatest enemies of carpets, not only clouding their beauty but shortening their lives as well. The best way to keep them looking their best is to use a vacuum cleaner with a rotating brush, says Ned Hopper, director of governmental affairs for the Carpet and Rug Institute in Washington, D.C. The right machine raises the carpet pile as it removes the

Secrets Revealed

FROM BAD WINE TO GREAT CLEANER

Some 10,000 years ago, some casual drinkers discovered quite by accident that wine, when left too long, turned sour. The chance discovery that fermentation of sugars created alcohol, then vinegar, led (indirectly) to the creation of dozens of products that cooks use for everyday cooking and preserving. And today's homemakers are rediscovering vinegar as a superb cleaning aid that will take coffee stains from china cups, deodorize the air in our rooms, and perform a host of other useful tasks.

Why is vinegar such a great cleaning aid? The answer is *acid*—specifically, acetic acid. "It's a naturally occurring organic acid," says Jane MacDonald, a technical manager for the Vinegar Institute in Atlanta, Georgia. "Because of its chemical structure, it can dissolve the mineral salts that leave unsightly films on surfaces. It's also mild, which is a definite advantage in cleaning."

soil. "You need good mechanical action in addition to suction to do a good job," he explains.

Miracle or Not? Tissue Sops Spots!

Many modern carpets have chemical coatings that make the fibers stain-resistant—but *not* stainproof. On carpets that have been treated, you can usually sponge up accidental spills with warm water. Some stubborn spots, though, require more intensive attention.

Hopper gives the following guidelines for removing spots.

1. Blot up as much liquid as possible with clean, white tissues or towels. (Remove semisolids by scraping them up with a rounded spoon.)
2. Apply spot remover or a detergent solution to a white towel and blot the spot thoroughly. *Do not scrub.* Work from the edges of the spot toward the center.
3. Continue until the spot is removed or until no more can be removed. Then place a ½-inch-thick layer of white tissues over the spot and weight it down.
4. Replace the tissues in half an hour. Leave the tissues on the spot overnight, letting them dry. Then remove. By dawn, there's a good chance the spot will be gone.

Secrets Revealed

COUNTERATTACK THE SPOTS AND GLOPS

Directly from the Carpet and Rug Institute in the nation's capital, here are appropriate treatments for common stains.

Mayonnaise Mop-Up. Scrape up mayo with a rounded spoon first, then blot with a commercial spot remover. Once the oiliness has disappeared, wipe the area gently with detergent on a folded tissue. Never use a detergent that has a bleaching or brightening ingredient, which may leave the cleaned area substantially lighter than its surroundings. (The mayonnaise mop-up method works on other greasy spills, too.)

Count Dracula's Housekeeper's Secret Formula. To remove blood, again use a rounded spoon to scrape it up, then wipe the area with warm water on folded tissues. Finish by gently sponging with a mixture of warm water and mild household detergent.

After the Party (and Kids' Party) Is Over... Stains from red wine and Kool-Aid *look* critical but can nearly always be removed if attacked immediately. Begin by placing a ½-inch layer of white tissues on the spill and weighting it down to absorb as much liquid as possible. As one pad takes on the color of the stain, replace it with another until no more color bleeds through. Then, using a mixture of 1 cup warm water to ⅛ teaspoon of detergent, rub the area with the fingers, not a brush. Blot it well with tissues. If the color remains, repeat the final step using 1 tablespoon of ammonia to 1 cup of water.

Booties for Chair Legs

When shampooing carpets, you don't have to move furniture to another room. David Schiller, owner of Coit Drapes, Carpets, Upholstery, Area Rugs, and Blinds in Tacoma, Washington, suggests you slip a plastic bag under each furniture leg, then tape it up to make a "bootie" before you start.

Move each piece of furniture slightly to one side as you come to it. Shampoo in the space, then move the furniture back immediately.

Revitalize That Vinyl

Vinyl sheet flooring looks wonderful when it goes down, so how come it doesn't keep looking that way? From Shirley Bomberger, consumer representative for Armstrong World Industries (manufacturers of many types of flooring), in Lancaster, Pennsylvania, come these suggestions.

- Sweep or vacuum the floor daily to remove surface debris. If vacuuming, use the vinyl or hardwood floor attachment (a rug beater bar can visibly damage sheet vinyl.)
- Wipe up spills as soon as possible.
- Wash with a no-rinse cleaner weekly.
- Apply a wax only if a high gloss is desired. (If your flooring has a no-wax surface, regular waxing is not needed at all.)
- Once or twice a year, clean with a heavy-duty cleaner.
- *Avoid* using scouring powders or steel wool pads, as they can scratch and eventually dull the floor's surface. And bypass soap-based detergents. It's hard to completely rinse soap from flooring surfaces, and the resulting film can dull the finish.

CLEAN TILE TIPS

Floor tiles come in a variety of materials, and each needs to be cleaned differently, says Rich Cecilian, manager of the Color Tile Company in Bremerton, Washington. Here are Cecilian's tile tips.

Vinyl floor tile. Also called resilient floor tile, vinyl tile demands much the same care as vinyl sheet flooring. "Don't use a powder-type cleaner," warns Cecilian, "because it doesn't completely dissolve. Rough granules are left suspended in the water, and it's like washing the floor with sandpaper. Such a cleaner can take as much as a year off the life of vinyl tile." Instead, Cecilian recommends the use of a concentrated liquid cleaner.

Urethane-finished wood parquet tiles. These tiles are prefinished at the factory for easy home maintenance. Sweep or vacuum to remove surface grit, then mop occasionally with water to restore their shine. These tiles should never be waxed.

Stain-and-wax-finished wood parquet tiles. Similar to urethane-finished wood tiles, these tiles do not have a hard finish and are susceptible to water staining. So any cleaning should be done quickly and with a mop wrung almost dry. Cecilian suggests finishing off with any good paste wax, but never with a water-emulsion self-polishing wax.

Asphalt tile. Many older homes today have at least one room floored with asphalt tile. According to Cecilian, any commercial floor-cleaning compound will clean asphalt tile satisfactorily. "Just be sure to wax afterward to add shine and protect the floor from future soiling."

Erase Black Marks

To rub out black heel marks on your shiny, clean floor, use a round type-writer eraser, recommends Jim Fowler of Merry Maids. The eraser can remove black heel marks from resilient or asphalt tile, but not wood. Rub the eraser *gently* across the mark, then wash the area. If your floor is the waxable type, you'll probably have to rewax that section.

FYI

WHAT DO VASELINE, SOAP, AND SUGAR HAVE IN COMMON?

Any one of them—or all—can help keep hands clean when you're cleaning up.

Ideally, we should wear rubber gloves whenever we tackle a cleaning job. But face it, sometimes that just isn't practical. You can protect your hands and arms from detergents and cleaning solutions, though, if you coat them liberally with petroleum jelly *before* picking up that first sponge and bottle of cleaner. And run your fingernails across a bar of bath soap, too. They'll be a breeze to brush clean later on. Or as Jim Fowler of the Merry Maids cleaning service in Omaha suggests, wash your hands with soap and a teaspoon of sugar to *really* get the pores clean!

Give Hardwood a Lotta Luster

Hardwood floors should be cleaned weekly with nothing more than a damp mop, says Rebecca Moore, owner/manager of a ServiceMaster franchise in Ashland, Oregon. "Then once a month, put 2 ounces of vinegar in a bucket of cool water and mop with that solution," she says. "Towel dry immediately, and buff with dry toweling. This will bring up the luster, and the floor will be beautiful."

Beating Bathroom Bothers

Smile! Clean Tile!

Usually, ceramic tile just needs an occasional wiping with any mild household cleaner to keep it gleaming. But when soap scum builds up, a slight escalation of effort is called for.

1. Wipe the tile with a mixture of one part water to four parts vinegar.
2. Rinse with clean water.
3. Buff the tiles to prevent streaking.

Did You Brush Your Grout Today?

To clean up the grout between ceramic tiles, follow the suggestion of ServiceMaster's Rebecca Moore, and scrub the grout with a toothbrush dipped in household bleach.

Caution: Never use bleach along with any other cleaner. Some combinations can produce extremely toxic fumes.

Shape-Up for Showers

Use a toothbrush with baking soda to get grime and mold out of a shower door track, suggests Fowler.

Go Soak Your Shower Head

Mineral deposits can build up inside a shower head, clogging holes and severely restricting the flow of water. Clean the shower head by soaking it in vinegar overnight, advises Moore.

Just unscrew the shower head and place it in a bucket. Pour in enough vinegar to cover and let it soak overnight.

A Citric Solution

Many experts recommend wiping shower doors with a vinegar/water mixture or with a fine steel wool pad and dishwashing detergent to eliminate soap film. Jim Fowler says one way to *keep* that film off is to rub or spray the clean doors with a light coat of lemon oil—sold as furniture polish and available at most hardware stores. After coating the doors, buff them dry.

For Finer Flushing...

Avoid commercial, in-the-tank cleaners, as they may affect the working parts of the flush valve, says Nancy Depotolla of the Kohler Company. Just clean the bowl regularly with any household cleaner.

Preserving Plastic Toilet Seats

Many of today's toilets come with color-matched plastic seats that should be washed *only* with a regular household cleaner, according to Depotolla. Be careful *not* to splash a strong bowl cleaner on plastic seats, she advises, especially around the hinge areas and the bumpers of the seat.

Want a shinier seat? Just spray the seat with a good-quality furniture polish and rub dry, Depotolla adds.

Less Toil, Less Trouble

Persistent brown stains in toilets require a good dose of household bleach, according to Martha Burlington, executive housekeeper for the Mark Antony Hotel in Ashland, Oregon.

Just pour 1 or 2 cups of bleach into the bowl and swish it around with a brush, she advises. Close the lid, wait an hour or so for the bleach to work, then flush.

Caution: Do *not* combine bleach with other bowl cleaners. The combination can result in toxic fumes.

Odd-Job Tactics

Don't Dry Clean Down

"We recommend *washing* down comforters," says Laura Zimmerman, manager of Scandia Down shops in Seattle, Washington. "Dry cleaning is not always good for down. The cleaning solutions can take the natural oil from down fibers and make them more susceptible to breaking down."

Dry cleaning will not actually *ruin* down, however. "If the cover of a comforter is badly stained," she says, "sometimes dry cleaning will remove the fabric stains better then washing. But washing is better for the down itself."

A down comforter can be cleaned in a normal washing machine. Set on a cool temperature and on the gentle cycle. Dry at low heat.

If Your Lock Locks Up...

"The best way to clean a stubborn lock," says Ilene Dyer, locksmith with Silverdale Locksmith in Silverdale, Washington, "is to squirt a product such as WD-40 into the keyhole and onto the bolt." Turn the handle back and forth several times as you squirt to distribute the WD-40 (available in hardware stores) throughout the tumblers, Dyer suggests. Your lock will work as good as new after that.

Shed the Soot from the Hearth

If the bricks around your fireplace look like the sooty face of a coal miner, follow the advice of Jerry Winslow, owner of Heritage Fireplace Shops in Bremerton, Washington.

- First, give those smoked-up bricks a good scrubbing with a half-and-half vinegar-and-water mixture or a mild detergent-and-water mix.
- If some stain remains after scrubbing, use a product called Brick and Stone Cleaner, available at fireplace shops. The mild cleaner comes in a pump bottle. Spray it on the bricks, then scrub with a brush.

- *Caution:* "You should test any cleaner on an inconspicuous spot first, especially if the brick is light colored," says Winslow. Even a mild cleaner may discolor some bricks.

Streak Beater

In spite of jokes to the contrary, most of us *do* do windows. And what other cleaning job causes so much frustration? Streaks are the bane of weekend window-cleaners. But there is a way to beat 'em.

"Use a squeegee to get the job done fast," advises Jim Fowler of Merry Maids in Omaha. "Wipe horizonally on one side of the window and vertically on the other side. That way, if you find a streak, you'll know instantly which side it's on. You won't have to keep going back and forth, trying to locate it."

Tumble the Curtain Dust Away

To spruce up dusty curtains, just toss them into a dryer with a barely damp towel, advises Fowler. Use the no-heat setting, and let the curtains tumble for 5 or 10 minutes. Hang them immediately to avoid wrinkling. (The same method works on small throw rugs. They'll come out fluffy and dust-free.)

Dip and Swish Your Blinds

Give mini-blinds a bath the easy way—just dunk them in a bathtub filled with warm water and detergent, says Fowler. After they're dunked, use a soft brush to loosen soil (if necessary). Drain the water from the tub and rinse the blinds in the shower. Hang them over the curtain rod to dry.

A Simple Wash for New Stained Glass

Modern stained glass is an extremely hard material and requires very little care. Any dishwashing liquid or an ammonia-and-water mixture will keep today's stained glass gleaming, says Kathy Schaeffer, a stained glass designer at the Mandarin Stained Glass Studio in Tacoma, Washington. "Lightly spray the cleaning mixture on the glass and rinse with plain water," she says. "Polish the leading by rubbing the panel again with a soft cloth such as an old T-shirt or sheet."

For Old Stained Glass, Gently Does It!

"If stained glass is antique, and has painted sections, you must be extremely careful," cautions Schaeffer. "Much of this glass was exposed to the elements for years, and the painted areas are very fragile. Use a soft brush to gently dampen the glass with a mixture that consists of 1 teaspoon ammonia to 1 quart of water. Then let the glass air dry."

Secrets Revealed

HOW TO BAN DIRTY BOOKS

There's a reason why books wear dust jackets—but whether they have their jackets on or off, they *always* gather their share of household dust. It's a good idea to clean your books about once a year to prevent build-up of dust and grime. Begin with the books on the top shelf and work your way down. (Of course, it's a lot easier if you can work with a partner on this annual dusting project!) To clean them safely, heed these suggestions from Nancy Little, assistant manager of the Preservation Unit at the Seattle Public Library in Seattle, Washington.

- "For dust, put a layer of cheesecloth over the nozzle of a vacuum, and go to it. The cheesecloth will keep the vacuum from sucking up loose pieces of paper."
- For smudges and spots on the covers, erase them away. "For minor spots, use the eraser called Pink Pearl, which you can get at an artist's supply shop or a stationer's store. It is similar to a pencil eraser, but not so abrasive. Just rub it on the spot."
- For larger smudges, Little recommends using the product called Opaline, also available from artist's supply shops. "Opaline is powdered eraser that comes in a bag. You squeeze the powder onto the book, then rub it onto the spot."
- To keep valuable books safe and clean, "the best solution," says Little, "is to enclose them in an acid-free case that will protect the paper from deterioration."

Lighten Up—Clean Your Shades

The best way to keep your lampshades free of dust (and therefore radiating the most light) is to brush them regularly, top to bottom. And the handiest tool for the job? A 4-inch-wide paintbrush, according to Fowler.

Dust That Faux-Gloxinia

"Never put liquids, even plain water, on your silk floral arrangements," says Dana McDonald, president of Silk Botanicals, in Surfside Beach, South Carolina, a firm that manufactures fine artificial plants. "These flowers are made of fabric, and the liquids can soak in and spot them. Instead, just dust them lightly with a feather duster."

FYI

HOW TO CLEAN LADY LIBERTY...WITH NAHCO3

Call it baking soda, call it sodium bicarbonate, or just call it "that box of stuff under the sink"—by any name, it's a natural cleaning aid homemakers have depended upon for generations. And today's environmentally concerned homemakers are rediscovering its virtues.

According to the Arm & Hammer Company, pure sodium bicarbonate is one of nature's safest chemicals. It is so pure, in fact, that more than 200 tons of baking soda were used to remove coal tar from the inside of the soft copper skin of the Statue of Liberty. The baking soda didn't harm the copper or pose any health risk to workers, even in that confined working space.

The Experts

Judy Anderson is the manager of Wicks and Sticks candle shop in Silverdale, Washington.

Bruce Barden is the technical director at GenCorp Polymer Products in Columbus, Mississippi.

Shirley Bomberger is a consumer representative for Armstrong World Industries, Inc., in Lancaster, Pennsylvania.

Christine Brosnan is consumer assistance representative for KitchenAid Dishwashers in Benton Harbor, Michigan.

Martha Burlington is the executive housekeeper for the Mark Antony Hotel in Ashland, Oregon.

Jeanne Byington is director of public relations for the Wallcovering Information Bureau in New York City.

Roy Carpenter is the owner of Carpenter Furniture Refinishing in Bremerton, Washington.

Brenda Cave-Grevious is manager of consumer relations at Formica Corporation in Cincinnati, Ohio.

Rich Cecilian is the manager of Color Tile in Bremerton, Washington.

Delores Chandler is owner of Designs by Delores in Port Orchard, Washington.

Una Ciardella is customer service manager for The Royal China and Porcelain Companies, Inc., in Moorestown, New Jersey.

Charlie Coffey is in research and development at the Classic Leather Company in Hickory, North Carolina.

Betsy Court is chief conservator of the Balboa Art Conservation Center in San Diego.

Sandra Davenport is administrative assistant at the Vinegar Institute in Atlanta, Georgia.

Nancy Depotolla is manager of public relations at the Kohler Company in Kohler, Wisconsin.

Ilene Dyer is a certified, registered locksmith at Silverdale Locksmith in Silverdale, Washington.

Jim Fowler is franchise service manager for Merry Maids cleaning service in Omaha, Nebraska.

David Gymburch is an account executive for Oneida Silver Company in Oneida, New York.

Ned Hopper is the director of governmental affairs for the Carpet and Rug Institute in Washington, D.C.

John Kolb is national accounts administrator for the Sherwin-Williams Company in Cleveland, Ohio.

Nancy Little is assistant manager of the Preservation Unit of the Seattle Public Library in Seattle, Washington.

Doris Loven is the former consumer affairs consultant at Henredon Furniture Company in Morgantown, North Carolina.

Dana McDonald is the president of Silk Botanicals in Surfside Beach, South Carolina.

Jane MacDonald is a technical manager for the Vinegar Institute, which is located in Atlanta, Georgia.

Katherine McGuire is showroom manager and national showroom coordinator for McGuire Furniture Company in San Francisco.

Rebecca Moore is the owner and manager of ServiceMaster of Ashland in Ashland, Oregon.

Pet Niebergall is restoration manager for the Marble Refinishing and Restoration Company in Seattle, Washington.

Shawn Norton is project manager/estimator for Northwest Marble and Terrazzo Company, Inc., in Seattle, Washington.

Todd O'Neill is manager of Arnold's Home Furnishings in Bremerton, Washington.

William H. Samenfink is instructor of hotel and restaurant management at Washington State University in Pullman, Washington.

Kathy Schaeffer is a stained glass designer at Mandarin Stained Glass Studio in Tacoma, Washington.

David Schiller is the owner of Coit Drapes, Carpets, Upholstery, Area Rugs, and Blinds in Tacoma, Washington.

Daryl Stegenga is a finisher at La Barge Mirrors in Holland, Michigan.

Carlene Weachock is marketing communications assistant for the Irish company Waterford Crystal, Inc., at its U.S. headquarters in Wall, New Jersey.

Jerry Winslow is the owner of Heritage Fireplace Shops in Bremerton, Washington.

Laura Zimmerman is the manager of Scandia Down shops in Seattle, Washington.

CHAPTER 4

Car Care

Good Ways
to Pamper Your Wheels

With the exception of your children, what do you suppose will be the biggest investment you make in your lifetime?

Did you say your house? Could be. But maybe not.

Assuming that you replace your car every five years, you'll probably sink more money and emotion into automobiles than any other object.

For you doubters, here's some quick math: A car buyer would be lucky to escape a dealer's showroom for anything less than $15,000. Let's say that between the ages of 25 and 70, you buy about ten cars—or about one every five years. Using those numbers, by the time you hit 70, your stock in the auto industry is likely to amount to a minimum of $150,00. And that's not counting gas, oil, tires, spark plugs, brake pads, clutch plates, and fuzzy dice for the rear-view mirrors.

Convinced?

Well, since cars *are* a major investment, it's important to get the most out of them. But how do you do that?

First, assume that the maintenance intervals recommended in your owner's manual are minimums—and follow them. Second, heed the expert advice that follows. And third, redefine your relationship with your car.

Relationship? Yes, but not the sort you're thinking. No need for candle-light and bubbly. A little consideration and an occasional checkup by a well-chosen professional will do it.

To initiate this new relationship, the first thing you'll probably have to do is break the insidious love/ignore/hate cycle that so many car owners fall into. The cycle goes like this: (1) You love the car when it's new; (2) you ignore it during the functional middle years; and, (3) you hate it when it finally breaks down from being ignored.

Instead of considering your car a hulking mechanical problem just wait-ing to happen, why not think of it as a friendly pet? You feed it when it's hun-gry, keep up its coat, and take it in for scheduled shots. Over time, you develop a trusting relationship. You know when something's not quite right, and after a while, you instinctively know when a problem is serious enough to seek the doc's attention. And you *expect* the critter to need more attention as it becomes older.

Like having a pet, owning a car never becomes entirely reciprocal. But if you get in tune with its needs, you'll come as close as possible to having a loyal friend.

Slick Answers to Your Oil Questions

For the Short-Hop Crowd: Frequent Changes

"There's no such thing as a standard mileage for changing your oil," says B. V. Alvarez, of Fletcher, North Carolina, who used to build engines for stock-car racing. "The frequency should depend on how you drive your car.

"The main problem with oil today is contamination from moisture. To get rid of the water inside the crankcase, you need to drive your car at least 7 miles (or 10 miles if you live in a cold climate) each time that you use it," says Alvarez. "Otherwise, the engine never gets warm enough inside to evaporate water."

The trouble is, most people don't drive that far. When they climb in the car, it's usually for short hops of just a few miles. Under those conditions, "Change that oil!" insists Greg Parham, owner of Import Connection of Arden, North Carolina.

According to Parham, who maintains and repairs Ferraris, Porsches, and Mercedes-Benzes, "Most people don't change their oil often enough. I know what the owner's manual says, but in real life most people make short trips and don't get their engines up to operating temperature. For the average person, oil ought to be changed every 3,000 miles. If the car is turbocharged, change it every 2,500 miles."

Secrets Revealed

WHO PUT WATER IN YOUR ENGINE?

"Wait just a minute," you're thinking. "You're telling me I need to change my oil because there's water in it. Where'd the water come from?"

Water sneaks into motors from two primary sources, says former NASCAR driver B. V. Alvarez. "First, when you burn a hydrocarbon fuel such as gasoline, water is one of the by-products. And when an engine—even one in perfectly good shape—is cold, water generated during combustion can slip past the piston rings and into the crankcase.

"Outside air is an even more important source of moisture in many climates," says Alvarez. "Although engines are well sealed to prevent noxious fumes from getting *out*, outside air can get *in*. When you turn off your engine, the gases inside the crankcase are hot. And as they cool, they contract, drawing in outside air. Often this happens in the evening, when air is especially moisture-laden."

Syns for the Long-Distance Driver

Are you a long-distance commuter?

Then you may not need to change your oil as often as the manufacturer recommends—especially if you use synthetic oils, engineered lubricants not based on petroleum.

Crankcase oil is no longer as simple as the black goo that oozed from a bullet hole in Jed Clampett's backyard. Synthetic oils are a good alternative for many car owners.

"Synthetics can withstand much higher temperatures than petroleum-based oils without breaking down," says Alvarez. "They stay cleaner longer than petroleum oils, and their viscosity [thickness] remains stable for many more miles.

"If you're driving far enough each day to thoroughly warm your engine, you should consider switching to a synthetic oil and changing it at the manufacturer's recommended intervals. In many cases these recommendations are as long as every 7,500 miles. But I wouldn't wait that long with a petroleum-based oil."

Synthetics are more expensive than petroleum-based oils, but with less-frequent changes, you'll end up buying less oil.

What about Oil Additives?

Many drivers believe that oil additives really help to "clean the engine" and keep the car running in peak condition. Is that true?

In a word, no.

According to David McManness of Denver, Colorado, an experienced Oldsmobile and Honda mechanic and a former vocational school auto-shop teacher, additives are mainly stop-gap measures for cars that really need *mechanical* attention.

"Most oil additives only mask a serious mechanical problem—and usually for a very short time. The typical oil additive just makes the oil thicker. That helps it to fill in the gaps between worn parts, keeping an engine that's essentially shot on the road a little longer.

"If you're out in the middle of nowhere and need to get somewhere, an additive may be a godsend. But remember that it's only postponing the inevitable repairs. And in the meantime, the car will very likely be spewing pollutants into the air because it's worn out. In my view, that's a crime against nature."

Getting More Miles for Your Money

Fill 'er Up...With Premium?

Do you get better performance from premium gasoline?

"It depends," says Dennis Simanaitis, *Road and Track* magazine's engineering editor (who is also an automotive engineer).

"First of all, there is no more energy in a gallon of premium gas than there is in a gallon of regular. The main difference between the grades is octane—the resistance to ping."

To work properly in an engine, gasoline must burn, not explode. And higher-octane gasolines have more resistance to explosion.

If your car's engine pings, you'll hear a rattling metallic sound when you accelerate. Ping can damage an engine if it's allowed to go on too long, and a higher-octane gasoline might solve the problem.

But there's another factor that can influence your fuel choice. "Some cars," Simanaitis says, "have a knock sensor that listens for ping. When it hears ping starting—generally before you're even aware of it—the knock sensor adjusts the ignition to eliminate ping."

Simanaitis says some cars may run acceptably on regular but perform better on premium because the ignition is able to adapt to the fuel. It all depends on the design of the knock-sensor system. Check your owner's manual to find out which fuels your car can use.

What's the Best Brand?

The *busiest* gas station may be your best bet regardless of the name on the sign, according to Bruce Black, of Hilton Head Island, South Carolina, a former manager for Pilot Oil Company.

Based on his first-hand experience in the oil business, Black says that modern-day petroleum economics have, in many cases, made the relevance of brand names pretty hazy. "At Pilot, we bought gasoline from whatever oil company was convenient, had supply, and was reasonably priced. In one region, that might have been Shell, in another Texaco, in another Marathon.

"Likewise, big oil companies—the ones that actually drill wells and refine crude oil rather than buying from another company—sometimes buy and sell refined products from each other. For example, if one company has more regular unleaded in one region than they can immediately use, and another has too much premium, they may very well work out some sort of trade."

When Black shops for gasoline, he says he looks at the quality of the particular station rather than seeking out one brand.

"I steer clear of shabby stations that look like they don't sell much gasoline," notes Black.

"When gas station storage tanks sit almost empty for extended periods, water can condense inside, fouling the gasoline. Now that's not necessarily a problem if the station owner checks for water—which should be done regularly—and pumps it out when necessary. But if he doesn't, well, you could end up buying a load of water."

Maintaining Your Car

Tired Trans? One Quick Sniff Tells All

If you're having a problem you think *might* be in your automatic transmission, there's a quick way to tell for sure. Environmental analyst David McManness, whose 1949 Studebaker pickup still runs smoothly after a quarter-century-plus of trusty service, suggests that you sniff the transmission oil.

"When an automatic is having problems, the transmission fluid develops a characteristic odor," says McManness. "Pull out the transmission dipstick and have a sniff. If it smells burned, it's time to see a mechanic."

Of course, to be an olfactory connoisseur, you first need to know the smell of *un*burned transmission oil. There's only one way to find out: Take a sniff when it's running well. That way, when you sniff later you'll have some scent to compare it to.

Eating Up the Miles

What's a reasonable life for a well-kept car?

"Just about any new car today should run at least 150,000 miles without major problems—if it's well maintained," according to Greg Parham of Import Connection. Parham, who fixes Ferraris but drives a Chevy pickup, says, "Unfortunately, most aren't well maintained, so most don't go that far. But they *can!*"

Change the Filters and Save the Injectors

"Fuel filters are cheaper than fuel injectors," Parham points out. That comparison is important to keep in mind if you own a car with a fuel-injection system.

If you don't change the fuel filter at regular intervals, the small orifices of the fuel injectors may get plugged up. Many people seem to think that the only time to worry about the filter is when it clogs up and the engine stops. But if you wait that long, you'll be looking at a very big repair bill for the injectors.

"Change that fuel filter at least every 15,000 miles," says Parham.

Change the Antifreeze and Save the Radiator

Parham again: "Antifreeze is less expensive than a radiator."

Because cars don't run at full operating temperature much of the time, cooling systems (especially those with aluminum radiators) can deteriorate. Changing the antifreeze helps to prevent that. But this isn't a do-it-yourself job, because antifreeze has to be properly handled and disposed of.

"Ask your garage to change the antifreeze every two years," says Parham. "It can dramatically extend radiator life."

Give Brakes a Break: Change the Fluid

"Brake fluid is subjected to tremendous heat in today's disk-brake systems," says Parham. "That fluid also has a tremendous affinity for water, which can corrode expensive brake parts from the inside out."

His recommendation?

"Change your brake fluid every two years."

Cold Out? Try Running Your AC

"Your air conditioner needs attention in the winter, as does your heater in the summer," says Import Connection's Parham. "If you turn the air conditioner on for a few minutes once a month during the winter, it spreads lubricant through the compressor, keeping parts coated. Likewise, turn the heater on once a month in the summer to keep heater valves from sticking."

Tips for Top Tires

American Car? Try Bigger Tires

Jan Davis, owner of the tire shop that bears his name in Asheville, North Carolina, recommends mounting the next-size larger tires that are labeled as "optional" in your owner's manual. When you're replacing old tires with new ones, consider putting on larger tires: They have a number of benefits.

- Because the tire diameter is larger, the engine will operate more slowly at a given highway speed—increasing fuel mileage and reducing engine wear.
- A larger tire may also last a little longer and ride better.

"Many American cars come with somewhat undersized tires," notes Davis. "If you read closely in the owner's manual, you'll find that larger-than-stock sizes are acceptable. We think it's a good idea, in general, to go to the largest recommended size."

Caution: Be sure to refer to your owner's manual first, and don't use a larger tire unless the manual lists an optional size.

Past Performance

Is It Safe to Rotate Radials?

When radial tires were first introduced, many manufacturers recommended *against* switching them from one side of the car to the other.

Does that rule still hold true? We asked Jan Davis of Jan Davis Tires in Asheville, North Carolina, for his opinion.

"That's no longer true, and it actually may never have been," he says. "When American tire manufacturers started building radial tires back in the early 1970s, they had some problems with tire cords coming apart. I was fairly new in the business then, and I saw it happen.

"I don't think the manufacturers could quite figure out what the trouble was at first. So they were desperately looking for anything that might solve the problem. And someone came up with the idea that changing a tire's direction of rotation might stress the cords. So they recommended against it.

"Maybe it did help back then, but tires are much better designed and built today. Not only that, cars are lighter and speeds are slower. Cord separation just isn't a problem anymore, and cross rotation can lengthen a tire's tread life significantly."

Frequent Swaps for Minimum Wear

Every car owner knows about rotating tires to minimize wear. But how often?

Jan Davis, the tire expert, recommends tire rotation every 5,000 miles. "This is especially important on front-wheel-drive cars," says Davis, "because the wear patterns on the front and back are so different."

(Reminder: Every 5,000 miles is when you should have the wear patterns checked for alignment problems, too.)

Try a New Rotation

What's the recommended way to rotate your tires?

"We've had the best luck using a modified cross-rotation pattern," says Davis. Here it is (for front-wheel-drive cars).

1. The right rear goes to the left front.
2. The left rear moves to the right front.
3. Both fronts go to the back on the same side.

For rear-wheel-drive cars, the rotation pattern is just the opposite in steps 1 and 2. So for rear-wheel-drive, it's:

1. The right front goes to the left rear.
2. The left front goes to the right rear.
3. Both backs go to the front on the same side.

This approach won't work for people who do it at home in the driveway, since both sides of the car need to be in the air at the same time. But according to Davis, it's worth a trip to your local garage to have it done this way.

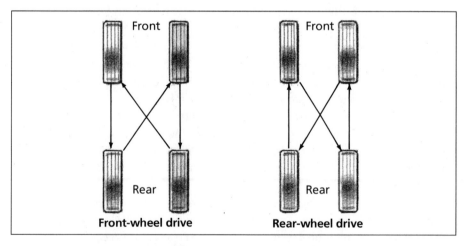

Rotation patterns for front-wheel-drive and rear-wheel-drive cars—to minimize wear and increase the life of your tires.

How Do They Line Up?

According to Jan Davis, owner of Jan Davis Tires in Asheville, North Carolina, and an active auto road racer, the number-one cause of premature tire wear is improper wheel alignment.

"Many people assume that they will feel something wrong in the steering if the alignment of their car needs adjustment. Actually, an alignment problem may not be at all obvious to the average driver, and a set of tires can be ruined very quickly."

An experienced tire technician can usually spot alignment problems just by looking at tire wear patterns. "Every time you have your tires rotated, ask the technician to check the wear pattern and recommend alignment if it's needed," says Davis.

Keep Up the Pressure

The number-two cause of premature tire wear? Davis points to improper inflation.

"Radial tires have made it more difficult for a driver to tell by looking or by the car's handling if a tire is low on air. Radial tires retain the same profile unless the air pressure is dramatically different," he says.

Gauge It Correctly

Get an accurate tire pressure gauge—and use it, recommends Davis. Check the pressure on new tires every two or three weeks. Check the pressure cold, before the car is driven. (If the car has been driven 5 miles or more, add 4 pounds per square inch to the manufacturer's recommended pressure.)

Managing Mechanics

How to Make Your Mechanic Mad

Just as you need to form a relationship with your car, so you need to learn to get along with your mechanic. A happy mechanic is one who will do your job well and quickly. According to Greg Parham, an import mechanic, the worst thing you can do is put off repairs until the last minute.

"It really gets my goat when people stop in and tell me they've had this problem for about six months—and now they need it fixed immediately because they're going out of town tomorrow.

"Please, *please* don't put off repairs until the last minute and expect your service person to take up your slack. It's really irritating when people don't have a serious problem until they have to go somewhere."

FYI

How to Avoid a Gender Bender

There's no pleasant way to put this: Men and women often aren't treated the same when they take a car in for repair.

Sexual bias is all too real in the auto repair business. A woman is likely to be assumed ignorant of mechanical matters unless she proves otherwise. It's not fair, but it's a fact.

Usually, the bias is instinctive rather than deliberate. Male mechanics, accustomed to being cross-examined by male car owners, imagine they're under less scrutiny when they're doing work for a woman. As a result, some mechanics get lazy.

How do you guard against the lazy or unscrupulous mechanic? Studebaker owner and former auto mechanic David McManness says, "Don't go in with an attitude of suspicion. It's very difficult to tell an honest mechanic from a crook at first glance, and you don't want to alienate a good technician.

"Basically, whether you're a man or woman, your only defense is to pay attention and be friendly and curious. When you're told that a part is worn out, ask whether it was defective or if there was some way the problem could have been prevented. Without saying, 'Show me the worn part and prove that it needs replacing,' ask the mechanic to show you what went wrong and explain the problem.

"I think the incidence of fraud in auto repair has dropped considerably in the last 20 years. More often, the problem is just that the mechanic isn't competent. Cars have become very complex, and wages have not kept up with the increased demands for tools, training, and knowledge. If you find someone good, latch on and don't let go!"

Don't Doubt—Learn!

Les Zimmerman, a Volkswagen and Porsche mechanic and writer from Venice, California, is irked by a tone of distrust from customers.

"Most people have no idea how their cars work, so they are naturally defensive when something goes wrong," says Zimmerman. "But treating a mechanic as a barely restrained crook does not bring out the best. Many mechanics are happy to talk about their work, but not if they feel like they're being interrogated.

"Instead of questioning whether a repair is justified, use the opportunity to learn more about your car. Instead of saying, 'Are you sure it really needs that?' say, 'What the heck does this weird-looking thing do?'

"Any good mechanic will be delighted to expound on his or her knowledge of the auto. Your best defense against the unscrupulous is to understand the problem."

For Greater Gratitude: Wash under the Hood

Ever think of washing your engine before you take it in to be fixed? If you do go to that slight extra trouble, you're likely to be greeted by one grateful mechanic.

"Very few people had the common courtesy to stop at a car wash and spray the engine bay before bringing a car in for service," says B. V. Alvarez, remembering the days when he owned his own shop. "I kept wondering, do they think I *like* getting greasy?"

According to Alvarez, all you have to do is lift up the hood and spray the engine—hard—before you bring it in. If you don't do it yourself, the mechanic may want to clean the engine before he works on it. Expect an extra charge.

Ever Thought of a Secondhand Engine?

Many car owners wonder whether it's worthwhile to have an engine rebuilt. Probably not, according to David McManness. But you might pick up a used engine that will give you many thousands of miles of satisfaction.

"There aren't many mechanics today who have the skills to properly rebuild an engine," says McManness. "I recommend that you look for a used engine from a junkyard instead. You can find engines from wrecked cars with low mileage, and many yards will guarantee a used engine. Even though the guarantee only lasts a short time, it's probably long enough to determine whether the engine has any serious problems.

"You'll pay less for a used engine, and in my experience, it will typically outlast a rebuild."

For Smarter Driving...

Steadddddddy on the Gas

Many drivers believe you'll save gas if you keep a light touch on the accelerator.

Not so, says B. V. Alvarez, who has designed alternative-fuel vehicles and managed teams of cars in fuel-economy contests.

"Because of the design of fuel systems and the nature of the combustion process, tippy-toeing on the throttle often isn't the most fuel-efficient technique. Depending on the car, you'll get the best mileage by accelerating at between one-quarter and one-half throttle with a steady foot—not by barely touching the gas pedal."

For Fuel Economy—Look Ahead

"The cardinal rule for fuel economy," Alvarez says, "is to avoid changing the position of the accelerator pedal. It follows from this that you want to avoid having to slow down and speed up again. Anticipating traffic and signals to maintain a steady speed will do more to improve your around-town fuel mileage than any other single technique."

Of course, you get another benefit from looking ahead; at the same time you're saving on gas, you also save wear and tear on brakes, clutch, and transmission.

Automatic Rule: Give That Left Foot a Nap

If you have an automatic transmission, *don't* use your left foot on the brake, says environmental analyst and mechanic David McManness, who counts a Mazda 323GTX among his around-town cars. "People who brake with their left foot almost always rest it on the pedal. This slight pressure speeds brake wear and, if it's enough to cause the brake lights to come on, can be very dangerous."

Don't Downshift to Decelerate

It takes practice to master downshifting. To downshift properly, you have to carefully synchronize pressing on the accelerator while letting out the clutch. Since most people can't do it correctly, McManness recommends that drivers generally should avoid trying to decelerate by downshifting. You may save wear-and-tear on the brakes, but if you downshift the wrong way, you'll stress the clutch and transmission.

"And brakes are much cheaper than transmissions and clutches," McManness observes.

A Lower Gear for the Long Grade

Whereas downshifting is not advised, car experts do suggest that you use a lower gear before you start down a long grade.

"Putting the transmission in a lower gear on hills is much easier on brakes," says Colorado resident David McManness. "Not only will it reduce wear, it will also keep your brakes cool so they'll be ready to work at full efficiency if you really need them."

Parked Uphill? Try This for a Start-Up

If your car has a standard transmission and you're parked on an uphill grade, here's advice for a smooth start-up.

"With the parking brake fully on, put the transmission in gear," says McManness, veteran of many Rocky Mountain drives. "Then gradually release the parking brake as you apply the throttle and begin to engage the clutch to go forward. After a couple of tries, you'll be able to do it without rolling backward at all."

But *don't* use your car's clutch to hold that position, he warns. "Slipping the clutch to avoid rolling backward is very hard on it. Unless you drive a car with 'hill-holder brakes' (some Subarus and old Studebakers have them), you should learn to use the parking brake to hold and start up on a hill."

Stop Before You Reverse

"You're putting your automatic or manual transmission under undue load if you change gears while you're still rolling," says long-distance commuter Les Zimmerman. "Since you're going to come to a stop anyway, why not wait?"

After the Start-Up—Git Up 'n Go

"*Don't* let your car stay in idle to warm up," says B. V. Alvarez. "It's better to get under way as soon as possible."

According to Alvarez, the first few moments after a cold start are some of the hardest on an engine, so you should drive gently. But getting under way quickly helps warm the engine and allows sensors to adjust fully to temperature changes.

"Though it's not as important with fuel-injected cars as it is with carbureted ones, this rule applies to all," says Alvarez.

Hints for a Classy-Car Look

How to Forestall Rust

Want to arrest the most-wanted rust culprit? Get the salt off. According to Bob Owenby—president of Harry's Body and Fender in Asheville, North Carolina, restorer of classic cars, and frequent judge at concours d'elegance—the main rust culprit is road salt used to melt snow and ice.

So how do you get it off your car?

"Thoroughly rinse salt from the inside of the fender wells and the underside of your car at least once a month," says Owenby. "Do-it-yourself car washes are very handy for this, and you need only use fresh water."

Is Your Undercoating Cracking Up?

If the answer is yes, you may need a new rust-preventive treatment.

"If your car is undercoated, keep an eye on the coating for cracks," says Owenby. "Salt can get into the cracks and be very difficult to rinse out. Rust can develop very quickly."

While Owenby is a fan of rust-preventive treatments such as Zebart, he adds, "Those treatments are no use at all if they aren't applied properly." Before you get an undercoating treatment, ask around. "I want to know a shop's reputation before I let someone in that shop treat my car."

Techno-Tip

CHEAP PAINT JOBS ARE ON THE WAY OUT

Bob Owenby of Harry's Body and Fender notes that the days of the bargain paint job are numbered. "Concern for the environment is changing the auto body business dramatically. To meet environmental requirements and do a decent job, a shop needs hundreds of thousands of dollars worth of equipment."

Car paints are now in the process of being entirely revamped, says Owenby. For environmental reasons, all 1992 Hondas come with water-based paint, and GM will soon be following suit. Other manufacturers will be close behind.

"On the one hand, this is good news. Current paints are very toxic, and they've been getting worse over the years," he says. "My paint men have to wear special suits and respirators to shoot the polyurethane clear coats that come on most cars today."

The problem is that water-based paints are very difficult to apply correctly. "I'm installing a special paint booth at a cost of over $100,000," says Owenby. "It incorporates radiant heat panels to bake water-based paint. And, just as important, it will capture paint dust, preventing it from getting into the outside air."

Without the radiant units, paint dries from the outside in, causing lots of problems. Water-based paints may not cure correctly, causing them to crack or peel.

"I think that the change to water-based paints is a good one, but it spells the doom of the backlot body man," noted Owenby. "It takes training and expensive equipment to paint a modern car."

Some Acid Remarks on Car Finish

"One of the biggest problems we see with paint today is damage from acid rain," says Owenby. "And unfortunately, there's not much you can do about it other than garage your car or move to a place without acid rain. And wax is no protection. The acidic water cuts right through it."

According to Owenby, fog is even worse than rain in those areas that are plagued by acid pollutants. "The fog lays a mist on the car, which then dries, leaving behind the residue of acid."

The damage can sometimes be repaired without repainting, according to Owenby. Most cars today are treated with a very tough "clear coat": someone at the body shop can grind out the marks with very fine sandpaper. But that's only a one-time solution. When it happens again, there's not enough clear coat left to sand.

"So if you live in an area with acid rain, get yourself a garage if you want your paint to last," advises Owenby.

Car Wash Techniques 101

Owenby says most people don't really know how to wash their cars. Here are the key elements of a perfect wash job.

- A detergent that really removes the film from paint.
- Lots of water.
- Soft towels that won't scratch the paint.
- A thorough rinse.

"Most people use soaps that won't remove the film from paint," notes Owenby. "I like to use a laundry detergent, which really gets the car clean." Any detergent—powder, liquid, or flakes—will do the trick. (But no bleach, even if you want your white car whiter.)

And next time you're about to throw away your raggedy old bathroom towels, save them instead. They're perfect for buffing.

Save the Polish for Your 6-Month-Old

Before you apply polish, the paint on your car should be 6 to 12 months old. That gives it time enough to cure.

Though body-shop expert Owenby prefers polyurethane compounds such as Nu-Finish, he says there are other good brands. "I basically agree with the top choices made by consumer magazines."

The ones to avoid are those that include abrasives for cleaning and those that seal too well, closing off the pores of the paint. Just looking on the label will tell the story. If the can says the liquid "has a mild abrasive cleaner" or "seals the finish," steer clear.

Nice Shades

We've all seen it. A haze accumulates inside the windshield, making the world look a bit fuzzy during the day and making vision really difficult at night. But what *is* that haze? And where does it come from?

"Over the last 30 years, car interiors have increasingly been made from plastics," says *Road and Track* editor Dennis Simanaitis. "The film you see on the window is from the solvents—often called plasticizers—in these materials. It's released by heat, and has been a real problem for manufacturers."

Although manufacturers have tried to seal the plastics to prevent outgassing, the problem still persists. One way to prevent the haze, however, is with a shade over your dashboard.

"It will prevent sunlight from shining directly on the dash and heating it," says Simanaitis. "And a white or silver shade will reflect some light back out through the windshield."

For No Film

To *remove* the tenacious, filmy windshield haze, Simanaitis suggests trying "high-proof" isopropyl alcohol. Conventional window cleaners, which are usually vinegar based, may have trouble dissolving the residues.

Good News about Newspaper

Les Zimmerman of California, whose five cars are approaching a combined total odometer reading of one million miles, has found that regular window cleaners work better when applied with newspaper. "I have no idea why, but the newspaper does seem to work," says Zimmerman.

Just spray on the window cleaner, then use crumpled newspaper to scrub the window.

Solving Everyday Problems

Lost Your Gas Cap?

It does happen. It's a rainy day. You're in a rush. You stop at the pump for a quick five dollars' worth, hop in the car, drive off...and the next time you fill up, you discover you left the gas cap behind.

Should you be concerned about water in the gas tank?

"Probably not," says B. V. Alvarez. "Cars built since the early 1970s have a system to prevent gas tank vapors from escaping into the atmosphere. You'll notice that there's a hinged flap inside the fuel tank's filler neck. Unless you're out in a hurricane, that flap should keep water from getting in your gas tank."

However, if you're concerned, add a bottle of fuel-line antifreeze (alcohol) to the fuel. The alcohol will dissolve any water and allow it to pass through without harm.

And, of course, get a new gas cap ASAP!

Uh, Houston, We Have No Lift-Off

You turn the ignition and...No lights. No horn. The engine won't even turn over.

"Chances are you have a bad connection at the battery negative terminal," says Les Zimmerman. "Try wiggling the clamp with your hand. If it's loose, that's probably the problem. And moving the terminal will usually restore the contact, if only temporarily."

Once the car's running again, drive directly to the shop and have it fixed, suggests Zimmerman. Otherwise, you'll just have to wrestle with the same terminal problem again...and again...and again.

Doors Locked? Keys Inside? Oops.

"It's not easy to get into a car nowadays," says Bob Owenby of Harry's Body and Fender in Asheville, North Carolina. "Even the specially designed openers won't work on every car. And the days of coat hangers are pretty much over. Many new cars have plastic pins in the mechanisms inside their doors. If you try to tug on them with a coat hanger, they just come apart."

So what *should* you do if you've locked your keys inside?

If you can read the serial number from your car (usually in a corner of the dashboard), call the nearest dealer. Using the number, the dealer can make you a new key—and it should cost you no more than a few dollars. (Of course, then you have to get from your car to the dealer to pick it up!)

If you *can't* read the number, or the nearest dealer is too far away...

"Swallow your pride and call in the experts." Owenby suggests you contact your local police department or, if you are a member, call the nearest American Automobile Association. Many police officers and American Automobile Associations are supplied with devices to help owners in distress, and they will at least know who to call.

Examine That Drip...With Care

A wet spot under your car? Some kinds of fluids are easy to identify, such as oil, antifreeze, and gasoline.

But if you're not sure what it is, don't touch it, cautions auto mechanic Les Zimmerman. A honey-colored or yellow fluid may be corrosive hydraulic fluid, brake fluid, or battery acid, which can burn the skin.

WHICH CARS ARE SAFEST?

The following tables from the Highway Loss Data Institute show the selective rates of injury for 1988 to 1990 cars. These tables show wide variations in injury rates: In some categories, cars with the *worst* records have twice as many injuries as those with the *best*. In general, most of the cars with the best record are the large models, while those with the worst overall results are usually small models.

Here's how the insurance industry keeps tabs on these cars.

- In the following tables, results are grouped according to five car body styles—station wagons and passenger vans, four-door models, two-door models, luxury models, and sports models. Different size models are listed within each style category.

- With each category, in the column headed Overall Injury, the number 100 represents the average for all cars. So an injury result of 130 is 30 percent *worse* than average; an injury result of 70 is 30 percent *better* than average.

- Cars identified with a * are equipped with air bags. Cars identified with a ♦ are equipped with automatic shoulder belts.

- For easy reference, here is how you can read the overall injury results for cars in these tables:

  Under 70 = substantially better than average
  70–79 = better than average
  80–120 = average
  121–130 = worse than average
  Over 130 = substantially worse than average

Station Wagons and Passenger Vans	Overall Injury	Station Wagons and Passenger Vans	Overall Injury
LARGE		**MIDSIZE**	
Plymouth Grand Voyager	56	Ford Taurus*	67
Dodge Grand Caravan	59	Toyota Camry♦	67
Dodge Caravan	64	Subaru Legacy 4WD♦	87
Plymouth Voyager	66	**SMALL**	
Chevrolet Lumina APV	68	Dodge Colt	105
GMC Safari Van	68	Ford Escort♦	109
Ford Extended Aerostar	70	Mitsubishi Wagon	110

Four-Door Models	Overall Injury	Four-Door Models	Overall Injury
LARGE		**MIDSIZE—***continued*	
Chevrolet Caprice♦	37	Ford Tempo 4WD♦	99
Mercury Grand Marquis*	57	Nissan Maxima♦	99
Ford Crown Victoria*	61	Buick Skylark♦	100
Oldsmobile Ninety-Eight♦	64	Oldsmobile Calais♦	104
Buick Electra♦	65	Acura Integra♦	105
Pontiac Bonneville♦	66	Subaru Legacy♦	105
Buick LeSabre♦	67	Chevrolet Corsica♦	108
Oldsmobile Eighty-Eight♦	73	Pontiac Grand Am♦	110
Chrysler New Yorker		Ford Tempo♦	112
5th Avenue*	75	Mercury Topaz♦	114
MIDSIZE		Mitsubishi Galant♦	114
Buick Century♦	65	Chevrolet Cavalier♦	130
Toyota Camry 4WD♦	68	Hyundai Sonata♦	130
Chevrolet Lumina♦	76	Nissan Stanza♦	132
Mercury Sable*	77	**SMALL**	
Oldsmobile Cutlass Ciera♦	78	Volkswagen Golf♦	101
Oldsmobile Cutlass♦	82	Honda Civic♦	112
Eagle Premier♦	84	Mazda 323♦	116
Pontiac Grand Prix♦	84	Volkswagen Jetta♦	125
Ford Taurus*	88	Toyota Corolla♦	129
Honda Accord♦	88	Ford Escort♦	131
Toyota Cressida♦	90	Geo Prizm♦	132
Plymouth Acclaim*	92	Dodge Shadow*	134
Mazda 626♦	94	Mitsubishi Mirage♦	135
Toyota Camry♦	94	Eagle Summit♦	139
Dodge Dynasty*	96	Hyundai Excel♦	173
Dodge Spirit*	96		

Two-Door Models	Overall Injury	Two-Door Models	Overall Injury
LARGE		**MIDSIZE—***continued*	
Buick LeSabre♦	71	Chrysler LeBarron	
Oldsmobile Eighty-Eight♦	72	Convertible*	96
Ford Thunderbird♦	80	Honda Accord♦	98
Mercury Cougar♦	89	Honda Prelude♦	98
MIDSIZE		Buick Skylark♦	102
Chevrolet Lumina♦	83	Acura Integra♦	103
Buick Regal♦	88	Ford Tempo♦	110
Oldsmobile Cutlass♦	91	Oldsmobile Calais♦	110
Pontiac Grand Prix♦	91	Chrysler LeBaron*	112

(continued)

WHICH CARS ARE SAFEST?—continued

Two-Door Models	Overall Injury	Two-Door Models	Overall Injury
MIDSIZE—*continued*		**SMALL**—*continued*	
Pontiac Grand Am♦	115	Mazda MX-6♦	115
Mercury Topaz♦	121	Nissan 240SX♦	123
Pontiac Sunbird♦	127	Plymouth Laser♦	132
Chevrolet Beretta♦	129	Toyota Celica*	132
Chevrolet Cavalier♦	146	Mitsubishi Eclipse♦	137
SMALL		Toyota Tercel♦	138
Plymouth Colt♦	105	Ford Escort♦	142
Ford Probe♦	106	Dodge Daytona*	147
Dodge Colt♦	111	Geo Storm*	147
Subaru Justy 4WD	113	Nissan Sentra♦	164
Honda Civic♦	114	Hyundai Excel♦	184

Luxury Models	Overall Injury	Luxury Models	Overall Injury
LARGE		**LARGE**—*continued*	
Jaguar X16♦	47	Cadillac Brougham♦	68
Lexus LS400*	47	Mercedes 300 SE*	70
Mercedes SEL/SDL Series*	49	**MIDSIZE**	
BMW 7351*	55	Volvo 740/760 SW*	44
Cadillac		Lincoln Continental*	56
Fleetwood/DeVille 4D*	59	Acura Legend 2D*	66
Lincoln Town Car*	59	Acura Legend 4D*	66
Mercedes 300/DE*	67	Volvo 740/760 4D*	84
		Mercedes 190D/E*	88

Sports Models	Overall Injury	Sports Models	Overall Injury
MIDSIZE		**SMALL**	
Chevrolet Camaro*	139	Nissan 300ZX♦	85
Ford Mustang*	145	Mazda MX-5 Miata*	86
		Honda Civic CRX♦	125

The Experts

B. V. Alvarez used to build engines and race stock cars in the National Association for Stock Car Auto Racing (NASCAR). He is president of Air Chek, Inc., a radon-testing firm in Fletcher, North Carolina. Since his retirement from NASCAR racing, he has been driving a Mazda RX-7 convertible and a Mooney 231.

Bruce Black is an urban planner from Hilton Head Island, South Carolina, and was formerly a manager with Pilot Oil Company. Although now out of the oil business, he still changes his own.

Jan Davis, owner of Jan Davis Tires in Asheville, North Carolina, drives a Porsche 911 and races a Volkswagen Rabbit.

David McManness, an experienced Oldsmobile and Honda mechanic and a former vocational auto-shop teacher, is an environmental analyst from Denver, Colorado. His transportation includes a 1963 Studebaker, a Grand Turismo Hawk, and a Mazda 323GTX.

Bob Owenby, president of Harry's Body and Fender in Asheville, North Carolina, is a frequent judge of classic car competitions.

Greg Parham, owner of Import Connection in Arden, North Carolina, says, "Ferraris don't do much for me." He drives a Chevy pickup.

Dennis Simanaitis, engineering editor for *Road and Track* magazine, drives a 1967 Austin Mini Moke.

Les Zimmerman is a writer, editor, car aficionado, mechanic, and long-distance traveler from Venice, California. His current collection of five autos tallies a collective 700,000 miles on their odometers.

CHAPTER 5

Home Maintenance and Repair

Streamline Your Patch-Ups and Fix-Its

Say hello to a new era in home maintenance! If yours is a new home, it's built with materials that are easier to maintain and repair, more resistant to the elements, and more bugproof than ever before.

If yours is an older home, you have the do-it-yourself advantage of new methods and materials any time you need to make repairs. That means that you may be able to do jobs singlehanded that you never thought you could tackle alone.

For better or worse, we now live in a world of snap-in wiring components, drop-in faucets, screw-in closet systems, and universal plumbing supplies easily mastered by amateurs. We now paint with space-age finishes that shrug off sun damage—and if we decide to remove paint, we can use safer and more effective strippers.

Need to replace a leaky old window? You might try a pop-in ready-made. Need to cover a hopelessly lumpy wall? Choose from dozens of panelings or heavily textured wallpapers. And if you need to hide wall damage, molded fiberglass escutcheons can add a Baroque or Victorian touch.

Re-side your home with a material you'll never have to paint. Fix leaks with caulks that are longer lasting and more resistant to ultraviolet rays than ever before.

Insulation is easier to install and more effective than ever. Even the little things, like wood filler and spackling compound, are easier to apply, more color true, and more shrinkproof. And almost every brochure or package you pick up at your hardware store or home center gives you a toll-free number to call for help with your project.

All things considered, there has never been a better time to be a homeowner who loves puttering around the house. In this chapter, with the help of a host of experts, you'll find a houseful of tips for grooming and fine-tuning, heading off troubles before they occur, improving inner and outer spaces, and beautifying your home from top to bottom.

Ending Seeps and Drips

Foil the Damp!

Suppose you have moisture in the basement, but you don't know where it's coming from. Is it seepage from *outside* or condensation from *inside*?

Here's a quick test to find the answer, recommended by John Molski, technical director of United Gilsonite Laboratories, makers of waterproofing products in Scranton, Pennsylvania.

Tape a piece of aluminum foil tightly to the inside of your basement wall. After several days, examine the foil. If the wall side of the foil is wet, you have seepage. If the room side is wet, the problem is condensation. If you have both, you need to seal the masonry with a waterproofer and also use a dehumidifier in the room.

Before You Seal—Check the Culprits

All the Drylok in the world won't keep water out of your basement if you have fundamental drainage problems, according to Molski. He suggests that you look for the following big three culprits.
1. Leaky gutters and downspouts
2. Improper grading around the home
3. Blocked drainage pipes

If any of these is the problem, correct it before investing in a masonry waterproofer, says Molski.

Moist Watch: Radiant Barriers Could Cause Drips!

Naturally, homeowners in cooler climates want to insulate their homes to save on heating bills.

But putting a radiant barrier over attic insulation is *not* the recommended way to do it, according to Howard Faulkner, associate professor of

TRICKS FOR THE SEAL IN YOUR BASEMENT

Getting ready to waterproof?

John Molski, technical director of United Gilsonite Laboratories in Scranton, Pennsylvania, recommends these steps for sealing the basement.

1. Wire brush the surface to remove all loose and broken mortar, dirt, dust, and deposits. It's best to remove any old paint by wire brushing or sandblasting.
2. Look for efflorescent stains—a chalky residue that will prevent a good bond between the masonry and the waterproofer. Where you find these stains, treat them with a 20 percent solution of muriatic acid. (Wear eye protection, gloves, and protective clothing.)
3. Patch cracks and holes, using a fast-setting hydraulic cement that will set even in the wet. A full-service paint dealer will carry a cement that's compatible with the waterproofer you're using.
4. The first place to seal is the joint between the floor and the wall. In basement construction it's common for cement floors to shrink slightly and pull away from the wall, leaving a space where water enters. Fill any spaces in the floor/wall joint with a sealing product such as Drylok Fast Plug.
5. Apply the first coat of waterproofer with a brush, advises Molski, and work it well into the pores of the cement.
6. Subsequent coats can be put on with a brush or a masonry roller. If possible, leave windows open and a fan going. During application, there should be plenty of ventilation. Apply the coating at a rate to cover 75 to 100 square feet with each gallon of waterproofer.

According to Molski, the waterproofer should not be spread too thin. Also, don't spread it on floors—waterproofers formulated for walls are not meant to withstand the abrasion of foot traffic.

A second coat may be necessary if you have a lot of seepage. "If seepage persists after several days," says Molski, "add another coat to these areas."

technology and the former executive director of the Energy Efficient Building Association (EEBA) at the University of Southern Maine in Gorham. Faulkner says radiant barriers should not be installed over attic insulation in cold climates.

Why not?

Those barriers can trap moisture in the ceiling, especially in older homes where a lot of rising warm air "leaks" through the ceilings.

"Although many brands of radiant barriers have perforations to allow moisture to escape, the effectiveness of these perforations has not been demonstrated in field applications," says Faulkner.

According to the EEBA, however, radiant barriers do save on air conditioning bills in hot climates. (See "What Is a Radiant Barrier?" on page 118.)

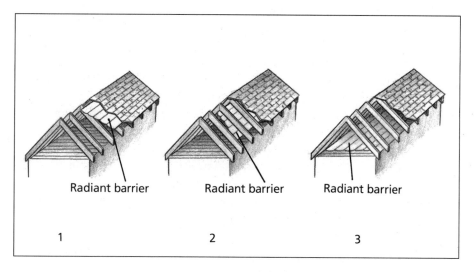

A radiant barrier helps save on heating bills, but it must be installed properly to avoid moisture problems. For homes in cold-weather climates, install a radiant barrier under the roof deck (1) or under the rafters (2), not on top of ceiling insulation (3).

Vent That Crawl Space

Is your unheated crawl space getting enough ventilation? If not, condensation and dampness can cause a long list of problems, from musty smells to wood rot.

John Kiker, who is spokesperson for the Mineral Insulation Manufacturers Association in Alexandria, Virginia, suggests a two-step solution to crawl space problems.

1. Cover the ground beneath the crawl space with a moisture barrier. To be effective, this barrier should be polyethylene sheeting, 4 mils or thicker. (Alternatively, you can use 55-pound asphalt roll roofing, with at least a 3-inch overlap between sheets of asphalt.)

FYI

WHAT IS A RADIANT BARRIER?

As we learned in ninth-grade science class, heat is transferred in three ways, through convection, conduction, and radiation. Traditional insulation—consisting of a puffy material like spun fiberglass—helps prevent convection and conduction heat loss.

But the shiny metallic films known as radiant barriers deal with another kind of heat loss—radiation. Radiant barriers are available in sheet form, and homeowners are often told (inaccurately) that these sheets can be laid on top of existing insulation. They're also available in the form of roll-batting, with a radiant barrier attached.

While insulators insulate, radiant barriers *reflect* heat. The problem is that metallic barriers do not breathe. Therefore, when used incorrectly, they trap dampness that rises from the home or that condenses out of the air as the attic cools. When condensation forms on a metallic film placed under shingles or under roof rafters, it can "feed" the fungi that cause dry rot in wood. When placed atop insulation on an attic floor, it traps moisture that rises from the home below.

If you have already installed a radiant barrier and you notice discoloration in ceilings, it's probably a sign of moisture caused by condensation. In order to solve the problem, remove the radiant barrier.

---

2. Vent the area. Kiker recommends 1 square foot of venting for every 1,500 square feet of crawl space. Ideally, vents should be on opposite sides of the crawl space, so there's good cross-ventilation.

Note: If you have $\frac{1}{16}$-inch screen over the vents (to keep out bugs and other basement invaders), you'll need twice as much vent per crawl space. In other words, 2 square feet of venting for every 1,500 square feet of crawl space. That's because the screen cuts down the air flow.

Exhaust Those Fungi

If someone in your family has a sniffly nose and itchy eyes long after the pollen season ends, there may be fungi breeding right inside your home.

"These microorganisms need very little moisture to flourish," remarks Donald Ahearn, Ph.D., professor of industrial and medical microbiology at Georgia State University in Atlanta. "A water pipe with condensation or a coffee pot brewing under a cabinet can provide enough moisture for many fungi to grow in the house."

If you want to get rid of them, adequate ventilation is essential, Dr. Ahearn points out. He recommends the following measures.

- Install attic or vent fans to help keep inside air circulating.
- Install exhaust fans in bathrooms to expel dampness from the shower.
- The kitchen also needs an exhaust to get rid of steam.
- If you have a crawl space, put down an insulating barrier and provide adequate venting (see "Vent That Crawl Space" on page 117).
- Is your heating or ventilating system on bare ground? If so, install a moisture barrier so fungal spores won't be sucked from the ground into the system.
- When insulating your home, be sure to put the moisture barrier *outside* the insulating fiber, not between the fiber and the heated area of the house. (Improper insulating leads to dampness.)
- As soon as the weather warms, don't forget to open roof vents.

Working with Wood

Picking Pine: Choose Your Grain

If you're using pine for a woodworking project, it pays to pick wisely. The following advice comes from Joseph C. Peters, national director of developing consulting for the real estate firm Cushman and Wakefield in New York City.

- Make sure boards aren't warped. When you're at the lumberyard, sight along the edge of each board you pick out.
- Choose boards that have grain close together, not widely spaced.
- When you select number 2 pine, make sure the knots are tight and not at the edge of the board.

Quick-Erase the Dents in Pine

Pine dents easily. However, you can raise the surface to erase those dents, just by applying warm water, says Peters. Reapply the warm water several times if necessary. Be sure to let the wood dry thoroughly before sealing.

Turp for the Tack

Want to remove sawdust from a project?

DO: Use a tack cloth dampened in turpentine, says Peters.

DON'T: Use paint thinner on the cloth.

The reason? According to Peters, paint thinner can leave a residue. Turpentine won't.

No-Strain Staining

Stain, Fill, Stain

When you're staining and patching a piece of wood, stain first, advises Dave Fuller, a product manager at DAP, a maker of caulks, sealants, and other repair products, in Dayton, Ohio. After the stain has dried, apply wood filler, let it harden, and sand it smooth. The final step is to stain the filler to match, using an artist's brush or cotton swab.

FYI

WHAT'S FIT TO STRIP WITH

Some wood-strippers are almost overpowering, as anyone can attest who has burned his fingers with the powerful stuff.

But new chemicals are constantly coming on the market. Next time you make a selection, take along the following stripper checklist.

1. Is it biodegradable? If so, it will say on the label.
2. Does it have a childproof cap?
3. Can you clean it up with soap and water? Some wood-strippers require expensive and dangerous solvents that make the cleanup job pretty miserable.
4. Does it contain carcinogens? Substances to be avoided include methylene chloride, acetone, toluene, methanol, and dibasic esters.
5. Is it flammable?
6. What's the performance time? Some strippers begin working in about 15 minutes; others take overnight or longer.
7. Which tools are needed? Some strippers can't be used with regular stripping tools.
8. Are the vapors toxic? If so, there will be a warning on the container: Take heed, and use in a *very* well ventilated area.

A Grain for Every Surface

On a newly installed steel or fiberglass door frame, you can create a wood grain that will match the surrounding woodwork.

"Create the wood grain with a graining tool," suggests United Gilsonite's John Molski.

A graining tool can be purchased in most paint and hardware stores. Apply stain to the door frame, then create the grain by drawing the tool along the wet stain. After staining and graining, add a protective coat of clear finish to complete the job.

Spraying the Stain Is Only Half the Job

If you spray stain or sealer onto a wood surface, you will need to take one more step to finish the job, according to Mike Stuhlreyer, merchandising manager of the Painting Systems Division of Campbell Hausfeld in Mount Juliet, Tennessee, makers of air compressors for home workshops.

Stuhlreyer recommends working in the stain or sealer with a brush or roller. For maximum color saturation with stain and thorough penetration with a sealer, mere spraying isn't enough.

Installations Made Easier

Hanging a Door? Quintuple Your Measures

The old carpenter's adage to "measure twice" needs to be multiplied if you're replacing an entry door, according to Scott J. Hanley, marketing man-

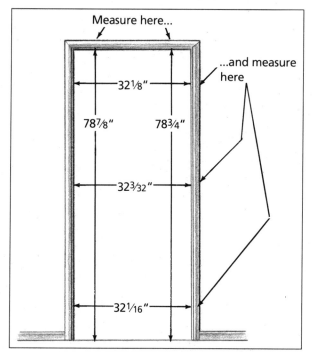

Measure here...

...and measure here

32⅛"

78⅞"   78¾"

32³⁄₃₂"

32¹⁄₁₆"

A recommendation for measuring a door frame: Measure in five places before you order a door. To order a door fitting the dimensions shown here, the correct measurement would be 78¾" × 32¹⁄₁₆".

ager at Stanley Door Systems in Troy, Michigan. In fact, Scott suggests measuring five different ways to get a door that will fit right on the first try.

"Working from the inside, measure the opening height in two places and the width of the opening in three places," says Hanley. "Then use the *smallest* measurement in each dimension when you're ordering the replacement door."

Of course, there's a good reason to get a door that will fit. A wood door can be scarred or ruined if you try to cut it to fit. Metal, fiberglass, or hollow-core doors can't be trimmed at all. On the other hand, if the door turns out to be slightly undersize, you can always fill in the gaps with shims, trim strips, and weatherstripping.

FOR YOUR TROWEL: A HANDY NOTCH GUIDE

Trowel and adhesive spreaders come in all sizes, with different notches. Which one you choose depends on what kind of adhesive you're using on which surface. And it's important: The depth and coarseness of the teeth make the difference in assuring lifelong adhesion.

Mike Sheridan, former senior test engineer and "Answer Man" on the consumer hotline at Red Devil in Union, New Jersey, supplies the following "notch guide" to help you choose a trowel or spreader that will be right for each kind of installation job.

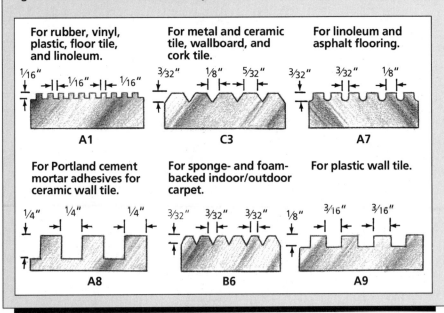

For rubber, vinyl, plastic, floor tile, and linoleum. — A1

For metal and ceramic tile, wallboard, and cork tile. — C3

For linoleum and asphalt flooring. — A7

For Portland cement mortar adhesives for ceramic wall tile. — A8

For sponge- and foam-backed indoor/outdoor carpet. — B6

For plastic wall tile. — A9

The A's, B's, and C's of Plywood Ease

If you're putting in a cabinet, countertop, or shelving, you can skip the sanding if you buy sanded plywood to begin with. Marilyn LeMoine, publications department manager for the American Plywood Association (APA) in Tacoma, Washington, explains how to choose presanded grades.

"First, look for the APA trademark stamped either on the back or the edge of the panel," she says. "You'll see a two-letter code, like A–C or B–B. The first letter tells the veneer grade on the face of the panel. The second letter tells you the grade of the backing." Here's how to interpret these codes.

Grades A and B are always sanded. Grades C and D are unsanded—but they may be acceptable for your project if the backing won't show.

And the ultimate grade? It's N—a select, natural finish–grade, free of open defects, for the most elegant installations.

For Smoother Laminate, Use Dowels

A supply of ¼-inch dowels will assure even, flat gluing when you're surfacing a large counter, table, or shelf with laminate, says Rick Mueller, a product manager with DAP in Dayton, Ohio. Here's the procedure.

1. Cut the laminate and apply contact cement, following directions from the laminate manufacturer and on the contact cement package.
2. Set dowels 8 inches apart on top of the surface.
3. Position the laminate on top of the dowels.
4. Carefully pull out the dowels one by one, moving from one end to the other. Work out the bubbles as you go.
5. Working from the center to the edges, use a roller or wood block to apply extra pressure.
6. After you've dressed the laminate edges, clean up any excess contact cement before it cures. (For cleanup, use the thinner recommended on the cement can.)

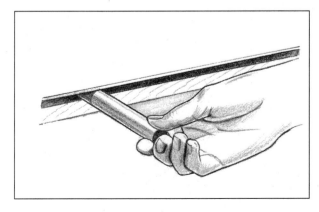

Here's an error-free way to position laminate. Set the precut laminate on top of dowels, with the adhesive side down. Then remove the dowels one by one.

Perfect Patterns for Panel Adhesive

For maximum stick-to-it-ive-ness, here are the ways to apply adhesive, recommended by Mueller.

- If you're installing paneling to studs or furring strips, run a continuous zigzag bead of adhesive down each strip or stud.
- When fastening panels to walls, put the adhesive on the panel first. Begin with a continuous bead around the perimeter of the panel. Then put a big "X" across the center of the panel, with crisscrossed lines running from corner to corner.

Faster Patching and Painting

For the Hole-in-the-Wall Gang

A small crack in plaster or wallboard is easy to fix. Just fill it with a layer of vinyl spackling, allow it to dry, then add a second layer.

But what about a major hole in a plaster wall? Before you can fix it, you need a backup support to receive the spackling. Dave Fuller, product manager at DAP, suggests the following procedure for patching drywall.

1. Cut a strip of wood 2 inches longer than the hole and narrow enough to slide easily inside. Drive a brad into the center of the strip as

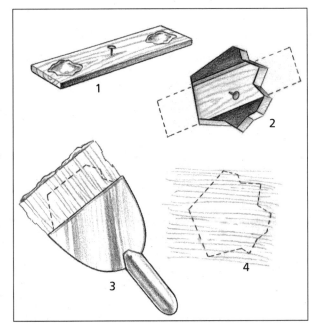

To patch a hole in plaster or wallboard, drive a brad into a strip of wood and apply adhesive at both ends (1). Insert the wood strip into the hole and pull it toward you (2) until the adhesive makes contact. Smooth over with spackling compound (3). Let dry and sand smooth (4).

shown in the illustration on the opposite page. (The brad should
stick out ¼ inch or so—just enough to hold with your fingers.)
2. Apply construction adhesive to each end of the strip on top, as shown.
3. Insert the wood through the hole, holding the brad to position it.
4. Ease the backup board into place and pull it toward you until the
   adhesive comes in contact with the back of the wall on each side of
   the opening.
5. Leave it in place until the adhesive dries. (Drying time is indicated on
   the adhesive package.)
6. Smooth on two layers of spackling compound, allowing drying time
   between layers.

CLEANER, BETTER SPRAYING

Using a spray gun is the way to go if you're painting a large surface.
But don't just spray and pray. Follow these tips for a smoother, better job.

Put your paint through the strainer. Always strain paint before
putting it through an airless paint sprayer, advises Mike Stuhlreyer, a merchandising manager for the Painting Systems Division of the compressor
manufacturer Campbell Hausfeld in Mount Juliet, Tennessee. "Even new
paint may contain coarse material that can clog the filter," he says. You
can use cheesecloth, a straining funnel (available at paint stores), or old
panty hose for straining jobs.

Keep shootin'! "Keep that spray gun in motion to prevent a buildup
of paint," says Campbell Hausfeld air tool engineer Chris Martini. "Start
the gun moving before squeezing the trigger. Release the trigger before
stopping the gun at the end of a stroke."

Bathe your gun with solvent. To clean oil-based paint out of a
spray gun, first wipe out the canister with rags, then wash it with paint
solvent, recommends Martini.

Keep the tip rust-free. "To prevent your spray gun tip from rusting
after spraying a water-based paint, wash the gun with soap and water
and give it a final rinse with lacquer thinner or mineral spirits," advises
Martini.

Keep track of your gallons. Eventually, spray gun tips wear out, and
when they do, you're likely to lose control and use more paint than necessary. Keep track of how many gallons have gone through your sprayer,
advises Stuhlreyer. Mark the box the spray gun is stored in, and replace
the tip after the fortieth gallon or so.

The same procedure will work with plaster. But before inserting the wood strip, clean away loose plaster around the inside edge of the hole so the adhesive will hold.

Picky, Picky

The challenge?

When refinishing an intricately carved mantelpiece or an overpainted antique chair, how do you get the last traces of paint and paint remover out of the tiny crevices?

Steve Honig, spokesperson for Woodfinisher's Pride Stripping Gels in Greenville, South Carolina, recommends a method used by old-time wood refinishers.

Wrap some steel wool around the end of a toothpick, then pick away the last vestiges of goo. With the steel wool on the end, you'll have a disposable goo-getter with just enough grip to gather up the last traces of leftover paint remover—and it won't gouge the wood.

GET THE LEAD OUT

Even though lead has been banned from paint products since 1977, lead-based paint was used in virtually all homes until the 1950s. So it continues to be a threat to people who live in older homes, warns environmental health consultant Mike Skinker, president of For Your Health Products in Chevy Chase, Maryland.

According to Skinker, children are especially at risk. Federal authorities estimate that one in six American children under age six suffers from some degree of lead poisoning, which can masquerade in many forms, from mental retardation to joint pains. A paint chip the size of a thumbnail contains 250 times the lead level that is considered acceptable by the Environmental Protection Agency (EPA).

For concerned parents, says Skinker, the best way to find out whether there's still lead in the home is by using one of the lead-check kits available through environmental supply stores and "green" catalogs. Some kits have simple swabs that turn color if lead is present in paint, pottery, and other household items that a child might put in his or her mouth.

If you find a lead-painted surface in your home, don't paint over it, because future flaking and chipping will continue to contaminate your home with lead. Consult a professional with expertise in lead paint removal, Skinker says.

Try a Match for a Brush

Need a very tiny paintbrush to touch up a hairline scratch? This suggestion comes from Evan Powell, a spokesperson for Southeastern Products Research and Development in Greenville, South Carolina.

Tear off a book match and dip the torn edge of the match into the paint, stain, or varnish you want to apply. Best of all, when you're done touching up with the matchbook paintbrush, just throw it away!

The Lineup on Paperhanging

Start Your Paper Plumb

You're about to hang wallpaper, and you'd like to begin from a true vertical. But you're not sure your walls are plumb.

What's the procedure?

Mike Sheridan, former senior test engineer at Red Devil in Union, New Jersey, manufacturer of painting tools and products, suggests that you *don't* start in the corner, especially if you have an old house where the walls are "untrue." Instead, measure out a distance ½ inch less than the width of the wallpaper and make a mark near the top of the wall. Suspend a plumb line at this point.

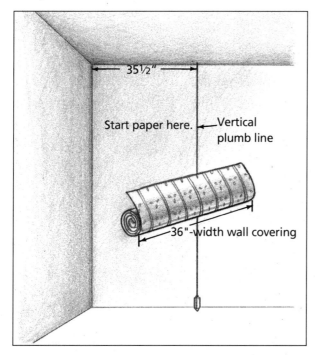

35½"

Start paper here. ←Vertical plumb line

36"-width wall covering

To guarantee that wallcovering is vertical, line up the edge with a plumb line as you hang it. (The edge at the corner of the room can always be trimmed to fit—even if that corner is irregular or out of plumb.)

Snap a chalk line or mark the plumb line using a straightedge, so you'll have an absolutely vertical line to start your paper on.

In older homes, where more settling has occurred and every wall may have slight irregularities, Sheridan suggests snapping a line on all four walls. This assures a fresh start on each wall so that any errors are not compounded as you move around the room.

Give Your Paper a Thorough Pasting

When brushing wallpaper paste on the paper, be sure to cover the entire strip, says Sheridan. Any unpasted areas will later show up as blisters or bubbles, and unpasted edges may curl.

Squash Those Bubbles

If you've got a few air bubbles you can't smooth out of your freshly installed wallpaper, try popping them with a pin. Then brush those bubbles smooth before the paste dries, suggests Sheridan.

"But be sure to clean that wallpaper *while* you're installing it," Sheridan adds. After each strip of paper is hung, use a damp sponge to clean up finger marks and excess paste before moving on to the next strip.

Past Performance

STEAM REMOVAL: A LESSON LEARNED

Ida Hawkins of Albany, New York, and De Land, Florida, discovered in the 1930s that steam heat is a sure-fire wallpaper remover.

It began with an accident.

"We had opened the valve in a steam radiator to let out excess air," she recalls. "Then we forgot about it and went shopping. When we got home, the steam had loosened the paper all around the room. It was sagging from all four walls and the ceiling.

"We laugh about it now, but we weren't laughing then. We had to scramble to brush the paper back into place and dry out the room."

Later, when the Hawkinses wanted to remove old paper, they used the same trick, but deliberately. They stoked up the furnace, opened the radiator valves, closed the door to the room, and let the steam flow until the paper was loose.

These days, of course, wallpaper steamers are available for sale or rent: different approach, same principle.

Outguessing Pesky Pests

Telltale Termite Tunnels

If you want to get the jump on termites, look for their tunnels around your house.

Contrary to what you might think, termites don't live *in* your house. They may be dining on your luscious homestead or your wooden porch, but they don't sleep where they eat, explains Kenneth T. Austin, chairman of the nation's largest home inspection company, HouseMaster of America, in Bound Brook, New Jersey. He says termites' favorite residence is moist soil *adjoining* their feeding grounds.

"Termites are sophisticated engineers," says Austin. "They figure out the best and safest route to and from your house. So take a periodic look around the outside of the foundation, above the soil, for termite tunnels. These are lines of mud about the thickness of a pen, leading from the soil to the sill plate or other wooden portions of the structure."

Periodic probing of basement beams and other low-lying lumber is also important, according to Austin. Use a flashlight to look for their tunnels, and an icepick or small screwdriver to test for soft, spongy wood.

To prevent termite infestation, clear away any scrap wood or firewood that's near the foundation of the house. It helps if crawl spaces are dry and well ventilated.

If you find evidence of termites, call in a professional.

Spare the Trap and Spoil the Ant

Carpenter ants have a reputation for dining on wood. But that's just not so, according to Austin—they eat what you do!

Meanwhile, they nest in damp wood, burrowing tunnels to harbor their eggs and nests. Austin says these ants are just as destructive as termites, as well as bolder and greedier.

To catch them, set ant traps near sinks, garbage pails, and other sources of discarded food.

Remember, though, that the nest must be destroyed. So if you find ants in the ant traps, you have to take one more step to get rid of them. Call in a professional to get the nest out of the wood, or make a bait that the ants will take back to the nest (see "Lead Ants into Temptation" on page 377).

If you're unsure of whether you've captured a *Camponotus* (carpenter ant) in your trap, take a six-legged sample to experts—either an exterminator or your county extension agent. They'll be able to ID the invader and recommend defensive action.

Garage Doors: On the Right Track

Safety-Check That Electric Garage Door

A garage door is probably the largest, heaviest piece of moving equipment in your home. That's why an automatic door should be tested periodically for safety. Jeff Molchan, spokesperson for Stanley Door Systems Division in Troy, Michigan, recommends a once-a-month safety check. Here's how.

- Place a 2 × 4 block of wood across the garage entrance, in the path of the door.
- Close the door.
- When the door hits the wood, it should stop immediately, then reverse.

If your door doesn't pass this test, Molchan says to disconnect the opener immediately. (The owner's manual will tell how.) Use the door manually until the system can be repaired or replaced.

Note: This is *not* a do-it-yourselfer's repair job.

The Manual Door: For a Smoother Glide

If a garage door doesn't move freely by hand, lubricate hinges, mounting hardware, and roller bearings. Molchan recommends spray lubricants such as CRC-666 or WD-40.

Caution: Don't lubricate the roller tracks. And don't try to adjust springs, cables, pulleys, or mounting hardware; these parts are under extreme tension at all times.

Sealing for Energy Savings

Every Crack Deserves a Caulk

Before winter chill sets in, many homeowners take a tour of the exterior with caulk gun in hand. Of course, the main targets of seasonal caulking are window frames, door frames, and roof joints.

"Don't forget to seal around water faucets, the dryer vent, and around porch or deck attachments, too," reminds Mike Sheridan, former senior test engineer at Red Devil.

Softer Putty: A Hair Dryer Assist

Want a new trick for getting old latex caulk out of windows?

"I heat the caulk with a hair dryer turned to medium," says Richard F. Tripodi, general manager at the Darworth Company in Avon, Connecticut, makers of caulks and sealants. When it's soft, pry it loose with a caulk knife.

FOR BETTER CAULKING, SERVICE THE SURFACE

"A caulk is only as good as the surface you apply it to," advises David Groene, a product manager at DAP in Dayton, Ohio. "Remove any chipped paint, and apply caulk to a clean, dry, solid surface."

Before applying the caulk, says Groene, you should vacuum away dust and chips, and wipe down metal, glass, or plastic surfaces with a solvent such as isopropyl alcohol.

Stuff-'n-Seal

Stuff scraps of insulation into deep cracks before caulking, says John Kiker of the Mineral Insulation Manufacturers Association.

Kiker suggests saving leftover scraps of insulation for these larger patch-up jobs. By stuffing the insulation in large cracks, you'll spend less money on expensive caulking materials—and also insulate better!

No-Jolt Electrical Tips

Handling Halogen

New, high-tech halogen lights generally burn twice as long as conventional bulbs, and they give a brighter light in the bargain. But they require different handling, according to Beth Lewis, a product manager for the Residential Lighting Division of Thomas Industries in Louisville, Kentucky.

- Halogen lamps burn very hot, so let the bulb and any protective screen or shield cool completely before changing bulbs. Keep halogen lamps away from draperies, bedspreads, furniture, and other flammables.
- When handling new bulbs, wear gloves or wrap the bulb in a towel. If body oils are left on the glass, they create "heat sinks"—that is, hot spots—that can cause a halogen bulb to fail prematurely. (When replacing a tubular, double-envelope bulb, special handling isn't necessary because the bulb has its own protective outer jacket.)

To Regenerate Halogen, Go to Brightest

A halogen bulb that's hooked up to a dimmer will last longer if you follow a simple turn-off rule: Always turn the dimmer to full brightness before turning off the light, says Lewis. That burst of brightness restarts the bulb's unique inner recycling process.

FYI

OUTDOOR LIGHTING TIPS

Planning some outdoor lighting around your home? Here are some strategic planning tips from Kathy Blessinger, manager of product development for the Residential Lighting Division of Thomas Industries located in Louisville, Kentucky.

- Floodlight a patio or an attractive outdoor scene. By creating a lit-up night landscape, you "open out" the night view from your windows. Net effect: Your home seems larger. Highlight a special tree, a flowering shrub, or a rock garden. An attractive architectural feature, such as a gazebo, also makes a beautiful focus in a nightscape.
- Set up "chore lights" for jobs you do after dark. For example, if you shovel the driveway at night during the winter, that's a good area to keep lit. Light the outdoor spot where you sort trash, or light up the driveway basketball court where the kids shoot hoops.

Don't Be Shocked: Obey Wordless Warnings

Many people don't realize that some electric items—microwaves and televisions in particular—can deliver a fatal jolt of electricity *even if they're turned off*. Some of these appliances have a condenser or capacitor that actually *stores* electricity: A lightning symbol on the side or back of the appliance tells you that it's not safe to tamper with it, even if it's unplugged. Call a professional!

Here are some other symbols approved by the Underwriters Laboratories (UL) that are often seen on electrical products and appliances.

An exclamation point in a triangle reminds you to read important instructions before proceeding.

If the product label shows a wavy line, it means that the appliance should only be connected to alternating current, never to direct current.

If you see a dashed line below a solid line, be warned that it means just the opposite: the appliance should be connected to *direct* current only, never alternating current.

A straight up-down line marks the ON position of a switch.

A circle marks the OFF position.

Super Storage Space

Double Your Closet Space

Is your clothing closet jam-packed?

If so, consider this rearrangement suggested by Judith Miley, president of JE Marketing Communications and founder of the Center for Home Organization and Interior Space Efficiency in Ocala, Florida.

- Divide the closet in half, with a center "partition" down the middle.
- On the left side of the closet, install a rod to hang full-length clothes. This is the area for robes, jumpsuits, full-length dresses, or pants and slacks on press hangers.
- On the right side, install *two* rods so you can hang an upper tier and lower tier of clothing. On the upper rod, hang shirts, blouses, and suit jackets; the lower tier can take skirts or slacks and pants that are folded over hangers.

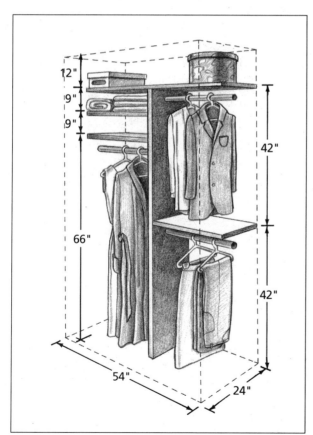

Multiply the storage space in a clothes closet by installing a divider, new shelves, and additional hanging rods.

Does Your Broom Have Too Much Elbow Room?

Miley has seen many broom closets where oodles of space is wasted: a broom or two hang all by their lonesome in a roomy closet, with unused space all around.

Her suggestion?

Take out the broom and fill the closet with shelving. You can create a pantry or linen closet that will hold mountains more than an unshelved closet. Then rehang your brooms on the back of the door. Or move them around the corner to another wall. (The wall of the garage or the stairwell to the basement or attic is just waiting to hold your long-handled friends.)

Storage Spots for Stormy Weather Gear

If you have an unused wall in the utility room, it can become an instant mudroom—a storage area for outdoor shoes, boots, umbrellas, and miscellaneous garden garb and trekking wear. Miley suggests where to begin: Look for varieties of ventilated shelving and shoe racks sold in many home centers. Here are some possible arrangements.

- Install a shoe rack that's just for outdoor boots and shoes. They'll dry faster if they're up off the floor. You can put plastic mats underneath to catch the drips from these wet-weather items.
- Add a waist-high shelf-and-rod setup for children's jackets and gear.
- Install a shelf-and-rod at the 6-foot level for adults' raincoats and umbrellas.

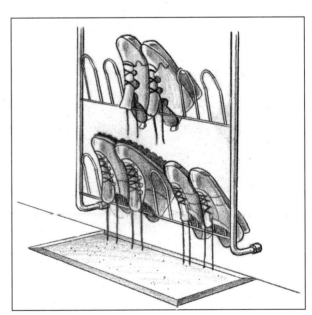

Put a wall-hung shoe rack near the back door, with a drip-mat underneath, and you have a drying-out area for wet boots and muddy shoes.

Bathroom Storage for Notions and Lotions

From Judith Miley come two ideas for storage of bathroom items.

1. Install a shallow rack on the back of the bathroom door to hold toiletries, soaps, and supplies. Many styles and sizes of shallow racks are available in hardware stores.
2. In a big bathroom where there's not enough closet space, consider a floor-to-ceiling storage tower. The tower can be a single column or, alternatively, a wall-separator between the toilet and the rest of the room.

A divider between sink and toilet is an ideal area for storing towels, washcloths, and other bathroom supplies.

Sunny Seating on Spiffy Storage

If your bedroom has a lousy storage-to-occupant ratio, consider the "found" space underneath a window.

Install a window seat with a lift-up lid, suggests Miley. It's an ideal place to keep extra pillows and blankets. Or you can dedicate that under-window storage space to extra shoes and slippers.

Better yet, add new closets on either side of the window seat. By framing the window, you'll create a comfortable window-seat nook for afternoon reading.

For additional storage space in the bedroom, install a window seat with a lift-up lid, and build in closets on either side.

Shelve Those Shoes

Shoes belong on the floor *only* when they're on your feet, declares Miley. She believes closets should have *shelves* to hold your shoes. If you shelve your shoes after you take them off, they'll get better air circulation, and you'll be able to vacuum the entire closet floor without lifting up every pair you own.

A Pipe Dream for Pigeonhole Storage

Your plumbing supply store may have the answer to compact storage for wine and other bottled goods.

- Purchase 6-inch-diameter PVC pipe that's cut into 14-inch lengths.
- Stack the PVC inside a box or cupboard, as shown in the accompanying illustration.
- Voilà—ideal storage for your favorite wine, soda, pop, or seltzer.

Wine or soda bottles

6" diameter PVC pipe

Lengths of PVC pipe become bottle holders: Lay the pipe on its side and stack inside a wooden box.

Better Climate Control

Shadow-Cleaning Your Heating System

When you have your furnace or oil burner cleaned and inspected, do an auxiliary cleanup at the same time, suggests Kenneth Austin, chairman of HouseMaster of America.

If you have forced-air heat, clean the registers and duct openings. Use the upholstery-cleaning attachment on your vacuum cleaner to eliminate last season's dust and grime. If the register is removable, take it outside for a thorough hosing. (Avoid spray-on cleaners, says Austin; they leave a residue that gloms on to dust.)

Hot-water radiators can use a good vacuuming, too, notes interior designer Diana Mizer of Saint Davids, Pennsylvania. With the first surge of heat, loose dust particles will rise on the warm air and head for your nasal passages. If you vacuum first, you'll catch the dust before it hitches a ride on the updraft.

Secrets Revealed

RADIANT IN-FLOOR HEATING: WHAT IS IT?

In Germany and Austria, 60 percent of homes have in-floor heating, according to David L. Weiner, executive director of the Plumbing, Heating, Cooling Information Bureau in Chicago. In the United States, that figure is 2 percent.

According to Weiner, in-floor heating had a brief heyday after World War II, particularly in the Northeast. GIs stationed in Europe picked up the idea and tried it out at home. But this kind of heating got bad press in the 1960s when, ridden with leaks and other problems, some systems broke down.

"Now, thanks to durable plastic piping, new high-tech flooring, and better construction practices, many consumers are reconsidering radiant floor heating," Weiner finds.

Here's how it works: Warm water from a central boiler runs through tubing that has been installed inside the floor or directly under flooring. The water circulates continually through a closed loop system, and the warm floor radiates heat evenly into the room.

New, high-tech plastic piping (much of it imported from Europe) is the secret to leak-free installation and long-lasting performance, according to Weiner. Installation costs are higher than for some other systems, but there's the interior-design advantage of no bulky radiators or unsightly registers.

An additional advantage: Heat levels in different parts of the home can be closely controlled, so nursery or playroom floors can be toasty warm while bedrooms stay cool. Net gain: lower fuel costs.

The Satisfying Hiss of Efficiency

At the start of the cold season, bleed hot-water radiators to let excess air out of the system. According to Austin, the system should be bled every year to assure even and thorough hot water circulation throughout your home.

Here's the routine.

- As soon as the system is hot, open the bleeder valve one-quarter turn on the radiator that's farthest from the furnace.
- Leave the valve open until air stops hissing and a tiny stream of water sprays out. Then close the valve tightly.
- Move to the radiator that's next-closest to the furnace, and repeat the procedure.
- Continue until all the radiators in the house have been bled.

The result: When the system is on, hot water will flow evenly through *all* the radiators, without excess air pounding through the pipes.

Avoiding Ah-Choo: Filter Out Allergens

Change heating and air conditioning filters regularly, says Dr. Donald Ahearn of Georgia State University. The filters collect dust, and dust harbors allergens. And while you're changing the filters, he suggests, vacuum the ducts as well.

Heat Pumps with Better Brains

Heat pump systems that provide heat, air conditioning, and hot water are not new. The systems can help save energy, but in the past they've had drawbacks. In many systems, the blower roars on, full speed, in nothing flat, which means you get a sudden blast of wrong-temperature air and things don't even out until the system has been on a while.

Now there are new heat pumps with graduated temperature control, according to Peter Cann, senior program manager for the Carrier Division of United Technologies Corporation in Syracuse, New York. Carrier's Hydro Tech, for one, uses microprocessor controls to operate the blower motor and compressor at whatever speed is right for the moment.

As soon as the desired room temperature is reached, the compressor slows down to maintain that temperature. Energy is saved because the unit runs at the lowest blower and compressor speed possible. This reduces the number of start-stop cycles, which in turn means lower energy costs because high, starting-load draw is minimized.

Because the transition is gradual, you won't get that blast of frigid air that usually accompanies the start-up of a heat pump in cold weather. In the new system, the blower stays at low speed until the coil warms up.

FYI

New Specs for Access: Allow for Wheelchairs

What if someone in your household becomes disabled? What if an elderly parent is confined to a wheelchair? Would that person have access to all the rooms and facilities in your home?

While this might not be a pressing issue at the moment, it's definitely something to keep in mind when you're making home improvements. Can you do the remodeling in a way that will make your home safer or more accessible for the aged or disabled?

George North, a disabled veteran, is advocacy director and architectural barrier coordinator for the Cal-Diego Paralyzed Veterans Association in San Diego, California. He suggests the following steps to help make your home a friendlier place for anyone who needs easier access.

Putting in a new door? Make it at least 36 inches wide. If the door has a sill, make that sill as low as possible.

Remodeling a bedroom? Why not install a full-length, sliding patio door with sections that are 36 inches wide or more. In case of emergency, this sliding door would be an escape route for anyone in a wheelchair. Better yet, outside the sliding glass door, install a patio, so you have a "privacy garden" with wheelchair access.

Adding a deck or porch? Consider a ramp rather than steps leading up to it. The recommended slope on the ramp is no more than 1-inch rise per foot.

Installing new wall switches or thermostats? They should be more than 3 feet 4 inches and less than 4 feet from the floor: That will make them accessible to an adult in a wheelchair.

Putting in base plugs? Recommended height from the floor is at least 12 inches.

Replacing a sink? Consider a pedestal sink, which is the most accessible. If you're installing a vanity-style sink, choose a cabinet with double doors in front. (If the double doors swing open so a wheelchair can roll under the sink, you'll be able to adapt the vanity later on to make it accessible.)

Replacing windows? Crank-type window openers are easier for the aged or handicapped to operate.

Adding new shelving in the kitchen? Slide-out shelves will be convenient any time, but especially for the wheelchair cook. If you install a shelf that pulls out from under the kitchen counter, anyone can use it from a seated position.

Adding new built-ins? Allow at least 36 inches for passage (around a kitchen island, for example) so a wheelchair can get through.

Laying floor covering? Any thick carpeting, or carpeting with heavy padding, will make things more difficult for someone who has trouble walking or is propelling a wheelchair. Consider friendlier alternatives—tile, hardwood floors, or tightly woven commercial carpeting.

Replacing doorknobs and handles? Lever-style handles are not only fashionable but practical. People with arthritis and others with limited strength or range of motion find it easier to operate handles than knobs.

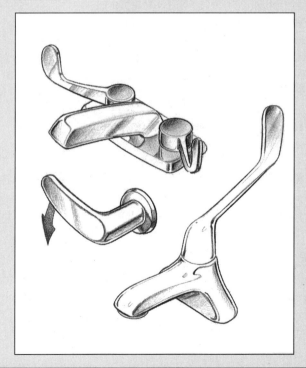

For family members who have trouble with regular knobs and faucets, install lever-style handles on doors and lever-handled faucets in kitchen and bathroom.

Dapper Decks and Fab Floors

The Floor-Sanding Alternative

Most homeowners know a few good reasons not to sand wood floors. It's expensive if you hire someone else to do it, and floor-sanding can turn into a horror story if you do it yourself. (A heavy-duty floor sander can leave your floor looking like a rippled pond on a windy day if you let it get away from you.) Also, newly sanded floors sometimes come out looking spanking brand new, which is the wrong look in an older home.

But what are the alternatives?

Bruce Johnson, moderator of the Minwax Home Planning Panel and author of the syndicated newspaper column "Knock on Wood" and The Weekend Refinisher, recommends a three-step method for refinishing your floors without sanding.

1. Begin with a refinisher, such as Minwax Antique Refinisher, to dissolve the old finish without destroying the patina of the wood.
2. Follow up with the stain of your choice. (Test a small out-of-the-way area first, before you apply the stain to the whole floor).
3. Finish up with a good polyurethane topcoat applied according to the directions on the can.

If you refinish instead of sanding, there's no dust or mess, and you keep the look of the original floor. "You'll still have the character that comes from nicks and scratches, but with a durable finish," notes Johnson.

Wood Preservative: 2 Definite Dos for Deck Owners

Applying wood preservative to your outdoor deck?

Scott Seman, a project manager at DAP in Dayton, Ohio, says it should always be applied with a brush or roller, not a sprayer. The sprayer creates a mist of preservative that could do serious harm to people, plants, and pets.

Another hint: Make sure the temperature is above 40°. At lower temperatures, the wood just doesn't absorb the stain as well.

Sap Stains on Deck?

If sap stains bleed through outdoor decking, you might be tempted to use steel wool to remove them. Seman warns against this method, because iron particles left behind on the wood can cause rust stains.

Instead, Seman recommends an oxalic acid solution to remove sap stains. Use a mixture of ¼ pound oxalic acid dissolved in a gallon of water. Brush away the sap stains, then immediately wash the acid away with water.

Caution: Always wear rubber gloves and eye protection when handling this harsh cleaner.

A Quick Patch for Vinyl Blights

Is there an ugly scar on the vinyl floor? Maybe someone clumped into the kitchen wearing football cleats or dropped a cast-iron pan. Before you go for a total replacement job, consider a patch-up.

According to Rick Mueller of DAP, vinyl *can* be patched. Here's how.

- Cut a replacement piece slightly oversize, taking care to match the texture or pattern of the original vinyl. Tape the patch over the damaged section and cut through both pieces, using a straightedge and a sharp utility knife. (Make sure the knife is held perpendicular to the floor. If it's angled, the seam will widen.)
- Lift out the damaged section, clean the floor underneath, and spread adhesive evenly onto the cut-out area, using a notched trowel. Press in the patch and smooth it from the center to the edges to remove air bubbles.

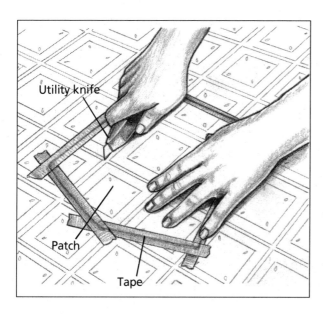

To cut a patch for a vinyl floor, lay an over-size patch-piece on top of the vinyl and tape it in place. Then cut through both layers (the patch piece and the vinyl underneath) with a sharp utility knife.

Smart Spruce-Ups

Ssssssshhhhh. Hints for a Hushed Interior

Want a quieter home?

There is much that can be done behind the scenes, according to Vince Powers, a representative of the North American Insulation Manufacturers Association in Alexandria, Virginia.

- Replace hollow-core doors with solid ones.
- With elastic, nonhardening caulk, seal wiring holes between connecting rooms or apartments. Caulk openings around electrical outlets.
- Isolate plumbing with resilient pads and sleeves. Seal for airtightness.
- Add water hammer mufflers where necessary. (See tip on page 151.) Appliances such as dishwashers and automatic washers that have solenoid shut-offs can cause plumbing to shudder and roar.
- Seal plumbing holes with caulk.
- Install one of the new, quieter toilets.
- Where possible, line ductwork with fiberglass duct liners.
- Check subflooring for cracks and seal them or add new subflooring.

Past Performance

THE SCENT OF COZINESS AND WARMTH

She was taught this trick by her mother, and now Beverly Margolis uses it any time she wants to make her home smell cozy and welcoming. Simply put an apple and a cinnamon stick in a pan of water and boil them together for 10 or 15 minutes.

"I used it just recently, when I had some plastering done and the whole house had that damp, funny smell," says Margolis, who operates Beverly Pac, a wholesale housewares business in Utica, New York. "In a few minutes, the whole house smelled like apple pie."

As Margolis points out, it's also a wonderful way to prepare a house for showing when you're selling or renting, or to refresh a home that has been sitting vacant for some time.

Remodeling? Moving In? Clean That Carpet First!

If you're getting ready to repaint the walls or remodel a room, clean the carpet first. That's the advice of Shannon Rench Tyler, spokesperson for the Host Consumer Division of Racine Industries in Racine, Wisconsin, manufacturers of the Host System dry carpet-cleaning method.

"If you start by bringing out the carpet's true color," says Tyler, "that can set up the color scheme for wall finishes and furnishings."

Tyler favors a dry extraction system, using a carpet-cleaning machine and a special dry cleaning powder such as Host or Capture. Sprinkle the powder on the carpet, then work it through the pile, using a machine made especially for dry-extraction cleaning.

Dry extraction machines are sold by Sears and other appliance stores and are also available through carpet cleaning rental sources. Professional services are also available.

Dream-Kitchen Fix-Ups

Make Room for Trash

Trash separation and recycling should be figured into any kitchen upgrade plans, suggests Joe Provey, former editor-in-chief of *Practical Homeowner* magazine. The one-stop, pull-out wastebasket is quickly becoming passé. Next time you're in a home store, look for slide-out double trash bins that you can easily install inside cupboards.

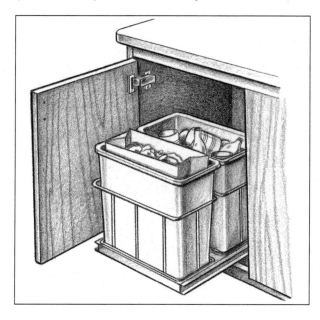

A slide-out tray for a pair of trash bins: One bin is for trash and the second for recyclables.

Getting the Kinks out of a Cabinet Door

According to Bruce Johnson of the Minwax Home Planning Panel, a warped door on a kitchen cabinet might be correctable. Try this to get it straightened out.

1. Remove the door.
2. Moisten the dried-out side by misting it with water or wiping with a wet cloth. Place the wood, cupped side down, on wet grass or on a damp towel in strong sun.

3. Place light weights on top of the wood.
4. When the shape has been restored, replace the damp towels with dry ones. Keep the wood weighted and well ventilated, changing towels as necessary until the wood dries.

A Flip Answer to Tight-Kitchen Woes

Storage spaces don't have to be permanent. Judith Miley of the Center for Home Organization and Interior Space Efficiency recommends some convenient flip-up and fold-out shelves for kitchen space.

- Install a flip-up shelf handy to the refrigerator. When you come in with a bag of groceries, pull out the shelf and set the bags on top. That way, everything's within reach when you're loading the fridge.
- Next to the kitchen sink, install a fold-out work shelf at stool height. Next time you're shelling peas or peeling apples, just pull out the shelf and pull up a seat. You'll ease back strain and take a load off your feet.
- Another flip-up shelf: A temporary snack-bar at the end of a counter. For kids or yourself, it's a good place to park a plate when you're having a quick bite. Afterward, just fold the shelf down out of the way.

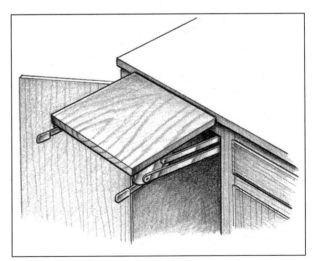

A flip-up shelf in the kitchen can be a holder for herbs and spices, a message-writing center, or a snack tray.

Breaker, Breaker on the Range

If your electric stove isn't heating fully, check the breakers in the main electrical box before anything else, says Macy Stern, a Houston homeowner who specializes in collecting antique cookstoves. Often *two* breakers are used to supply adequate current to the range. If one fails, the stove may continue to heat, but only partially.

Past Performance

THE KEY TO STOVE PRESERVATION: CLEANLINESS

Macy Stern of Houston, Texas, now retired from a television acting career, collects and restores antique cookstoves. She has discovered that old cookstoves will last almost forever, if you watch out for their number-one enemy.

And what's that?

Dirt and spills.

"It's funny," says Stern, "but dirt is still the biggest enemy of stove operation. If spills aren't wiped up immediately, they can bake on, obstruct gas passages, corrode electrical terminals, and cause all sorts of problems. What your mother taught you is still true, no matter how new or old your cookstove. Keep it clean!"

Tile in Style

Rout That Grout

Replacing ceramic tile? Half the battle is to *thoroughly* remove the old grout, says Rick Mueller, product manager at DAP.

If the tile has simply fallen out and needs replacing, dig out the old grout using a carbide-tipped utility knife.

If you have to dig out the old tile, don gloves and safety glasses and shatter it with a nail set and a hammer.

Before installing the new tile, scrape out the remaining mortar or adhesive with a chisel. Remove any bits of grout still sticking to the surrounding tiles, then vacuum to remove remaining debris. You'll now have a clean, dry, sound surface to accept the new tile.

Sticky Tile Tips

Tile adhesives have different characteristics. Be sure to read the manufacturer's directions on how much tile adhesive to apply at one time, cautions Mike Sheridan, former senior test engineer at Red Devil, manufacturer of painting tools and products in Union, New Jersey.

"Some adhesives harden faster than others, and they all harden faster in hot, dry weather," says Sheridan. "Take the job in small bites, so it doesn't get ahead of you."

Wood Helps Tile Jobs

When setting a tile floor, place a flat board over the surface and tap gently with a hammer to make sure each tile is firmly set, Sheridan recommends.

A new tile floor should not be walked on. Place plywood over it, and walk on that.

An essential step in setting a tile floor: Tap the board with a hammer to make sure each tile is firmly set.

Tile Won't Bend

Don't put ceramic tile over a floor that has any "give" in it, Sheridan warns. "Ceramic tile can't take movement."

Before laying any tile, nail down loose flooring. If necessary, cover the old flooring with a new plywood subfloor.

Concrete floors should be filled and leveled with a suitable cement filler compound before tile is laid.

PUTTING OUT AIRS

The kitchen hearth can easily become your central air-pollution center *unless* you vent away familiar cooking fumes like smoke, odors, heat, and moisture.

Ann Vaughan, director of consumer relations at Jenn-Air Company in Indianapolis, warns that good kitchen ventilation is especially important in today's tightly constructed, energy-efficient homes. "The best place to capture and dispose of destructive fumes is right at the source—the kitchen range or cooktop," she says.

Here are the comparative advantages of two kinds of ventilation systems, updraft and downdraft.

Updraft ventilation. A fan above the range pulls fumes up from the cooking surface, through a filter, to the outdoors. Ventless models use a filter and recirculate the air back to the kitchen, but they remove only *some* grease, smoke, and odors and none of the steam and heat. Arrange for outside exhaust if at all possible.

An updraft exhaust can be routed vertically through the ceiling and up to the roof, directly outside through the wall, or to the ceiling and along a joist to the outside wall or eaves. The exhaust ducts can also run up an inside wall, then to the roof with wide-angle bends.

An updraft system is efficient, since heated air rises naturally, and it's generally easier to install in an existing home than a downdraft system. The exhaust fan can be located inside the hood over the stove or mounted outside. The interior fan draws better, but it's also noisier.

Downdraft ventilation. A large selection of downdraft gas and electric stoves and cooktops is available. In a downdraft stove, a fan pulls cooking fumes *down* from the range top, usually through an air grill built into the stove surface. A filter traps some of the airborne grease; smoke, dampness, and odors are carried through a duct to an outside vent.

Downdraft ventilation can go directly through the wall to the exterior or down between the floor joists and through the crawl space or basement to the outdoors. Ductwork can also be installed through the cabinet toe space to the outside, or up inside walls or cabinets and through the roof.

Because the fan is so close to the stovetop, the downdraft system captures smoke, odor, moisture, and grease before they can escape and disperse into a room. And a fan under the stovetop is generally less noisy than a hood fan.

Save-a-Mint Plumbing Hints

The Right Pipe: Be Brand Loyal

If you're doing a major plumbing project around the house, make sure *all* plastic pipes and fittings are the same brand, warns Richard Day, author of *Do It Yourself Plumbing...It's Easy with Genova.*

Different brands have subtle variations in pipe-wall thickness. Even though two different brands may meet specifications as ½-inch or ¾-inch systems, they may have differences in ID (inner diameter) or OD (outer diameter) sizing. If you stick to the same brand for all your piping, you can be far more certain of an all-compatible system with leak-free installation, according to Day.

For Instant Repairs, Keep a Universal Kit

New universal plumbing repair supplies are more versatile than ever. Brands like Uncopper, Spring, and Genogrip can be used to join metal to metal, plastic to plastic, or metal to plastic.

Author Richard Day recommends keeping a kit on hand, *just in case* you have a problem with a frost-split pipe or other plumbing headaches. Repairing a frost-split pipe can be as simple as adding a single coupling. If you always have two couplings of each size on hand in your workshop, you can bridge over a larger split with PB (polybutylene) tubing.

Welding in a Chill?

If you're planning to weld PVC pipe in the depths of a cold snap, look for a special, low-temperature welding product such as Articweld P cement. Richard Day points out that most welding solvents are formulated to work in mild temperatures; the products formulated for low temperatures will set up despite freezing weather.

Branching Out? Find a Tee That Fits

Shopping your local plumbing supplier for a tee? Make sure you ask for the right size. There are two measurements you need to specify—the through opening and the branch size (see illustration on the opposite page).

In industry lingo, the first through opening is given first; the second through opening, second; and the branch size, third.

If you need a reducing tee with a run size of ¾ inch at one end and ½ inch at the other, plus a branch size of ½ inch, ask for a ¾ × ½ × ½-inch tee.

If you need a tee having a uniform run of ¾ inch (that is two ¾-inch through openings) and a branch of ½-inch, ask for a ¾ × ¾ × ½ -inch tee.

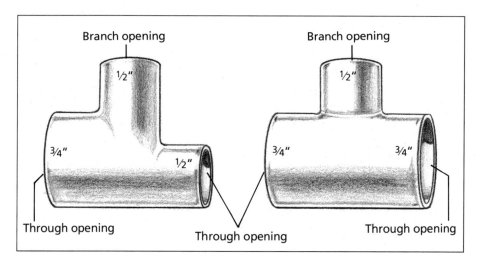

If you're buying a tee for plumbing work, always give the size of the through opening first, then the branch size. At left is a reducing tee ¾" × ½" × ½". At right is a ¾" × ¾" × ½" tee.

Muffle That Water Hammer

Do you hear crashes and roars when your dishwasher changes cycles or when the water turns off in your automatic washing machine? You can mute the mayhem with a water hammer muffler, according to Richard Day.

The "muffler" is simply an air chamber that gives the excess pressure a place to go. Many homes already have them, but if you hear the pipes hammering in your home, you definitely need another one.

Look for the new, universal models that can be installed in any metal or plastic pipe system. Place the muffler as close as possible to the shut-off device that is causing the noise—usually a clothes washer or dishwasher, but mufflers are often needed on lines leading to sinks and showers, too.

Been Working on Pipes? Give Them a Flush

If you or your plumber has been working on your plumbing system, give it a thorough flushing before drinking the water, says Day. Sending water through the plumbing system hastens the curing of the solvents used in joining pipes, and it washes away any impurities you introduced when working on the system. Here's how to flush the pipes.

1. Close the home's main shutoff valve.
2. Open all the faucets.
3. Reopen the main valve just enough to let water flow slowly into the system.

4. When water starts flowing from the lowest-level faucet, close the spigot until the water's just coming out at a steady trickle.
5. Move up through the house, turning each spigot to a trickle.
6. Let water trickle from each faucet for 10 minutes. Then turn off faucets.
7. Close the main valve for half an hour, let the water stand in the system, then open the faucets for 10 more minutes of trickling.
8. Repeat the cycle one more time.

As a final step, pressurize the system by turning the main valve on full. Opening one faucet at a time, flush each for a few seconds, close again, then flush each toilet. Your new plumbing should now be clean and ready to use.

This Is a Turn-Off

If you're adding any water-using appliance to your home—like a water softener, washing machine, or automatic icemaker—be sure to add a valve in the water line near the appliance, says Day. That way, you can easily turn off the water if you need to service the appliance.

Air Gaps Give Pipes a Chill

When you're insulating pipes against heat loss or freezing, don't leave any air gaps, warns Richard F. Tripodi, general manger at Darworth Company, a manufacturer of caulks and sealants in Avon, Connecticut.

Insulation should be butted as closely as possible when you're wrapping the pipes. Then fill in all gaps with a PVC-based adhesive caulk.

Making Your Workshop Work

Saw Blade Shopping

The circular saw is a basic tool in most home workshops—but many owners wonder which is the right blade for many jobs.

Different blades are needed for different tasks, according to Jim Luebbers, a manager in the Craftsman Group at Vermont American Corporation in Louisville, Kentucky. You will need to answer these questions before you go shopping.

- Are you cutting hardwood or softwood?
- Are the cuts across the grain, or with the grain? (That is, ripping or crosscutting?)

Once you get to the supply store or hardware store, let someone help you find the right blade for the job. By using the correct blade, your cuts will be cleaner, less sanding will be required, and the blade will last longer.

FYI

PUTTING AIR TOOLS TO WORK

These days, home air compressors, air tools, and accessories are affordable and compact. The air compressor is the basic power unit, and the air tool is hooked up to it with a long, flexible air hose.

Just pick up an air tool to find out why owners like them. Since they don't have built-in motors, they're lightweight, ideal for working overhead or getting into hard-to-reach places.

Since the tool runs off an air hose, not an electric cord, the tool that you hold in your hand does not pose a shock hazard. And an air tool generally lasts longer than its motorized equivalent, because it has fewer working parts.

Jim Kregel, spokesperson for the Power Air Division of Thomas Industries in Sheboygan, Wisconsin, lists some of the air tools that are available for easier home repairs.

Staplers. You can control staples so they secure the material, not shoot through it. Light and maneuverable, air staplers are easy to use in tight attic spaces.

Pneumatic nailers. For trim work or paneling, you can adjust the air pressure, according to the hardness of the wood, to drive the nails just the right distance into the surface. "These nailers work so quickly, the wood doesn't split. You don't have to drill pilot holes," says Kregel, "nor do you get the bounce-back or scarring you get when using a hammer."

Spray nozzles. With a simple spray nozzle attachment on the air hose, you can blow sawdust, plaster dust, and other debris out of corners and hard-to-reach crannies with a high-power stream of air.

Paint sprayers. These are probably the most familiar of the air tools—indispensable for tricky painting tasks such as shutters, wicker, heat registers, stencils, and the like.

Caulk guns. With a trigger-operated air caulk gun, you have excellent control in making a steady, even bead for a foolproof seal.

If you're unsure about how much use you'll get from air tools, rent them at first, suggests Kregel. Then buy only the compressor and the attachments you'll use often around your home. And, for greatest control, Kregel also advises getting a compressor that has a pressure adjustment valve.

Battle Blade-Warp

"Prolonged, continuous use can warp a blade so that it runs untrue, spoiling the cut," Jim Luebbers points out.

How do you know if a blade is overworked? It heats up. "Excessive overheating can burn both the blade and the workpiece," adds Luebbers. "Do not overwork a blade or force it to cut."

Putting the Lock on Threads

At the very least, loose bolts and screws are an annoyance; at worst, a loose bolt on a wheelbarrow, swing set, or exercise bike can be downright dangerous.

To put an end to the annoyance and the dangers, look for chemical threadlockers, which are sold in hardware stores and home centers, advises Beverly DeJulio, spokesperson for the Automotive and Consumer Group of the Loctite Corporation in Cleveland, Ohio. Just place a drop of the threadlocker on the threads before tightening the screw or bolt.

Threadlockers such as Loctite and other brands are available at different strengths to tolerate various temperature extremes.

Drywalling the Pro Way

Drywall Time? Leave Colored Tape to Pros

The best tape for drywall joints is a white mesh, according to Craig Christman, national sales manager of the Consumer Products Division of Custom Tapes, in Harwood Heights, Illinois. For homeowners who aren't used to taping drywall joints, Christman *doesn't* recommend a colored mesh tape.

"Professionals use colored mesh because it gives them a sanding guide," he observes. "However, amateurs can sand too deeply, leaving too much color to show through the finished job. This results in shadows under the painted or papered walls."

Drywall Taping in 5 Acts

The trick in putting up drywall is to get smoothly taped joints: You want to make those seams disappear so they never show under paint or wallpaper.

But don't expect to get a perfect job in one easy step. Taping drywall is a five-act drama, according to Mike Sheridan, formerly of Red Devil. Filling and fairing is a job that requires time and a deft hand as you apply thin coats of drywall joint compound, wider with each application, until the joint can no longer be seen.

Here are the steps recommended by Sheridan.

1. Apply a generous amount of compound to the joint, about 15 to 20 feet at a time, using a taping knife. Cover about 3 inches on each side of the joint.
2. While the compound is still wet, lay the tape directly over the center of the joint, using a taping knife to press tape into the compound.
3. Applying firm pressure with a taping knife held at a 45-degree angle to the wall surface, force out excess compound at the edges. Start at the middle of the tape and work out to both edges.
4. Let it dry for one full day. Then apply a thinner coat, feathering it out 6 or 8 inches with a wider, 10- to 12-inch taping knife.
5. After the compound has dried completely, finish up with a third, thin coat, feathered out 12 to 14 inches.

When it's dry, sand lightly with medium-grit sandpaper. The joint should now be invisible after it's painted or papered.

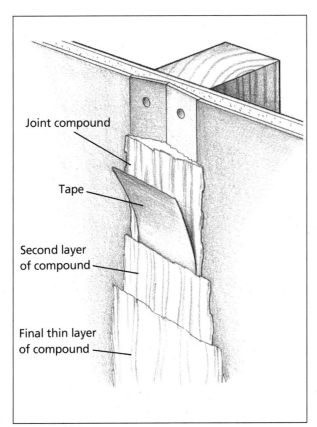

Joint compound

Tape

Second layer of compound

Final thin layer of compound

For a smooth seal in drywall, apply joint compound, then lay tape on compound while it is still wet. Apply two additional coats, allowing time to dry between each coat.

The Experts

Donald Ahearn, Ph.D., is professor of industrial and medical microbiology at Georgia State University in Atlanta.

Kenneth T. Austin is chairman of HouseMaster of America, a nationwide home inspection service headquartered in Bound Brook, New Jersey.

Kathy Blessinger is manager of product development for the Residential Lighting Division at Thomas Industries in Louisville, Kentucky.

Peter Cann is a senior program manager for the Carrier Corporation Division of United Technologies Corporation in Syracuse, New York.

Craig Christman is the national sales manager of the Consumer Products Division of Custom Tapes, Inc., in Harwood Heights, Illinois.

Richard Day is the author of *Do It Yourself Plumbing...It's Easy with Genova.*

Beverly DeJulio is spokesperson for the Automotive and Consumer Group of the Loctite Corporation in Cleveland, Ohio.

Howard Faulkner is associate professor of technology and the former executive director of the Energy Efficient Building Association at the University of Southern Maine in Gorham.

Dave Fuller is a product manager at DAP, Inc., maker of caulks, sealants, and other repair products, in Dayton, Ohio.

David Groene is a product manager at DAP, Inc., in Dayton, Ohio, maker of caulks, sealants, and other repair products.

Scott J. Hanley is a marketing manager for Stanley Door Systems in Troy, Michigan.

Ida Hawkins of De Land, Florida, and Albany, New York, is a housewife and avid do-it-yourselfer.

Steve Honig is spokesperson for Woodfinisher's Pride Stripping Gels in Greenville, South Carolina.

Bruce Johnson, author of the syndicated newspaper column "Knock on Wood" and of *The Weekend Refinisher*, is moderator of the Minwax Home Planning Panel.

John Kiker is spokesperson for the Mineral Insulation Manufacturers Association in Alexandria, Virginia.

Jim Kregel is spokesperson for the Power Air Division of Thomas Industries in Sheboygan, Washington.

Marilyn LeMoine is publications department manager at the American Plywood Association in Tacoma, Washington.

Beth Lewis is a product manager for the Residential Lighting Division of Thomas Industries in Louisville, Kentucky.

Jim Luebbers is a manager in the Craftsman Group at Vermont American Corporation in Louisville, Kentucky.

Beverly Margolis is the owner and operator of Beverly Pac, Ltd., a wholesale housewares business in Utica, New York.

Chris Martini is an air tool engineer for Campbell Hausfeld, a compressor manufacturer in Mount Juliet, Tennessee.

Judith Miley, president of JE Marketing Communications, is the founder of the Center for Home Organization and Interior Space Efficiency in Ocala, Florida.

Diana Mizer is an interior designer in Saint Davids, Pennsylvania.

Jeff Molchan is spokesperson for Stanley Door Systems Division in Troy, Michigan.

John Molski is technical director at United Gilsonite Laboratories, in Scranton, Pennsylvania.

Rick Mueller is a product manager at DAP, Inc., manufacturer of caulks and sealants, in Dayton, Ohio.

George North is advocacy director and architectural barrier coordinator for the Cal-Diego Paralyzed Veterans Association in San Diego, California.

Joseph C. Peters is the national director of developing consulting for Cushman and Wakefield Realtors in New York City.

Evan Powell is a spokesperson for Southeastern Products Research and Development in Greenville, South Carolina.

Vince Powers is a representative of the North American Insulation Manufacturers Association in Alexandria, Virginia.

Joe Provey is former editor-in-chief of *Practical Homeowner* magazine.

Scott Seman is a product manager at DAP, Inc., maker of caulks, sealants, and other repair products, in Dayton, Ohio.

Mike Sheridan is a former senior test engineer for Red Devil, Inc., in Union, New Jersey, manufacturer of painting tools and products.

Mike Skinker is an environmental health consultant and president of For Your Health Products in Chevy Chase, Maryland.

Macy Stern, of Houston, Texas, is a specialist in antique cookstoves.

Mike Stuhlreyer is merchandising manager of the Painting Systems Division of Campbell Hausfeld in Mount Juliet, Tennessee.

Richard F. Tripodi is general manager for the Darworth Company, manufacturers of caulks and sealants, in Avon, Connecticut.

Shannon Rench Tyler is spokesperson for the Host Consumer Division of Racine Industries, Inc., in Racine, Wisconsin, manufacturers of the Host System dry carpet-cleaning method.

Ann Vaughan is director of consumer relations for the Jenn-Air Company in Indianapolis.

David L. Weiner is executive director of the Plumbing, Heating, Cooling Information Bureau in Chicago.

CHAPTER 6

Kitchen and Cooking

Skills and Tools
for Tasty Cuisine

You've learned a lot in your kitchen through the years. Your cooking now is faster, healthier, and probably a lot easier than it used to be. There's no doubt about it—when it comes to preparing food, experience *is* the best teacher.

Experience teaches those who earn their living in the kitchen, as well. Food writers, gourmet chefs, caterers, bakers, and other professionals who spend their workdays slaving over that proverbial hot stove can't afford to waste their time. Whether making initial selections at the market or cutting that perfectly baked cheesecake into 16 perfectly even pieces for 16 fussy guests, they make every motion count.

We've talked to a number of food professionals, who willingly share some of their trade secrets. Meet a caterer from Chicago who has great advice on barbecue cooking and tips on preparing buffet meals for dozens. For that fresh citrus flavor in key lime pie, heed an expert dessert chef from New York City. Want the tastiest beans, the fluffiest rice? Learn some secrets from a pressure-cooking specialist.

Here you'll find tips for everything from selecting the right tools for the job to turning out a perfect pie crust every time.

Microwave Wisdom

Think Healthy

"The good news is that low-fat, high-moisture–content foods—fish; skinless, boneless chicken; vegetables; and fruits—are the best items to microwave, and the best for us, so it's a great choice for the health-conscious cook," says Judith Benn Hurley, a food columnist for the *Washington Post* and author of *Healthy Microwave Cooking* and *The Every Day Herbal*.

When the microwave was first introduced, the word *oven* led many people to think that the appliance will do everything a regular oven does, only faster. "It's different. It cooks with moist heat, so things don't brown and crisp," she explains. But if you "think health" when you're wondering what you can whip up in the microwave, you'll be on the right track.

Is This Dish Micro-Safe?

Here's how to test that pretty casserole, according to Thelma K. Snyder, of Bellmore, New York, who along with Marcia Cone, is the author of *Mastering Microwave Cookery* and *Microwave Diet Cookery*.

1. Place the empty dish in the microwave.
2. Put ½ cup of water in a heatproof glass measuring cup and place it next to the dish.
3. Run the microwave on high for 1 minute.

After that time, the water (which has attracted the microwave energy) will be hot, but the dish you are testing should stay cool. If the dish is hot, it might crack during use, so it should not be used in microwave cooking.

Protect Those Tender Tips

Want even micro-cooking for irregular foods? Position is everything, says Hurley. Asparagus or broccoli, for instance, should be arranged in a starburst pattern, with tender tips at the center and thicker, tougher ends toward the outer rim of the plate.

The same arrangement can be used for boneless chicken breasts or fish fillets: Even them out as much as possible by pounding the chicken lightly or folding under the thin tips of fish fillets. If there's still some unevenness, place the thicker parts to the outer edges.

Sizing Things Up

For the most even and successful microwave cooking results, have your ingredients in equal-size pieces, advises Hurley, or else tiny pieces will overcook. "Items of the same texture and size, such as chunks of carrots, turnips,and parsnips, will all become tender within the same cooking time.'

Worry-Free Sauces

"If you use your microwave for nothing else," advises Snyder, "do try it for sauces. There's much less stirring involved, and no worry about scorching or burning."

Great for the Grill

The microwave gives you a great head start on outdoor grilling. Use it to precook chunks and slices of different vegetables.

"Once each is tender, I set them aside, then brush them with a bit of oil, sprinkle with herbs or seasonings, and finish them on the grill," says Snyder, adding that everything from eggplant to onions can all be placed on the grill at the same time, and each turns out perfectly cooked.

A Whisk for Ease

How convenient—a whisk that can stay right in a bowl or cup, even when the microwave is on!

"Of all the microwave gadgets I've seen, this is the one I'd recommend," says Chicago newspaper columnist Patricia Tennison, author of *Glorious Vegetables in the Microwave* and other books about microwave cookery.

Look for a durable, "microwave transparent" whisk that can be safely used in foods heated up to 400°.

"It's very convenient for repeated stirring," Tennison explains. "You leave it right in the mixture, so you eliminate drips and extra utensils."

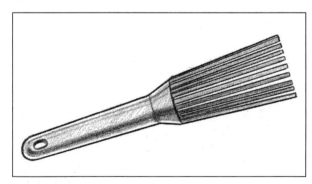

One of the most useful items for cooks who use microwave ovens—a microwave-proof plastic whisk.

Entertaining Excellence

Organize, Organize, Organize

Whether you're a professional party planner or a once-in-a-while host, there's no denying that entertaining a crowd is a big job. "The big crunch starts an hour or so before the party, getting everything assembled and ready to serve," according to Carlyn Berghoff, president of Carlyn Berghoff Catering in Chicago. She offers some practical strategies for staying organized.

- Keep all the food items that go together in one spot. For example, for a vegetable pasta salad, place the cooked pasta in the fridge and right alongside, on the same shelf, place all the bags and containers of vegetables, herbs, and dressing.
- Mark and label items clearly—for instance, mark all the pasta salad items with a large P. When it's time to put the salad together, you (or a helper) can grab all the P items, toss them together, and the pasta salad's done.
- Do the same with each item on your menu, remembering to include garnish and any special items, such as toothpicks or dipping sauce, and marking everything clearly, so there's no last-minute confusion.

FYI

ESCHEW SOME ENTERTAINING ERRORS

Common mistakes can make entertaining an ordeal rather than a pleasure. Here are a few to avoid.

- Reheating cream-sauced pastas can result in a gluey, overcooked dish, says Carlyn Berghoff, president of Carlyn Berghoff Catering in Chicago. And, she adds, "Don't serve buffet salads with leaves of lettuce large enough for King Kong."
- Any buffet foods that are too juicy and drippy are "unkind to your table linens, your guests' clothing, your furniture, and your carpeting," warns Hannelore Dawson of Newark, Delaware, author of *Great Food for Great Numbers.*
- Don't run out of dishes or glasses, says Arno Schmidt, former executive chef of the Waldorf-Astoria hotel in New York City. "When planning a dinner party, people forget that they may need more than the basic service for 12," he explains. "If you serve an appetizer and a salad, you may not have any clean plates for dessert. If you try to run them through your home dishwasher, it will take 45 minutes, and you'll be stuck with hot plates for ice cream." Instead, he advises, visit a restaurant supply house and purchase some plain, inexpensive plates and flatware. Do the same with all-purpose wine glasses, so when you entertain, you won't have to worry about having enough tableware.

Let the Herd Graze

A "grazing" buffet is the best way to feed a large crowd, says Berghoff. As a guideline for total amounts of food, she gives these suggestions.

- For a 2-hour cocktail party, allow 12 bites per person; for a 3-hour party, about 18 bites per person.
- Count portions from the cheese tray and crudité display as "bites" as well.
- Plan on a bit more of certain very popular items like shrimp—a bit less of more exotic or unusual foods.

Chilling Facts about Ice

Don't forget ice in your party planning, says Berghoff. Follow these guidelines to make sure you have enough.

- For a 2- or 3-hour cocktail party, about a pound of ice per person is sufficient.
- In the summer, double that amount.
- If you plan to chill wines, soda, and beer in tubs of ice, you'll need extra for that purpose.

For an impressive buffet table: Create a "riser" in the center, covered with a small cloth, where you can place dishes or a centerpiece.

Set the Stage

To give your home buffet a more professional look, create the dramatic, tiered look of the grand hotel buffet. "It's simple to do at home," says Berghoff.

Simply spread a tablecloth over your table as usual, then place a stack of one or two telephone books, or an overturned bowl, or even an empty milk crate, on the table surface.

Cover that "riser" with another small cloth and use that surface as the focal point of the buffet. You might place a food platter, a still life of fruits and vegetables, or a tumbled basket of pretty breads and crackers on the raised surface.

Scatter Ye Rosebuds

To give your buffet table that sophisticated "catered" look, place single blossoms and leaves here and there among the food platters on your table, suggests Berghoff. Don't use a bouquet of flowers in a vase or centerpiece. The free-form scattering of flowers will make your table setting look lavish and extravagant for the same cost.

Rationing the Rations

How much is too much when you plan a buffet for a large group? Will there be enough?

"Most people overplan," says Hannelore Dawson of Newark, Delware, author of *Great Food for Great Numbers*. "Consider the whole menu when planning portion size and total amounts of food."

If you have only one entrée or meat dish, you should allow for approximately a 6-ounce portion per person. On the other hand, if you offer a choice of main courses, such as a meat dish, a poultry dish, and a fish dish, then the most you would need of each would be about 2 ounces per person.

BEFORE YOU GO ALL OUT: CHOOSE YOUR ROLE

Will you play hostess or chef at your next dinner party? It's important to understand the difference, says Arno Schmidt, former executive chef of the Waldorf-Astoria hotel in New York City. "Cooking for a dinner at home is really much harder for the home cook than for the professional chef," he contends.

"The home host or hostess has so many distractions—phone calls, work, and family needs—it's difficult to concentrate. Trying to be both charming hostess and gourmet chef is the most common entertaining error. People plan an overcomplicated restaurant menu, with each course requiring lots of last-minute touches and precise timing.

"For a relaxed and successful party, plan to serve items that can easily be done ahead, that just need finishing or reheating before serving, even for a small dinner party. Guests can't enjoy themselves if the hostess keeps running into the kitchen every 10 minutes."

The Fast Stack

Does the thought of making enchiladas for 50 people make you yearn for a long siesta? Well, take Dawson's timesaving advice: Don't roll them, stack them! "Prepare enchiladas as you would lasagna, layering the tortillas and the filling in large, shallow baking pans. When they're baked, cut them into neat squares to serve." Dawson suggests using the same stacking system for sweet or savory crêpe dishes as well.

Read My Menu

It is standard procedure in a hotel banquet room to post a menu for all to see, says Brooklyn author, culinary consultant, and Certified Executive Chef Arno Schmidt, former executive chef of the Waldorf-Astoria hotel in New York City. And it's a good idea in a home setting as well. "Even today, when I entertain at home, I always write out a detailed menu and place it on my refrigerator," he says. "It's a good reminder for the cook as you go through the final prep to get ready for each course. And it's great fun for guests to read."

It's helpful in another way as well. "When guests arrive," says Schmidt, "you're usually busy with a few last-minute details. I can offer guests a glass of wine and let them read the menu while I finish my work."

Give Your Salad a Big Spin

The next time you have a mountain of salad greens to prep and wash for the big family reunion or block party, give this do-ahead trick a whirl.

Place one cotton pillowcase inside another, fill the inside case with trimmed and washed greens, and head for your laundry room, says Nancy Stern, a teacher, consultant, and kitchen designer who runs The Uncomplicated Gourmet Kitchen Design Studios in Westwood, New Jersey.

REUSABLE TOWELS (WOW!)

Tired of using up money (and trees!) buying roll after roll of paper towels? Why not take the advice of Nancy Stern, a consultant and kitchen designer who is owner of The Uncomplicated Gourmet Kitchen Design Studios in Westwood, New Jersey. Stern's advice: Buy some inexpensive cotton dish towels. To keep them handy in the kitchen, roll them up and store them within easy reach in a cute basket.

At the end of the week, toss them into the white laundry load with some chlorine bleach to keep them sweet-smelling and sanitized. You'll be surprised at the savings.

Securely fasten your giant "salad bag" and place it in your washing machine along with a clean bath towel. Set the washer on the spin cycle for a few minutes. "When it's over," says Stern, "you'll have crisp, dry salad leaves and wet pillowcases." For ideal storage, transfer the greens to a dry, clean pillowcase and store in the fridge. Your greens will stay in perfect shape for at least 24 hours.

Spill the Salt

"When you're serving a large crowd in a rush, you may get a little sloppy," says Schmidt. "If you should have a little greasy spill, dump some salt on it to keep anyone from slipping until you have a chance to clean it up."

Strategies for Safety

Banish Bacteria

Wash away your concerns about bacterial contamination the easy way, advises author Hannelore Dawson. Make a simple solution of 1 gallon of water and 2 tablespoons of household bleach. "Use this to wash off your utensils and all cutting and preparation surfaces immediately after preparing your raw poultry, for instance," she says. "Everything, including your hands, will be properly sanitized."

TRACKING AND TRICKING TRICHINELLA

There's good reason to take special care when cooking pork—trichinosis is a nasty disease. The culprit, *Trichinella spiralis,* is a parasite that can take up unpleasant residence in the human body. *If* you ingest the meat of an infected hog, and *if* that meat has not been adequately prepared, you can find yourself playing host to an unwelcome invader.

Now, let's clear up those *if's* with information from the Pork Producer's Council, the U.S. Department of Agriculture (USDA), and the Centers for Disease Control.

1. Infection in U.S. hogs is a clinical rarity, so the likelihood that any pork you purchase harbors the evil villain is almost negligible.
2. Trichinella is destroyed at temperatures above 137° or below 15°.
3. No one should take even a long-shot chance of ingesting a harmful parasite, so cook pork to an internal temperature of 160°—a good safety margin—and stop worrying!

The Acid Test for Safe Picnic Fare

Concerned about food spoilage at your summer buffet or family picnic? Your best protection is an acidic dressing or marinade, suggests Dawson. She gives the following suggestion.

If you're planning to grill teriyaki chicken strips when you reach your picnic site, marinate them overnight in soy sauce, lemon juice, sherry, and ginger. Then you can safely transport them raw and chilled.

Knives: Sharper Is Safer

Are razor-sharp knives dangerous? Nope. The real danger is from dull knives, says Brooklyn chef Arno Schmidt. The dull edge requires more pressure and is more likely to slip and cut you instead of the carrot. Schmidt's safety advice:

- Buy professional-quality knives.
- Clean them immediately after use.
- Store them in a heavy knife block.
- Keep them well sharpened.

Quick-and-Easy Eats

Precook Fabulous Fish

Want to have delicious fare all ready when the guests arrive? Poach or bake boneless chicken breasts or fish fillets in advance, says Dawson. Dress them with a zesty vinaigrette or top with a sauce of marinated vegetables and chill for at least an hour or overnight. These can be safely served at room temperature and will be moist and delicious.

Quick Chicken Barbecue

Get a head start on your cookout this way, advises Dawson: Bake or roast your chicken pieces completely at home. Don't overcook them, but do cook each piece completely through. Then freeze them. When you're ready to head for the picnic site, pour barbecue sauce over the frozen chicken. By barbecue time, the chicken will have thawed and absorbed the sauce and will just need to be heated through on the grill. It will be perfectly cooked and perfectly safe to eat in much less time.

Freeze Your Own

Don't waste time and money shopping for frozen convenience foods or prepackaged meals in your supermarket. Make your own! "I don't put uncooked food in my freezer," says The Uncomplicated Gourmet's Nancy Stern.

"Use at least half, if not more, of your valuable freezer space for precooked, ready-to-heat-and-eat meals you've prepared yourself." If you do that, here's the payoff.

- You control the purity of the ingredients, eliminating additives and fillers, and limiting the salt and fat content.
- You can customize the seasonings and portion size to your family's needs and preferences.
- You, or any family member, can have a meal in minutes at the end of a busy day, rather than starting from scratch.

Think Big

Grab your largest pot and fill it up when you have the time and urge to cook, says Stern. "It makes no sense at all to go to the trouble of preparing a soup, stew, or casserole and have it all gone after one meal."

Add just a little more time for preparing and cooking a large batch of a family favorite, and reap the benefits from your freezer for weeks to come.

Make sure to pack and freeze in small portions, advises Stern. Then you can whip up a fast dinner for one or two, or grab a whole bunch of packages for a last-minute dinner party.

For Scintillating Flavor

Add Something Special to Saltless Sauces

To lend flavor to salt-free tomato sauce, author Judith Benn Hurley suggests the following additions.

- Minced carrot or some marjoram for a bit of sweetness.
- A splash of wine for sour or acidic taste.
- Garlic for some aromatic flavor.

"With these additions, you'll stimulate a lot of taste sensation," says Hurley, "and the sauce will be far more interesting and exciting, rather than bland."

Herbs: How to Store 'Em

To keep fresh herbs at their best at home, suggests Hurley, treat them like fresh flowers. Stand them in a glass of water and loosely drape a plastic produce bag over their tops to keep in moisture.

Sally Schneider, of New York City, author of *The Art of Low Calorie Cooking* and a contributing editor for *Food and Wine* magazine, suggests an alternate method for conserving freshness in herbs: "Wrap them loosely in damp paper towels and then place them in a plastic bag, as you would salad greens."

Burnt Offerings

When grilling foods, especially those that have been marinated with herbs, try tossing some extra herb sprigs, like rosemary or thyme, on the coals during the last few minutes of cooking, suggests Hurley. "This trick is especially good if you have an herb garden," she points out. "Burning the coarse, woody stems adds flavor and fragrance to the food on the grill."

Exchange Peppers for Salt

Chili peppers are a great way to compensate for salt. Fresh serrano or jalapeño peppers are Schneider's choice: "Add a little minced chili pepper (about ½ to 1 teaspoon) while you're sautéing," she suggests. "You won't generate firepower, but you will enhance the overall piquancy of your recipe."

Marvelously Mashed

Buttermilk, which (despite its name) is naturally low in fat and carlories, is Schneider's secret ingredient for making rich-tasting mashed potatoes.

Use a combination of buttermilk and some of the water the potatoes were boiled in instead of whole milk and butter as you mash your potatoes. Then, at the very end, add just a touch of unsalted butter.

"You'll get real butter flavor from that final touch," she says, "and you won't have added all those extra calories in the mashing process."

Nut Oils: A Little Dab Will Do

Imported nut oils are wonderful for getting a nutty taste in recipes with far fewer calories than you would from the nuts themselves. Adding ½ cup of chopped nuts to a recipe can cost 350 to 400 calories, but nut oils have 40 calories per teaspoon, explains Schneider. (And the imported kinds have the "nuttiest" flavor.)

She suggests using the nut oils as great flavor substitutes in salad dressings, applesauce or other fruit purées, or in baked goods. "For a real treat, try hazelnut oil in chocolate pudding," she suggests, "or add a teaspoonful to a sponge cake."

Healthy Eating

Here's the Skinny on Beef

You don't have to ban beef from your diet in order to be healthy. Choose the leanest cuts—those from the round are the lowest in fat—and trim every bit of exterior fat you possibly can, advises Tom Ney, director of food service at Rodale Press in Emmaus, Pennsylvania.

Make a Little Go a Long Way

Top loin and top sirloin have slightly higher fat levels than cuts from the round and will cook up juicier and more tender, says Ney. They're okay as a meal choice, especially if used in dishes that make smaller portions go further—like a stir-fry or fajitas.

Add a Touch of Class

A little luxury can be lighter than you think. Despite the elegant image (and price) of filet mignon, says Ney, it's not a bad choice as a once-in-a-while beef treat. "Beef tenderloin (its proper retail name) is a lean cut. Just be sure it's trimmed completely clean of any fat." It's a far better choice than any other to satisfy that occasional craving for a steak dinner.

Trim That Pork

A well-trimmed pork loin is as healthful a choice as a lean beef round, says Ney. "Trim the pork of any visible fat. And don't overcook it, so it can retain its flavor and tenderness."

Quick 'n' Healthy Pork

After you've trimmed pork loin, here are three quick and healthy ways to prepare it, suggested by Tom Ney.

- Slice it into ¼-inch medallions (small, coin-shaped pieces) and sauté them for 1 minute on each side in just a tiny amount of oil. Create an elegant entrée by combining the meat with fruit slices, such as apple, pear, or orange.
- Cut the meat into julienne (matchstick) strips, then marinate it for stir-fries.
- Use leftover cooked roast sliced in sandwiches or in strips for salads.

Bring on the Beans

Beans are both good and good *for* you. They contain both soluble and insoluble fiber, are delicious, and have a rich, satisfying taste. And, says Ney, if you think it takes too much time to include them in your meal plan, use these shortcuts.

- Keep some canned beans on the shelf. At mealtime, just drain and rinse them and toss them into a salad, a soup, or chili. In no time at all, you enhance the nutrition of a dish.
- Keep frozen lima beans on hand. They're often overlooked as a good fiber source.
- Combine lentils or other beans with rice or pasta to give you a complete protein.

Techno-Tip

WHAT'S COOKING IN THE FUTURE?

It's not so much "what" as "how," says Carol Lamkins, a certified home economist and kitchen designer with Design Vision located in Fullerton, California. In the search for a cooking method that is safe, fast, nonpolluting, and energy efficient, the magnetic induction cooktop seems to win the prize.

A sealed cooktop, powered by electricity, stays cool to the touch during use but gives a cooking response similar to a gas burner. The cookware must be of metal that can attract a magnet, since it acts as a transformer for the energy generated by the cooktop. The cooking process takes place in the electromagnetic field within the vessel, not exactly like microwave cooking but similar in its instant-on, instant-off operation.

"You could place a paper napkin between the pot and the surface," she explains. "Water in the pot would boil, and the paper, since it's non-magnetic, would be unaffected."

Pressure Cooker Cookery

The Oil Cure

Cooking dried beans in the pressure cooker is supposed to be a no-no, since they tend to foam when they cook and may clog the pressure vents. Lorna Sass of New York City, author of *Cooking under Pressure*, has devised a simple solution: "For every cup of dried beans, you should add 4 cups of water and 1 tablespoon of oil." Oil prevents the foam-up, and the beans cook perfectly, she explains.

Steamed Brown Rice Is Nice

If you like the nutty flavor and health benefits of brown rice but find it tricky to cook, try steaming it in the pressure cooker, suggests Sass. It's as easy as one, two, three.

1. Combine 1 cup of long-grain brown rice and 1½ cups of water or stock in a 4- or 5-cup casserole or heatproof dish, and place the uncovered casserole on a rack in the pressure cooker.

Techno-Tip

COOKING IN A CLOSED SYSTEM

A pressure cooker is a closed system that uses high-temperature, pressurized steam to do the cooking. As liquid in the cooker is heated and converted to steam, pressure builds up, raising the boiling point of water from 212° to 250°.

So when you pressure cook, the higher temperature and pressure shorten overall cooking time. The force of the steam itself permeates and tenderizes the fibers of the foods.

2. Add 2 cups of water to the bottom of the cooker and lock the lid in place.
3. Cook under high pressure for 20 minutes, remove from the heat and wait an additional 20 minutes for the steam to release naturally. The rice will be fluffy, not sticky.

Better Baking and Dessert-Making

Scale Up for Easier Measure

If you bake a lot, your best baking assistant could well be a large-size kitchen scale, according to Flo Braker of Palo Alto, California, author of *The Simple Art of Perfect Baking* and *Sweet Miniatures*.

Braker recommends purchasing a scale with a 2-pound capacity that is large enough to hold a good-size mixing bowl. Next time you make your favorite recipe, says Braker, jot down the weight of each ingredient as you measure it out and add it to the bowl. So any time you make that recipe, all you have to do is set the bowl on the scale and do the measuring by weight. Of course, you'll still have to measure the minor ingredients (teaspoons and tablespoons, for instance), but all the major ingredients can be done on the scale. That saves you the bother of using lots of bowls and measuring cups.

Any Power in That Baking Powder?

"Please, please test your baking powder, especially if you don't bake often," urges Braker.

It's done in one easy step. Add 1 teaspoon of baking powder to ½ cup of boiling water. If the powder foams vigorously, it's still good for baking.

Foolproof Yeast Proofing

Want to make sure your yeast will rise? Test it first. With all her baking experience, Braker still proofs her yeast before she uses it. Here's how.
- Dissolve the yeast in warm water (about 100° for fresh yeast; 110° for dry).
- Add a pinch of sugar or ground ginger.
- Keep the yeast and water mixture in a warm place for about 10 minutes.

If the yeast is viable, it will begin to foam and bubble. If it shows no signs of life, toss it out and buy some fresh.

Take Your Oven's Temperature

Have trouble turning out perfect cakes and pies, even though you follow the recipe to a tee? Well, your oven's temperature may not be accurate, says Rose Levy Beranbaum of New York City, author of *The Cake Bible* and *Rose's Christmas Cookies*.

"Bake a packaged cake mix, and if the cake is underbaked or overbaked in the allotted time, your oven temperature is off," she says. Manufacturers test those instructions exhaustively, she explains. Try a 25° correction the next time you bake, and you may find you've set things right.

Secrets Revealed

CAKE FLOUR IS NOT ALL-PURPOSE

"When a recipe calls for cake flour, use it," advises Rose Levy Beranbaum, author of *The Cake Bible*. "It makes a big difference in your finished cake."

"All-purpose" flour is a misleading name, she explains. Cake flour is really an entirely different product. The only cake flours available in the United States at present are Softasilk and Swans Down brands. While cautioning that substitutions are never ideal, Beranbaum suggests that if you can't get cake flour, buy bleached (not unbleached) all-purpose flour, and use the following formula: 1 cup sifted cake flour equals ¾ cup sifted, bleached all-purpose flour plus 2 tablespoons cornstarch.

And don't confuse cake flour with self-rising flours, which contain measured amounts of leavening agents and salt. Self-rising flour will greatly alter a recipe if used in place of regular flour with no other changes.

Secrets Revealed

GET UP AND DOUGH

Accomplished bakers turn out large volumes of cookies in short order. Flo Braker, author of *Sweet Miniatures,* offers this bag of tricks to make volume production of cookies and small desserts easier and more efficient. These will come in handy when you're faced with holiday baking or unexpected guests.

To prepare a variety of doughs for cut-out cookies and pastries in volume, follow these easy steps.

1. Roll out the dough into sheets of appropriate shape and size.
2. Make stacks of the dough sheets with waxed paper between them.
3. Label each stack, wrap in plastic wrap, then freeze or refrigerate.
4. When you're ready to bake, remove the dough sheets from the refrigerator or freezer, let them warm for a few minutes, then cut out the shapes and bake. The cold dough gives a neat, clean cut, even for the fanciest shapes.

To prepare large quantities of drop cookies (like chocolate chip or oatmeal cookies), use this method to save time and washing up.

1. Cut out pieces of parchment or foil the size of a cookie sheet.
2. Portion the entire batch of dough onto the parchments.
3. As you bake, just slide a cookie sheet under each piece of parchment and pop it in the oven.
4. When the cookies are done, slide the parchment onto a cooling rack, and proceed to bake the other parchments.

"The cookies slide right off the parchment or foil, and you can reuse the paper," says Braker. "You'll only need a few cookie sheets and may not even have to wash them."

Whipping the Whipped Cream Blues

Have you ever been left flat by runny whipped cream? Look for the answer to that problem in the dairy case, suggests Susan Purdy, author of *As Easy as Pie* and *A Piece of Cake.* "In order for whipped cream to hold its shape, it needs a butterfat content of 36 to 40 percent," she explains.

Since percentages aren't listed on cream containers, look for the word *heavy* on the label. That indicates a minimum of 36 percent butterfat. Don't select a container that says *whipping cream* unless it also says *heavy.* "Whipping cream will whip, but it won't hold," she warns.

Hold Those Pretty Peaks

"Stabilize whipped cream for extra-long holding by using a bit of gelatin," Purdy suggests. Use this tip when you want to decorate pies or tarts in advance and hold them in the refrigerator for several hours.

Place 1 teaspoon of gelatin in 2 tablespoons of water in a saucepan and heat just until the gelatin is dissolved. Then add it to 1 cup of heavy cream during the whipping process.

Zestier Zest

What's that special citrus flavor that makes lemon meringue pie more lemony and key lime pie more limey? It's citrus zest—the colored outer rind of citrus fruit that is a source of pure flavor.

Now here's the challenge: How do you get the best of the zest without picking up the bitter white pith from underneath?

"Rub a sugar cube hard all over the skin of the fruit," says Nick Malgieri, author of *Perfect Pastry* and *Great Italian Desserts* and director of the pastry program at Peter Kump's New York Cooking School in New York City. The sugar cube, he explains, "extracts the essential oils—where the flavor is." Then dissolve the flavored cube in whatever liquids are added to the recipe.

Some Nutty Advice

Want perfect results when you bake with nuts? Pastry expert Nick Malgieri offers some pointers.

- Taste before you buy, unless you're buying a vacuum-packed brand you trust.
- Keep nuts in the freezer, not the refrigerator.
- Add a bit of the sugar from your recipe to the food processor along with the nuts to prevent the nuts from clumping together and getting too oily.

Get Rid of Pesky Nut Skins

Toasted hazelnuts lend a delicious flavor to baked goods, but it's always a bit of a nuisance to remove the skins after toasting. Flo Braker uses this procedure.

1. Toast a large batch in the oven.
2. Turn them out onto a kitchen towel and rub to remove some of the skin.
3. Transfer them to a sieve and rub them around on the screening to remove more skin.
4. Then freeze them. The change in temperature will cause all the remaining bits of skin to loosen.

Save the Best for Later

Here's a riddle: How many cans of nuts must be opened to find 50 perfect nut halves for holiday cookies? Answer from Braker: None. Just open your freezer!

Take her simple advice: Each time you bake any recipe that calls for ground or chopped nuts, sort out the perfect specimens first and reserve them in a container in your freezer. When the time comes for specialty baking, you'll have a stockpile of beauties ready to go.

Chocolate Takes to Buttering Up

When melting chocolate and butter together, let the butter begin to melt first, then add the chocolate, suggests Braker. The butter protects the chocolate from scorching.

Try the Squoosh Test

How soft is "softened" butter? It should still feel cool but not be so soft that it puddles or is melting, says baking expert Rose Beranbaum.

Having butter at the right temperature and softness will make a big difference in the texture of the finished cake. "You should just be able to 'squoosh' it with your fingers," she says.

Defrosting a Cake? No Sweat!

When defrosting a frozen cake layer, Malgieri places it on a cooling rack and covers it lightly with a kitchen towel. The towel absorbs the condensation, preventing the cake from getting soggy, he explains.

Cool It for Glass

Lower your oven temperature by 25° when baking in glass, advises Beranbaum. Glass absorbs heat faster and might scorch or burn the cake bottom at the higher temperature.

Feel the Chill

Braker makes a good point about room temperature, as it's referred to in recipes. "Average room temperature is about 70°," she says. "Body temperature is 98.6°. So something that is at room temperature will feel slightly cool to the touch."

The Egg Standard

Unless the recipe specifies otherwise, you should always use large eggs when baking, says Beranbaum. That's the accepted standard size used in recipe writing.

FYI

GLUTEN BAKIN'

Ever wonder how some people get perfect pie crusts every time? They have the goods on gluten.

Gluten—the protein in flour that gives strength and elasticity—is the substance that produces a tough crust, explains Susan Purdy, author of *As Easy as Pie* and *A Piece of Cake*. "When you make bread, you do everything to encourage gluten development: mixing in liquid, vigorous kneading, and warmth," she says. "For pastry, you do the exact opposite to prevent and inhibit the gluten." Here are her perfect-pie pointers.

- Keep everything ice cold. You can chill your flour in the refrigerator or freezer, work on a chilled surface, and use cool fingertips or utensils, rather than the warm palms of your hands.
- Include some type of acid in the liquid called for in the recipe—2 tablespoons of white vinegar, for example, or 2 to 3 tablespoons of lemon or orange juice.
- Use a minimum of liquid, just enough to form a dough mass, since liquids activate gluten.
- Keep handling to a bare minimum. Do just enough to form the dough and no more. Extra manipulation or overprocessing by machine really strengthens the gluten.
- Use a high initial baking temperature. Preheat your oven for at least 10 minutes to 425°. Bake the pie on the lower third of the oven for 12 to 15 minutes, then lower the temperature to about 350°, raise the pie to the center rack, and complete baking. The initial high heat sets the crust. Purdy explains: "The high heat causes the liquid in the dough to convert immediately to steam, which forces the layers of pastry apart, creating flakiness. At lower temperatures, the liquid will melt out of the dough and be absorbed into the flour, re-energizing the gluten and creating strength and toughness."

The Perfect Pan

Use heavyweight dull aluminum pans for best baking, advises Beranbaum.

"Dark pans cook too quickly," she explains. "Shiny surfaces reflect heat, and neither gives you the good, even baking results you want."

Keep Your Cake

To keep a delicious cake moist and fresh, you need to protect it from exposure to air.

"Use a truly airtight plastic wrap, like Saran Wrap," Beranbaum advises. "Most plastic wraps have microscopic pores, which is fine for vegetables but not good for cake."

The Incredible Shrinking Pie Crust

Frustrated with pie crusts that shrink out of shape? Both you and your dough need to chill out and relax, says Malgieri.

Many people roll out pie crusts right after they mix the dough, then struggle to stretch the dough into the pan. Instead, take Malgieri's advice for creating a crust that won't shrink.

"Make sure the dough has an adequate opportunity to chill until firm. This chilling time firms up whatever fat is in the dough, making it easier to handle." Cold also relaxes the gluten in the flour, so the finished crust will hold its shape and come out flaky and tender.

Once rolled out and fitted in the pan, it's good to chill it once again before baking to ensure a perfectly shaped crust.

Secrets Revealed

MAGIC TO SMOOTH A CAKE HUMP

Sometimes, flat, even cake layers are essential to your baking needs. But often cakes come out with unsightly humps in the middle. Here are some strategies from New York cookbook author Rose Levy Beranbaum, that will help you avoid those humps.

"There are times, of course, when the recipe is at fault, but in most cases, it's simply the result of uneven heat transfer," she explains. "The metal sides of the cake pan conduct higher heat to the edges before the center of the cake has had enough time to cook through. The center continues to rise, and the finished cake is domed instead of flat.

"If the dome is slight, you can simply shave it flat with a long sharp knife. But if your goal is a level layer straight from the oven, you must equalize the heat. Some people wrap strips of wet towel around the edges of the cake pan; they're easy to use and last for years." Wrapped around the sides of a pan, they modulate the temperature to promote even rising and perfectly level cake layers.

Pound Your Dough

It sounds brutal, but using your rolling pin to gently pound chilled pie dough is a good idea, according to Malgieri.

"It softens the dough slightly without stretching it and gets it close to the shape you want." So pound first, then roll it, and you'll avoid rips and tears.

No More Soggy Bottoms

Do your pies suffer from damp bottom crusts? Use Malgieri's secret formula the next time you bake: To every cup of flour in any pastry recipe, add ¼ teaspoon of baking powder.

"The baking powder causes the dough to expand, and since it has a weight on top of it, namely the filling, it presses hard against the bottom of the pan," he explains. Maintaining that contact with the hot surface of the pan ensures a well-baked bottom crust.

One before All

"Before baking a whole batch of cookies or tiny pastries, always test-bake one," Braker advises. "Then you'll know if you need to make any small changes in the recipe or timing." At most, the test will take about 10 minutes, but it will ensure that your whole batch is perfect.

Freeze before Baking

What a cool idea: Prepare a batch of fruit pies in summer, pop 'em in the freezer, then bake 'em when winter winds blow.

Freezing fruit pies before baking yields a crisper bottom, but only if you bake them straight from the freezer, according to Beranbaum. "The bottom crust will bake faster since it's thinner and closer to the oven heat than the filling, and the thawing fruit juices won't get a chance to penetrate the crust," she explains.

Something to Chew On

Braker has a secret for weight control while baking: "I always chew gum when I'm baking, so it's less convenient to nibble."

Hands off Those Taps

Before you begin a baking project that will leave you with messy hands, place little plastic produce bags on your faucet handles, suggests Braker. It will let you use the faucets as you need to and save you the bother of cleaning sticky batter and bits of dried bread dough from the faucet handles afterward.

Floss Your Cheesecake

Beranbaum (possibly influenced by her dentist Mom) claims that dental floss is her secret weapon for avoiding the mess and waste of cutting cheesecake. "Simply hold the floss taut and cut down into the cake," she says. "When you reach the base, pull the floss free with one hand, and repeat the steps for as many portions as you need. The slices are perfect and neat, and there's no need to wet and wipe a knife."

This technique works well for any custard or mousselike dessert.

The Experts

Rose Levy Beranbaum of New York City is author of *The Cake Bible, Rose's Christmas Cookies,* and *Rose's Celebration.*

Carlyn Berghoff is the president of Carlyn Berghoff Catering in Chicago, Illinois.

Flo Braker, author and baking instructor, lives in Palo Alto, California. Her books include *Sweet Miniatures* and *The Simple Art of Perfect Baking.*

Hannelore Dawson, the author of *Great Food for Great Numbers,* lives in Newark, Delaware.

Judith Benn Hurley of Reading, Pennsylvania, is a food columnist for the *Washington Post.* She is the author of *Healthy Microwave Cooking* and *The Every Day Herbal.*

Carol Lamkins, a certified home economist and certified kitchen designer, runs Design Vision in Fullerton, California.

Nick Malgieri is director of the pastry program at Peter Kump's New York Cooking School in New York City and author of *Perfect Pastry* and *Great Italian Desserts.*

Tom Ney is the director of food service at Rodale Press in Emmaus, Pennsylvania, and author of *The Health-Lover's Guide to Super Seafood.*

Susan Purdy is the author of *As Easy as Pie* and *A Piece of Cake.*

Lorna Sass of New York City is the author of *Cooking under Pressure* and *Recipes from an Ecological Kitchen.*

Arno Schmidt, author and culinary consultant, is a Certified Executive Chef from Brooklyn, New York, and the former executive chef of the Waldorf-Astoria hotel in New York City.

Sally Schneider of New York City is the author of *The Art of Low Calorie Cooking* and a contributing editor to *Food and Wine* magazine.

Thelma K. Snyder is the author, with Marcia Cone, of *Mastering Microwave Cookery* and *Microwave Diet Cookery.* She lives in Bellmore, New York.

Nancy Stern, owner of The Uncomplicated Gourmet Kitchen Design Studios in Westwood, New Jersey, is a teacher, consultant, and kitchen designer.

Patricia Tennison, a Chicago-based columnist, is author of *Glorious Vegetables in the Microwave, Glorious Fish in the Microwave,* and *Sumptuous Sauces in the Microwave.*

CHAPTER 7

Money Management

What You Save
Is What You Win

Money. It takes so long to earn it and so little time to spend it. Sometimes we don't even know where it went.

But it doesn't have to be that way. With planning, the wise use of credit, a few money-saving techniques, negotiating savvy, and well-honed sale-seeking skills, we can all get more value for our dollar.

We can stretch that dollar by using coupons and credit wisely. Phone calls (comparison shopping by phone!) may take a few minutes, but they can save you hundreds of dollars on major purchases. We can keep more of the dollars we earn by maximizing our tax deductions, and we can double or triple our money, over the long term, by making investments that pay off.

In this chapter you'll find practical negotiating tips to help you buy and sell a car or a home. For many people a new home is *the* major investment decision of a lifetime—and some practical hints can help you buy low, sell high, and make the most of your real estate.

You'll also find practical tips from money management experts about how to save and invest so your money accumulates safely for your future goals. And they offer some sage advice about insurance, too.

Whether you're trying to establish a balanced budget, get more for less, or multiply what you have, here's some expert advice to begin with.

Cutting Costs to Save More

Oops—Where'd It All Go?

Money has a way of disappearing out of our wallets. That's why Paul Richard, vice president and director of education at the National Center for Financial Education in San Diego, recommends developing a family spending plan. "Most people routinely waste 20 to 30 percent of their money because of poor spending practices," says Richard.

To avoid that, recognize where you're spending it by keeping receipts over a month-long period. "If your money is not going into savings, it's going somewhere," Richard says.

Secrets Revealed

THE KESSLER ACCORDION ACCOUNTING SYSTEM

If you don't have a system for paying your bills, it's likely some of your payments will arrive late. That means interest charges. Stuart Kessler, chairman of the Personal Financial Planning Division of the American Institute of Certified Public Accountants in New York City, offers this advice.

- Keep an accordion file for bills. Use the first slot for unpaid bills and the second slot for charitable contributions you will make in the future.
- File paid bills either alphabetically or by category in the rest of the slots.
- Pay the bills twice a month, even if that means you pay some a couple of weeks early.

A note from Kessler: Consider using a computer program. Besides writing your checks, the simple program will also do your recordkeeping, alert you as to when your CDs mature, and make tax preparation a simpler task.

Enveloping Your Family Budget

Here's a simple method for keeping records, recommended by Richard.

Mark three business envelopes "household expenses," "auto and travel expenses," and "business-related expenses."

At the end of each month review the spending patterns with the family. Then put the three envelopes into an 8½ by 11-inch envelope and mark the month on the outside. At year's end you can easily trace where your money went.

"Look for ways to spend smarter and get more for your dollars," says Richard. "Everyday spending decisions are far more critical to our financial future than any investment decision we'll ever make."

Get the Jump on Purchase Prices

Knowing what you'll need ahead of time gives you the best opportunity to spot a bargain or take advantage of a sale, says Amy Dacyczyn, mother of six and publisher of *The Tightwad Gazette* in Leeds, Maine. Make a list of five purchases you're likely to make in the next six months. Then keep track of prices on those items. That way, you'll recognize a genuine sale or bargain when you see one.

"The most important thing people need to do is anticipate their needs as far in advance as possible," says Dacyczyn.

Dacyczyn suggests that you start shopping for a kindergarten wardrobe when your child is three years old. For predictable purchases such as new tires, get acquainted with prices, then watch for sales. Just buy when the price is right and store the items until you need them.

Let Your Fingers Do the Shopping

Your telephone can save you hundreds of dollars if you call around for prices, notes Dacyczyn. Planning a major renovation project? Call around for competitive bids. Need a new televison? Be sure to make *at least five phone calls* to check prices on the model you want to buy.

Although she says "a bargain is partly research and partly luck," Dacyczyn leans toward research. When she started printing her newsletter, she called all 70 printers listed in her local Yellow Pages directory.

Net savings?

Thirty percent in printing costs.

Why Rush to Spend?

Patience is more than its own reward. Often there's a multibuck bonus as well.

Jim Dacyczyn, Amy's husband, visited 22 car dealerships before buying a new Chevy Suburban. Time spent with dealers: 9 hours. Savings: $4,000 off the sticker price. Translated: $444.44 per hour.

Wait as long as you can before purchasing any high-ticket item, says Amy Dacyczyn. "That allows you time to recognize a genuine bargain when you see it, and you feel confident in snapping it up."

Keep a List of Rock-Bottom Prices

"When we do our grocery shopping we keep a price book," says Amy Dacyczyn. "We know the bottom price of every item. By having a system, you know to buy only when an item is at the bottom price."

Spend Cash, Not Promises

For trips to the supermarket or local discount store, spend cash. That will dissuade you from buying impulsively.

"Take the time to get cash before going to the store," recommends Paul Richard. He points out that many people who use credit cards or checks really don't know exactly how much they spend. When you actually see the cash leave your hand, it makes you think twice.

Don't Shop Piecemeal

Make a list of what you need at the supermarket and shop once a week, recommends Stuart Kessler, chairman of the Personal Financial Planning Division of the American Institute of Certified Public Accountants, and a senior tax partner in the accounting firm of Goldstein, Golub, Kessler, and Company in New York City.

"Part of the problem with convenience stores is you go in to buy a gallon of milk, and you end up buying three or four items," says Kessler.

Credit Card Interest—Ripped-Up Dollars

Don't charge more on your credit card than you can pay off in a month. "Credit card interest is a killer to a budget," says Kessler. "Whatever money you're paying out on credit card interest (often about 19 percent annually) is ripped-up dollars, especially since the interest is no longer tax deductible." He also suggests getting rid of all plastic cards you don't use. Just having them in your wallet creates a temptation that could end up costing you a *lot* in interest.

Credit Card Buying: What Does It Really Cost?

Elgie Holstein, president of Bankcard Holders of America, a nonprofit national consumer organization in Herndon, Virginia, points out that the high interest on credit cards is enormously expensive. He offers this example: Suppose you have a $1,000 outstanding balance, and the credit card company is charging you 21 percent interest. If you make only the minimum payment on that balance each month, it will take you about five years to pay off the debt on the card and *you'll pay nearly $5,000 in interest!*

"High-rate debt, paid back slowly, is a bottomless pit," says Holstein.

Secrets Revealed

CHECK YOUR OWN CREDIT RATING

Your credit record is your lifelong financial report card—and every time you apply for a car loan, a mortgage, or any other kind of new credit, *someone* is looking at your report card. So it's important to make sure the information is accurate.

The three major credit reporting companies in the country are TRW, TransUnion, and Equifax. To get a copy of your credit report, look up the number of one of those companies in your phone book. When you call, you will be told how to send in a written request for your credit record. (The cost usually ranges between $5 and $20 for the report, unless you've recently been denied credit—in that case, it's free.)

When you get the report, examine it carefully for errors. You have the right to take certain actions to correct the record if you find errors.

Thanks to the federal Fair Credit Reporting Act, you have these rights.

- Any credit bureau *must* provide you with a complete report of the information in your credit file when you request it.
- You can dispute any information in your file or get missing data added to your file. You can put your side of the story in the credit file.
- If you request it, all potential creditors and employers who have made inquiries into your file in the past two years must be notified of errors that have been corrected.
- Any negative information about you will be removed after seven years, and any bankruptcy information after ten years, provided you request it.
- You can insist that only legitimate members or users of the credit reporting agency have access to information in your file.
- You are entitled to know why you were denied credit.

Another reason to correct your record: A potential *employer* can also check it.

Household Cutbacks? Watch for Warnings

It's time to seriously curtail your spending if certain "red flags" show up. According to O'Neill, the warning signs include:

- Spending more than 20 percent of your take-home pay on repayment of installment debt other than your mortgage.

- Borrowing on your credit card to pay for food, mortgage, or car payments.
- Delinquency on your mortgage, rent, utility bills, or car payment.
- Making only minimum payments on credit card bills. ("You *should* be paying more than the minimum due because it only covers interest and a small amount toward the principal," says O'Neill.)

IF YOU CAN'T PAY YOUR BILLS—DON'T HIDE

When you find yourself in over your head, most lenders are willing to work out a revised spending plan with you, says Elgie Holstein, president of Bankcard Holders of America, a ten-year-old nonprofit national consumer organization in Herndon, Virginia. But if that fails, you may need the help of a credit counselor from a nonprofit credit counseling service. A credit counselor works with a debtor to come up with a budget and a revised payment plan. These counseling services also act as mediators between debtors and creditors. Usually, there is no charge. In addition to the Consumer Credit Counseling Service, a national organization with many local branches, most large cities have publicly funded services that offer counseling to those who have overextended their credit.

Best Nest for Your Eggs

Pay Yourself First

If your financial goals are not just dreams, you've got to plan to meet them. But how?

"Pay yourself first," says Cooper. Before the mortgage or any other bills, put the money aside for your future. Some employers help you do this by offering direct deposit into a 401K plan or mutual fund.

If your employer has a 401K plan, *use* it! If you want to find out about other kinds of funds, check at your library for information on:

- Aggressive growth funds
- Growth funds
- Growth-and-income funds
- Balanced funds
- Income funds
- Bond funds
- Municipal bond funds

- Specialty funds
- Money market mutual funds
- Tax-exempt money market funds

Tithe Yourself Over

Everybody should save something from every paycheck for the curveballs life sometimes throws. Thomas O'Neill, president of the Consumer Credit Counseling Service in Philadelphia, suggests saving 10 percent of your take-home pay.

"If you can't save 10 percent, save what you can," he says. "It's important because we all have emergencies such as needing a new transmission, a medical expense that insurance doesn't cover, or braces for the kids." O'Neill says everyone should have three to six months of take-home pay saved in case they lose their job.

Try Having Some Fund

Mutual funds offer the small investor not only the chance to get in on stock market earnings, but better-than-inflation earnings as well, according to Robert L. Butler, a vice president of marketing with Phoenix Equity Planning Corporation in Hartford, Connecticut. They provide an excellent way to save for retirement or your children's education because the mutual fund earnings are likely to be well ahead of inflation.

"If you look at the stock market history of any 10-year period over the last 60 years, stock market earnings outpaced inflation 90 percent of the time," observes Butler. "Over any 20-year period, stock earnings outpaced inflation 100 percent of the time."

Inflation usually runs at about 3 to 4 percent, says Butler, while in the overall history of the stock market, earnings are a little over 10 percent.

Mutual Fund Tactic: Make It a Habit

It can be an act of faith sometimes, but one way to save in mutual funds is with dollar cost averaging. That means you put the same dollar amount into a mutual fund every month, regardless of how the stock and bond markets are doing. If the market is down, you get more shares for your dollars; if the market is up, you get fewer shares.

"The real advantage is you're not trying to outguess the market," says John E. Cooper, a certified financial planner with Provident National Bank in Philadelphia. And for long-term investors, it doesn't make any difference what the market is doing tomorrow. Its long-term earnings are historically good.

Secrets Revealed

How Soon Will Your Investment Double?

One easy way to figure out how much your investment will be worth in the future is to apply the Rule of 72, says John E. Cooper, chartered financial planner with Provident National Bank in Philadelphia. If you divide the interest rate of an investment into 72, you get the number of years it will take for that investment to double.

For instance: If you deposit $1,000 in a regular savings account earning 6 percent interest, it will take 12 years for it to double (72 divided by 6 equals 12).

At 9 percent interest, it would take 8 years to double (72 divided by 9 equals 8).

Cooper suggests you use the same rule to gauge the effect of inflation on your money. "If you divide the rate of inflation into 72, it will tell you how long it will take *prices* to double." At a 5 percent inflation rate, it will take 14.4 years for prices to double (72 divided by 5 equals 14.4).

Does This Interest Interest You?

"Shopping around" for the best interest rates on savings accounts may seem time-consuming. How much does it really matter, you may wonder, if interest is a point or two higher?

Here's how much: Julie and Joe invest identical amounts of money, but Julie earns 3.6 percent more interest than Joe. At the end of a 20-year period, Cooper points out, Julie will have *twice* as much money as Joe.

So...whether you're saving for vacation, retirement, education, or a new house, *do* pay attention to interest.

Tackling Tax Matters

The IRS Can Check a Check

Keep careful records of your deductible expenses. That way, you'll have them all on your tax return and you'll be able to substantiate them if you're audited.

And what's the simplest way to do that?

"Pay for deductible items by check," says Paul Huth, certified public accountant and partner in the firm Ernst and Young in Cleveland, Ohio. As long as you save your checks, you'll have a permanent record of payment.

Note: If your bank *doesn't* return your checks at the end of the month, it's worthwhile asking for that service just to have those canceled checks in your files.

Sort Your Deductibles

Keep a *separate* checking account for your deductible expenses, and sort those checks by category each month, adds Huth. Charitable contributions go in one pile, business expenses in another, and so on. That way, when you get to income tax time, your checks are already separated.

Save for Retirement with Before-Tax Dollars

Your employer can deduct money from your paycheck and invest it directly in a 401K retirement plan. By saving the money *before* it reaches your paycheck, you save tax dollars, according to Provident National Bank's financial planner John Cooper. For instance, if you're in the 28 percent tax bracket, you'd have to earn $139 in order to save $100 after taxes. With a 401K you'd be saving the *full* $139 that you earn!

Self-employed people can get the same savings by making a contribution to a Keogh Plan.

Secrets Revealed

YOUR AUDIT ODDS

Every three years, the Internal Revenue Service randomly selects between 50,000 and 55,000 returns for a thorough examination, says Frank Keith, IRS spokesperson from Washington, D.C. This random checking of returns is done to measure how well taxpayers comply with the law. And the results of these audits are used by the IRS to see what kinds of returns are most likely to be incorrect and need an audit. That information goes into the computer and helps in deciding which returns get selected for audit in future years. Keith says the number of audits done "for cause" each year is about 0.8 percent.

Check Your Math—Before the Revenooers

Errors in arithmetic are the most common mistakes people make on their income tax return, according to Frank Keith, a spokesperson for the Internal Revenue Service in Washington, D.C. So double-check your math before sending in your return.

(And while you're at it, Keith advises, make sure you didn't check off a wrong box or use a wrong table for reference—two common trouble spots in the tax-filing process.)

FYI

THE IRS GIVEAWAY: FREE ADVICE!

There is free telephone assistance available from the IRS. You can call the toll-free number 1-800-829-1040. Or look on your tax mailing for a list of free publications and find out how you can send for them.

Report Only Taxable Income

Don't report income that is not taxable, as many people do. According to Judy C. Keisling, an assistant vice president and director of tax training at H & R Block headquarters in Kansas City, Missouri, the following income is *not* taxable.

- Inheritances
- Life insurance proceeds received because the insured died
- Worker's compensation
- Tax-exempt interest
- At least one-half of your Social Security benefits

Number-One Tax Goof? Here It Is

According to Keisling, "The biggest mistake people make in preparing their taxes is failing to claim *all* the deductions and credits for which they are eligible."

Use the Most Beneficial Filing Status

The standard deduction amount you can claim varies. And it's partly determined by your filing status.

"Be sure your filing status is one that's most beneficial to your personal situation," says Keisling. "For example, if you're single and provide a home for your child, you may be eligible to file as 'Head of Household' rather than 'Single.' This will allow you to claim a higher standard deduction and thereby reduce your tax bill."

Profiting from Property

Buy a Home When Others Aren't

In general, people think of spring as the best time of year to buy a home, but "business is a lot less cyclical than it used to be," according to G. William Fox, president of the Philadelphia-area real estate firm Fox and Lazo, which has been family run for three generations.

Although March is still the busiest month, he says, peak activity now runs February through August. It's true that those who shop at off-peak times have fewer houses to choose from. Nevertheless, home buyers looking in the slow weeks between Thanksgiving and New Year's Day can sometimes get a bargain.

"Smart money buys when no one else is buying," adds Dorcas Helfant, president of the National Association of Realtors and president of Coldwell Banker Helfant Realty, in Virginia Beach, Virginia.

In a Hot Sellers' Market, Act Quickly

When the "Sold" signs are dotting more lawns than "For Sale" signs, you're probably in a hot sellers' market. That calls for quick decisions and aggressive negotiating, notes Fox. To snap up the house you want, says Fox, you may have to offer the full asking price, and in some cases, even go above that.

In a Soft Sellers' Market, Be a Shopper

When the "For Sale" signs are many and the "Sold" signs are scarce, you have time to be a shopper. It's also a good time to be a negotiator. To do this well, Fox says, "It's extremely important to try and figure out what houses in the area are really worth."

Big Improvements May Not Pay

An inground pool, a luxurious bathroom, a remodeled kitchen—those are all nice additions that may help your house sell more quickly. But those improvements are *not* likely to add significantly to the price of your home, says Helfant, and you probably won't even recover their cost.

Mechanical updating, on the other hand, is extremely important. "Central air, for instance, will make the home more valuable, as will updated plumbing and wiring," says Helfant.

A Little Sprucing Will Boost the Price

Selling your home? To give yourself a market edge and perhaps get a higher price, Fox recommends the following ways to spruce up your home inexpensively.
- Throw out now what you'll discard when you move.
- Paint the front door.
- Paint the basement walls, if they need it.
- Wash windows, baseboards, and sills.
- Paint rooms that need it, but use neutral colors.
- Mow and fertilize the lawn, edge, trim hedges, and put mulch in the flower beds.

Be on the Lookout for Bargains

"You can sometimes find bargains in estates and divorces," says real estate expert Edith Lank, who writes the syndicated column "House Calls," and is the author of seven books on real estate. A seller under pressure to sell quickly may authorize the broker to tell buyers he wants a fast sale. If you're a prequalified buyer, you may find a good deal!

Facts to Bid On

Before you bid on a house, Lank says you should know:
- Property taxes
- Square footage of the interior
- Lot size
- What comparable houses in the neighborhood sold for recently

Also, you should have an engineer inspect the property, and make the agreement of sale subject to a satisfactory report, recommends Lank.

Make a Reasonable Offer

If you did your homework by learning the selling prices of comparable homes in an area, you know just about what the house is worth. Lank says it's not wise to make your initial offer too low, because it can evoke negative emotional reaction from the seller.

"Make your first offer close to what you'd really pay," she suggests, "enough to tempt the seller to close the deal and be done with it."

Car-Shopping Strategies

Before You Do a Wheels Deal...

Know what you want in a car before you walk into the showroom, advises George Giek, managing director of automotive engineering and road services for the American Automobile Association in Heathrow, Florida. He suggests making this at-home checklist.

- Decide what the car will be used for—long-distance trips, commuting to work, running local errands, transporting Little Leaguers to ballgames, or hauling heavy loads, for example.
- Figure out how many miles a year you drive.
- Decide how much money you are willing to spend.
- Decide what kind of fuel economy you are interested in.

FYI

IF YOU SOUR ON YOUR CAR, IT MAY BE A LEMON

Most states and the District of Columbia have lemon laws to protect people who buy cars that are defective and can't be fixed.

If you've followed instructions in your owner's manual and the car is still not working right, consider these steps recommended by George Giek, managing director of automotive engineering and road services for the American Automobile Association (AAA) in Heathrow, Florida.

1. Take the car back to the dealership and describe the symptoms to the service manager.
2. Make sure the service manager *writes down* your complaints and describes the dealership's efforts to fix the car. (That way, you develop a paper trail.)
3. Give the service department two tries to fix the car, then talk to the dealer.
4. If you're still not satisfied, get the manufacturer involved.
5. If you're *still* not satisfied, call AAA.

A manufacturer should replace the car if it can't be repaired after four or five attempts, says Giek. Every state has slightly different regulations, but generally a third party go-between makes a decision about what should happen with the car. By using the third party, you can avoid the cost of going to court to get the matter settled. But if you disagree with the third-party decision, you can still sue, according to Giek.

Narrow Your Search through Research

Read about the makes and models of cars that are available in your price range. But be sure the books or articles you consult are looking at cars from the consumer's point of view, recommends AAA's Giek. (Many automotive magazines rate a car by its engine performance and speed tests, while you may be most interested in gas consumption and trunk space.)

Giek suggests that you narrow your potential choices down to three kinds before you begin visiting showrooms.

Take a Road Test—Alone!

Of course you want to drive the car before you buy it—but test-drive the car *without* the salesperson, says Giek. Otherwise, the salesperson will be talking while you're driving, and that makes it difficult for you to do an objective evaluation or even to discuss the car with your spouse.

If the dealer won't allow you to take the car for a drive alone, find another dealer who will, suggests Giek.

Shop without a Checkbook

Don't take a checkbook or more than a $20 bill with you when you're car shopping, says *Chicago Tribune* auto editor Jim Mateja, whose syndicated column appears in more than 150 newspapers. That way, you can't be talked into making a deposit on a car until you've finished shopping.

Avoid Car Salespeople Who...

...Demand a deposit before they will quote you a price, says Mateja. (In fact, they shouldn't demand a deposit at all!) Mateja also recommends avoiding salespeople who:

- Quote you *only* monthly payments when you ask for a price.
- Ask what it will take for you to buy a car today. (Those salespeople are trying to match what you can spend with a car they have.)

Mateja says your best defense against these salespeople are your two feet. "Turn on your heels and get out as fast as you can," he says.

Watch Out for Double Stickers

More than one sticker on the window should sound an alarm, says Mateja. The second sticker is for the added options. And the thing to remember about options is that they are *optional*. You don't have to buy them to buy the car.

Know What Options You Want

If you have decided ahead of time which model car you want, with which options, you have a tremendous advantage in getting the best price. Have each dealer give you a price on the car *complete* with local taxes, title fees, and destination charges, suggests Haig Aznavoorian, sales manager for Nationwide Auto Brokers in Southfield, Michigan. Just be certain that each one is pricing the same car with the same options and including all fees and other charges.

Shop for Financing

Dealers are glad to offer you financing because that's another way they make money. Sometimes their financing package is a good deal, but the only way to know is to shop around. See what your bank or credit union would charge you for an auto loan.

Mateja says if the dealer quotes you an interest rate, make sure you see that rate written down on the contract. *Don't* sign a contract unless that space is filled in.

Also, Mateja says, check the dealer's math. Mistakes do happen. (And sometimes they aren't mistakes.)

Finance for as Short a Time as Possible

"The longer you finance, the longer it takes to build equity in your car," says Mateja. If you finance for five years, at some point you may owe more on the car than the car is worth.

Insurance-Buying Insights

How Much Life Insurance?

To find out, just multiply your income, suggests James H. Hunt, a life insurance actuary in Vermont who is a member of the board of the National Insurance Consumers Organization.

The most compelling reason to buy life insurance is to protect your dependents if you die. Young families have the greatest financial need for insurance and often have the least buying power.

For those young families, Hunt recommends annual renewable term life insurance. He points out that young families struggling with other expenses can afford to buy the coverage they need if they get term life insurance.

And how much *does* a young family need? "Roughly seven to eight times their annual income," Hunt calculates.

Secrets Revealed

A Hint about the Hereafter

A lot of people may tell you otherwise, but the original copy of your will belongs in your safe deposit box, in the opinion of John J. Lombard, Jr., past chairman of the Real Property Probate and Trust Law Section of the American Bar Association and a senior partner in the law firm of Morgan Lewis and Bockius in Philadelphia. He names only two other places where a will is safe: your lawyer's vault and your bank's vault, if your bank is the fiduciary—that is, the trustee.

Lombard notes that keeping the will in a lawyer's vault may make an executor feel that he must use that attorney to probate the will. In fact, says Lombard, the executor is free to choose any attorney, no matter where the will is kept.

A Healthy Lifestyle Can Mean Insurance Savings

You'll save dollars on your life insurance coverage if you maintain a healthy lifestyle.

Debbie Randolph Chase, a senior communications associate at the American Council of Life Insurance in Washington, D.C., says you may qualify for a discount on your premium if you:
- Are a nonsmoker.
- Maintain a normal weight.
- Exercise regularly.
- Maintain a moderate blood pressure (even with medication).

If you fit the bill for fitness in any or all of these areas, be sure to find out whether you get a policy advantage.

Save $$$ on Auto Insurance: Buy Only What You Need

According to the National Insurance Consumers Organization (NICO), you'll save dollars on your auto insurance if you:
- Increase deductibles. By increasing your deductible on collision and comprehensive insurance from $100 to $250, NICO estimates you could save almost 20 percent. By making your deductible even higher, you'll save more.
- Don't buy incidental coverages. You don't need medical payments coverage with your auto insurance *if* you have that covered under a health

plan. Substitute transportation, towing, and labor are not a good value for your money either.

- Shop around. Rates vary from company to company.

Up Your Insurance for Some Possessions

Most policies cover your home's contents and personal possessions separately. Many items such as silverware and jewelry are covered only up to a certain value, and then you must buy additional insurance. Robert J. Gibbons, Ph.D., vice president for the American Institute for Chartered Property Casualty Underwriters in Malvern, Pennsylvania, suggests asking your agent if you need additional insurance to cover these: jewelry and furs, silverware, firearms, home office equipment, and any other high-value personal property.

PUT THESE IN YOUR SAFE DEPOSIT BOX

In addition to your will, there are many other items you may want to keep in a deposit box. Just remember that the size of the box is a factor in the rental fee charged. If you want to minimize costs, rent a box that's at least big enough to hold the essential items. These include:

- Valuables and important papers you don't need to access regularly. Chester B. Myszkowski, vice president, marketing, at Chase Manhattan Bank in New York City, suggests keeping such items as a coin collection and the title to your home in the box, but not your auto insurance policy or birth certificates that you may need occasionally.
- Lists of home furnishings and where you bought them, as well as photographs of valuables. They would be helpful in a claim to your insurance company in the event of fire or burglary, according to New York financial planning expert Stuart Kessler.
- Any bearer bonds that are negotiable as cash belong there, says John J. Lombard, Jr., probate and trust expert of the American Bar Association. Also store stock certificates and anything that can not easily be replaced if it is lost.

How Much Is Enough Health Insurance?

Health insurance offered by a large employer is probably all you need, according to Mark V. Pauly, Ph.D., professor at the University of Pennsylvania's Wharton School of Business. Pauly, who is chairman of the

Health Care Systems Department, advises against buying any more. "If you buy as an individual, you'll be paying for a lot of red tape costs that you'll never get back."

If you're self-employed, Dr. Pauly says, "try to buy as little as you can tolerate." He recommends taking large deductibles in exchange for smaller premiums. Also, he suggests shopping around because prices vary, and you may be able to get less expensive coverage by checking with your chamber of commerce or merchants association.

FYI

Joining an **HMO?**

Here are some basic questions to ask before committing to such a health insurance service. "Some cover a lot more than others, particularly with regard to prescriptions, mental health care, and substance abuse," says Mark Pauly, Ph.D., professor of health care systems at the University of Pennsylvania's Wharton School of Business in Philadelphia. Among the questions worth asking:

- Will I have to change my doctor?
- How are disputes between patient and the "gatekeeper doctor" resolved? (The gatekeeper doctor is the doctor who can refer the patient to other doctors or specialists.)
- If I do use health care outside the HMO system, will HMO pay anything?
- What's the premium? Compare the HMO premium with that of a conventional insurance company. But be sure you consider how much you would pay in a year to the insurance company for deductibles, says Dr. Pauly.

Getting Steals and Deals

What to Ask before Buying a Computer

Even though computer prices have crashed in the last decade, some are still expensive. So, before plunking down your money for the computer, you should ask the dealer a few questions, according to Russ Walter, one of the founding editors of *Personal Computing* magazine and the publisher of *The Secret Guide to Computers*. Among the questions to ask:

- What the dealer charges for shipping.
- If there's a surcharge for buying with a credit card.
- What, if anything, the advertised price does *not* include.
- Whether you are buying the *newest* version of the model.

Find Software That Works for You

More important than price when purchasing software is finding the right program to do the job.

"If it doesn't do what you want, it's worthless," says Vincent Gale, vice president of The Boston Computer Society, an association of 100 computer clubs in Massachusetts.

To get the best prices in software, the standard answer is to buy from a mail-order catalog, says Gale. But his recommendation is to join a user group where you can get technical help.

Cheap Fix-It—The 800 Way

Before getting a repairman in to fix your broken dishwasher, or anything else on the fritz, check to see if the manufacturer has an 800 telephone number that customers can call to get help. Most large manufacturers offer a service that tells you how to operate, hook up, or repair an appliance. For instance, the General Electric Answer Center handles about three million calls a year. The answer center will help you diagnose the problem and sell you a needed part over the phone.

Answer centers for some companies will even "walk you through" the repair over the phone.

Join a Fuel Cooperative to Cut Heating Costs

Call it a fuel cooperative, a consortium, or a buyers' group—the purpose is the same: saving money on fuel bills. Richard Altomonte, director of Flushing Fuel Consortium in the New York City area, says most cooperatives can save homeowners between 10 cents and 25 cents per gallon on oil. "If the average person uses 1,000 gallons and they're saving 15 cents a gallon, they'll save $150 dollars over the course of a year," Altomonte points out.

Check your phone book for such a group in your area. But before you join, Altomonte recommends you find out who the supplier is, how good the service is, and what the fuel price was during peak season the previous year.

Timbe-r-r-r...Almost Free

Federal and state forest managers often allow individuals to take all the firewood they want for free or for as little as $5 per visit.

"Check with local ranger districts to find the free-use areas," advises Ron Lewis, staff specialist for timber sales administration with the United States Department of Agriculture Forest Service in Washington, D.C.

Buy Unassembled Furniture and Save

Buy furniture in a kit, put it together, apply the finish yourself, and you get the dual benefits of furniture customized to your liking and lower cost. "The difference between kit and finished price is 25 to 50 percent," says George Moore, president of the 47-year-old Yield House Company of North Conway, New Hampshire, which sells both kits and finished furniture.

Many companies offer furniture kit catalogs: Just look in the classified sections of a do-it-yourself magazine to find sources of furniture kits.

Shopping for Refunds? Go for a Triple

Looking for notices of sale items? One place to check is the bulletin board of the store where you're shopping, according to Jean Kwiatkowski, publisher of *Money Talk*, a national refunding newsletter published in the town of Larksville, Pennsylvania.

If you can buy an item on sale, use a coupon, and take advantage of a manufacturer's rebate, it's called a "triple play," says Kwiatkowski. With the right triple play, you may end up getting an item for free—or almost free.

The Coupon Caper

You're not saving money if you "spend to save," so use a coupon *only* for an item you planned to purchase anyway. Consumer specialist and author Barbara Salsbury of Santa Clara, California, takes that advice one step further. "Many times there are alternatives to national brands at a lower price," says Salsbury, reminding shoppers that coupons are an advertising tool. "Comparison shopping means comparing not only stores, but also brands."

She suggests checking out the store brand of an item because, "If the house brand is on sale, there are even greater savings available."

In addition, she says you should compare supermarket prices for non-food items with those of the local discount drugstore or mass merchandiser.

Buy When the Season Is Right

Appliance manufacturers often put current models on sale just before a new one is introduced. Marion Joyce, a syndicated news columnist who writes on consumer matters, recommends calling a manufacturer's 800 number to find out when models will change. For air conditioners and lawn furniture, she also recommends checking out retailers' preseason and Fourth-of-July sales.

Factory Outlets Offer Big Savings

Although some items in factory outlets are imperfect, that imperfection can be barely perceptible. But the savings are large.

"At factory outlets you can save 50 percent or more," says Joyce. She says discontinued items from some manufacturers are also available in outlets, providing savings on china, cut glassware, crystal, and some appliances.

Buying a Camera? What's Included?

If you're comparison shopping for cameras, be sure you get prices for identical equipment, says Gary Haynes, assistant managing editor for graphics at the *Philadelphia Inquirer*. "Big-city prices can save you a lot of money, but make sure that the price you're quoted includes all the batteries, straps, and accessories that the equipment is packaged with," says Haynes. "For example, an 8mm Sony handycam won't run without a power supply. Some New York stores quote a terrific price for the camera, but unless you ask, they don't tell you that the battery it's packed with—and which you need to run the camera—is an extra $60 or $75."

How to Save on Film

"No matter what kind of film you use, the cost per picture will be about 15 percent less if you buy 36-exposure rolls instead of 24-exposure rolls," says Haynes. "If you buy 20 rolls of the same film at a time, you can save even more—20 to 25 percent over the single-roll price at most camera stores."

Haynes recommends storing the film in your refrigerator until you're ready to use it.

The Experts

Richard Altomonte is director of Flushing Fuel Consortium, a ten-year-old fuel-buying group for homeowners in the New York City area.

Haig Aznavoorian is sales manager for Nationwide Auto Brokers in Southfield, Michigan, an organization that sells printouts of information about the availability and pricing of various car models.

Robert L. Butler is a vice president of marketing with Phoenix Equity Planning Corporation, a subsidiary of Phoenix Mutual located in Hartford, Connecticut.

Debbie Randolph Chase is a senior communications associate at the American Council of Life Insurance in Washington, D.C.

John E. Cooper, a certified financial planner with Provident National Bank in Philadelphia, counsels bank customers about retirement planning.

Amy Dacyczyn publishes *The Tightwad Gazette* from her Leeds, Maine, home. The newsletter is sent to consumers like herself who believe in being thrifty.

G. William Fox is president of Fox and Lazo, a Philadelphia-area real estate firm started by his grandfather in 1886.

Vincent Gale is vice president of the ten-year-old Boston Computer Society in Boston, Massachusetts, an association of 100 computer clubs. He works with software groups and IBM and PC user groups.

Robert J. Gibbons, Ph.D., is vice president for the American Institute for Chartered Property Casualty Underwriters in Malvern, Pennsylvania. He holds the professional designations of Chartered Life Underwriter (CLU) and Chartered Property and Casualty Underwriter (CPCU).

George Giek is managing director of automotive engineering and road services for the American Automobile Association (AAA) at the club's national headquarters in Heathrow, Florida. An automotive engineer, Giek has been in the automotive business since 1951.

Gary Haynes is assistant managing editor for graphics at the *Philadelphia Inquirer.*

Dorcas T. Helfant is the 1992 president of the National Association of Realtors. A realtor since 1967, Helfant is president of Coldwell Banker Helfant Realty, Inc., a Virginia Beach, Virginia, firm specializing in single-family brokerage.

Elgie Holstein is president of Bankcard Holders of America, a ten-year-old nonprofit national consumer organization in Herndon, Virginia, that focuses exclusively on consumer credit.

James H. Hunt, a life insurance actuary, is a member of the board of the National Insurance Consumers Organization. He served as Vermont state insurance commissioner from 1965 to 1969.

Paul Huth is a certified public accountant and partner in the firm Ernst and Young in Cleveland, Ohio.

Marion Joyce is a syndicated consumer news columnist whose column appears in more than 1,000 newspapers.

Judy C. Keisling is assistant vice president and director of tax training at H & R Block headquarters in Kansas City, Missouri. An Enrolled Agent, she has been with the company for 15 years.

Frank Keith is press spokesperson for the Internal Revenue Service in Washington, D.C.

Stuart Kessler is chairman of the Personal Financial Planning Division of the American Institute of Certified Public Accountants. He is also a senior tax partner in the accounting firm of Goldstein, Golub, Kessler, and Company in New York City.

Jean Kwiatkowski is publisher of *Money Talk*, a national refunding newsletter that is published in her hometown of Larksville, Pennsylvania.

Edith Lank is an award-winning, nationally syndicated real estate writer whose column, "House Calls," appears in more than 100 newspapers. The author of seven books on real estate, she also gives advice on the radio to listeners of Public Radio and Financial News Network.

Ron Lewis is a staff specialist for timber sale administration with the United States Department of Agriculture (USDA) Forest Service in Washington, D.C.

John J. Lombard is immediate past chairman of the Real Property Probate and Trust Law Section of the American Bar Association and a senior partner in the Philadelphia law firm of Morgan Lewis and Bockius. He has been practicing law for 32 years.

Jim Mateja is auto editor of the *Chicago Tribune*. His syndicated column appears in more than 150 newspapers around the country. Besides writing for numerous magazines, he also does the auto entries for *Encyclopedia Britannica* and *Compton's Encyclopedia*.

George Moore is president of Yield House, Inc., in North Conway, New Hampshire, which sells both kit and finished furniture.

Chester B. Myszkowski is vice president, marketing, at Chase Manhattan Bank in New York City.

Thomas O'Neill is president of the Consumer Credit Counseling Service in Philadelphia.

Mark V. Pauly, Ph.D., is a professor at the University of Pennsylvania's Wharton School of Business, where he is chairman of the Health Care Systems Department.

Paul Richard is vice president and director of education at the National Center for Financial Education in San Diego, a nonprofit education organization to help people save and plan for their financial future so they can be less dependent on Social Security or Medicare.

Barbara Salsbury is a self-employed consumer specialist in Santa Clara, California, who teaches about economical money management.

Russ Walter is the publisher of *The Secret Guide to Computers* and is one of the founding editors of *Personal Computing* magazine. He is the owner of 40 personal computers and works out of his Boston home.

CHAPTER 8

Beauty and Grooming

The Skinny on Skin, Nails, Hair, and the Package That Says *You*

Living, breathing, and exposed, your skin is the packaging that holds you together.

Every human body is handily covered by about 2 square yards of skin. In fact, skin is your largest organ—and it serves a multitude of purposes. It safeguards your internal organs, and it's the all-in-one container that holds in all your precious bodily fluids.

But skin has a lot more responsibility than keeping your parts in place. Whether we like it or not, we are often judged by how our skin looks to others. So, in addition to being an A-1 packaging and protective device, your skin needs to be pampered, soothed, and cared for to keep you looking your best.

Of course, there are other elements to the *you* that meets the eye of the beholder. In the pages that follow, you'll find out what the experts say about special ways to get that extra *something* into your hair. You'll discover the lowdown on fingernails—what to do about persistent problems such as cracked nails, and how to have hands like a model's. From the makeup artists who cater to celebrities, you'll discover makeup tips that make stars photogenic—and find out the best ways to flatter your features.

What are the real ramifications of beauty and grooming? For most of us, the total look is actually a great combination of how we look plus how we feel.

That quick glance in the bathroom mirror as we start the day may tell the whole story. And if the story we see there is a happy one, we're likely to start out the day saying, "Hey, not too bad!"

Hair beyond Compare

Using Your Head When You Look for a Hairdresser
What's the best way to find a hairdresser who's right for you?

According to superstylist Londoner Dale, owner of the Dale International Salons in San Diego, you should *interview your new hairdresser.*

"Don't make an appointment for service," explains Dale. "Make an appointment for a free consultation."

Dale suggests that you ask the hairdresser at least five questions.
1. What style would you suggest?
2. If I do my hair in that style, how easy will it be to maintain?
3. How often will I need a hair appointment?
4. What products do I need and how expensive are they?
5. What's the cost of the service(s)?

Other things you can find out during the consultation: How long has the hairdresser been at that location? Where did he or she train? Does the salon provide ongoing training for its hairdressers?

"You want a hairdresser you can trust," says Dale, "and someone who has been in that location for a long time."

FYI

CURL UP WITH SOME HAIR-RAISING FACTS
1. What's the entire life span of a single healthy hair?
2. How many hairs fall out every day?
3. What's the number of hairs on an average head?
4. How fast does a hair grow?
5. Growing at this rate, how many years would it take for a hair to reach the moon?

Answers: (1) 3 to 5 years; (2) 50 to 70 a day; (3) Approximately 100,000; (4) Approximately 1 centimeter (0.39 inches) per month; (5) 3,200,566,666 years.

Past Performance

COMBING THROUGH HISTORY

Everything that's old seems to be new again, including trends in hair-dressing.

Did you know...

- Ancient Egyptians shaved their heads as clean as a Sphinx's hide. Two reasons for that: relief from the heat (Cairo can be sweltering), and cleanliness (who needs shampoo when you have a bald pate?).
- In the very old, trendy days of ancient Greece and Rome, the affluent sprinkled their hair with gold dust.
- Among high-class Greeks, to bleach was chic. As a matter of fact, they became experts in elaborate braids and trumped-up styles. Spiral curls and long, intricately fashioned wigs were the norm in the forum.
- Saxons, early Germanic peoples, dyed their hair blue, green, and orange.
- The daring Gauls, who lived where France is now, decided "bright was right" and dyed their hair fire-engine red.
- Predating crew cuts, Afros, perms, and bobs by half a millennium, style-conscious coquettes of the 1400s often plucked the hair high on their foreheads to achieve the illusion of a receding hairline. The reason for this rampant tweezing? A stunningly high forehead was considered the essence of fashion.
- In the 1700s, women sported massive do's decorated with flowers, jewels, and ornaments.

And today? Put in this context, Madonna's bleach is just a throwback to Greek techniques. Hennaed hair is a reminder of days of yore when Gauls went wild with the dye—and the shaved heads, jewels, and bangles of today's trend-setters are basically a repeat (yawn) of centuries ago.

At the root of it all, nonetheless, hair probably hasn't changed much. It's fundamentally just what it was when our ancestors yanked it back and tied it with a strip of reed to form a prehistoric ponytail.

A Snip and a Promise

Suppose your hair looks fine *except* for the bangs. How can you do some quick-snip styling without going to the trouble and expense of going to a hairdresser?

Hairdresser Sam Brocato, president of Brocato International Salons and Beauty Schools in Baton Rouge, Louisiana, suggests that you invest in a pair of small, sharp 4-inch scissors. Proceed as follows.

1. Part the bangs in the middle, directly at the midline of your face.
2. Grasp one portion of the bangs over one eyebrow, and begin.

If you want straight bangs: Press the bangs against your forehead with one hand. Slide the edge of the scissors under the bangs, and make a horizontal cut. Repeat on the other side.

For layered bangs: Lift a portion of the hair at a 45-degree angle away from the face and cut.

For extra-fluffy bangs: Hold a portion of the hair straight up and snip the ends.

Brocato cautions against cutting too much. But if you just cut lightly (not more than ¼ inch), "a proficient hairdresser can straighten out a do-it-yourself trim."

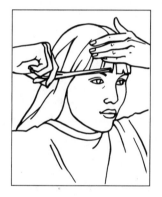  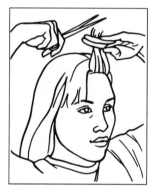

How to cut straight bangs.   *How to cut layered bangs.*   *How to cut extra-fluffy bangs.*

Do Your Tresses Pass the Silk-Scarf Test?

The best advice for beautiful hair? Hairdresser Bontempo says to treat it like an expensive, precious silk scarf. He points out:

- You would never yank on a silk scarf; don't pull on your hair when you're brushing or combing.
- You would never wash a scarf with harsh detergents; use salon products specifically designed for your hair type and condition.
- You would never toss a silk scarf in a dryer that's turned on high; dry your hair lightly.

"To keep hair beautiful," he says, "treat it with TLC."

Split Ends: The End Result of Overdoing

What's the surest way to end up with split ends?

Overdoing anything with your hair, according to David Patrick Bontempo, owner of Bontempo's Salon in Pasadena, California. Bontempo, who has coaxed the hair of Miss Universe into prizewinning form, lists the following common "overs."

- Overdrying
- Overperming
- Overdoing with curling irons or hot rollers
- Overtime in the pool (chlorine is wicked to hair)
- Overexposure to sunlight

And you're just asking for split ends if you regularly use a brush with broken bristles.

Concludes Bontempo: "Be moderate."

THE 5-STEP GUIDE TO BUYING A NEW BRUSH

Frank Chirico of Allen Edwards Salons in Santa Barbara, California, suggests these tips for buying a new hairbrush.

1. Buy an inexpensive one and see if you like the shape of the handle in your hand and the bristle formation in your hair. If it doesn't grab, it could be a keeper. A costlier brush won't necessarily do a better job.
2. If you have fine hair, select a soft brush, with bristles spread farther apart. Many people prefer brushes that have plastic, ball-tipped synthetic bristles.
3. For coarser hair, bristles that are closer together will do a better job. Try a natural boar-bristle brush.
4. For extra comfort, a flexible rubber cushion which connects the bristles to the brush will help.
5. When you're drying your hair with a blow-dryer, select a brush with bristles that are widely spaced.

Cure: Stand Up and Be Snipped

How do you snip the split ends without trimming the neighboring hair?

"To trim *just a few* split ends," says Bontempo, "twist a section of hair. Strands with splits will stand out."

When you see the strands that stand straight up, just snip them off—and you're done.

A QUESTION OF CLEAN

According to David Cannell, Ph.D., vice president of corporate technology of Redken Laboratories in Canoya Park, California, all contemporary shampoos and soaps are formulated to work well, even if you're in an area that has hard water. But what are the ingredients that *make* them work?

They're called surfactants. These reduce water's surface tension, lifting off dirt and oil simultaneously. And the grime suspended in water is rinsed away.

Some surfactants are mild—such as those contained in baby shampoos. Others are more powerful, containing such ingredients as ammonium lauryl sulfate and sodium lauryl sulfate that are effective in removing heavier oils and residues from mousses, gels, sprays, and conditioners.

What does this mean to you? Well, if you use many hair products, a mild baby shampoo may not clean your hair very well. So you might need one of the more powerful products with a stronger surfactant.

Note: If your tap water is so hard that you can't get suds with *any* commercial shampoo, try lathering up with distilled water.

The Right Chemistry for a Great Perm

Why is it, you may ask, that a second perm rarely takes as well as the first?

Eric Serena, owner of the Eric Salon in Beverly Hills and the man who does perms for many of Hollywood's biggest stars, cautions, "Hair that has been permed but is 'growing out' still has permanent wave chemicals on the ends."

According to Serena, many perms are made for "virgin hair"—that is, hair that's never been permed before. But hair that's already permed is certain to react differently from the virgin hair that's just growing in.

The solution?

Look for one of the new perms that are *specifically designed for previously permed hair*. According to Serena, these new perm products are formulated to do double duty.

- They produce a good curl in virgin hair that is close to the scalp...
- But they react more slowly on hair that still has some permanent wave chemical on the ends of the strands.

Quintuple Treatments for Damaged Hair

Sometimes hair is damaged by too many perms and treatments. For those in big trouble with this kind of "overprocessed hair," Sam Brocato has a go-all-out solution.

For severely damaged hair, he recommends four or five home treatments with a protein-rich conditioner—all in the same day.

Seem time-consuming?

When you consider that it's *your hair* you're restoring to its natural beauty, what Brocato calls "the shotgun approach" may be the best. If hair is overprocessed, he says, "it is in desperate need of help."

Budget Beauty: The Price Is Right

How would you like to receive the perfect pampering—an all-round beauty treatment for *less than* $25?

Yes, it's possible—if you visit a cosmetology school and become a live model for a student, says Brocato.

"The advanced students are well-informed," he observes, "and the quality of work performed in beauty schools is excellent and at good prices. After a whole morning of pampering, you can walk out of the school with beautiful nails, a great cut, and a top-of-the-line perm—plus a bottle of shampoo—for under $25."

Better Styling with a Dollop of Gel

A styling gel may be just what you need to make the most of your hair style. And if you put it in *just* the right place, a little can go a long way.

Alan Benfield-Bush, the award-winning hairdresser who is founder of ABBA International Academy in Irvine, California, has a four-step method he recommends for using a gel-lotion product correctly.

1. Place about a dime-size dollop of product in the palm of one hand.
2. Dab a tiny amount with the fingertips of the other hand—but *just* a dab. Leave most of the gel in your palm.
3. Starting in back of your head near the scalp line, start working the gel from your fingertips into the root area of your hair.
4. Continue the fingertip application until that dollop is gone.

Snoozing the Frizzies Away

Does your hair have a case of the frizzies?

It could be your case that's contributing to the problem. Your pillow-case, that is.

According to hairdresser Tina Cassaday of Tina Cassaday Creations in Hollywood, what you need is satin. "If you switch to a satin pillowcase, your problem could be over by tomorrow morning."

With that satiny smoothness, hair glides over rather than sticks to the pillowcase, and the frizzies are reduced to zero.

Underdry for Better Bounce

If you're using a hair dryer, keep your locks on the damp side.

Frank Chirico, partner with Allen Edwards at the exclusive Allen Edwards International salons in Santa Barbara, says, "Most people use a hair dryer too long, overdrying hair. Dry the hair until 90 percent of the moisture is removed—then stop. If your hair is well cut and healthy, the style should fall into place."

According to Chirico, overdrying steals hair's body and bounce, causing split ends, frizzies, and dull colors.

What Do the Beatles and Jamie Lee Curtis Have in Common?

"Condensed milk," says Cassaday.

The Beatles were her former clients. Jamie Lee is a more recent one. To all, Cassaday recommends conditioning hair with sweetened, condensed milk. Apply as you would conditioner.

"Because of the protein in condensed milk, you get extra shine."

But don't forget to rinse when you've finished, she cautions.

An Egg's Worth of Extra Body

Want extra body in your hair—without resorting to high-priced products with a multitude of chemical compounds?

Cassaday suggests the following:

1. Whip a raw egg with a small amount of shampoo.
2. Apply and leave on for 5 minutes.
3. Rinse well.

Add Vim with Vinegar

Who needs expensive hair-care products to add shine and sparkle to their hair! Tina Cassaday says the best for zest may be right in your cupboard—your kitchen cupboard.

To help neutralize the scalp and bring out natural red highlights in your hair, use one part apple cider vinegar and two parts very warm water.

Rinse with plain water afterward.

Sun-Streaked Glory—With Honey and Alum

You know the look—gorgeous wavy locks with streaks of sun-bleached blonde. And voilà, you look as if you just returned from an incredible sun-and-surf week in Hawaii.

But there's a natural way to get the beautiful streaks without leaving home. Try the following steps, doing a "patch test" on one part of your hair first. Then, if you like the effect, go ahead with sun-bleached streaks. According to Cassaday, about 45 minutes in the sun is all it takes.

Here's the trick.

- Mix honey and alum—an aluminum compound sold in drugstores, often used as a styptic. Mixed together, they should form a paste that's the consistency of pancake batter. (That is, not too runny; about thick enough to fall from a spoon in globs.)
- In front of the mirror, "paint on" the highlights with your fingertips.
- Then go sit in the sun for about 45 minutes (with some protective sunscreen on your skin, of course).
- Shampoo and rinse your hair.

The result: streaks that are about three shades lighter than your natural hair color.

NATURAL RINSES WITH GORGEOUS RESULTS

The goal?

To create hair that shimmers and gleams.

Tina Cassaday, who caters to stars in her Hollywood salon, Tina Cassaday Creations, has come up with a selection of special formulas that are all natural.

Whether or not you have a starring role, here's what she recommends.

For blondes: Make 1 pint of chamomile tea and add the juice of half a lemon. Let cool, and use it as a rinse.

For brunettes: One pint of rosemary tea, with thyme and nettle added. Strain out the thyme and nettle before you use it as a rinse.

For redheads: Rosemary tea with cinnamon chips.

Getting Gray? Why Hide It?

Many women think about heading for the hair salon at the first sign of gray hair—with plans to restore it to a darker color.

That may be the wrong approach, according to Edward Jiminez, a hair color expert in Beverly Hills who specializes in beauty makeovers.

"At a time when hair color is lost with graying, the complexion also tends to fade," says Jiminez. "Thus, if you select a hair coloring that's too dark in order to hide gray, you'll get a hard, fake look."

Put New Light in Gray Hair

Jiminez points out that advertisers would like the consumer to believe that color is *always* the answer when hair begins to gray. But, he insists, "It's simply not true. A new style may be all you need to put pizzazz into a new fantastic look."

What does Jiminez recommend as an alternative?

"Try one shade *lighter* with a nonperoxide rinse." That way, the natural lightening of the complexion will be complemented by lighter hair with better styling.

GOT A YEN FOR HENNA? BE WARNED...

"It's almost impossible to 'un-henna,' " says fashion expert and hairdresser Brian Thomas, owner of Blue Monday Salon in Hillcrest, California.

Henna first hit the news when the Nile's most famous beauty, Cleopatra, reportedly daubed it on her Egyptian locks. Derived from *Lawsonia inermis,* a shrub grown in Asia and the Far East, henna looked like a novelty: Suddenly there was a whole new Cleopatra on the throne. Cut to...the 1960s, when henna had another resurgence in popularity. And why not? It comes "all natural," since the dye comes from the henna plant. It's easy to apply. And it drew gazes.

Tempted?

Well, Thomas says henna could turn into a hair-coloring nightmare. The label may say the tint comes out, but Thomas says "Not so." True, it fades, but as it does, the color becomes even more counterfeit.

Thomas observes, "There's little a hairdresser can do but sympathize when a client comes in with a coating of henna on her hair—pleading for help."

Henna also doesn't take to perms, colors, or tints. You'll have to wait until the henna grows out. Since hair grows less than an inch a month, that's quite a commitment regardless of how dedicated you are to things natural.

Fresh New Looks Made Easy

What can you do if you like your cut but yearn for a change? Coloring virtuoso Scott Cole, educator and owner of Color Cutting USA, based in Atlanta, says, "Nothing drastic...just a few highlights here and there can bring a whole fresh appeal to your favorite hairstyle."

Cole suggests adding a touch of highlights at the sides and on a few bangs. "See if you like the look before having all your hair highlighted."

A Shampoo Should Be Forever

John Paul Jones DeJoria, co-founder and CEO of John Paul Mitchell Systems in Saugus, California, says a shampoo is right for you when it "gives your hair a feeling of softness and manageability." And, if a shampoo *is* right for you, there's no reason why you should ever change brands.

"If a shampoo is 'not working' for you, that's because it's leaving an unseen deposit on the hair shaft. A good shampoo will not do that," he says.

Beware the Scent That Clashes

Before you use a shampoo, take a good sniff, suggests Alan Benfield-Bush. "Select a shampoo with a fresh floral or berry fragrance," he says. "Steer clear of shampoos that smell like cheap perfume." Benfield-Bush says that highly perfumed shampoos will linger and change throughout the day—and their scent may clash with your cologne.

Smooth as Satin

Do you know how hair feels when it's really healthy?

Frank Chirico says, "Feel your hair about an inch from the scalp line...that's what all your hair should feel like if it's healthy." If all your hair doesn't feel that way, Chirico says to switch to a new program.

- Use a protein shampoo every day.
- Follow up with a moisturizing conditioner.
- Try to keep drying and chemical services to a minimum.

Stop the Rubadub

Do you know how to use a towel to dry your hair? "Most people don't," says David Patrick Bontempo.

He gives his clients two rules to dry and comb by.

1. "Never, ever rub your hair dry; you'll damage it. Instead, *blot* the moisture out."
2. "To reduce the possibility of damaging the hair, comb when it's still wet. Start combing at the ends, then work your way up until you're combing the whole length of hair."

In a Pinch, Stop by the Kitchen

No shampoo in the house. And you *have* to get ready to go...pronto?

LeMaire, owner of Los Angeles' LeMaire/Hair, admits it's even happened to her. So she went to the kitchen and found...

"I can't recommend it for everyday use, but in a beauty crisis, a small amount of liquid dishwashing soap is an acceptable shampoo substitute."

"Rinse *really* well," she adds.

In a Pinch Again? Creme Rinse With...

Here's LeMaire, handling another beauty crisis—this time, looking for a rinse. Why not look in the laundry room?

Fabric softener??

"It's fine for an emergency," says LeMaire. Pour out a dollop about the size of a 50-cent piece for a one-time rinse after shampooing. Then rinse well under the shower.

If You Hate That New-Perm Smell...

No other smell on this planet can compare to the odor of a fresh perm. You can try to ignore it, of course, but that usually doesn't work. Instead, why not follow hairdresser David Patrick Bontempo's advice.

"A rinse of diluted apple cider vinegar helps neutralize that smell," he says. The perm solution is alkaline; vinegar is acidic; with the blend, you get a neutral pH—and that neutralizes smell as well.

The proportions Bontempo recommends are ½ cup apple cider vinegar to 2 cups of water. Then rinse well with water.

Preview a Perm

A perm can give you a whole new look. But will it be the *right* look?

There are two ways to get a quick preview, using off-the-shelf hair-care products. Edward Tytel, vice president of Genoa International in Mukilteo, Washington, recommends one of these methods.

1. Set your hair in small hot rollers. Then spray with an extra-holding hair spray to finish the quick-perm.
2. To attain that wild and sensual look? "Use an extra-holding, water-soluble hair spray," says Tytel. "Spray a handful of hair and crush the hair into your palm. Still holding the curl of hair, open your palm just enough to blow it dry." Repeat in sections—spraying, holding, and drying until you achieve the curly look.

Either method gives you a sneak peek at a perm. If you don't like it, just shampoo your "perm" away. And if you *do* like it...head for the salon for a longer-lasting perm.

SEXY, MASCULINE, AND BALD

Men who are bald or balding often think hair replacement is the way to look young and sexy again.

Better think again, suggests Jeanne Braa, artistic director for John Paul Mitchell Systems in Saugus, California.

"Baldness is the ultimate symbol of masculinity," says Braa. "There's an outdated belief that the scalp is an unattractive, private part of the body. But that's not so."

She likes to see bald men *stay* bald—the natural look. (And staying naturally bald is less expensive, to boot.)

Need role models? Consider...

- Sean Connery
- Gerald McRaney
- Rob Reiner
- Michael Jordan
- James Taylor
- Telly Savalas
- Yul Brynner
- Kareem Abdul-Jabbar
- Lou Gossett, Jr.
- Pernell Roberts
- Danny DeVito
- Bruce Willis
- Jack Nicholson
- Prince Philip
- Mr. Clean
- Willard Scott
- Homer Simpson

Mastering Makeup

Knock Their Socks Off

Attending your high school reunion? Meeting a former flame? Going to a big party after work?

Whatever the occasion, you might want a trick to make your eyes irresistible. This one comes from Doreen Milek, president of Studio Make-Up Academy, located in a working Hollywood television studio.

"After you've applied makeup and dusted the eyelid with a light powder," says Milek, "apply a fingertipful of gold or silver eye shadow to the center of your eyelid, just above the lash. Blend in slightly."

Voilà...instant glamour! And your eyes will look this big!

Check Out That Package

Shopping for new cosmetics?

Become a smart consumer—and don't use products that might be contaminated with bacteria.

"Cosmetics actually have a long shelf life," says Lisa Kraayenbrink, spokesperson for the Color Cosmetic Division of Aveda Indra Corporation in Minneapolis. "Problems arise when bacteria contaminate the products."

What's a consumer to do? "Never buy a product that has been used or looks questionable." Just as with food or medication, you should not use a product if:

- The seals appear to have been broken.
- The contents do not seem to be hygienic.
- There are traces of the product around the edge of the opening.

One more tip from Kraayenbrink: If you're having a complimentary makeup session, look before you leap. Watch the cosmetologist, and make sure the brushes are cleaned for each client.

Using a Blusher? Go for Natural

The oldest form of makeup is the natural blush that comes to your cheeks when you're smiling.

When you highlight your cheeks with blusher, complement your smile, suggests Jim Schwartz, manager of public affairs for Clarion Cosmetics in Hunt Valley, Maryland.

- For a realistic blush, smile your biggest smile, then apply blusher to the puffy tops of your cheekbones.
- *Stroke* on the color, brushing slightly upward and outward to the hairline.
- Don't stop where the cheekbone ends. Lightly blend into the hairline.

For a Softer Eyeliner

Is your eyeliner pencil soft enough for your skin?

"To make sure, first draw a line on the tender part of your hand—the area between your fingers," says Charles Busta, vice president of marketing for Cover Girl Cosmetics in Cockeysville, Maryland.

If the pencil tugs at your skin when you draw on this part of your hand, it means you need to warm up the pencil tip before applying it to the delicate eye skin.

How?

Just hold the pencil in your hand until it warms up, suggests Busta.

For Longer-Lasting Lipstick Color

Would you like to have lipstick's color last longer?

Jim Schwartz says, "Dust a light coating of powder over bare lips, then apply lipstick." Blot any excess color with a tissue.

SPRUCING UP FOR A SUPER PHOTO...THE NIGHT BEFORE

Getting set to have your picture taken? If it's a portrait that's going to be done professionally, you'll want to look your very best.

San Diego photographic makeup artist and freelance photographer CeCe Canton says what you do the night *before* the photo shoot may be a lot more important than how you say "cheese." Here are her suggestions.

- Before the shoot, try out the makeup and clothing you'll wear. When you go, take two or three different wardrobe changes and ask the photographer's opinion of clothing and jewelry. Unless you're going for a fashion statement look, blend makeup well and dress conservatively.
- Get a good night's sleep before the shoot and schedule it for the morning. To avoid bleary or puffy eyes, don't drink alcohol the night before. Keep coffee to a minimum (if you must drink it) and your appearance will be more peaceful.
- A shiny look on the face, forehead, hairline, or nose will make you look nervous. Use a light skin-toned color powder on a puff, pressed into the skin, then distributed gently into the shiny areas. (Canton says this goes for men as well as women.)
- Advice for men: Make sure your collar is crisp and loose enough. A tight collar is unattractive. Shave close. Use petroleum jelly if the lips are dry.
- Advice for women: Choose earrings and other jewelry that isn't too bold—and with a matte finish. Flat gold or silver jewelry will reflect the flash.
- For those who wear glasses: Have a few shots done with and without your glasses; make the decision about which you like better when you see the proofs.

Sometimes, says Canton, it makes sense to hire a professional makeup artist, if you can afford one. She especially recommends this if you want to camouflage specific skin or facial imperfections.

Pamper Your Skin

Hide That PMS Pimple

Yes, even high-fashion models do get an occasional blemish. So how do *they* hide it?

"Red neutralizer is the answer," responds makeup expert Lisa Tully, of Laguna Beach, California, who specializes in print work for fashion layouts.

Although it's called "red," the neutralizer is often a greenish color. You can pick it up in beauty supply stores and some department stores. Just put a dot of the neutralizer under your foundation makeup.

Sunburn Strategy

Preventing a sunburn is first priority, according to Vera Brown, owner of Vera's Retreat in the Glen and Vera's Retreat in Tarzana, California. The internationally known skin care authority recommends that you find a sunscreen with the right sun protection factor (SPF) for your coloring. Use it whenever your skin is going to meet the sun.

But what if you get a light burn?

"Place cold aloe vera juice compresses on your face, lips, and anywhere else you're pink," says Brown. "Leave the compress on for a good 10 minutes." And... "After the aloe dries, swear you won't do this to your body again. Period."

For severe sunburn?

"Seek medical help," suggests Brown.

Declogging Smogged Pores

Whether you live in Malibu, Manhattan, or Madison, your face comes in contact with pollutants.

"Cleansing with a natural cold cream, followed by a rosewater and glycerine rinse will help remove pollutants," says Brown. "Regardless of how exhausted you are, always cleanse your face and neck well twice a day."

Moisturize All Over

Dry, wrinkled skin can be a problem anywhere—on elbows, knees, and around your fingernails. What's the best relief?

Darrell Doughty, senior research scientist at the Oil of Olay Skin Care Center in Shelton, Connecticut, suggests a facial moisturizer.

Just because it says "facial" doesn't mean it can only be used on the face, he points out. "The best moisturizer a consumer can use is the one he or she will use regularly."

Skin Care: Look in Your Kitchen Cupboard

Skin care authority Vera Brown suggests that you look around your kitchen for beauty-treatment ingredients. Everything you need may be right on hand.

Here are some of her favorite formulas.

A cleansing mask: Combine well: 1 tablespoon plain yogurt with l teaspoon sesame oil. Apply to your face and neck. Leave on 15 minutes. Massage gently and remove with a washcloth and very warm (almost hot) water, rinsing two or three times.

A mask for dry skin: Combine one well-mashed banana with a small amount of honey. Apply to your face and leave on for 15 minutes. Rinse well.

A mask for oily skin: Combine 3 teaspoons Fuller's Earth (available at pharmacies and health food stores), 1 tablespoon aloe vera juice, and ½ teaspoon plain yogurt. Work into a paste and apply. Leave on 15 minutes and rinse well.

A tightening mask: Combine 1 tablespoon mashed avocado, 2 tablespoons raw honey, and two egg whites in the blender. Process until smooth. Massage gently onto your face, then relax while the mask tightens skin and increases circulation. Leave on for 15 minutes and rinse well.

An all-over skin softener: Combine equal amounts of wheat germ or sesame oil and apple cider vinegar. Add to warm bathwater. After the bath, pat your skin dry.

A Breakfast Mix for Beautiful Skin

Want some help for chapped skin?

Here's a soothing cereal from Vera Brown: Soak 2 tablespoons raw barley and 2 tablespoons oatmeal in 1 cup of warm water for 10 minutes. Simmer the mixture for 10 minutes and cool to lukewarm. Beat in 1 tablespoon liquid lecithin. Add 1 cup hot water. Pour all ingredients into a blender and mix well. Strain through gauze and use in the bathtub with warm (not hot) water.

Caution: Skin softeners that contain slippery ingredients tend to make the tub slippery when added to bathwater. Take care climbing in and out.

The Ingredients of Better Skin Care

With all do-it-yourself masks, soaks, and cleansers that are made with natural ingredients, Brown emphasizes:

1. Always use fresh ingredients.
2. Never apply the ingredients close to your eyes.
3. Make sure your face is clean before applying any mask.
4. Always rinse well using a soft terry washcloth and warm water.

A Neck without Oil Needs a Helping Hand

Do you know that the neck area has no oil glands?

"To keep your neck soft and youthful looking, make sure you include it in your moisturizing program," says Charles Busta of Cover Girl.

Great Grooming

Tweeze When the Skin Is Softest

"To make tweezing as pain-free as possible, tweeze *only* after a hot shower," suggests Deborah Medina, founder of UBU Cosmetics in Carlsbad, California. Medina notes that the skin is softer after you've taken a shower or bath or been in a steamy room.

And after tweezing?

"Rub the area with an ice cube—or apply witch hazel with a cotton ball," Medina says. Both treatments tighten the pores and reduce any discomfort.

Facial Hair Bleaches Can Burn

Yes, a special bleach will make dark facial hair turn almost invisibly pale. But the bleach can burn your lip, unless you start out right.

Medina, who does makeup for ABC, NBC, and CBS, suggests that you start with a half-treatment first. "The first time you use the product, cut the time to half."

Afterward, soothe the area with witch hazel and ice.

Medina explains that women often leave the bleach on too long and damage the skin.

Underarm Lesson, Part 1

If you want maximum protection from an underarm product, choose an antiperspirant. If you're concerned with odor, choose a deodorant.

In a nutshell, that's the advice of John Seifert, who does consumer research for Procter and Gamble in Cincinnati.

"Odor is caused by the bacteria that feed on chemical components in underarm sweat," explains Seifert. "A deodorant works by controlling the population of that bacteria and does not help control wetness."

An antiperspirant, on the other hand, helps control *both* odor and wetness. The active ingredient in an antiperspirant is aluminum—a mineral that does a lot more than just control bacteria. In fact, aluminum travels to sweat glands, where it reacts to obstruct the flow of perspiration.

Underarm Lesson, Part 2

Scott Gilpin, a member of the product development team of Procter and Gamble's Beauty Care Council in Cincinnati, says that it's not necessary to use a *lot* of antiperspirant.

If you're using a solid or roll-on antiperspirant, just a thin layer will give maximum protection, he observes.

Underarm Lesson, Part 3

"The best time to apply an antiperspirant for maximum protection is when your underarms are a little warm and moist," says Seifert. "This enables the active ingredients to enter the sweat glands more readily."

One good time is just before bed, since your arms are usually close to your sides when you sleep. Also after a warm shower or bath.

UNCOMMONLY GOOD SCENTS

If you're buying expensive perfume, you might as well get the most out of it. Here's how to save money and enjoy your fragrance longer— from Larry Flanagan, a scent expert based in New York City who is associate advertising manager for Navy Fragrances.

1. Refrigerate a fragrance. It can last up to two years. (If a fragrance is exposed to heat, air, or sunlight, it starts to change immediately.)
2. The fragrance fades faster in a larger bottle. Therefore, buy two smaller bottles versus one large one.
3. Keep all perfume bottles out of the sun.
4. Keep the bottle tightly capped. (Fragrance stored in an atomizer has a shorter life.)

Thumbs-Up Hand Care

Quick Fix for a Split Nail

Hand model Tivoli Frick of Los Angeles suggests using a "tiny amount" of nail glue to fix the crack in a nail.

"Then file the nail to smooth the edges," she suggests. Usually the glue is enough to hold until the break grows out.

(Caution: Nail glue is made of an acrylic resin that has been found to cause allergic reactions in some people.)

How to Unpolish

Anyone who has ever removed nail polish knows how difficult it is to eliminate the infinitesimal traces that cling to the sides of nails.

How does a hand model get rid of the remains of unwanted polish?

"An orange stick dipped in polish remover does it every time," says Frick.

A Moisturizer for Cuticles

For healthier nails and cuticles, there's a simple once-a-day beauty treatment.

Bella Haroutunian, owner of LaBella's Nails in Beverly Hills, says, "Rub a small amount of petroleum jelly into the cuticle and skin area around your nails every evening."

HOW TO MAKE HANDS LOOK PICTURE PERFECT

Some models have hands so beautiful that they are photographed time and again for ads and catalogs. Tivoli Frick, of Los Angeles, is one of those models.

What does she recommend for well-pampered hands?

- If I have any sign of chapping or even a tiny cut, I rub an antibacterial ointment into my hands and nails before bed. Otherwise, I use petroleum jelly.
- Heat mittens, found in beauty supply stores, are wonderful for softening the skin on your hands. First apply some petroleum jelly, then relax with the mitts on. It's like giving your hands a facial...they'll look that youthful.
- To remove any stains on the nails or underneath the top edge, use a cotton swab dabbed in a small amount of peroxide or bleach. Then rinse well.
- Don't cut your cuticles; you could introduce bacterial infection. Instead, soften them first, using the heat-mitts treatment. Then gently push back the cuticles with an orange stick.
- Don't file your nails after using heat mittens. They'll get softer and moister inside the mittens—and you want nails as strong and dry as possible when you file.
- *Special* hand creams may be wonderful, but I use whatever is on sale at the store. I use a cream on my hands two or three times a day.
- The use of sunscreen, gloves for sports, and gloves in the garden and the kitchen are absolutes for every person who wants attractive hands.

A Second Look at Artificial Nails

Artificial nails are sculpted from the same plastics that dentists use to fill teeth. Ingredients include vinyl compounds (such as methyl methacrylate), a catalyst, and a plasticizer.

The Food and Drug Administration provides these tips for the use of artificial nails.

- If there's any question about sensitivity to the material in the sculptured nails, have one nail done as a test and wait a few days to see if any reaction develops. Some people are allergic.
- Never apply an artificial nail if the nail or tissue around it is infected or irritated. Let the infection heal first.
- Read instructions before applying nails. Save the ingredient list for your doctor in case of an allergic reaction.
- Treat artificial nails with care. They may be stronger than your own, but even so, they can break and separate. Protect them from harsh detergents and microbial contamination.
- If the artificial nail separates from the natural nail, place the fingertip into rubbing alcohol. That will clean the space between the natural and artificial nail. It's important to do this before reattaching the artificial nail, in order to help prevent infection.
- Don't use household glue on your nails. Use only products intended for use on natural and artificial nails.

How to Get a Smudgeproof Manicure

There's a top-model procedure for fine manicures that never smudge. This advice comes from Hollywood manicurist Haroutunian.

1. Always use a nail base coat first.
2. Apply two thin coats of polish.
3. Apply one thin coat of top coat.
4. Hold your fingers in front of a small fan to set the polish. (Alternatively, dunk your fingers into ice water.)

The key, according to Haroutunian, is to apply thin coats and *always* make sure the polish is completely dry between applications. If you want to avoid smudging your nails, don't drive, go to bed, or do anything else until the polish is absolutely dry.

The same tips apply to smudgeproof pedicures, too.

What's the Vintage of That Polish?

If you really want a smooth-as-silk application of nail polish, you must become date conscious. "For beautiful nails, you need fresh polish," says Haroutunian.

"Old polish will not give an even, glossy look," she says. She suggests that you write the date on the label as soon as you bring the polish home from the store—and discard the polish after two months.

The Experts

Alan Benfield-Bush, award-winning hairdresser, is founder of the ABBA International Academy for hairdressers and co-owner of ABBA Liquid Styling Tools hair care products in Irvine, California.

David Patrick Bontempo is owner of Bontempo's Salon in Pasadena, California. His clients include Miss Universe and other beauty pageant contestants.

Jean Braa is artistic director for John Paul Mitchell Systems in Saugus, California, the creative source for Paul Mitchell World Training and Advancement Center and Paul Mitchell Associates worldwide.

Sam Brocato is president of Brocato International Salons and Beauty Schools in Baton Rouge, Louisiana and the creator of Brocato International hairstyling products, sold exclusively at salons.

Vera Brown, internationally known skin care authority, is owner of Vera's Retreat in the Glen and Vera's Retreat in Tarzana, California.

Charles Busta is vice president of marketing for Cover Girl Cosmetics in Cockeysville, Maryland.

David Cannell, Ph.D., is vice president of corporate technology of Redken Laboratories in Canoga Park, California.

CeCe Canton is a makeup artist and freelance photographer in San Diego; her work has been seen internationally in consumer and trade publications.

Tina Cassaday is owner of Tina Cassaday Creations, Inc., a Hollywood salon with its own hair care product line. Catering to many celebrities, she specializes in the natural approach to beauty and hair care.

Frank Chirico is co-owner of the exclusive Allen Edwards International Salons in Santa Barbara.

Scott Cole is owner of Color Cutting USA, based in Atlanta, Georgia.

Londoner Dale is owner of the prestigious San Diego–based Dale International Salons. He has trained extensively with Vidal Sassoon and has styled for Sting, Carol Burnette, Vanessa Redgrave, and others. His work has appeared in *Vogue, Cosmo, Self,* and *Glamour.*

John Paul Jones DeJoria is co-founder and CEO of the professional beauty product company John Paul Mitchell Systems in Saugus, California.

Darrell Doughty is a senior research scientist at the Oil of Olay Skin Care Center in Shelton, Connecticut.

Larry Flanagan, a scent expert, is the associate advertising manager for Navy Fragrances in New York City.

Tivoli Frick is a hand model in Los Angeles who has had her hands photographed for advertisements for jewelry, toys, cat food, computers, records, movies, shoes, clothing, and credit cards. Her hands appeared in the movie *Galaxy of Terror*.

Scott Gilpin is a member of the product development team of Procter and Gamble's Beauty Care Council in Cincinnati, Ohio.

Bella Haroutunian is the owner of LaBella's Nails in Beverly Hills.

Edward Jiminez, a Beverly Hills hairdresser, color expert, and educator, has worked extensively with major hair-care product companies including Clairol and Pantene. He also does work for television, theater, and the print media, with Disney among his clients. Beauty and grooming makeovers are his specialty.

Lisa Kraayenbrink is spokesperson for the Color Cosmetic Division of Aveda Indra Corporation in Minneapolis, Minnesota.

LeMaire is a comedian and owner of the Melrose Avenue LeMaire/Hair Salons in Los Angeles, California.

Deborah Medina, founder of UBU Cosmetics in Carlsbad, California, does makeup for film actors and actresses. She also does work at ABC, CBS, and NBC networks, and makeup for the Super Bowl commentators.

Doreen Milek, founder and president of Hollywood's Studio Make-Up Academy, is an award-winning makeup artist.

Jim Schwartz is the manager of public affairs for Clarion Cosmetics in Hunt Valley, Maryland.

John Seifert conducts consumer research for Secret and Sure antiperspirants at Procter and Gamble in Cincinnati, Ohio.

Eric Serena, owner of the Eric Salon in Beverly Hills, is hairdresser to some of the film industry's leading performers, including Cher. He specializes in creating hairstyles for actors' roles in movies and on television.

Brian Thomas, fashion expert and hairdresser, is owner of Blue Monday Salon in Hillcrest, California, and a partner at Margarita White's salon in Mexico City. His work has appeared in all leading women's fashion magazines.

Lisa Tully of Laguna Beach, California, is a makeup artist who does fashion, sportswear, and beauty makeup for models who appear in print advertising.

Edward Tytel is vice president of Genoa International in Mukilteo, Washington.

CHAPTER 9

Country Living

Working Your Own Land

Life in the country is certainly different from life in the city, although the two are certainly intertwined. Fax machines, computer modems, and overnight express mail link one population to the other, and the old stereotypes of rural folk as backward and less educated is getting a long-overdue revision.

By its very nature, what most separates rural living from urban living is *land*. In the country, folks commonly live in close contact with a landscape. In the cities, people have less chance to experience trees, crops, and the vagaries of weather. Country living is most often shared with other creatures, too—domesticated farm animals, household pets, and wildlife of all kinds. Residing in a rural neighborhood requires a respect for animal life and an appreciation for the ecology of living things: It's all interconnected.

Because there are fewer public utilities and government services in the country, rural people are forced to be more self-reliant than their urban cousins. They may service their own machinery, grow their own vegetables, or find alternative sources of energy when the need arises.

It's a special way of life, to be sure, and not meant for everyone. But for those with an affinity for nature and a sense of independence, the rewards can be great.

Secrets Revealed

METES AND BOUNDS

Legal descriptions of property defy quick interpretation. They are decipherable only with the aid of a government survey map.

Rural land descriptions differ from city lots, and precise locations are sometimes difficult to determine without the aid of a surveyor. When a description reads Section 16, T5N, R30W what does that mean?

Most areas of the United States have been divided into townships (T). These are 6-mile by 6-mile blocks, which are subsequently divided into 1-mile by 1-mile blocks called sections. Townships are measured from a known point such as a state border. T5N, consequently, refers to the fifth (5) township north (N) of the state border

Ranges (R) refer to the number of townships east or west of a designated meridian. R30E would be the 30th township east of that meridian.

Sections are numbered from 1 to 36 within each township, beginning in the northeast corner and progressing in the manner shown below:

6	5	4	3	2	1
7	8	9	10	11	12
18	17	16	15	14	13
19	20	21	22	23	24
30	29	28	27	26	25
31	32	33	34	35	36

Section 16, therefore, lies near the middle of the township.

A single section covers 640 acres. Smaller parcels, such as 20 acres, are described by their location within that section. For example, the notations $N\frac{1}{2}$, $NW\frac{1}{4}$, $NW\frac{1}{4}$ indicate that the 20-acre parcel lies on the north half of the northwest quarter of the northwest quarter of Section 16.

Properties that don't conform to subsections so easily are described from a known point—a section corner, for instance—with what are known as metes and bounds. This description begins at the known point and measures the boundaries of the land in feet from there: commencing 500 feet north of the southeast corner of said section, thence east 600 feet, thence north 100 feet, thence west 600 feet, thence south 100 feet.

Boundaries that bend and curve at odd angles will require a professional surveyor to precisely measure or identify.

Lessons on Livestock

Ask Your Grandparents

"Back in the horse-and-buggy days of our grandparents, most everybody knew how to take care of their animals. It was just common knowledge," says Donna Ewing, president and founder of the Hooved Animal Humane Society in Woodstock, Illinois. "Problem is, most of our parents weren't too interested in horses or other farm animals, and there's been a generation gap. People moved away from the farms. Now that some are coming back, we're having problems because people don't have the same kind of education they once did. The love of the animals has been passed down, but not the care."

Before buying horses or other farm animals, consult a local veterinarian, Ewing suggests. Join animal organizations. Talk to neighbors. Take lessons. And, if you have grandparents who know the ways of pets and livestock, ask them for their advice!

Techno-Tip

TOP HORSES ARE MULTIPLYING

It's not cloning exactly, but through embryo transfer, a single mare can mother a dozen or more foals. Horse breeder Bini Abbott obtained a grandson of Triple Crown winner Secretariat through an embryo-transfer process performed by veterinarians at Colorado State University.

"First they breed the mare, and then, after seven days, they flush the embryos out of the mare," Abbott explained. "They have other mares cycling at the same time so their bodies are ready to receive an embryo." The embryos are implanted in the surrogate mares, who then carry the foals to term.

The procedure costs $5,000, according to Abbott, and is available at animal reproduction labs throughout the country. "They've been doing embryo transfers with cattle for years, but with horses this is rather new," she observes.

Shoe and Trim

"Horses need to be reshod or trimmed, on the whole, every six weeks," advises Bini Abbott, a veteran horse breeder who lives on an 85-acre ranch in Arvada, Colorado. "It's not like buying shoes for a person."

Just in case you need to find a local smithy, "horseshoers" are usually listed in the Yellow Pages—or you can call a veterinarian for recommendations. New shoes may run about $40, but it's just $15 or so for a trimming.

Save These Numbers

Animals react differently than humans to toxic substances, and between separate species there can be great variability, says William Buck, D.V.M., director of the University of Illinois National Animal Poison Control Center in Urbana, Illinois. The center maintains a 24-hour national hot line providing expert advice on animal poisonings. Two numbers are available: A fee of $30 per case is charged via credit card for calls to 1-800-548-2423. Or you can call 1-900-680-0000 and pay by the minute (about $2.75 per call—but ask the charge when you call).

Choose Your Horse Carefully

Buying a horse? "Be really cautious," says Abbott. "It's not like getting a puppy." If you have a small homestead, be sure to look for an animal with a gentle disposition. Thoroughbreds are stunningly beautiful but usually too high strung and jumpy for the average rural lot. Percheron and Haflingers are good working breeds—that is, wonderful at pulling hay wagons or sledging a load of wood. "And don't be afraid of a horse with age on it," Abbott adds, "because they can be marvelous—the salt of the earth."

Vitamin C Helps Dogs Whelp

Dogs need a vitamin C supplement approximately three weeks before they whelp, says Bea Lydecker, a practicing animal psychologist who lives near Oregon City, Oregon. She markets herbal animal care products through her company, Bea Lydecker's Naturals. She drew this conclusion after watching her pregnant bitches eat orange peels and the blossoms off roses. "An animal left to nature will find the things that it needs," observes Lydecker, "but not if you just keep it in the house and feed it processed foods."

Bring in Some Bees

Homesteading teacher and self-sufficiency advocate Glenn Simmons of Scio, Oregon, recommends beekeeping on a small acreage, both for a personal supply of honey and for commercial reasons. "Honey brings a good price," he says. "And it doesn't take long to get acquainted with the different problems that arise in the keeping of bees."

Want to locate a hive? It could be as near as your local orchard: Fruit growers like hives on their property to ensure pollination. Contact your extension agent about state permits and beehive inspections.

Plant Fish

Fish can be planted, raised, and harvested in a farm pond. If the water is deep and cool, plant trout; if it's shallow, try catfish or perch, suggests Simmons. He says he feeds his trout a daily ration of soybean meal, fish meal, and ground dried liver in a pellet form with vitamins. Tiny fingerlings planted in mid-May can be harvested as 9-inch trout in September.

Techno-Tip

CHICKENS CAN DO DOUBLE DUTY

Chicken farmers can create a reliable composting floor system in the chicken house to provide humus-building fertilizer, suggests Teresa Maurer, former associate program director and reseach coordinator at the Kerr Center for Sustainable Agriculture in Poteau, Oklahoma. To demonstrate, the Kerr Center created a chicken house that produced 220 cubic feet of fertilizer in 500 days.

An old 20-by-60-foot hay barn was modified with wood slat sides for ventilation. A thick layer of hardwood sawdust, purchased from a local sawmill, was spread over the dirt floor as bedding. A compost starter was added to the sawdust and 200 chickens contributed nutrients. The floor was watered down when it got dry and tilled once or twice a month with a hand rototiller. The result: 220 cubic feet of fertilizer all ready to go on the garden.

Milking Is a Commitment

Are you harboring romantic notions of warm milk, fresh cream, and home-churned butter? Having a milk goat or a milk cow is like being in jail, says Simmons. "You are going to have to milk them in the morning and again every night, seven days a week."

An Apple a Day Keeps Mastitis Away

Mastitis, or inflammation of the udder, is a serious and often costly ailment in milk cows. Marv Ruffing's 100-cow dairy in Woodburn, Oregon, has been free of the disease for five years, he says, because of daily supplements of apple cider vinegar added to the cows' feed. "Now my cows need less feed, their coats have a higher gloss, their calves are bigger, and they calve easier," he says. Ruffing's prescription for success: Add 4 ounces of apple cider vinegar per cow per day, sprinkled over hay or grain.

Remove Flies without Insecticides

The horn fly, a serious pest of grazing cattle, can be controlled without pesticides using a walk-through fly trap, field tested at the Kerr Center for Sustainable Agriculture in Poteau, Oklahoma. "You set the structure between a pasture and water or shade—someplace the cow is going to need to get to regularly," explains Teresa Maurer, former assistant program director and research coordinator at the center.

As cows walk through the device, a series of canvas strips hanging in the pathway rub against their hides and disturb the flies. Attracted by outside light, the flies try to escape through holes in louvered screens. When the cow exits, the flies are trapped between the inside and outside screens.

"The flies collect in a nice little trap and you feed them to your fish or you throw them out on the pasture," says Maurer. "It's not total eradication, but it certainly helps."

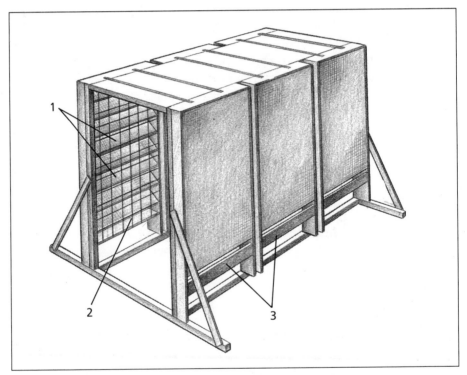

A walk-through fly trap to control horn fly. As cows walk through the fly trap, they rub against canvas strips. The flies are attracted by light on louvered screens that have holes punched in them (1). When the cow leaves, the flies are trapped between panels and screens (2) and fall to the "fly cleanout" at the bottom of the trapping elements (3).

Let Goats Get Your Weeds

The Kerr Center has also experimented with using grazing animals for weed control. Conclusions: Alternating sheep, goats, and cattle on the same land reduces the need for herbicides. "We let the goats come in and work on the brush for a bit, then let the sheep come in and work on the ragweed that comes in after the brush," says Maurer. "After the brush and the ragweed have been knocked back a bit, we let the cattle in to work on the grass."

Past Performance

COMPOST ON THE HOOF

Seems that Americans have been devising better ways to make compost since—well, since before the United States of America was the United States of America, according to horticulturist Peter Hatch, director of gardens and grounds at Monticello outside Charlottesville, Virginia.

"One interesting method for composting was published in 1771 in *Transactions of the American Philosophical Society*, in 'Essay on the Cultivation of the Vine' by Edward Anthill," says Hatch. "Anthill suggested that 'a fenced pen be built adjacent to the vineyard site for hog, sheep, or cattle. The pen would be constantly filled with straw, river mud, leaves, buckwheat, reeds, salt meadow hay, soap suds, dried blood, pork and beef pickle, corn cobs, cider and beer emptyings, and greasy dishwater, all of which would be mixed together by the livestock, especially the hogs, and eventually rot into a rich and beneficial compost.'"

Never one to lack for a good idea, Thomas Jefferson in 1794 proposed a similar, but portable, pen for cows. The pen could be moved from field to field or orchard to orchard, where the animals would help renew the soil right on the spot.

The ABCs of Soil and Stream

Test for Quality

Unlike their urban cousins, country landowners have to take responsibility for their own water quality. Most get their water from wells, which should be tested annually for bacteria and (less often) for other contaminants.

County health departments or extension agents will direct you to a lab for testing, according to Jim Peterson, Ph.D., professor of agricultural engineering and chairman of the Environmental Resources Center at the University of Wisconsin in Madison and water quality specialist for the University of Wisconsin Cooperative Extension Service. Tests for nitrates and bacteria typically cost between $5 and $15.

Get a Well Report

When buying rural property, always ask for a well construction report, recommends Dr. Peterson. This will include details on the date of installation, depth, size of casing, and pump capacity for the well. Good records also include a history of well and plumbing maintenance, and water testing. This information will help you assess the quantity and quality of your groundwater supply. "The shallower your well is, the more local your water supply is," Dr. Peterson points out.

Water Can Be Treated

If you discover contaminants in your water supply, various home water treatment systems can help. Three types of systems—activated carbon filters, distillation, and reverse osmosis—are proven and reliable. County health officials will know which to recommend.

But Peterson warns against more exotic purification systems: "If you hear of something electromagnetic that realigns the molecules such that it does wonderful things for the water, it's very unlikely to work," he says.

Know Your Enemy

Before buying rural land, ask an extension agent or private consultant for a botanical inventory, suggests Richard Old, Ph.D., a weed diagnostician at the University of Idaho College of Agriculture Weed Diagnostic Center. "You could buy a piece of ground for $100 an acre and acquire the legal responsibility for a noxious weed problem that could cost you $1,000 an acre."

On undeveloped ground, compare the prevalence of native versus nonnative species of plants. On ground that has been tilled, most species will be nonnative—and nonnative plants are more likely to be on the "noxious" list. So be wary.

Brainstorm Before You Change Your Land

Before making changes on your land (especially if it's for a new land use), consult local authorities. That is the recommendation of a riparian systems consultant, Bruce Lium, whose private firm, the American Water Resources Company, is headquarted in Hailey, Idaho. Lium, who helps people plan water use, suggests talking to county planners, extension agents, fish and wildlife biologists, and environmental quality specialists. "Tell them what you have in mind and ask for their advice. You'll find they have some good ideas. And if there's a need for a permit later on, it will go through easier if they know your project personally."

Follow the Beaver

The best pond engineers are beaver, says Lium, who is a former United States Geographical Survey (U.S.G.S.) research biologist. If you have a stream on your land, you can make a beaver-style dam by blocking a section with rocks or logs. Add to the dam until the pond reaches the desired depth. "You want to keep the water moving so that you don't get stagnation or algae growth," says Lium. "Longer and narrower is better than round."

Restore Damaged Stream Banks

Livestock grazing and heavy recreational use has denuded many stream banks, leading to erosion and flooding. To restore these riparian environments where there's flowing water, Lium suggests planting willows at the stream's low-water mark and hardier woody plants—aspen, dogwood, alder, currants—higher up the bank. The intertwining roots of these plants will bind the soils together and resist erosion. "Then I'd overseed the entire river bank with native grasses and wildflowers. This will give you a good surface root mass and improve the visual characteristics."

Diversify for Wildlife

Wildlife appreciate "vertical structure" in a landscape—patches of tall trees and brush separated by open fields—according to Warren Snyder, wildlife research biologist for the Colorado Division of Wildlife based in Sterling, Colorado. "The layering effect will attract more species and increase the density of wildlife."

Save Wetlands

Ponds, marshes, and swampy places are critical wildlife habitat, Snyder points out. Leaving them intact will preserve and attract flocks of waterfowl, as well as many other species of birds and animals.

Fish Out Mosquito Problems

Wetlands are often associated with mosquitoes, but there are environmental side effects to pesticide spray. Is there an alternative?

According to entomologist Alan Eaton, Ph.D., professor at the University of New Hampshire in Durham, a biological control agent known as Bti, available at many garden centers, has proven to be effective with about 30 species of mosquitoes, and it doesn't harm other aquatic life. Bti is applied directly on the water, remains active for about three days, and requires frequent reapplications.

Another option? Plant mosquito-devouring fish. Fish that eat mosquito larvae are common in tropical southern states. In the north, try stocking a pond with guppies, Dr. Eaton suggests. (Since guppies won't survive the winter in a northern pond, you'll have to restock annually.) Other larvae eaters include goldfish, dragonflies, and frogs.

Forget the Zappers

Tired of slapping mosquitoes? Ready to get an outdoor "zapper"?

"For gosh sakes, don't waste your money on one of those electrocuters," says Dr. Eaton. "They're of absolutely no benefit whatsoever in controlling mosquitoes."

Better Barns and Buildings

Make Reparations

Don't tear down that old barn or outbuilding. It can probably be repaired for less than the cost of a new one!

"We've always repaired things instead of replacing them," says fourth-generation rancher Russell Wilkerson of Cambridge, Idaho, whose ranch won the 1991 Farm Heritage Award from the National Trust for Historic Preservation. "It's just an attitude we've had in the family for a long time."

FYI

REHABILITATION CAN BE LESS TAXING

Investment tax credits are available for rehabilitation of old farm buildings, according to Mary Humstone, director of the Barn Again! program of the National Trust for Historic Preservation. To qualify, the building must be used for income-producing activities. (So barn-to-house conversions aren't eligible.)

State historic preservation offices have details on the federal tax credit, as well as information on state or local incentives. To find out more, contact the office in your state before you begin a rehabilitation project.

The Wilkerson Ranch has three huge, gable-roofed barns dating back to 1866. Using their own labor, the family recently spent $10,000 renovating and painting a barn that would have cost them $40,000 *in materials alone* if it were built from the ground up.

Seek Experience

Unless you have the know-how and equipment to do the job safely, leave the structural work on buildings to experts, suggests Mary Humstone, director of a program of the National Trust for Historic Preservation called Barn Again! Neighbors can often suggest a good contractor for farm buildings. And local historical societies can recommend builders with restoration experience.

FYI

BARN REHABILITATION CHECKLIST

With diligent care, most barns and outbuildings will last for generations. Neglect them, though, and deterioration sets in fast.

Mary Humstone, Barn Again! program director with the National Trust for Historic Preservation, recommends the following checklist to determine the condition of a barn and to decide what rehabilitation work needs to be done.

Framing. Are posts, beams, sills, rafters, and joists solid and free of rot?

Foundation. Check for cracks, settling, and shifting out of place. Also look for loose or missing mortar.

Roof. Check roof covering and flashing for damage. Inside, look for water stains and rot on sheathing and beams.

Exterior walls. Eyeball the length of the barn at eave level: Is it straight along the eaves? Note where siding or battens need to be replaced.

Interior. Check the condition of the floor. Make sure it slopes to a drain or gutter.

Location. Does the barn allow good access to other buildings and the farmyard? Are water and electricity available? Is there room to expand?

Environment. Is the barn airtight and insulated? If necessary, can heating and ventilation systems be installed?

Utilities. What is the condition of the plumbing and wiring? Does it need to be updated?

ROUND BARNS

"They were really kind of an architectural oddity," says Portland, Oregon, architect Steve Nys of the circular barns that were promoted and built during the late 1800s and early 1900s. Some historians believe that round barns originated among the Shakers in New England. It was said the round barn could "keep the devil from hiding in the corners."

Aside from protecting farmers from evil, modern-day architects have rediscovered the practical advantages of a round design.

- Livestock penned in a circular arrangement of stalls can be fed from a central location, saving time and effort.
- The aerodynamic shape can better withstand high winds. Also, snow is less likely to drift up against its walls.
- A cylindrical shape encloses the most area with the least amount of material.

"A lot of people purchased stock plans for these barns and, in their own unique way, modified them to meet their needs," said Nys. Early twentieth-century farmers eagerly experimented with ways of making their operations more convenient and efficient.

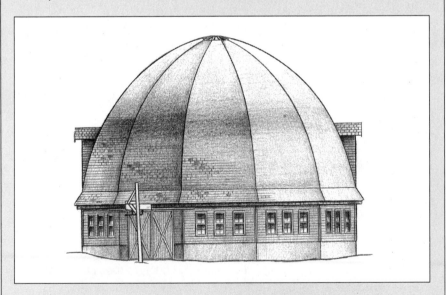

Typical design for a round barn, originally designed by Shakers. Rectangular barns were easier and less expensive to build: Few round barns have been constructed since the early 1900s.

Keep the Water Out

"Water is the worst enemy of old barns," says Steve Nys, an architect with the firm DiBenedetto-Thomson in Portland, Oregon. Patching up holes in the roof and weatherpoofing are the first order of business in any farm building rehabilitation. Once wood rot sets in, deterioration can be rapid.

How Firm a Foundation?

A decaying foundation may look intimidating, but don't give up on the barn just yet. Using anchor rods and hydraulic jacks, the barn frame can be lifted and the foundation rebuilt underneath.

"Trim off the bottom of the sill that has been decayed from weather and rot, and put in a concrete foundation," suggests Russell Wilkerson. "That gets a barn straightened up so it stands the way it was meant to."

Grade for Drainage

Where does the water flow during a heavy rain or spring runoff? If an acreage is properly planned, the water should drain away from the barn or other buildings, says Steve Nys. If necessary, grade the land to channel water away from foundations.

A Hoe-Down...Before Painting

Veteran rancher Russell Wilkerson paints the buildings on his Idaho ranch every five years or so. He recommends scraping off the old paint with a modified long-handled hoe. "We straighten that hoe and put it on a grinder," says Wilkerson. "Then we use that hoe to scrape down the buildings."

Keep a Paintbrush Ready

"We always keep a paintbrush and a bucket of high-quality exterior latex paint handy," Wilkerson says. "If we find ourselves with a spare hour—or if we're between jobs—we just grab a brush and go out and paint a while. When we're through, we put the brush back in the water and walk away. Pretty soon you look over, and you've got a whole building painted. You'd be surprised how much three or four people can paint in an hour."

Old Barns Accommodate New Uses

Old hay and dairy barns can still be useful, even on a farmstead without livestock, says preservationist Mary Humstone. With a concrete floor and a little electrical wiring, a barn can be converted to a machinery shop or a retail operation. And she has no objection to metal roofs, which are a practical and relatively inexpensive way to cover a barn. (The Barn Again! program collects case histories of successful conversions. For information, call 1-800-274-3694.)

Keep the Essentials Handy

Whether you're a master carpenter or just a home handyperson, there are certain tools that no country farmsteader should be without, according to Tom "Rusty Rooster" Henscheid, a West Seattle, Washington, master carpenter and contractor. "A lot of people spend an awful lot of money on fancy tools they rarely use, while at the same time they lack the absolute rudiments," he says.

Henscheid's basic toolkit includes the following:

Shovel: Good quality and well-sharpened, long-handled shovel.

Hammers: A 16-ounce claw hammer, a 24-ounce framing hammer, and an 8-pound sledgehammer.

Handsaws: An eight-point crosscut and a four-point ripsaw.

Measuring tools: Good squares with staircase fixtures (for marking repeated angles), compass, tape measure.

Plumb bob: "This is a $5 tool that saves carpenters hundreds and hundreds of hours," says Henscheid. "Rather than running back to the truck and looking for a level to make sure something is straight, you pull the plumb bob out of the pouch that you're carrying with you and drop it down. That will give you an absolutely perfect vertical line."

Chisels: "One of the primary tools for a carpenter or a homebuilder."

Planes: "You can shave 1/16 or 1/4 inch off a piece of wood real fast."

Spokeshave: "Old wagon wheel makers used them for cutting spokes." Handy for fitting handles and carving chair legs or posts.

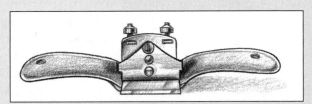

Spokeshave.

Circular saw: "Thank God they were invented; I would never want to be without one."

Electric drill: A small hand drill is essential. "Buy drill bits as needed."

Clamps: C-clamps and lightweight bar clamps. "You can never have enough clamps."

Duct tape: "Have it on hand for instant repairs."

Flashlight: A commonly needed device that too many carpenters forget to pack in their toolbox, says Henscheid.

Keep Animals Downwind

"It is wise to build your barn downwind from the house so that the majority of the time the wind will blow odors from the house to the barn, and not vice versa," says Glenn Simmons, Oregon homesteader and educator.

Build for Multiple Use

"I prefer a two-story hip roof barn," says Simmons. "This permits storage space in the upper area." By storing hay and grain in overhead lofts, the ground floor is free for animal stalls and shop space.

The Right Tools for the Tasks

A 2-Way Ax

Down east woodcutter Philip McBrien of Liberty, Maine, recommends a two-faced ax for anyone who's clearing trees and chopping firewood. One side has a sharp, thin blade; the other side is blunter. Use the sharp side for cutting and splitting wood and the blunt side for chopping branches and bushes, McBrien recommends. A busy woodcutter can switch from one side to the other without having to set down his ax.

Get a Good Handle

"I like a white oak handle not more than 30 inches long on my ax. A lot of hickory handles are too stiff," says McBrien. To make the handle especially limber, soak it in a pan of linseed oil for about three months. According to McBrien, this makes the handle more shock absorbent.

Keep It Limber

"My grandfather took old crankcase oil, mixed it with an equal portion of kerosene, and put it in a long piece of plumbing pipe that was sealed at the bottom. He would periodically dunk the handle of his shovels in that pipe, then wipe them off with a rag," says Tom Henscheid, whose remodeling business, Rusty Rooster Company, is located in West Seattle, Washington. "I never remember seeing any of his shovel handles cracked or split. They lasted forever."

Stay Sharp with Waterstones

"You have to have sharp tools," says master carpenter and contractor Henscheid. "If you don't keep them up, they won't perform well and you won't do good work." He recommends using oriental waterstones instead of oilstones for sharpening because they are softer and less expensive, cut steel faster, and are easier to take care of.

Crank an Edge

"My preference is to use a hand crank grinder to sharpen tools," adds Henscheid. "They're still available and not very expensive." The master carpenter has found that a hand-cranked grinder does a much better job than an electric grinder.

Test Tractor Fluids

When buying used tractors, have the oil and transmission fluid tested in a laboratory for signs of dirt and metal shavings; if you find either, it's a forewarning of mechanical troubles. "We do it on a periodic basis on all our tractors," says part-time wheat farmer Jim Shepherd of Walla Walla, Washington, who is a professor of economics at Whitman College.

Get a Cat for the Grades

Mechanized farming came late to the hilly wheat country of southeastern Washington because the steep grades were too much for early wheeled tractors, says Shepherd. The development of diesel-powered Caterpillar tractors in the 1930s quickly modernized the wheat farms, and they are still being used today. For farming on steep hillsides, check out the new Caterpillar tractors with rubber tread.

Have Winch, Will Harvest

A small woodlot on your land can provide a sustainable source of wood heat as well as supplement your income. John Garland, Ph.D., a forestry extension agent at Oregon State University in Corvallis, recommends the type of small, tractor-powered winch systems used in Scandinavia for harvesting trees. A winch system mounts to the three-point hitch of a common farm tractor and is used to haul and stack logs by remote control. "You match the winch size you need to the size of timber you're going to cut," Dr. Garland explains. Costing $2,300 to $10,000, the systems are manfactured by two Scandinavian companies, Farmi and Igland.

Keep It Clean

The most important rule of farm machinery maintenance, according to Idaho farmer-rancher Russell Wilkerson, is "keep it clean." That includes all engine and mechanical parts that could be cracked or have leaks. When the engine is clean, it's a lot easier to repair broken parts or fittings. "If you can't see it, you can't fix it," notes Wilkerson.

Power Up for Rural Living

Conserve First

"Before you change your energy supply, *do efficiency*," suggests Amory Lovins, vice president and director of research at the Rocky Mountain Institute in Snowmass, Colorado, and the author of *Soft Energy Paths*. "Then, whatever you need for supply will be smaller and simpler," suggests Lovins. Efficiency begins with insulating drafty buildings and installing lights and appliances that draw less power.

Techno-Tip

LOOK TO THE SUN

Many rural properties lie off the beaten track and far from the nearest electric utility power supply grid. Connecting a new home to that grid can be expensive. If the grid is more than a quarter-mile away, a photovoltaic (PV) power supply may be more cost-effective than a hookup, says Amory Lovins, vice president and director of research at the Rocky Mountain Institute in Snowmass, Colorado.

The initial cost of installing the PV system's silica panels can be high (around $5,000 for a moderately sized home system), but once installed, they operate almost without cost. Only the rechargeable batteries ("fed" by the panels) will have to be replaced periodically.

A sunny climate is critical to solar power, of course, but a woodstove can supply backup heat during cold, cloudy spells. Finding a consultant to help you set up a home PV system is much easier than it used to be, as there are now more than 20,000 solar-powered homes nationwide.

"Another option for rural people would be microhydro," says Lovins. Requirements include a source of gravity-driven, flowing water and permits from local water resource agencies. (Consult a hydrological engineer.)

And..."There are very reliable small wind machines, both new and recycled old ones, that can be a good power source if you're in a windy area such as the Great Plains," says Lovins.

Get a House Call

"If you have a drafty old house, you should probably get hold of a house doctor who will diagnose your house's chills and fevers," suggests energy expert Lovins, who has served on the U.S. Department of Energy's senior advisory board. The "house doctor" uses special diagnostic equipment like blower doors and infrared viewers. To find a house doctor, consult your state energy office.

Look to Your Windows

Most folks know that south-facing windows achieve more solar gain, but new superefficient windows have many times the insulating capability of conventional panes. With well-insulated windows "it doesn't matter which way the window faces; it will still gain more heat than it loses," says Lovins.

Pump It with Solar

For watering livestock, the Meadowcreek (an environmental educational center in Fox, Arkansas) uses a solar-powered pump. "When the sun is out, the pump comes on and you can pump out of a pond, a stream, or a shallow well," explains Luke Elliott, director of the center. "We have the pump mounted on a trailer so you can pull it to wherever you need to provide the water. It's a real slick little system. No batteries and minimal things that can go wrong."

Distill with Solar

A solar water still, available from McCracken Solar Company in Alturas, California, is another good application of solar energy in rural areas, Elliott says. Operated entirely on photovoltaic (PV) panels and long-life rechargeable batteries, it will distill about 2 gallons a day, withdrawing chlorine and other chemicals from well water or municipal supplies.

Past Performance

COOL THE PERSIAN WAY

Persian draft towers are an ancient method of air conditioning that could have modern applications. Begin with a tall tower or chimney that has an opening at the bottom: the rising air creates a natural draft. Then try a modern addition to this Persian invention: "Up near the top you have a very small atomized water spray," explains energy expert Amory Lovins, who has served on the U.S. Department of Energy's senior advisory board. "The water instantly evaporates into cool air, which sinks down the chimney. You get cool, slightly moist air rushing out the bottom of the tower."

Successful Sowing and Growing

Revere the Elders

For home gardening, many old-time varieties of fruits and vegetables are hardier and better tasting than new ones, says Kent Whealy, the founder and co-director of Seed Savers Exchange in Decorah, Iowa. "So much plant breeding these days is entirely for commercial applications," he points out.

Many old or heirloom nonhybrid varieties of plants have been dropped from seed catalogs and are available only through networks of collectors.

Save Your Seeds

Preserve your favorite vegetable varieties and save money by collecting and growing your own seeds from year to year, says Kent Whealy, founder and co-director of Seed Savers Exchange in Decorah, Iowa. Hybrid plant varieties won't reproduce true to form, but nonhybrids passed down from grandparents or obtained from fellow seed savers are worth harvesting for their seeds alone. Here are the steps for saving seeds.

1. Identify and mark the most "true-to-type" plants in your garden. Plan to save some of their seed when it matures.
2. With large-fruited plants, scrape the seeds out of the fruit. With small fruits, crush and ferment the fruit before collecting the seeds.
3. Dry seeds quickly to prevent germination or growth of mold. Seeds may be dried either in direct sunlight or by placing them on a tray in a low setting in the oven. (Don't let the temperature get above 95°, says Whealy, as that will damage the seeds.)
4. Store seeds in airtight containers (jars or plastic pouches) in a refrigerator or freezer. Avoid moisture as much as possible. Most seeds can be stored for many years with little loss of germination or vigor.
5. Thaw out containers before opening. Otherwise, moisture will condense on the cold seeds and damage them. Expose seeds to the air for a few days before planting.

For more information on saving or obtaining heirloom and unusual seeds, write to the Seed Savers Exchange, R.R. 3, Box 239, Decorah, IA 52101.

Buy Certified Seed

An important rule for anyone putting in a crop is to "buy clean seed," says University of Idaho College of Agriculture weed expert Richard Old. "Lots and lots of weeds come in as contaminants with other seeds. Many farmers are planting wild oat with their crop seed, and wild oat is one of our major crop weeds." Certified seed is more expensive, but it will save money and heartache in the long run, according to Old.

A WEATHER REPORT...ON THE WING

Before there was a National Weather Service, folks in the country observed animal behavior to help with their weather forecasting. Folklorist Hubert Davis of Portsmouth, Virginia, has collected many of the old meteorological aphorisms, including these observations on wild birds.

When swallows fly high,
Clear weather is nigh;
But when swallows fly low,
'Twill rain or snow.

When loons loudly cry,
A windstorm is nigh;
When sea birds leave the bay,
A storm is on its way.

When geese honk high,
Expect a clear sky;
Cold weather is in sight
When geese fly at night;
But good weather 'twill be
When geese go out to sea.

When the cuckoo with the owl jowers,
It's a sure sign of coming showers.
Blue jays loudly cry
When a shower is nigh;
But look for a downpour
When birds sing no more.

The crow with loud cries
A sudden shower foretells,
As in single file he flies
Up over the hills.

If crows pitch and blunder
In their morning flight,
Expect wind and thunder
To come before night.

When birds feed late in the day,
Sure sign that snow is on the way.

Get a Budget

The best way to estimate the costs and potential returns of a crop in a specific area is to consult an "enterprise budget," says Tim Cross, Ph.D., an agricultural economist with the Oregon State University Extension Service in Corvallis. Enterprise budgets break down the costs associated with a crop (labor, machinery, materials) and the likely income based on current prices. Not only good for estimating the profitability of a crop in a given area, they also provide a handy guide to the equipment and labor requirements for land preparation, planting, and harvesting a particular crop. Cooperative extension service offices in most areas of the United States have enterprise budgets available free of charge for a variety of crops and livestock operations.

Weather-Watch for Growers

Some states have implemented computerized links to remote weather stations. "Anybody with a home computer and a modem can call and get up-to-the-minute weather data," says Mike Willett, a tree fruit specialist with the Washington State University Cooperative Extension Service in Yakima. This data can be used to plan irrigation schedules, anticipate frosts, determine spraying conditions, or monitor weather changes. In the state of Washington, the system is called Public Agriculture Weather System (PAWS). Systems go by other names in other states; ask for details from your county extension agent.

The Experts

Bini Abbott lives on an 85-acre ranch near Arvada, Colorado, where she raises thoroughbred horses and miniature donkeys.

William Buck, D.V.M., is director of the University of Illinois National Animal Poison Control Center in Urbana, Illinois.

Tim Cross, Ph.D., is an agricultural economist with the Oregon State University Extension Service in Corvallis, Oregon, who specializes in teaching farm management skills.

Hubert J. Davis, a retired science educator, from Portsmouth, Virginia, writes full-time about science and folklore. His "What Will the Weather Be?" booklets are published by Pocahontas Press in Blacksburg, Virginia.

Alan Eaton, Ph.D., is a professor of entomology at the University of New Hampshire in Durham.

Luke Elliott, formerly the director of the Energy Office in Grand Junction, Colorado, is now director of Meadowcreek, an environmental educational center in Fox, Arkansas.

Donna Ewing is president and founder of the 20-year-old Hooved Animal Humane Society in Woodstock, Illinois. She has also organized Hooves Across America, a nationwide organization of people concerned with horse welfare.

John Garland, Ph.D., is forestry extension agent at Oregon State University in Corvallis.

Peter Hatch is director of gardens and grounds at Monticello, Thomas Jefferson's historic home outside Charlottesville, Virginia.

Tom Henscheid is a master carpenter and contractor. His ten-year-old remodeling business, Rusty Rooster Company, is located in West Seattle, Washington.

Mary Humstone is director of the Barn Again! program of the National Trust for Historic Preservation. Her office is in Denver, Colorado.

Bruce Lium, a former United States Geological Survey (U.S.G.S.) research biologist, is a riparian systems consultant. His private firm, The American Water Resources Company, is headquartered in Hailey, Idaho.

Amory B. Lovins is vice president and director of research at the Rocky Mountain Institute in Snowmass, Colorado. The author of *Soft Energy Paths*, he has served on the Department of Energy's senior advisory board.

Bea Lydecker is a practicing animal psychologist who lives on a rural lot near Oregon City, Oregon. She markets herbal animal care products through her company, Bea Lydecker's Naturals.

Philip McBrien is a veteran New England woodsman who worked as a logger long before the age of the chainsaw. He lives in Liberty, Maine.

Teresa Maurer is former assistant program director and research coordinator at the Kerr Center for Sustainable Agriculture in Poteau, Oklahoma.

Steve Nys is an architect with the firm DiBenedetto-Thomson in Portland, Oregon.

Richard Old, Ph.D., is a weed diagnostician in the University of Idaho College of Agriculture Weed Diagnostic Center. He grew up on a family farm near Albion, Washington

Jim Peterson, Ph.D., professor of agriculture engineering, is chairman of the Environmental Resources Center at the University of Wisconsin in Madison and is a water quality specialist for the UW Cooperative Extension Service.

Marv Ruffing operates a 100-cow dairy farm near Woodburn, Oregon. He is the former president of Farmer's Cooperative Creamery in McMinnville, Oregon.

Jim Shepherd is a professor of economics at Whitman College and a part-time farmer. He raises dryland wheat on 1,000 acres of land near Walla Walla, Washington.

Glenn Simmons is a veteran homesteader and educator who lives in Scio, Oregon. He teaches classes in self-sufficiency and has written a self-published book on homesteading called *From the Ground Up*.

Warren Snyder is a wildlife research biologist for the Colorado Division of Wildlife based in Sterling, Colorado.

Kent Whealy is the founder and co-director, with his wife, Diane, of Seed Savers Exchange. They operate a 57-acre farm north of Decorah, Iowa, where thousands of endangered vegetables and hundreds of old-time apple varieties are raised. They also raise rare poultry and cattle.

Russell Wilkerson is a fourth-generation rancher in Cambridge, Idaho. The Wilkerson Ranch won the 1991 Farm Heritage Award from the National Trust for Historic Preservation.

Mike Willett is a tree fruit specialist with the Washington State University Cooperative Extension Service in Yakima, Washington.

CHAPTER 10

Exercise and Sports

Tips to Guide
Your Get-Up-and-Go

Whether you're aiming to improve your health, enhance your looks, lose a few pounds, or get lean, keen muscles, this chapter is for you. Our experts' tips and tricks will help you enjoy exercise that is safe, comfortable, and time-efficient. Best of all, this is the kind of exercise that can add a real spark of pleasure to your day.

Need help choosing a bicycle, hiking shoes, a health club, or indoor equipment? Confused about what and when to eat or drink for peak athletic performance? Wondering whether you should exercise if you're prone to asthma? Looking for the best sit-ups, tips for starting a weight-training program, or advice for over-40 runners? Need some tension-easing stretches? You'll find answers to all these questions and many more in this chapter. (And to balance all our up-to-the-minute information, we've got some dandy exercise recommendations first published in 1903!)

Whatever your age or fitness level, you're likely to feel healthier, live longer, and get more enjoyment out of everything you do if you add some regular exercise to your schedule. This chapter will help get you *and* your exercise program in shape.

Exercise: For the Health of It

Avoid People-Movers

"You can't delay aging," says Walter Bortz II, M.D., a gerontologist and associate professor at Stanford University School of Medicine in Stanford, California and author of *We Live Too Short and Die Too Long.* "Nobody knows how to stop time. But you can absolutely undo the adverse effects of muscle disuse. Throw off the bedclothes and get out and exercise."

Dr. Bortz suggests that you find activities that you're using automated techniques to perform, and substitute muscle power. "Don't ride the golf course in a golf cart. Walk the course instead. Don't take the escalator at the airport. Climb the stairs! Anytime you see something that attempts to move you, say that you're going to move yourself."

Run Less, Get Fit

What is the biggest mistake people make when they're running for fitness?

"They run like they're training for competition," says veteran runner Joe Henderson, of Eugene, Oregon, West Coast editor of *Runner's World* magazine and author of 14 books on running. If you're running for fitness, according to Henderson, all you need are 2 to 3 miles of track or road work, three to five days a week.

Hearts Don't Know the Diff

When weather conditions interfere with a running program, use a treadmill indoors to simulate running outdoors, suggests Henderson.

Of course there's slight sensory deprivation: You might miss the scenery, sights, and smells of the great outdoors. But apart from that, "your heart doesn't know the difference," says Henderson. "It craves the activity—it's not particular about how you get it."

The H2O Alternative

Running in water is a great training alternative, especially if you're recovering from an impact injury, says Henderson.

You'll need a flotation device made for water running, such as the Wet Vest or Aqua Jogger, to keep you upright while you churn up the laps. Talk about easy on the ankles: There's no impact, because your feet don't touch bottom.

If you stay in the pool as long as you normally run, you'll get a good training session. And if you're traveling, remember to take the flotation device in your suitcase: You can kick up the miles in the hotel pool.

FYI

BEST BETS FOR BURNING FAT

Want to burn fat?

If you consistently exercise aerobically, your fat-metabolizing system gets ever more efficient. In fact, it burns with a higher flame even at rest.

Exercise physiologist Greg Phillips, author of *The THINK LIGHT! Low-Fat Living Plan,* explains, "The actual amount of fat you burn during a typical aerobic workout isn't substantial. Most of the benefit comes when you exercise consistently for an extended period of time."

As Phillips explains, people metabolize fat during the workout *and* for hours afterward. "In the long run, you become a better fat burner."

Phillips recommends the following exercise plan to help burn up fat in the most effective manner.

- Exercise four to five times a week.
- Each time you exercise, continue for 30 to 60 minutes.
- You want low to moderate intensity: Go for a heart rate that's roughly 60 percent of maximum.
- Exercise using the large muscles in a rhythmic and continuous manner. Walking, jogging, cross-country skiing, bicycling, aerobic dancing, or rowing are ideal.

In addition, Phillips recommends some muscle strengthening exercise to preserve or increase your muscle mass. "Muscle is the tissue that does most of the fat burning. Focus on aerobic activity, but try to build in some strengthening work as well."

Indoor Turbo-Action

If you already own a bicycle, you don't need to invest in a second, stationary bike, says JoAnn Dahlkoetter, Ph.D., a psychologist in Redwood City, California, who specializes in sports psychology and stress management. Turn your *outside* bike into an *inside* bike with a turbo-trainer, also called a wind trainer or track stand.

Just quick-release the front wheel and fit the front forks into the turbo-trainer frame. The back wheel runs on a roller that provides resistance. "It just takes a minute to set it up," says Dr. Dahlkoetter, "and you're ready to go."

Tennis for Fitness, Not Fierceness

To get the most fitness benefits from tennis, don't play competitively.

"Playing to *win* in tennis is not very good aerobic exercise," notes Larry Kassman, M.D., of Waterville, Maine, a multisport recreational athlete who cycled cross-country in 1982. The reason: In highly competitive tennis you're always trying to put the ball away. If you want tennis to be an aerobic exercise, you have to keep the ball in play.

Also, play singles, so you run more. Your best bet, says Dr. Kassman, is to choose a partner of the same ability level and with the same exercise goals.

Martial Your Forces

"There are as many kinds of martial arts as there are body types," says Lisa Frazer, a martial arts instructor from Walnut Creek, California, with a third-degree black belt in jujitsu. Some demand great strength and flexibility, others are gentler and more comfortable for people with physical limitations. T'ai chi is often recommended for people getting back in shape after back or knee injuries.

"Martial arts is 75 percent mental and 25 percent physical," says Frazer. "It stresses the unity between the mind and the body. It allows people to surpass the limits they thought they had."

If you're interested in taking up martial arts, Frazer suggests you look at your goals and your strengths and weaknesses. Then visit studios, talk to instructors, and watch classes. "See what's going on. See how physical it is. Look at the relationship between the instructor and students."

Halting and Healing the Hurts

Warm Up First, Stretch Second

Warming up and stretching are two different activities. Both are recommended, but there's definitely a preferred order.

"Warming up does not involve stretching," says Mona Shangold, M.D., professor of obstetrics and gynecology at Hahnemann University in Philadelphia and author of *The Complete Sports Medicine Book for Women* and *Women and Exercise: Physiology and Sports Medicine.* "When you're warming up, you're raising the muscle temperature by using the muscles. The purpose of stretching, on the other hand, is to elongate the muscles."

The bottom line? Warm up your muscles with light rhythmic movement *before* you stretch. "Stretching muscles when they are cold may lead to a greater risk of injury," warns Dr. Shangold.

FYI

INJURY PREVENTION TIPS

Make changes gradually to avoid injury, advises James G. Garrick, M.D., medical director of the Center for Sports Medicine at Saint Francis Memorial Hospital in San Francisco. Here are some examples of changes that can cause injury from overuse.

Running and cycling: A sudden increase in mileage.

Swimming: Using a new stroke for the whole workout.

Racquetball: Playing in a tournament when you're used to playing twice a week.

Golf, skiing, and tennis: Going on vacation and starting to play every day, when you're used to playing only on weekends.

In all sports, it pays to buy your new shoes before the old ones wear out. "Do part of the workout in the new shoes, then switch to the old shoes for the rest of it," recommends Dr. Garrick. "By the time the old ones are worn out, they're abnormal. Going into new shoes is like putting a wedge in your shoe."

High-mileage runners are especially vulnerable to change. "If you're running 70 or 80 miles a week, you have to be careful about changing from used to new shoes, even if it's the same brand," says Dr. Garrick. "You have to be careful about adding hills. You're probably working close enough to your maximum capabilities that you can get tipped over the edge really easily."

The 5-Minute Cool-Down

Done exercising? Don't just stop. Cool down gradually by continuing to move, but with smaller, slower movements, advises Dr. Shangold.

By cooling down gradually—for about 5 minutes—you avoid dizziness. This routine also helps to protect the heart from irregular heartbeats.

Heads Don't Roll

Stretch the neck by tipping the ears towards the shoulder, then dropping the head forward, says Daniel Kosich, Ph.D., president of EXERFIT Lifestyle consulting in Albuquerque, New Mexico.

Don't let the head roll backward, warns Dr. Kosich, or you may put too much pressure on the areas where the nerves exit from the vertebrae. "These nerves are critical, not only for movement, but even more so for heart function." Reduce risk to a minimum by not dropping your head backwards.

Squat Like a Native

Deep knee bends are bad, but squats are fine if you do them correctly, according to Lockridge.

Here's how:

1. Squat with your legs wide apart and the buttocks hanging down.
2. When you get up, lead with the head, not the buttocks.

"What's wrong with our deep knee bends is that our heels come up off the floor with the knees pointed forward. That action smashes the inside of the knee from the inside," says Lockridge.

Rising from a squatting position, pull your chin in slightly and rise straight up. Keep your feet flat on the floor.

Back Up a Minute

Sore back? Here are some strategies to soothe your flip-side, suggested by Alice Lockridge, exercise physiologist at Pro-Fit in Seattle, Washington.

To stretch the back, sit down with crossed legs, then gradually bend forward, rounding your back. Or stand with slightly bent knees and round your back, with your hands on your thighs for support.

"The back isn't meant to hold all your weight," observes Lockridge. People with long backs should be particularly careful, she adds, since they have more chance of injury.

Lockridge adds: "Don't ever do two functions of your back at once. Don't bend and twist. Don't touch the toes and bounce. Don't lean sideways and forward."

To stretch back muscles, sit cross-legged and bend forward. Another good stretching exercise for the back: Bend your knees, lean forward, and place your hands on your thighs.

For Asthma: Second Wind

If you suffer from exercise-induced asthma and you think you have to abandon your workout when it triggers an attack, here's good news. Shortly after an exercise-induced attack may be the *best* time to exercise, advises Neil F. Gordon, M.D., Ph.D., director of exercise physiology at the Cooper Institute for Aerobics Research in Dallas, Texas. Dr. Gordon specializes in exercise prescription for people with chronic medical conditions.

"Once a bout of exercise triggers an attack and you stop exercising to recover from it," Dr. Gordon explains, "you can return to exercise within the next hour—possibly up to 4 hours later—secure in the knowledge that another attack is unlikely."

If another attack does occur, it will be milder. The period after the initial attack is called the refractory period, when the threat of a follow-up attack is greatly reduced. Stop just long enough to recover (with medication, if necessary), then get back to your workout.

FYI

HOW DRY AM I?

Don't wait until you get thirsty before drinking water, says triathlete and author Ellen Coleman, clinical dietitian at Riverside Community Hospital in Riverside, California. By the time you feel thirst, you're over 2 percent dehydrated—more than enough to impair your athletic performance and possibly lead to overheating.

Don't go by thirst to determine how *much* to drink, either. If you drink just enough to quench your thirst, you're likely to replenish only two-thirds of what you need.

To avoid dehydration, Coleman recommends this watering schedule.

- Drink 8 to 12 ounces of water 10 to 15 minutes before moderate exercise of an hour or less.
- Drink 14 to 20 ounces of water 10 to 15 minutes before running an hour or more, or before any endurance event.
- Drink 3 to 6 ounces of water every 10 to 15 minutes during exercise.
- Drink 16 ounces after exercise for every pound lost. (Weigh yourself before and after your workout to know how much water you sweated away.)

Avoid the Wheezes

Exercise-induced asthma is often triggered by high-intensity exercise that lasts longer than 6 minutes, says Dr. Gordon. Here are his tips for lessening the risk of an attack—without sacrificing your workout.

- Avoid exercising in cold, dry air. If you must, cover your mouth with a scarf or face mask, or breathe only through your nose.
- Warm up for at least 10 minutes—longer if you need to. A long warm-up creates a refractory period, leaving you less at risk for an attack.
- Lower the intensity by exercising less strenuously, but for a longer time.
- If you must exercise at high intensity, do so intermittently. Limit your high intensity to 30- to 60-second bouts, resting or lowering your intensity in between.

First Aid Kit: Diapers and Frozen Peas

If you get injured playing sports or exercising, says James G. Garrick, M.D., medical director at the Center for Sports Medicine at Saint Francis Memorial Hospital in San Francisco and the author of *Peak Condition* and *Be Your Own Personal Trainer*, "Put ice and compression on the injury. If you can't get ice, compression is still good."

Dr. Garrick suggests using padding to localize the compression before wrapping the injury. "Put something smooshy under the wrap, like a couple of layers of disposable diapers. The padding fills in the hollows."

Dr. Garrick recommends icing with a sack of frozen peas or frozen corn. "It contours nicely, and you can reuse it."

Pain Is a Stop Sign

Never ignore pain or try to work out in spite of it. "That is a dangerous thing to do," warns Dr. Shangold of Hahnemann University. "Pain is always a signal that something is wrong. When you feel pain, stop exercising."

Heal Thyself

It is frustrating to wait for a sports injury to heal, but if you don't, it will just get worse. Dr. Shangold recommends the following steps for healing a sports injury.

1. Stop participating in the sport that caused the injury.
2. Avoid that sport until you can participate without pain.
3. Find another sport that you can practice without pain, so you can maintain your fitness level.
4. Correct the cause of the injury to avoid repeating it.

Rehab Riding

Cycling is great rehabilitation for many injuries, particularly those that come from pounding the pavement, says cyclist Dr. Larry Kassman. "There's no shock, so it's good for many knee and ankle injuries and many back problems. You can get good aerobic exercise without any wear and tear."

But it pays to be careful, he warns. Biking can make certain kinds of knee problems worse. And improper biking—such as pedaling in too high a gear—can *create* knee problems. Check with your physician before you hop on a bike to work out an old injury.

Cycling through Carpal Tunnel

Biking may make carpal tunnel syndrome worse, because you're leaning on your wrists. To prevent a worsening condition, relax the pressure on your wrists and shift position as much as possible.

Should you switch to upright handlebars? Dr. Kassman says no. Drop handlebars allow you several choices of position. With upright handlebars, you're stuck in one position, he notes.

Take a Load off Your Hands—For Safety

Will hand weights during aerobics help you get fit faster? "They'll only help you get injured faster," says Carl Powell, an international master aerobics instructor from Atlanta, Georgia, who has taught exercise to overweight, formerly sedentary people enrolled in the Optifast program at St. Mary's Hospital in San Francisco.

Weighting down your arms while performing fast aerobic movements can cause rotator cuff injuries—painful problems in the shoulder.

"Weight training and aerobic training are two separate entities," says Powell. "You've got to do both, and they've got to be separated. There is no quick fix."

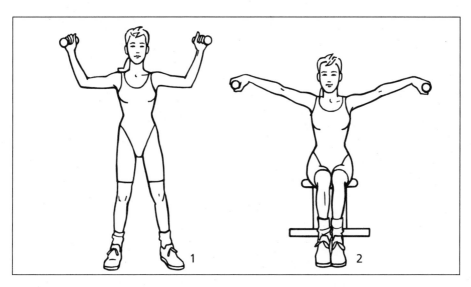

When doing lateral raises (see tip below), lead with the thumbs up (1), not with the back of the hand leading up (2).

Lateral Raises? Thumbs Up!

Lateral raises are standard lifting exercises performed with dumbbells to help strengthen the shoulders. But many people do lateral raises incorrectly because they lead with their "knuckles up," according to Pro-Fit's exercise expert Alice Lockridge.

The correct way? Leading with the *thumb up*, lift your arms from a horizontal position up to your shoulders.

"It's old-fashioned and hurtful and wrong to have the back of your hand lead up," says Lockridge. "When you lift your arm up, out to the side, and your elbow is above your wrist, you're apt to hurt the inside of your shoulder." Lockridge says if you lead with the thumb up, "the proper form follows automatically."

What's Your Line-Up?

When you're working on strength training, it's important, for safety's sake, to practice correct alignment at all times, according to EXERFIT's Dr. Daniel Kosich. Dr. Kosich says these points are the most important ones to practice.

- Shoulders at equal height, not one raised higher than the other.
- Chin in neutral in a comfortable position, not jutted out or pressed into the chest.
- Back neutral, not arched.
- Abdominals and buttocks slightly tightened.
- Knees slightly bent.
- Feet about shoulder-width apart.

Possible Hazards: Body Positions

According to Lorna Francis, Ph.D., a physical educator and researcher who teaches exercise instructors at San Diego State University, a number of body positions are just plain hazardous and may result in injury. Avoid the following whenever you are working out.

- Knees forward of the toes.
- Lifting the arms overhead with the palms down.
- Locking the joints.
- Bending forward without support.

Over 40? Less Is Better

If you're a runner over 40, your performance might rival that of younger runners, but chances are you'll get hurt faster and heal more slowly, according to *Runner's World* editor Joe Henderson. "The one penalty of age that seems almost universal is that your recovery rate slows down."

Avoid the risk of injury by taking more rest days. In your twenties, you might have needed only one day off a week. But from your forties up, says Henderson, you'll run safer if you take two or three days off a week.

Fitting In Exercise...Anywhere!

Deplane—And Take a Hike

About to take a plane flight from here to nowheresville, with one or two layovers in between?

You can burn calories *and* decrease travel stress during an airport layover, says David Essel of Sarasota, Florida, a business speaker and producer of workout videos who spends 40 out of 52 weeks a year in transit. Pull on your walking shoes, stash your carry-on luggage in a locker, and hoof it around the terminal. "You can burn 150 to 300 calories just walking around the terminal while you wait for a plane," says Essel.

A Workout with a View

You're in your hotel room with only 10 minutes to spare. Not enough time for a workout...Right?

Wrong, says Essel, a specialist in "portable" workouts.

"You can do a program in 10 minutes with no equipment." He suggests these exercises for a 10-minute workout that will reduce stress, increase mental performance, and help you feel better about yourself.

Squats. To do squats, start with your feet placed shoulder-width apart and your hands resting on your hips (1). Slowly lower your body into a squatting position as you bring both arms out in front (2). When your buttocks are a little above knee-height, hold that position. Then return to a standing position, bringing your hands to your hips.

Heel raises using the phone book. To do heel raises, stand with the balls of your feet on the edge of a thin phone book, with your heels on the floor (1). Raise your body, lifting your heels from the floor, and hold (2). Then slowly lower your heels to touch the floor.

Triceps dips using the chair. To do these triceps dips, place your hands on the front edge of the seat of the chair. Lower yourself to the position shown, then push up again.

Modified push-ups on the floor or against the wall. To do modified push-ups, lie face down with your knees bent, your feet crossed, and your hands flat on the floor just outside your shoulders (1). Push your body away from the floor, extending your arms without locking the elbows (2). Hold that position, then slowly lower your body to the floor.

Abdominal crunches on the rug. Lie on the floor with your feet on a chair and your arms crossed on your chest (1). Raise your shoulders off the floor (2), hold, then slowly return to starting position.

Shrug Off Office Stress

Don't just stretch after exercising—stretch to release tension while you're working at your desk, too. Bob Anderson, of Palmer Lake, Colorado, is the author of *Stretching*. He has taught stretching to the Denver Broncos, New York Jets, and Los Angeles Dodgers, and recommends this shoulder shrug.

1. Bring the shoulder points up toward the earlobes.
2. Hold the shoulders up for 3 to 4 seconds.
3. Let go and relax the shoulders down.

"The shoulders are designed to do just one thing—hang," Anderson says. "You breathe a lot better and you have a lot more relaxation in your upper body when your shoulders are hanging down. A shoulder shrug is like yawning with your shoulders."

Working Up to Working Out

Get the Doc's Okay

Be sure to check with your physician before beginning an exercise program, says James M. Rippe, M.D., cardiologist and director of the Exercise, Physiology, and Nutrition Lab at the University of Massachusetts Medical School in Worcester, Massachusetts. Your doctor may recommend an exercise tolerance test if:

- You have been sedentary.
- You are over 45.
- You smoke cigarettes.
- You have high blood pressure.
- You have elevated cholesterol.

Catch a Racing Pulse

Wondering how *much* to exercise?

One way to gauge your fitness level is to clock how quickly your elevated heart rate drops after you stop exercising, according to Dr. Shangold of Hahnemann University. A fit person's heart rate returns to normal quickly after an all-out exercise session. Here's Dr. Shangold's recovery rate test.

1. Exercise maximally for at least 3 minutes.
2. Immediately after stopping, record your pulse for 5 seconds. Multiply that number by 12 to get your heart rate per minute. (Don't take your pulse for more than 5 seconds, because you want to find your rate before your pulse has a chance to slow down.)
3. Wait 60 seconds, then do this pulse check again. The second reading should be appreciably lower than the first.

4. Subtract the second number from the first to get the difference. As you get fitter, the difference between the two should increase.

Pumping Pencil

Once you've started exercising regularly, motivate yourself to continue: Write your workout plans in pencil in your appointment book or exercise log, suggests sports psychologist Dr. JoAnn Dahlkoetter. Be specific, including the number of miles or the amount of time you plan to do. Then when you complete your exercise session, write over your entry in pen.

One Step at a Time

If you're just starting an aerobic dance program, don't try to do the whole class the first time. "Do the warm-up and the first 10 minutes of the aerobic portion, then just walk around the room," suggests Dr. James Garrick. of the Center for Sports Medicine at Saint Francis Memorial Hospital in San Francisco.

Join the class again for the floor exercises. Each successive day, add on 2 more minutes to the aerobic portion. In two weeks you'll be doing the whole class safely. This system also works with a home workout video tape.

FYI

CLUB CHECKOUT

Thinking of joining a health club? Carl Powell, international master aerobics instructor from Atlanta, Georgia, offers this checklist for choosing a club.

- Make sure the instructors are certified. Certification means that the instructors have been educated and tested on their exercise knowledge.
- Make sure the club has all the services you need.
- Be cautious if a club gives you a high-pressure sales pitch. Even if you think it's right, *don't* sign on the dotted line the first time you visit.
- Visit the club at the time you want to exercise. Don't visit on your lunch hour if you'll want to work out at night. If you need to fight the crowds to use the facilities, it's better to find that out before you join.
- Check the cleanliness of the locker rooms.
- Talk to the trainers. See how helpful and informed they are.
- Phone at a busy time and ask a question. If the club is managed well, the staff will be polite, friendly, and helpful to each person who calls.

Do-Si-Do and Waltz to Fitness

Here's a novel idea for getting started on your aerobic exercise: Grab your honey and go out dancing! According to workout video producer David Essel, you can burn as many calories ballroom dancing and square dancing as in a brisk, 30-minute walk. Here's the catch, though—don't take breaks in a 30-minute dance period if you want the maximum aerobic benefits.

Don't Run Wild

How much should you run if you're just beginning? Running expert Joe Henderson advises that you begin by walking *or* running for half an hour, three to five days a week.

First see if you're capable of walking steadily for 30 minutes. If that's easy, add some running to the walking. "Gradually increase the amount of running and decrease the amount of walking, until you've reached the point of running 3 miles in the 30 minutes," says Henderson.

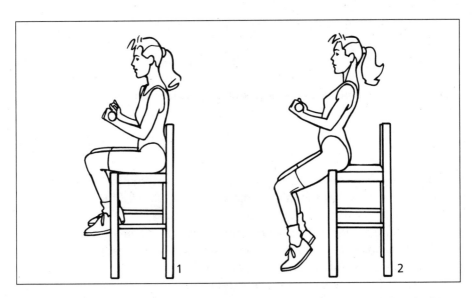

Use proper technique when doing strength training (see tip below). For the biceps curl, maintain upright posture (1). Avoid leaning back (2), which puts undesirable strain on the lower back.

Proper Pumping

Just starting a strength training program? "Be careful not to overdo it," says exercise physiology expert Dr. Daniel Kosich. "Spend three or four weeks just learning proper form and technique." Instead of trying to increase the weight-load at each session, Dr. Kosich recommends that you work on these basics.

- Learn the proper technique for each movement.
- Concentrate on isolating the muscle that you're strengthening.
- Avoid cheating—using extraneous muscles to accomplish the lift, such as throwing your body into the move, or leaning back to help on the biceps curl.
- Learn a breathing rhythm. Keep your mouth open, and don't hold your breath and exert force. Exhale on the effort and inhale on the recovery.

Find Your Comfort Zone

"Exercise is one of the very best ways of reducing anxiety and tension and improving your mood," says cardiologist Dr. James Rippe. And you don't need to exercise intensely to make this happen: Dr. Rippe has observed that people who exercise at a comfortable, enjoyable level end up feeling more relaxed.

If you don't experience decreased anxiety and improved mood, you may be exercising too hard or too competitively, says Dr. Rippe. An exercise that requires hard concentration may not be right for you.

Also, any exercise that involves risks can make you more anxious, rather than less so. "Look at it piece by piece to see what you might be doing wrong if you're not experiencing reductions in anxiety and tension."

Pointers from the Pros

Say Ahhhhhh

When people are under stress, they unconsciously clench their jaws, intensifying the stress.

"Keep your face relaxed if you want the rest of your body to follow along," says stretching expert Bob Anderson. "The key area for relaxation is the jaw. When you're stretching, running, cycling, or sitting at the computer, you don't want your teeth to touch."

Fuel Your Engines

For energy, stamina, and muscle strength, athletes should make sure 60 to 70 percent of their diet comes from carbohydrates, recommends triathlete Ellen Coleman, clinical dietitian at Riverside Community Hospital in Riverside, California, and author of *Eating for Endurance*.

A diet high in complex carbohydrates enhances athletic performance because the muscles need them to make muscle glycogen. If you don't get enough carbohydrates, your muscles will lose their glycogen stores, resulting in fatigue.

"When muscle glycogen stores deplete, fit people slow down and unfit people have to stop," says Coleman. So be sure to eat plenty of complex carbohydrates such as grains, legumes, pasta, potatoes, fruits, and vegetables.

Breakfast before Exercising?

How important is eating before an early-morning workout? Not very, if you exercise for an hour or less, says Coleman.

However, if you get dizzy from working out on an empty stomach, have a small meal of carbohydrates, such as bread, cereal, or fruit, an hour or so before exercising.

And if your workout is going to last more than an hour, be sure to eat a high-carbohydrate breakfast. Don't skip it, says Coleman, or you'll sacrifice performance.

Better Seating

For women who think cycling is a pain in the derriere, try a new seat.

"Get a woman's seat," suggests cyclist Dr. Larry Kassman. "It makes all the difference in the world."

A good bicycle usually comes with a good *man's* seat. But women are built differently. A woman's bike seat is designed to accommodate a woman's wider pelvis and make cycling more comfortable.

If you're a woman buying a new bike, ask the bike shop to exchange the seat: You probably won't be charged extra. "If you end up buying it," says Dr. Kassman, "it costs very little, and it's the best investment you can make for riding comfort."

Stretch a Leg

Just got a new bicycle?

Before you ride, adjust your seat height, says world-class endurance athlete Dr. JoAnn Dahlkoetter. "It's important to have your seat high enough so that when your foot is at the bottom of the pedal stroke, your knee is slightly bent." If your leg is completely stretched out, it pulls the tendons behind the knee.

Fasten Your Feetbelts

Riding a bicycle—or an exercise bike?

Be sure to use toe straps or clip-in pedals, says Dr. Dahlkoetter. "You want your whole foot attached to the pedal, first for stability, so you stay on the pedals better, and second so you can get a full stroke all the way around the pedal."

Each part of the stroke uses different muscle groups when your foot is attached to the pedal. By working your muscles all the way around the pedal, your legs will get a better workout—and so will your heart.

FYI

A BICYCLE BUILT FOR YOU

How do you choose a bike these days, with all the choices available? "First, decide what you're going to use the bike for," says Larry Kassman, M.D., a multisport recreational athlete from Waterville, Maine, who cycled cross-country in 1982. Decide where your interests lie—then choose the bike that best suits your needs.

Racing bikes. These are made for riding fast. They have narrow tires and turn easily but don't absorb shock well, especially when loaded down. They're not recommended for touring or riding off the road. Get this kind of bike only if you plan to race, suggests Dr. Kassman.

Sport bikes. This type is made for long-distance touring, camping, and recreational distance riding. They used to be called "10-speeds," although now they're more likely to have 12, 18, or 21 speeds, making hill climbing easier. Their additional gears and slightly thicker tires make them more comfortable than racing bikes.

Mountain bikes. These are also called off-road or all-terrain bikes and are versatile for hills, dirt roads, and city riding conditions. Although they don't go fast, they have plenty of low gears for hill climbing, thick tires for traction and shock absorption, and upright handlebars. "They're excellent for riding over bumpy roads, potholes, or glass in the road," says Dr. Kassman. "They don't get flat tires easily. They're made for comfortable riding and bad roads."

Inventing a Better Sit-Up

The best sit-up is a curl-up, says Dr. Garrick. Lie down with your knees bent and your feet flat on the floor, with your arms behind your head or crossed on your chest.

"You don't have to go all the way up. Just clear your shoulders from the floor. Curl up slowly, hesitate at the top, and then come down as slowly as you went up," he says. The traditional sit-ups aren't as effective for flattening the abdominals.

Curl-ups are most important because they strengthen the back, says Dr. Garrick. "If you get a flat stomach, too, that's just an additional benefit.'

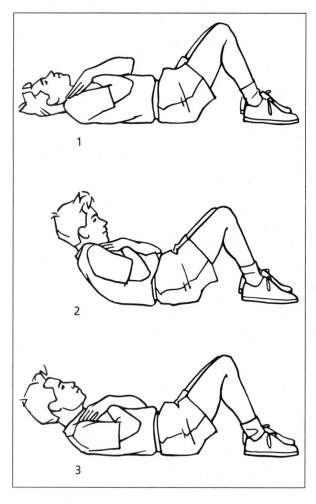

To do curl-ups, begin by lying on your back with your knees bent, your feet flat, and your hands crossed on your chest (1). Press your lower back to the floor and "curl" your shoulder blades off the floor (2), keeping your chin tucked close to your chest. Then lower your shoulders to the floor again (3).

Mind Your Muscles

When you work out with weights or other resistance devices, pay special attention to form to be safe and get the most power from each pump.

Dr. Lorna Francis of San Diego State University suggests these resistance training guidelines.

1. Warm up the muscles by taking them through their range of motion without weights. Then stretch.

2. Choose the correct amount of resistance. Choose a weight you can lift at least 8 times, but less than 12.
3. Perform one set of 8 to 12 repetitions.
4. Move slowly and with control.
5. Use the muscle's full range of motion. If you can't, the weight is too heavy. (If you use music, keep the tempo slow enough to perform the move completely, no more than 130 beats per minute.)
6. Maintain a neutral posture. Don't throw your body into the movement—move just the muscle you're working.
7. Create a balanced workout by working both sides of the joint. For example, if you do the biceps (front of the upper arm), also do the triceps (back of the upper arm). If you do the quadriceps (front of the thigh), also do the hamstrings (back of the thigh).
8. Inhale and exhale with each repetition. Don't hold your breath.
9. Lower the weight even more slowly than you lifted it. Control the weight—don't let the weight control you.

FYI

SHOES AND SOCKS FOR DEWS AND ROCKS

If you plan to hike over rocks, cross raging streams, or trudge through swamps and snow, you'll need heavy, sturdy boots that you can weatherproof, says Pat Lyons, R.N., an outdoor recreational athlete. Start hiking in them a month before your backpacking trip.

Running or walking shoes are fine for hiking on park trails with a few hills. They don't do well on steep trails, however. "The soles aren't made for dealing with steepness," Lyons cautions. "Downhill is the problem: You can slide and fall."

The best shoes for steep trails will have soles designed for good traction. When you try them on, wear the same kind of socks you'll hike in. A good sporting goods or camping store can recommend sport socks that wick away moisture. Wool used to be the best, but now some of the synthetic fibers, such as those used in Thor-Lo sports socks, may keep you even more comfortable.

"The most important thing is that the sock and shoe combination really fits so that you're not getting friction or pressure points," says Lyons. "Take moleskin along so that if you do get blisters, you can stop and do repair on your feet immediately."

Exercise for the Overweight

Equipment Expertise

If you're an overweight exerciser looking for home exercise equipment, try this advice from fitness consultant Gail Johnston, executive director of Curves Unlimited in Walnut Creek, California.

- Look for equipment that can tolerate greater weight. Cheap equipment won't do it. Be cautious about ordering equipment that you can't try out first.
- Considering a cross-country ski machine? First check out the track width. Is there enough space between the skis? You want to be able to move your thighs without uncomfortable friction.
- Exercise bikes: Ask to exchange the standard seat for a larger size.
- A rowing machine makes sense if you can get up and down comfortably. If not, you're probably better off with another type of exercise equipment to start.

"The bottom line," says Johnson, "is don't buy a piece of exercise equipment because it's good for you. Buy it because every aspect of it feels comfortable, and you feel safe and secure and well supported when you're on it."

Impact: Less Is Better

Johnson suggests that overweight exercisers should avoid high-impact activities, such as running, jumping, and high-impact aerobics. "But experiment with any other activity that interests you," says Johnson, "such as baseball, recreational dance, or t'ai chi."

Stay Cool

Many overweight exercisers work out in sweats. But Johnson warns that sweats are heavy and can lead to discomfort and overheating. "Wear light, comfortable, loose-fitting clothing that breathes," she advises.

Larger Needs

If you're an overweight person, be careful about taking a class designed for the average-sized exerciser, says Pat Lyons, R.N., coauthor of *Great Shape: The First Fitness Guide for Large Women.*

"A woman with a bigger body is already working out with weights. She doesn't have to do as much to get her heart rate up."

Look for a class for overweight people, or join up with friends and dance together in a room. "That's as much exertion as a larger body needs," says Lyons. "We don't need to jump or do strenuous moves."

Past Performance

THOSE WERE THE DAYS

Just in case you think physical fitness is something new, here's an entry from *Ladies Home Companion* published in 1903:

PHYSICAL CULTURE

Games, such as rowing, skating, lawn tennis, handball, boxing, fencing, polo, curling, quoits, football, golf, baseball, basketball, bowling, and all gymnastic exercises are very beneficial. Such games bring the muscles into proper action and thus cause them to be fully developed. They expand and strengthen the chest; they cause a due circulation of the blood, making it bound merrily through the blood vessels, and thus diffuse health and happiness in its course. If games were more patronized in youth, so many miserable, nervous, useless creatures would not abound. Unfortunately, in this enlightened age, we commence at the wrong end—we put the cart before the horse—we begin by cultivating the mind, and we leave the body to be taken care of afterward. The two are inseparable. They should be trained together....Exercise in the open air, take long walks and vigorous exercise, using care not to over-do. Housework will prove a panacea for many of the ills which flesh is heir to. One hour's exercise at the washtub is of far more value, from a physical standpoint, than hours at the piano.

The Experts

Bob Anderson, of Palmer Lake Colorado, is the author of *Stretching*, as well as videos, charts, and computer programs about the stretching program described in the book. He has taught stretching to the Denver Broncos, New York Jets, and Los Angeles Dodgers, and has set up stretching programs for many college football teams.

Walter Bortz II, M.D., is a gerontologist and associate professor at Stanford University School of Medicine in Stanford, California. The cochairman of the American Medical Association–American Nursing Association (AMA-ANA) Task Force on Aging, and a marathon runner, Dr. Bortz is the author of *We Live Too Short and Die Too Long*.

Ellen Coleman is a clinical dietitian at Riverside Community Hospital in Riverside, California, and holds a master's degree in public health. She is the nutrition columnist for *Sports Medicine Digest* and is the author of *Eating for Endurance*.

JoAnn Dahlkoetter, Ph.D., a psychologist in Redwood City, California, specializes in sports psychology and stress management. She is a world-class endurance athlete.

David Essel, of Sarasota, Florida, is a frequent presenter for IDEA, the Association of Fitness Professionals, and a keynote speaker for numerous business meetings and conventions. He has produced and has been featured in more than ten workout videos. As a frequent traveler (he is on the road 40 weeks out of the year), he specializes in portable workouts.

Lorna Francis, Ph.D., is a physical educator and researcher at San Diego State University in California.

Lisa Frazer, of Walnut Creek, California, is a martial arts instructor with a third-degree black belt in jujitsu.

James G. Garrick, M.D., is medical director of the Center for Sports Medicine at Saint Francis Memorial Hospital in San Francisco and the author of *Peak Condition* and *Be Your Own Personal Trainer*.

Neil F. Gordon, M.D., Ph.D., is director of exercise physiology at the Cooper Institute for Aerobics Research in Dallas, Texas. He is a specialist in exercise prescription for people with chronic medical conditions.

Joe Henderson lives in Eugene, Oregon. He is the West Coast editor of *Runner's World* magazine, a marathon runner, and the author of *Run Farther, Run Faster, Total Fitness: Training for Life,* and other books on running and fitness.

Gail Johnston, executive director of Curves Unlimited in Walnut Creek, California, specializes in marketing and education for the large exerciser.

Larry Kassman, M.D., is a multisport recreational athlete from Waterville, Maine, who cycled cross-country in 1982.

Daniel Kosich, Ph.D., is president of EXERFIT Lifestyle consulting in Albuquerque, New Mexico. Author of many articles on exercise physiology, Dr. Kosich is a consultant to the Jimmie Heuga Multiple Sclerosis Center.

Alice Lockridge is an exercise physiologist at Pro-Fit in Seattle, Washington.

Pat Lyons, R.N., of Oakland, California, is the coauthor of *Great Shape: The First Fitness Guide for Large Women*.

Greg Phillips, an exercise physiologist and weight management specialist and president of Speaking of Titans, Inc., in Durango, Colorado, is the author of *The THINK LIGHT! Low-fat Living Plan*.

Carl Powell, based in Atlanta, Georgia, is an international master aerobics instructor who has done three workout videos. He has taught exercise to overweight, formerly sedentary people enrolled in the Optifast program at St. Mary's Hospital in San Francisco, California.

James M. Rippe, M.D., a cardiologist, is director of the Exercise, Physiology, and Nutrition Lab at the University of Massachusetts Medical School in Worcester, Massachusetts.

Mona Shangold, M.D., is professor of obstetrics and gynecology at Hahnemann University in Philadelphia, Pennsylvania, and is the author of *The Complete Sports Medicine Book for Women* and *Women and Exercise: Physiology and Sports Medicine.*

CHAPTER 11

Clothing

The Choice and Care
of What You Wear

Clothing has been part of the human experience since we first roamed the earth.

From fig leaves to primitive fur cloaks, from The Gap to Gucci, fashion is much like fine art—a reflection of a society and its values, economy, lifestyle, and beliefs.

Clothing also expresses who you are and how you feel about yourself. Whether you're shopping, browsing through catalogs or making something for yourself, your choices express your individuality. Of course, trends and fads come and go, and often it's hard to decide whether the style that's *au courant* is also a style that suits you personally. But whether you decide to stay with the traditional, go with the new, or combine the two, the clothes you wear are distinctly *you*.

Winding up the twentieth century, we have more choice in fabrics and styles than ever before. During any shopping spree, consumers are exposed to a varied world of colors and chemistry. The natural fabrics are still with us, of course, but now there are thousands of different fibers, blends, dyes, fabric constructions, and finishing techniques.

If this makes for great shopping, it sometimes makes for great confusion when it comes time to clean the clothes we've purchased. What should be dry cleaned? What needs to be hand washed? And which clothes require *special* handling?

In this chapter, you'll find tips on purchase, care, handling, storage, cleaning—as well as some great hints on fashion, bargain-hunting, and packing for travel. Whether you're looking for better ways to care for the clothes you like best, or beginning to ponder a whole new wardrobe, here are some words of wisdom from the experts we consulted in the fields of fashion, cleaning, textiles, and conservation.

Stain-Free Clothing

Speed, the Best Defense against Stains

Treat stains *immediately* and your clothes will have a better fighting chance.

Kay Obendorf, Ph.D., professor and chairman of the Department of Textiles and Apparel at Cornell University in Ithaca, New York, says that a quick response to spills and dribbles is not only common sense but also very good chemistry.

Oil, wine, and other stain-makers oxidize if they're allowed to set on your clothes, according to Dr. Obendorf. Research has shown that the oxidation process actually changes the chemical composition of the cloth.

"Since stains can act as a dye," she says, "the longer a stain sits, the more difficult it will be to remove."

So treat any stained clothes as soon as you can. If you let them lie overnight, it may be too late! Before last night's fine burgundy wine sinks deeper into your lapel, get a head start on stains. Act now!

Give Your Clothes a Long-Life Boost

Everyday practices can help protect your investments in clothing. Here are some cautions from clothing experts.

- Don't press garments until they have been cleaned. Heat from an iron will set stains and perspiration, according to Daniel Eisen, chief garment analyst of the Neighborhood Cleaners Association in New York City, a dry cleaner entrusted with such garments as The Metropolitan Museum of Art's costume collection. Once set, those marks will be difficult or impossible to remove.
- Don't wear treasured garments when you get your hair permed or colored. Fumes from these chemicals can discolor and degrade some fabrics, according to Beth Minardi of Minardi Minardi Salon in New York City, a hair-color specialist and consultant for the Clairol Company.

- Wait until your underarm deodorant or antiperspirant has completely dried before putting on clothes. Chemicals in these products can cause fibers to weaken, according to Procter and Gamble spokesperson Marie-Laure Salvado of Cincinnati. They may also cause colors to change in some dyes.

FYI

TRY ANYTHING—BUT READ THIS FIRST!

Removing stains is a complex business, according to Velda Rankin, national program leader at the United States Department of Agriculture (USDA) Research Service, Washington, D.C. The problem, according to Rankin, is that "each substance, fiber, and fabric reacts differently."

To make sure your clothes get the special handling they deserve, here's how to proceed.

- Always read care labels, but proceed with caution anyway. Required by law, care labels are usually but not always accurate, says Karen Puffer, women's wear merchandising manager for BASF Fibers Division in New York City. According to Puffer and other experts, garments made abroad are especially likely to be mislabeled.
- Before trying any stain remedy, first test an inconspicuous part of the garment, says Norma Keyes, manager of textiles services laboratory for Cotton Incorporated, in Raleigh, North Carolina. She suggests using the inside of a hem, a pocket, or cuff.
- If you're dealing with an heirloom or a highly valued garment, you should consult a specialist in clothing care, according to Christine Paulocik, associate conservator at the Costume Institute of the Metropolitan Museum of Art in New York City. Rapid deterioration can occur if an old garment comes in contact with soap, tapwater, or bright sunlight. Since valued heirlooms need special cleaning and storage care, Paulocik recommends visiting a reputable dry cleaner who specializes in restoration work. Better yet, call your local museum for conservation tips and referrals.
- If you decide to have a valuable garment dry cleaned, first remove ornate buttons, fancy trims, and attached accessories.

If you follow care instructions printed on a label, and the garment is damaged, contact the manufacturer or the store, advises Keyes. "You definitely have a legitimate claim," she says.

Rx for Wool: Tips for Removing Stains and Spots

Getting stains and spots out of wool clothing requires special procedures. Here are some ways to attack some specific problems before they leave a permanent blotch on your wool garment.

Alcohol or food: Place a towel under the area of the stain. Gently rub carbonated water (club soda) toward the center.

Blood: Blot with a paste made with water and common starch. Soak through from back to front with soapy water and rinse.

Butter and grease: Sponge the area with a dry cleaning solvent such as Afta.

Chocolate: Sponge with soapy water. Then rinse.

Coffee and tea: Sponge with glycerine. If none is available, try warm water.

Egg: Scrape off as much as you can, then sponge with warm, soapy water and rinse.

Glue: Sponge with rubbing alcohol.

Ink: Immerse the garment in cold water.

Iodine: Treat with cool water followed by alcohol.

Iron rust: Sponge with a weak solution of oxalic acid until the stain disappears. Then sponge carefully with household ammonia and rinse with water.

Lipstick: This stain may often be erased by rubbing white bread over the area with a firm, gentle motion.

Mud: Let it dry. Then brush and sponge from back with soapy water.

Red wine: Immerse in cold water.

Road oil and tar: Sponge with a dry cleaning solvent, available from fabric and hardware stores.

Make Stains Disappear from Delicate Fabrics

Makeup is smudged across your fine silk dress, and dinner guests are due to arrive any minute. Dry cleaning fluid to the rescue, says Lynda Joy, a New York–based evening wear and bridal designer who does biannual runway shows at the Plaza Hotel.

If your organza is sullied, saturate it with a store-bought fluid like Afta, which can be found in many fabric stores and hardware stores. Joy has used it on last-minute occasions to get stains out of silks, bridal laces, taffeta, and shantung—as well as many designs with intricate beadwork.

Club Soda and Stains: A Bad Mix?

Many people believe in using seltzer or club soda to remove stains—and club soda does work on many fabrics. But think twice before using soda to take spots out of fine ties. Andy Tarshis, president of New York–based TieCrafters, which specializes in cleaning, restoring, and altering ties, says using club soda can lift more than just the stain. On men's ties, where dyes and prints are often unstable, "seltzers and club soda can blur the dyes."

Stains in That Tag-Sale Special?

If you want to wash and wear that fabulous "it's me" dress that you found at a yard sale, by all means give it a try. Jeanne McIvor, a New York fashion model who formerly operated a New England retail store for antique and restored clothing, has successfully practiced a slew of restoration tricks on cotton, linen, and wool over the years.

Take note, however: McIvor's methods are for "found" garments only—not for a valued heirloom. Results may vary. If you picked up a linen or cotton garment, and you're willing to take some chances, here's how.

1. Choose a sunny day.
2. Hand wash the garment in cool water, using a mild detergent.
3. Spritz stains with a mixture of water and fresh lemon juice.
4. Line dry the garment in the sun.

You can repeat the process as often as necessary until the stain comes out. McIvor says she has never noticed any visible deterioration.

Dry Clean or Wash?

Be Swayed by This Advice

Any suede garment is very difficult to clean, so be sure to send it to a cleaner who specializes in suedes, suggests G. Bruce Boyer of Bethlehem, Pennsylvania, a fashion editor for *Town and Country* magazine and the author of *Elegance, A Guide to Quality Men's Wear*. If a suede garment is dry cleaned without special attention, you may end up with something that resembles cardboard, Boyer warns.

When the Label Says Soap, Use Soap

Chemically, soap and detergent are two very different compounds, points out Patricia A. Beegle, fashion marketing manager for the DuPont Company Fibers Division in Wilmington, Delaware. But you can't tell the difference unless you read the label on the individual product. For instance,

Ivory liquid is a soap, while a green-tinted dishwashing liquid is a detergent. When a care label says to use one or the other, be sure to do so, says Beegle. The life of your garment may depend on it.

Hosiery: Handle with Care

Want to protect your hosiery investments? Here are two tips from Sara Maness, manager of consumer relations for the Kayser Roth Corporation in Greensboro, North Carolina, manufacturers of Calvin Klein, Burlington, and No-Nonsense hosiery.

- Hand wash only, using well-diluted, mild liquid facial soap.
- Line dry. (Maness doesn't recommend machine washing or drying, even if you encase hosiery in a pillow slip—the machine treatment hurts the nylon fibers, and hosiery won't last as long.)

Extra Care for Wool Knits

Multicolored wool knits need extra care when you're hand washing, says Eleanor Kairalla, president of the Kairalla Agency in New York City, which does research and public relations for the Luxury Animal Fibers Industry. (Luxury animal fibers include angora, cashmere, wool, and mohair.) She recommends:

- To avoid possible bleeding of colors, don't let the garment soak.
- After hand washing and rinsing, spread the knit on a towel. Also, layer a towel *inside* the body and sleeves to keep surfaces from touching each other.

Caring for Rayon—A Finicky Fiber

Rayon, a cellulosic fiber made from wood pulp, is used to create silkier, shiny fabrics, including worsted suiting, knits, and gabardines. Karen Puffer, women's wear merchandising manager for BASF Corporation's Fibers Division in New York City, warns that consumers should be particularly careful when cleaning clothes made from this fiber. What works for one rayon garment may lead to the demise of another.

Rayon is weak when wet, explains Puffer, so it should usually be dry cleaned.

But not always. "One rayon shirt may be hand washable," she says, "while another, although very similar in appearance, must be dry cleaned or it will shrink, fade, or wrinkle beyond recognition."

Pay *special* attention to care labels when you're cleaning anything made with rayon.

GENERAL CARE FOR MAN-MADE FIBERS

The following man-made fibers can be hand or machine washed. To find out the fabric content, check the label of your garment. The label may also list care instructions; if not, here are general guidelines.

Acetate: Many acetates need to be dry cleaned. If the garment can be hand washed, use warm water with mild suds. Do not twist or wring the garment, and don't soak colored items. Press while still damp on the wrong side with a cool iron. If you press the right side, use a pressing cloth.

Acrylic: Delicate items should be hand washed. Acrylic does tend to pill, so turn the garment inside out before washing and drying. Reduce static electricity by using a fabric softener in every third or fourth washing. Gently squeeze out the water, smooth or shake out the garment, and let it dry on a plastic hanger.

If machine washing, use warm water and add fabric softener during the final rinse. Machine dry at a low temperature, then remove garments from the dryer immediately. For wrinkles, use a moderately warm iron.

Nylon: Machine wash and tumble dry at low temperature. Use warm water, and add softener to the final rinse cycle. Remove nylon articles from the dryer as soon as the cycle is complete. If any garment needs ironing, check the care label—but never use an iron set higher than warm.

Polyester: Most polyester can be machine washed and dried. Use warm water and add a fabric softener to the final rinse cycle. Machine dry at a low temperature, and remove articles as soon as the cycle is complete. If ironing is needed, use a moderately warm setting. Most polyester items can be dry cleaned: Follow the instructions on care labels.

Rayon: While some rayons can be bleached, others are sensitive to chlorine bleach—so check the care label and, if in doubt, don't use bleach. Wash in mild suds, using cool or lukewarm water. Gently squeeze suds through the fabric and rinse with lukewarm water. Smooth or shake out the garment (no wringing or twisting!), and hang it on a plastic hanger to dry. (Rayon sweaters, however, should be dried flat.) While damp, press on the wrong side with an iron set at moderate. Use a pressing cloth if you need to finish on the right side.

Spandex: Hand or machine wash in lukewarm water. Do not use chlorine bleach on any fabric containing Spandex; instead, use an oxygen or sodium-perborate–type bleach. Drip dry or machine dry at low temperature. If ironing is required, do it rapidly, passing the iron quickly over the garment. Use the lowest temperature setting.

HAND WASHING WOOL OR CASHMERE

Jean Raney, wool education expert for the American Wool Council, and Eleanor Kairalla, a luxury fiber specialist in New York City, suggest the following steps for hand washing wool or cashmere sweater knits.

1. Make a paper pattern of the garment: Before washing, lay the garment flat on a piece of tissue paper and trace around it with a pencil.
2. As a safeguard against pilling and friction, turn the sweater inside-out.
3. Wash in lukewarm to cold water. Use a mild soap or nonbleach liquid detergent, following directions on the container.
4. Soak for 3 to 5 minutes. Gently squeeze suds through without twisting or wringing the garment.
5. Rinse twice in clean water. Make certain the rinse water is the same temperature as the wash water.
6. A tiny drop of bath oil can be added to the final rinse. It lends a pleasant scent to wool or cashmere sweaters and also makes the fibers more resilient.
7. Gently squeeze out excess water. Roll the garment in a towel (or towels) to absorb excess water.
8. To dry, turn right-side-out, then lay the knit on a dry sheet of plastic. Place the tissue pattern on top of the garment with the pencil outline facing up. Smooth the garment until it returns to its original shape. Line up all seams and ribs by pressing firmly with your fingers.
9. Allow to dry, keeping the garment out of sunlight and away from direct heat.
10. Finish by touching very lightly with a warm iron. Use a pressing cloth between the iron and the garment.

Intro to Hand Washing

Yes, hand washing is certainly easier on clothes than the mechanical action of an electric washing machine—and proper hand washing can save delicate fibers that would be ruined by harsh detergents and hot water.

Textile expert Dr. Kay Obendorf has the following hand washing tips.

- The water should never be warmer than tepid. The cooler the better.
- Use a basin large enough to allow the garment and fibers to relax.
- Add only enough mild soap or detergent to create minimal suds.

The Creme de la Creme of Solutions

The ultimate in chemically stable, museum-quality washing solutions?

According to Christine Paulocik, associate conservator for the Costume Institute at the Metropolitan Museum of Art in New York, you can't go wrong with Orvus WA Paste. Orvus is pH neutral and free of perfumes, colorants, and optical brighteners—all of which Paulocik likes to avoid. Detergents that contain bluing or optical whiteners can weaken fibers, she says.

Orvus is sold in small quantities, by mail order from Talas, a division of Technical Library Service. A detailed consumer price list is available for a small charge. For information, write to Talas, Technical Library Service, 213 West 35th Street, New York, NY 10001.

Cleaning Alternatives

What's the best procedure if the care label on your favorite silk blouse says it can be *either* dry cleaned or hand washed?

Do both. That's the recommendation of Dr. Obendorf at Cornell and Patricia Beegle of DuPont.

It makes good sense, in terms of chemistry, to alternate cleaning methods. Clothes will come out brighter, colors will remain more vibrant. Dry cleaning removes excess body oil from the fabric. But after three or four dry cleanings, hand wash the garment to help remove the buildup of excess fluid from the dry-cleaning process.

Hand washing provides a special bonus for a white silk blouse. While dry cleaning fluids may cause white blouses to yellow, hand washing can take the dull yellow away—leaving your blouse just as white as before.

$200 SILK PAJAMAS FOR LESS THAN $20

Love those washed silk pajamas in the window at Bergdorfs?

By shopping in Chinatown and washing it yourself, you can enjoy your sweet dreams in the luxury of silk for about $20 instead of $200, according to Jeanne McIvor, showroom fashion model for Anne Klein Coats in New York City, who also owned and operated a New England retail store for antique and restored clothing.

Here's how. Visit Chinatown and buy a pair of bright, stiff silk pajamas in a solid color. Toss them into the washing machine and wash on the hot water setting with regular detergent. Then tumble dry at high heat.

Presto, soft silk pajamas in a beautiful washed-down tone. "They will shrink, so buy the pajamas rather large," adds McIvor.

Give Your New Cleaner a Trial Run

Moving into a new neighborhood? Choose a new dry cleaner carefully, warns Daniel Eisen of the Neighborhood Cleaners Association.

Before sending your finest Italian cashmere overcoat to the new cleaner, try a test run with less valuable garments. When the clothes return, scrutinize the color, pressing, pleats, and seams. Eisen also checks the "hand" of the garment (that is, how it feels to the touch), and he looks it over to make sure the cleaner has removed all stains.

Mistreatment can lead to deterioration, shrinkage, fading, and other damage.

The More Sorting the Better

Unless your family has a penchant for pink-tinted white underwear, you undoubtedly sort whites from colors before machine washing.

But Dr. Obendorf goes even farther: She teams white cotton with white cotton, dark terry with dark terry, and bright acrylics *only* with bright acrylics.

Why all this trouble? According to Dr. Obendorf, the result is better cleaning and less transfer of lint. She says the drying action is also improved, since everything in the same load has equal fiber content and similar volume.

FYI

HEIRLOOM CARE

Where do you turn if your local museum is stumped by the stains on Aunt Tess's collection of hand-embroidered silks?

What if you don't trust your dry cleaner with a priceless cashmere coat that's been splattered with ink?

Both sound like jobs for specialists.

If you don't have one in your neighborhood, you can write to the Neighborhood Cleaners Association (NCA), 116 East 27th Street, New York, NY 10016. Describe the garment and ask for advice.

Since the association has 4,000 members nationwide, there's probably someone who can analyze your garment. When you send in the garment for inspection and advice, there's likely to be a minimal charge.

If an NCA dry cleaner is not within range, the New York office will take phone inquiries. Average waiting time for the New York lab to complete examination of a garment is about three weeks.

Machine Action on Cotton Sweaters

Many cotton sweaters can be safely washed in a machine, says Norma Keyes, manager of the textiles services laboratory for Cotton Incorporated in Raleigh, North Carolina. She recommends a gentle setting in warm water and "your usual detergent."

There are some exceptions, however. Keyes says you shouldn't try machine washing cotton sweaters that have loose, delicate, or open-knit construction.

No-Fuss Drying and Pressing

A Gentle Dryer—With Legs

Vintage-clothing restorer Jeanne McIvor found the perfect "gentle dryer" in a dime store.

It's a plastic screen that stands on tiny legs, allowing for ventilation from below. McIvor, who gives her clothes a lot of TLC, flat-dries her garments on the plastic screen.

Cut Down on Static

Some people use commercial static reducers to keep static buildup to a minimum.

Not necessary, according to Dr. Obendorf. Fabrics build up static when they're dried beyond their original moisture content. To prevent this:

- Remove laundry from the dryer *before* it has completely dried.
- Finish drying the load by hanging the clothes on a line.

The Inside Story of Better Drying

Is your dryer in the habit of hammering your clothes into submission?

Here are some ways to avoid prolonged pummeling and improve wearability.

- If you're looking for softness of hand, remove cotton garments from the dryer before they're completely dried, advises Norma Keyes of Cotton, Incorporated.
- You can reduce the drying period for small loads if you add three small, clean, dry white towels. According to Procter and Gamble spokesperson Marie-Laure Salvado, the towels increase the "tumbling effect" and the whole load will dry faster.
- Avoid overloading your dryer. Clothes need to be able to circulate. According to Salvado, overloading can result in excessive wrinkling. Heat damage can occur if the dryer vent becomes blocked.

Silks and Linen

When you're pressing silk and linen, a steam iron will do the job. But you must keep the fabric moist and apply plenty of pressure, advises Steven Stipelman, a fashion illustrator for *Women's Wear Daily* and an illustration instructor at Parsons School of Design in New York City. But *never press fancy raw silk*, the kind typically used for bridal dresses and expensive evening attire, Stipelman says. That's a job for professionals.

Steam Up the Wool

Wool responds extremely well to steam, says Jean Raney, wool education consultant for the American Wool Council in Englewood, Colorado. She recommends "the old steamy bathroom trick"—that is, putting your woolens in a steam-filled bathroom to help restore them.

When dealing with wool, adds Raney, it's best to keep pressing to a minimum: steam press on the wrong side of the fabric by lowering and lifting the iron rather than sliding it back and forth.

Pressing Precious Fabrics à la Italia

Carmela Sutera, a New York–based bridal designer and owner of Carmela Sutera designs, is descended from a long line of Italian couture makers. She offers the following tips on steam pressing wool. It's a trick she learned from her aunts in the homeland.

- For a professional wool finish that's as smooth as zabaglione...First wet a clean, white linen dish towel, then wring it dry: This is to use as a pressing cloth.
- Lay the pressing cloth on top of the garment. With a very hot, no steam iron, press the cloth and the wool underneath. (It's okay to press the right side of the garment when you're using this method.)
- Immediately after lifting the wet linen towel, lay a *dry* linen towel on top of the wool and lightly press again. And, presto, your treasured garment has a magnificent finish.

More Smooth Moves from the Homeland

For gentle care of silks and linens, Sutera suggests: Sprinkle linens with an ample amount of moisture, then roll them up like a jelly roll in a *slightly* damp (not soaking wet) towel. Allow the package to rest 10 to 15 minutes at room temperature. (For very stubborn wrinkles, pack this linen roll in your freezer during that time.) Then set your steam iron on the linen setting, unroll the package, and press. To press washable silks, roll a clean, damp garment in a towel and allow it to rest overnight. Then press with a very hot iron the next day.

Smart Storage

The First Commandment of Storage...

...Clean your clothes!

Ready to put your winter clothes away for their long summer nap?

Clean them first, insists Cornell's Dr. Kay Obendorf. She says moths and other six-footed enemies are most likely to chomp on clothes that are soiled with food. Those same munchers scorn the taste of dry-cleaning residue.

And don't assume that man-made fibers and blends are pestproof. Actually, they're prime targets for some insects, according to Velda Rankin, national program leader at the United States Department of Agriculture (USDA) Research Service in Washington, D.C.

Sort Your Store-ables

Shirley Eng, conservator at The Fashion Institute of Technology in New York City, suggests that you sort your clothes after you clean them and before you store them.

Says Eng: Separate the *protein fibers* (silk, wool, cashmere) from *cellulosic fibers* (rayon, linen, cotton). That's to prevent transfer of pests from one set of clothes to the other.

To prevent dyes from being transferred, separate the darks from the whites, suggests Eng.

Shedding Light on Drier Garments

Control moisture by using a low-wattage light bulb inside closets, says Rankin, who has done extensive research on mildew. Turn the light on every once in a while to generate dry heat and ward off excess moisture.

In addition, Rankin suggests that you open up and air out storage closets every now and then.

She notes that moisture and mildew can occur during any season— summer or winter.

What's That Stain on My Linen Suit?

Bridget Coughlin, fashion promotion specialist of the International Linen Promotion Commission in New York City, may have the answer.

If you put your linens into storage without cleaning them, invisible stains may oxidize. The result: unsightly, irreversible discoloration.

Mothproofing without Mothballs

Mothballs have been getting a bad rap for two reasons. First of all, they're not great for the environment. (See "A Mothball Assessment" on page

290.) And they're also dangerous for kids: Doctors have reported thousands of cases of children under six who have been poisoned by mothballs. The good news is, you *don't* have to use mothballs as long as you store freshly laundered or dry-cleaned clothes in a clean, airtight storage container.

Jean Raney of the American Wool Council defines *airtight*: It's an environment that does not allow for the exchange of air or incoming critters, she says.

But what about that trusty cedar closet or chest? Doesn't the cedar automatically drive them away?

Not by scent alone. Raney points out that a cedar closet or chest is only as good as it is airtight.

STORING IN PLASTIC

For seasonal storage, most people think plastic. And that's fine—as long as you get the kind of plastic that will do the job right.

On that score, here are three hints from our experts.

1. **A clear choice for the short term.** For regular seasonal storage, use a *clear* plastic bag, suggests Jack Levy, the head buyer for the Madison Avenue–based store Cashmere-Cashmere. For small items, like gloves, a resealable plastic sandwich bag will do the job. For larger items such as winter coats, suits, and dresses, use a garment bag from a good notions store.

2. **Long-term storage? Tape up some poly.** Shirley Eng, conservator at the Fashion Institute of Technology in New York City, has this recommendation for long-term storage. Purchase some polyethylene plastic sheeting, then make a sealed container to hold the clothes. Cut the sheeting to size, put the clothing inside, then squeeze the air out,and tape the outermost edges. Unless you're using acid-free tape (a conservationist's item), be sure the tape doesn't come in contact with the clothes you're storing.

3. **Silica gel—before you seal.** The final step, before you seal up clothes for storage, is to make sure they stay dry. Add a pack of silica gel to *any* storage area. The gel soaks up excess moisture, ensuring that your clothes stay free of mold and mildew. In most climates, silica gel will last a season. But be sure to replace it with a dry packet before you put your clothes away for storage the following year. Packets of silica gel can be purchased in the household goods section of most department stores and hardware stores.

FYI

A MOTHBALL ASSESSMENT

Yes, mothballs and mothproofing sprays help keep moths from lunching nonstop on valuable clothing, says Jean Raney, wool education expert for the American Wool Council in Englewood, Colorado. However, these products do have their drawbacks—from a strong unpleasant odor to mounting evidence of their high toxicity. Here are some facts on mothballs and their use.

Hang 'em high! Mothballs or crystals should be hung in the top of the storage area, where they have no direct contact with your clothing. Raney notes that mothballs can discolor your garments.

Out of tyke-grasp. Keep those mothballs well beyond reach of children and infants. One accidentally ingested mothball can cause severe seizures or worse.

Environmentally speaking... Mothballs may not be such a hot idea. According to the nonprofit citizens organization, the Clean Water Fund of Washington, D.C., some mothballs contain p-dichlorobenzene, a known carcinogen and toxic substance. In some U.S. communities, legislation has been passed forbidding mothballs from being dumped in regular trash.

Bulkies without the Hang-Ups

Bulky sweaters should not be hung on hangers: they'll stretch from the shoulders. Instead, always store bulky knits folded, says Eleanor Kairalla, representative of the Luxury Animal Fibers Industry.

Hey, Moth Eggs, Chill Out!

Want to eliminate moth eggs and larvae before you store your woolens and cashmeres? Try some freezer burn.

According to Raney, a 24-hour hiatus in the freezer is enough to eliminate any lingering moth offspring. Just put the clothing in a plastic bag and let it freeze. After a day or so, take it out and put it in airtight storage. It will be moth-free all summer long.

Take Away Their Library Card

If you've been saying some unprintable things about silverfish, it could be that you're unintentionally feeding their appetites. Though not heavy-duty readers, silverfish love to munch on magazines and newspapers. If you're storing such stuff in your clothes closet, get it out soon, suggests Rankin.

Silverfish have a passion for cellulosic fibers, including cotton, linen, jute, rayon, and ramie. And any paper product makes a favorite side dish.

Coddle Your Treasures with Acid-Free Storage

Paulocik offers the following tips on storing your most treasured garments, from wedding gowns to christening outfits and ballroom dresses.

- Wrap and box treasured garments in acid-free paper only. Ask a local cleaner or conservator where you can find acid-free tissue paper and boxes. Other papers eventually break down and cause discoloration.
- Nix the blue tissue. Your grandmother may have recommended using blue tissue paper for storage, but the dyed stuff is dangerous for your clothes, says Paulocik.

STALKING THE WILD MILDEW

Have you noticed more problems with mildew in recent years? Those airborne spores may be more than a figment of your clothes-concerned imagination.

Mildew *is* a bigger problem these days, according to Velda Rankin, national project leader at the United States Department of Agriculture (USDA) Research Service in Washington, D.C. Her extensive research on this subject has shown that it's an ever-increasing problem due to the growing world market for imported clothes. Deep in the holds of ships—where those clothes are often packed—are perfect breeding grounds for moisture-loving spores.

Advice from Rankin:

- Keep air moving. Frequent exchange of fresh air can help prevent the growth of mildew.
- Going away on vacation? Ask someone to come in and open the windows every so often. (Again, the key is moving air.)
- Try triage—fast. If any items are attacked by mildew, get them out of the house pronto. *Don't* try to brush them off, and don't vacuum them inside your home.
- Once items are outside, brush off mildew briskly, using a commercially prepared compound that eliminates mildew. Hope for the best. If any signs of mildew remain after treatment, you're better off bidding farewell to your garment.

- Store smaller garments folded and boxed in the acid-free materials. To avoid permanent creasing, remove the item on a seasonal basis; refold and store again.
- Don't hang any garments on wooden hangers. Over time, the acid in the wood can have a chemical reaction with fabric, and stains appear in the shoulders of the stored clothing.
- Yes, wire hangers are bad for your clothes. Instead, use padded hangers, preferably padded with unbleached muslin or cotton (see the illustration below).

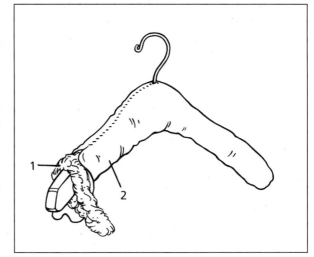

Cover wooden hangers with padding to avoid stains on garments. Wrap polyester or cotton quilt batting around the hanger (1). Cover with unbleached muslin or cotton (2).

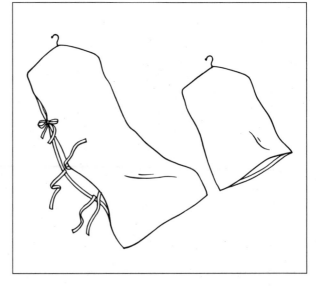

To make a closed dust cover, cut two pieces of unbleached muslin or cotton fabric to fit around the garment. When you sew the pieces together, leave a small opening at the top for the hanger and a large opening on the side to insert the garment. An "open" dust cover is open at the bottom, with a small hole in the top for the hanger.

Although plastic wrap is fine for everyday storage, the ultimate covering is unbleached muslin. Paulocik says most of the garments at the Metropolitan Museum are stored in unbleached cotton or muslin—never plastic. (You can make your own coverings for treasured garments with an unbleached muslin or cotton dust cover as shown in the illustrations on the opposite page.)

Avoid That Attic-Broiled Look

In storing clothes, as in storing fine wines, temperature and climate control is essential. Christine Paulocik of the Metropolitan Museum of Art explains that all fibers possess a natural moisture content. Blasts of heat can cause fibers to become brittle.

FOR ZIPPIER ZIPPERS

Keep zippers gliding and sliding easily by rubbing on a thin film of candle wax suggests evening wear and bridal designer Lynda Joy of New York City, who designed costume accessories for the Broadway show "Harlem Nocturne." She notes that commercially prepared zipper glides are also available.

In a sticky situation, suggests men's fashion writer Bruce Boyer, use soap or pencil lead on zippers.

Tucks, Mends, and Alterations

Insta-Hem

With only moments to spare before you leave the house for your big appointment, you suddenly notice that the hem appears to be falling out of your jacket. But luckily...

You have *fusing tape* on hand.

You can find it in any good sewing and notions store. Steven Stipelman, couture sewing expert and fashion illustrator, says all you need is a hot iron and the directions on the package. Before you step out the door, just iron your hem in place.

To Avoid a Social Gaffe...

Here's another way to mend a hem in a moment of dire need: Use gaffers tape—the kind found in photo-supply stores. Architectural photographer Carla Breeze, author of NY *Deco* and LA *Deco*, says she's used it to tape up all sorts of bothersome trouble spots, from the hems of heavy woolen coats to the soles of her shoes. It's not for filmy fabrics, since it shows right through. But for hefty garments that need makeshift repair, it's perfect.

SMART ALTERATIONS

In men's clothes, some alterations are a great idea—and others are likely to lead to trouble.

"It's easy to ruin a garment by attempting to narrow a lapel or collar," says *Town and Country* fashion editor Bruce Boyer, of Bethlehem, Pennsylvania. Also: Don't allow a tailor to ease the chest on a jacket. And the tailor shouldn't take anything in, or let anything out, more than 2 inches.

So what alterations are most likely to be worthwhile?

According to Boyer, worthy alterations include relining a coat, easing a seat, widening or tapering legs, removing cuffs, tightening a sleeve, and taking in or letting out a trouser waist.

For a Trimmer Tie: Mail for Renovations

What man is going to take the time or trouble to alter a tie—even if it's an old silk beauty?

On the other hand, why throw away favorite neckwear just because it's unfashionably wide or a little frayed at the seams?

Here's an alternative recommended by two fashion experts—fashion illustrator Stipelman and fashion editor Bruce Boyer.

Pack your needy neckwear off to TieCrafters, 116 East 27th Street, New York, NY 10016, for sprucing up and mending. Prices run about $10 for combined cleaning and alterations, but you should write to check that price before you mail off your tie.

Pattern Play: Measure the Max

If you're buying a home-sewing pattern, *don't* buy according to your dress size. Instead, buy a pattern that fits your largest measurement, says

Stipelman, who began sewing at age 13 under the tutelage of his mother, a milliner.

Stipelman recommends: When you have someone take measurements, ask that person to measure the *fullest* part of the bust, hip, and waist. Also be sure to measure the length from base of your neck to your tailbone. Then compare these measurements to those given on the pattern.

Hosiery Hints

For a Better Fit, Figure on Spandex

If longer wear, less tear, and a personalized fit are top priorities, look for hosiery that has a blend of Spandex in it.

"Spandex makes nylon hosiery fibers stronger and longer wearing," says Sara Maness of Kayser Roth Corporation. Also, there's less chance of snagging, since the Spandex fibers cling to your skin.

(If you dislike the clingy feel of the Spandex fibers, you may still opt for all-nylon, Maness notes.)

HOTLINE TO HOSIERY

Hosiery delivery by remote control?

It's easy—using one of the many hotline numbers.

Givenchy and Round The Clock brands will mail directly to your home, office, or hotel. The minimum order is three pairs. Call 1-800-926-4022.

ShowCase Products offers a catalog with a bounty of branded hosiery and intimate apparel—Hanes, L'eggs, Bali, and Henson Kickerknit, at 50 percent off. All merchandise is slightly imperfect. Call 1-800-522-1151.

Or you can order discounted hosiery directly from the manufacturer. L'eggs, for instance, has a 24-hour phone-in number: (919) 744-1170. Delivery takes about eight days. But if you're in a big hurry, you can have overnight delivery via Federal Express.

On the Go? Or Just for Show?

With the huge selection of hosiery available in all textures, fabrics, and patterns, you have a wide range of choices for all occasions.

For the office: Maness suggests wearing semiopaque or semisheer hose.

To create a sleek look: Choose hose that match the color of your shoes, dress, skirt, jacket, and blouse. "It's very sophisticated," observes Cathy Volker, vice president of fashion and merchandising for Hanes Hosiery in Winston-Salem, North Carolina. "You can never go wrong when you match the color of your hose to the color of your hemline."

To look more slender: Wear dark-color hose in semisheers or opaques (as long as it works with your outfit).

To make legs look longer: Select ribbed hosiery, sugests Joni Zeller-Claxton, vice president of designing for Calvin Klein Hosiery in New York City.

To look sleek and sexy: Wear skin-tone hosiery, says Volker. She suggests nude-tone hose with slingback mule shoes (for day), sexy, strappy footwear (for night), or super-sleek pumps (whenever). But, she warns, be critical: Sometimes nude hose *may* look matronly. If the nude look doesn't work, go for color instead.

The Thigh-High Alternative

Want an alternative to waist-high panty hose?

Zeller-Claxton suggests trying thigh-high styles. Thigh-highs have elastic tops and silicone grippers: Many styles are available in department and hosiery specialty stores.

Join a Hosiery Club!

Did you know that your local department store may have a hosiery club?

Bloomingdale's, for instance, offers its customers price-off incentives on multiple purchases of hosiery. Image consultant Brenda York, president emeritus of the Association of Fashion and Image Consulting and a consultant for Liz Claiborne, is a happy member of one such club: She has hosiery mailed directly to her home.

Footwear Tips from Heel to Toe

Look for Handsewn Uppers

With proper care and maintenance, men's quality shoes can last a lifetime. But if you're going to pay top prices, know what to look for.

You want a shoe with a leather sole that's been sewn on rather than glued, says fashion editor Bruce Boyer. "Quality leather should be used on the upper, as well as on the inside of the shoe."

Because quality men's shoes can be resoled on a regular basis, top-of-the-line footwear makes economic sense. "A really good pair of shoes can last 20 to 30 years," says Boyer.

Brush Up on Brushes

For leather shoes, use a horsehair brush, says Scott Griffin, store manager for Hanover Shoes in Whitehall, Pennsylvania. Horsehair helps push polish into the pores of the leather, while man-made bristles will scratch the surface. (For suede, use a brush specifically designated for suede shoes.)

After a Hard Day—Or Night

Slip off those oxfords, let those weary dogs breathe, and get ready to...

Wait, don't settle into that armchair yet! "Most people think of polishing *before* they wear their shoes," says Boyer. "I do it the other way around."

He recommends a quick brushing with a horsehair brush to prevent dirt and dust from settling into your leather shoes.

THE SHINING: 10 SURE-FIRE STEPS TO GLEAMING UPPERS

Scott Griffin, manager of the Hanover Shoe Store in the Lehigh Valley Mall in Whitehall, Pennsylvania, shines more than 40 pairs of shoes each week. Here are his hints for the ultimate in shining perfection for leather shoes.

1. Insert a shoe tree. Nontreated cedar is the best: It provides the proper drying vehicle and prevents the upper from excessive creasing. (You can also stuff the shoes with newspaper, advises Griffin, but don't use plastic trees—they don't allow the leather to breathe properly.)
2. Brush off dirt and soil with a horsehair brush.
3. With a soft cloth, apply commercial shoe cleaner to remove old dirt, dust, and wax.
4. Brush again, bringing back some shine.
5. Apply lanolin-based shoe polish with a soft cloth, and allow it to soak in for several minutes. (Lanolin-based polishes are creamy in texture and saturated with dye.)
6. Again, brush shoes vigorously, using a horsehair brush.
7. Apply Kannebo wax polish in the correct color. (This is a stiffer wax than the lanolin-based compound.)
8. Rub rapidly with an old T-shirt, tube sock, nylon panty hose, or chamois.
9. Apply specially made heel and edge dressing to the edges of the heels and soles. (You'll find these dressings wherever shoe-care products are sold.)
10. Allow shoes to dry at least overnight—preferably for 24 hours.

After the Downpour

Fine business or dress shoes don't need waterproofing. But if they *do* get wet, keep them away from direct heat, says Boyer.

Insert cedar shoe trees, or stuff them tightly with newspaper—then let them dry naturally.

A Waterproofing Tip for Trekkers

What's the best waterproofing product for hiking shoes and boots?

Look for silicone-based products, suggests Dave Butler, national sales manager for Adidas Outdoor in Warren, New Jersey. A mountain climber for more than 22 years, Butler cautions against mink oils and other waterproofing agents. "They can either dry out or make the leathers too soft," he says. As for trusty saddle soap: "It's for saddles only! It simply doesn't work on most footwear."

Give 'Em a Rest

Shoes always need a day off, says Boyer. If you allow 24 hours for the leather to dry out, shoes also have a chance to recover their original size and shape.

"Save Your High Heels for Evening..."

That's advice for women from Adrienne Weinfeld-Bert, the style director and fashion editor of *FootWear Plus* and other trade magazines. Weinfeld-Bert says high heels look entirely out of place during the day, "unless they're very tailored or you're wearing them to a special dressy occasion."

For day wear, she recommends shoes with more secure, lower heels. She also points to the many comfort shoes for women that come in a full range of styles and prices.

Men's Shoes for Women

For long-lasting, quality shoes with a casual look, more women should try shopping in men's shoe stores, suggests Weinfeld-Bert. She herself wears an expensive pair of French-made men's black loafers for casual attire.

"In France," she observes, "one of the biggest trends is for women to wear men's Gucci loafers."

Puddle-Hopping in Style

Keep an eye out for fashionable footwear in water-resistant materials, suggests Karen Puffer of BASF Corporation.

Better shoe stores and department stores carry many styles of fashionable, rain-resistant shoes in a variety of materials—from patent leathers to high-tech waterproof fibers. Puffer herself makes it a habit to carry a pair of lightweight designer shoe boots made with Gore-Tex, a breathable, waterproof coating.

Fashioning Your Wardrobe

Color-Code before You Shop

Before you head off to the shopping mall, spend time arranging your own closet. "You'll end up saving time and money," says Monika Tilley, an Austrian-born designer of leisure wear and swimwear. Arrange your closet by color, rather than by item.

Hang the light blues and whites in one area and bright oranges and yellows in another, with a third area for blacks and navies.

Color coordination will make it easier to see where the gaps are before you go shopping, and easier to pull together an outfit when you're dressing.

Kids' Stuff for You

Save big by going small, suggests fashion consultant Brenda York, founder of the Academy of Fashion and Image in McLean, Virginia.

She often takes clients into the girls' or boys' departments of upscale stores like Neiman Marcus, Saks, or Nordstrom's. "They stock all the right accessories at lower prices," she notes. On behalf of her clients, York checks the youth departments for scarves, bags, and oversized cotton fleece activewear.

Go Simple, Go Chic

Following the latest fashion trend?

Patricia Beegle of DuPont urges women to think about how that trendy necklace or bracelet fits in with the whole look.

"Keep things simple," she says. "Less is more when it comes to being well dresssed. A woman who always follows a trend without thinking about how it fits with her entire look usually comes across as a fashion victim."

Color Speaks

Color not only enhances skin tones, it also evokes certain moods. That's why York recommends certain colors for certain effects.

- A soft periwinkle blouse under a business suit reads "approachable and even-keeled."
- Want to appear more businesslike and powerful? Wear blackened colors like burgundy, eggplant, or deep navy.
- Spirited and energetic? Try a bright, pure orange.

Nothing Beats a Great Scarf

French women look divine in them. They're simple and elegant—and with just the right amount of color, you can catch that air of sophisticated joie de vivre.

That's why Hanes vice president Cathy Volker recommends a "wardrobe of scarves."

Any time you need an extra something, just put on a scarf...with flair.

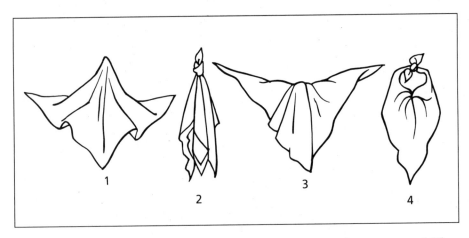

To make a "knotted bib," lift the center of the wrong side of a square scarf (1). Make a knot at that point (2), then flip the scarf right-side-up, holding the corner so it forms a triangle (3). Tie it behind your neck (4).

For a "rosette" effect, place an oblong scarf around your neck and make a double knot in front (1). Twist the ends to coil the scarf (2), then wrap the coiled portion around the knot (3). Tuck the ends behind the rosette (4).

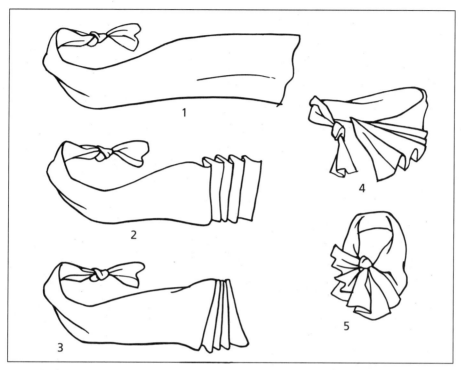

To form a scarf into a "pleated wrap," make a simple knot close to one end of an oblong scarf (1). Make accordion pleats in the opposite end (2) and continue to hold the pleats while you bring that end around your neck to the front (3). Push the pleated end upward through the knot (4), then tighten the knot and fan out the pleats (5).

All about Wool

Bald Shoulders?

When you're wearing a mohair coat or sweater, avoid carrying a shoulder bag, warns Madeline Daddiego, director of promotions for the Mohair Council of America, with headquarters in San Angelo, Texas.

The weight of the bag and friction of the shoulder strap can wear a bald spot on the top of your shoulder. Instead, carry a hand-held purse.

Give Wool the Brush-Off

Use a natural-bristle coat brush to dust off your wool after every use, suggests *Town and Country* fashion editor Bruce Boyer. That way, soil, dust, and grime won't get a chance to settle into the wool.

R & R for Wool

Jean Raney of the American Wool Council says your wool garments will look better and last longer if you allow them to rest for at least 24 hours after each wearing. Hang them in a well-ventilated area to give the wool fibers enough space to relax.

Shaving the Pills

Pills are those tiny, stubborn little nodules that cling to the surface of natural fibers like wool and cashmere and synthetics like polyester and acrylic. You can carefully shave pills off of wool and cashmere using a hand or battery-operated sweater shaver, says Jack Levy, head buyer for the Madison Avenue–based, four-unit store, Cashmere-Cashmere. Levy says to make sure you purchase a shaver especially designed for shaving pills. Also, go slowly.

Less Pilling for Cashmere

Freezing cashmere in a plastic bag in your freezer for up to a week can prevent excess pilling, says Levy.

Lint Busters

Here are two ways to spruce up wools that are hit by the blizzard of mid-winter lint.

1. Use a scotch tape lint roller. According to Jeanne McIvor, showroom fashion model for Anne Klein, the tape roller won't cause pilling.
2. Or use a slightly damp natural sponge, suggests Eleanor Kairalla, whose agency does research for the Luxury Animal Fibers Industry.

You Can Beat Cashmere...

Into shape, that is. If your cashmere sweater has stretched out a bit around the waist, you may be able to whap it into shape again. Levy says cashmere will recover its original shape if you repeatedly slap the stretched-out part against the side of a smooth desk or tabletop

Groom Your Mohair

Different kinds of mohair need different grooming to keep it looking good, according to Madeline Daddiego of the Mohair Council of America.

For mohair with a long, hairy nap, Daddiego suggests a natural teasel brush or a fine baby brush. "Gently coax the fibers to ease any tangles out."

If you have a mohair garment with a nubby texture (called a boucle), use a vacuum with a brush attachment, says Daddiego. Just put a clean attachment with a narrow opening on the end of a vacuum base and run it over the mohair. A vacuum also works well on mohair blends with a boucle weave.

Travels with Cashmere

From the foothills of Outer Mongolia to the innards of your closet space, cashmere travels an exotic route.

The soft fleece grows under a thick coat of coarse hair on the belly of Outer Mongolian goats. Since each goat produces only about 4 ounces of fleece a year, it takes about three goats-worth of fleece to create enough wool for a single-ply sweater.

A man's overcoat? You're looking at the fleecy annual production of 24 goat bellies.

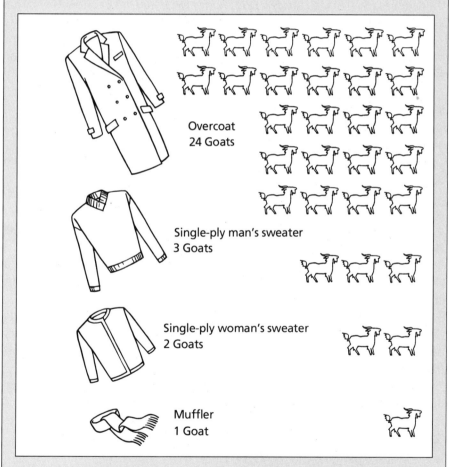

Overcoat
24 Goats

Single-ply man's sweater
3 Goats

Single-ply woman's sweater
2 Goats

Muffler
1 Goat

How many cashmere goats to the garment? At the rate of 4 ounces of fleece per year, this is how many goats it takes to produce some typical cashmere garments.

The Experts

Patricia A. Beegle, fashion marketing manager for the DuPont Company Fibers Division in Wilmington, Delaware, has worked for several major New York advertising firms.

G. Bruce Boyer, from Bethlehem, Pennsylvania, a fashion editor for *Town and Country Magazine,* is the author of *Elegance, A Guide to Quality Men's Wear* and *Eminently Suitable.* He has also written about men's clothes for the *New Yorker, Harper's Bazaar,* and the *New York Times.*

Carla Breeze is a New York–based architectural photographer and author. Among her books are NY *Deco, Pueblo Deco,* and LA *Deco.* Her work has also appeared in *L'architettura, House Beautiful,* and *Southern Accents.*

Dave Butler, a Portland, Oregon–based wilderness trekker and mountain climber for over 22 years, is the national sales manager for Adidas Outdoor, a line of outdoor clothing and footwear in Warren, New Jersey.

Bridget Coughlin has worked as a fashion promotion specialist for the International Linen Promotion Commission in New York City.

Madeline Daddiego is director of promotions for the Mohair Council of America, with headquarters in San Angelo, Texas.

Daniel Eisen is chief garment analyst for the Neighborhood Cleaners Association in New York City.

Shirley Eng is conservator at the Fashion Institute of Technology in New York City.

Scott Griffin is store manager for Hanover Shoes in the Lehigh Valley Mall in Whitehall, Pennsylvania.

Lynda Joy is the evening wear and bridal designer for Lynda Joy, Inc., in New York City. She has designed for a number of theatrical productions, including costume accessories for the Broadway show "Harlem Nocturne."

Eleanor Kairalla is president of the Kairalla Agency in New York City. The agency is the research and public relations arm for the Luxury Animal Fibers Industry. (Luxury animal fibers include angora, cashmere, wool, and mohair.)

Norma Keyes is manager of the textiles services laboratory for Cotton, Inc., in Raleigh, North Carolina.

Jack Levy is head buyer for the Madison Avenue–based, four-unit store, Cashmere-Cashmere.

Jeanne McIvor is a showroom fashion model for Anne Klein Coats in New York. A former showroom model for Paris-based designer Kenzo, she has also owned and operated a New England retail store for antique and restored clothing.

Sara Maness is the manager of consumer relations for the Kayser Roth Corporation in Greensboro, North Carolina. (Kayser Roth makes Calvin Klein Hosiery, Burlington, Interwoven, and No-Nonsense hosiery brands.)

Beth Minardi is the co-owner of Minardi Minardi Salon in New York City. A hair-color specialist, she is also a consultant and spokesperson for the Clairol Company.

Kay Obendorf, Ph.D., is professor and chairman of the Department of Textiles and Apparel at Cornell University in Ithaca, New York.

Christine Paulocik is associate conservator of the Costume Institute at New York's Metropolitan Museum of Art.

Karen Puffer is women's wear merchandising manager for BASF Corporation's Fibers Division in New York City.

Jean Raney is wool education consultant for the American Wool Council in Englewood, Colorado.

Velda Rankin is national program leader at the United States Department of Agriculture (USDA) Research Service in Washington, D.C. She has done extensive research on mildew.

Marie-Laure Salvado is spokesperson for Procter and Gamble Company in Cincinnati, Ohio.

Steven Stipelman has been fashion illustrator for *Women's Wear Daily* for over 25 years. An instructor of illustration at Parsons School of Design in New York City, he is a couture pattern-maker and sewing expert.

Carmela Sutera, owner of Carmela Sutera Designs, is a couture bridal designer in New York City.

Andy Tarshis is president of Tiecrafters, a 40-year-old New York firm that specializes in cleaning, restoring, and altering ties.

Monika Tilley is an Austrian-born designer of leisure clothing and swimwear.

Cathy Volker is vice president of fashion and merchandising for Hanes Hosiery in Winston-Salem, North Carolina.

Adrienne Weinfeld-Bert is the style director and fashion editor for *Foot-Wear Plus, Earnshaw's Review, Plus Sizes,* and *Small World,* trade magazines that serve the footwear, children's wear, and women's large-size industries.

Brenda York is president emeritus of the Association of Fashion and Image Consulting, founder of the Academy of Fashion and Image in McLean, Virginia, and consultant for Liz Claiborne, Inc.

Joni Zeller-Claxton is vice president of designing for Calvin Klein Hosiery in New York City.

CHAPTER 12

Pets

Healthier, Happier
Furry Friends

Man's Best Friend? He chews the furniture, soils the rug, and slobbers over everything else. Some pal! Barking when we're trying to sleep, hogging our favorite chair when *we're* the ones who are dog tired...

And Kittypuss? This descendent of the King of Beasts spends most of her waking hours ignoring us, as if dignified arrogance were her noble birthright. And the rest of the time? Usually she's choking on her own furballs in front of your dinner guests.

But we love 'em anyway. So much, in fact, that American households have more pets than children. We spend more than $7 *billion* each year on food for dogs and cats alone, and at least another $2 billion on other pet paraphernalia like flea collars, litter boxes, and aquariums. What's all this pet care add up to? We have brought into our homes some 210 million pets—nearly one pet for every man, woman, and child in the United States.

With all this pet love going around, there are sure to be times when we wonder: Am I doing right by Fido? Is Kittypuss getting the care she deserves? And when they misbehave, we surely wonder why they *sometimes* make trouble right on their own home turf.

For answers to these and many other questions about pet care, we turned to the experts—veterinarians and trainers—to ask for sound advice and helpful hints. Here you'll find tips on feeding, training, care, and grooming. You'll even get a glimpse behind the scenes—a pup's-eye view of his master's pats, a kitty's rationale for friendly leg-rubs. Whether you have pets, want pets, or wish to do right by the ones you live with, here are the experts' dos and don'ts.

Choosing Your Best Friend

Pooch Picking I: Look for the Droopy Tail

Let's say you go dog-shopping at your local animal shelter. You come across a little pooch that stares at you with sad brown eyes. Sure, he's a cutie, but that tail between his legs is a dead giveaway: "He's too submissive," you say—and look for a livelier Fido.

Too bad, says Liz Palika, a dog obedience trainer from Oceanside, California, and a columnist for *Dog Fancy* magazine. You just blew your chance of getting what was probably going to be an incredibly trainable, loving, and ever-devoted dog.

"When we see a dog being submissive, we think he's afraid," she observes. "But in dog language, showing submissiveness doesn't mean fear or weakness: It acknowledges that *you're* the leader, which is the best thing a dog owner can get from a pet. You can train a submissive dog with much less difficulty than a dog who isn't submissive."

Pooch Picking II: Shun the Bold and the Runty

"If you're picking from a litter, never choose either the boldest or the runt," Palika adds. "The boldest will be difficult to train, and runts tend to be sickly."

Pooch Picking III: The Belly-Up Test

Down to the final selection process?

"Pick a dog that appears healthy, roll him over on his back, and hold him there," says Paul Donovan, V.M.D., a longtime veterinarian and director of the Alburtis Animal Hospital in Alburtis, Pennsylvania. "If he's a submissive dog, you should be able to hold him in that position (with his belly facing upward) without much struggle from him. A dog who's aggressive will probably fight to get out of that position."

Your Pooch Pick May Pose Problems

Certain breeds are prone to certain illnesses—so keep that in mind when you're looking for a dog. According to Dr. Donovan, here are some of the most common problems.

- Golden retrievers, German Shepherds, and Labradors are prone to hip dysplasia.
- Schnauzers get bladder stones and pancreas infections.
- Dachshunds are prone to slipped disks and paralysis.

Teaching Fido Manners

Dog Discipline: Don't Let Him Dominate

Dogs, being pack animals, try to dominate the "pack" around them—and that includes you. "When a dog jumps on you, or stares at you, or nuzzles you, or barks or gently bites your hand, these behaviors are signs of displaying dominance," says Myrna Milani, D.V.M., a veterinarian in Charlestown, New Hampshire, and author of *The Body Language and Emotions of Dogs*. "Acknowledging these behaviors is a sign of submission. Although you may think the dog is being cute or affectionate, in the dog's mind you are showing your submissiveness to this animal, telling him that *he's* in charge." When Fido runs into the house before you, "it's because he sees himself—*not* you—as head of the pack," explains Dr. Milani. "And your allowing him to be first, in his mind, just reinforces that behavior."

The Right Pitch for Training

"The single biggest mistake people make in trying to train their pets is assuming the animal knows what they're saying," says Palika. "Dogs don't understand *words*. They understand *tones*. That's why when your dog does something right, you should *praise* him in a high-pitched tone of voice. For *correcting* a behavior, use a low, growling tone of voice."

You may sound silly to yourself, with those falsettos and growls, but these are the tones your dog understands.

Leash Your Pooch's Potential

"You *must* teach your dog to walk on a leash without pulling," Palika says. "Teach the dog to pay attention to *you, only* you, and not a tree, another dog, or anything else." Here's how to start.

1. Put the leash on the dog and hold it in one hand with a "treat" in the other. (The treat could be a food he likes or his favorite toy.)

2. Tell him "Watch me," and start walking. Every time he steps in front of you or diverts his attention to something other than you, give the leash a snap to get his attention and say, "Fido, I've got the ball." He'll pay attention to the ball or the treat, and you can transfer that attention to you.

3. Praise him (in a high voice!) for the attention, and continue walking.

"If you're having serious problems with a dog walking on a leash, get a choke collar," suggests Palika. "It gives the dog a real snap."

Doorstep Training: The "Come" Command

"One of the easiest ways to teach your dog the 'come' command is have a box of doggie cookies or biscuits by the door," says Palika. "Tell him, 'Fido, I've got a cookie' and as soon as he starts running toward you, tell him to 'come.' When he gets there, pop a cookie in his mouth. After a while, he will learn that this box of cookies, combined with the word, 'come' means he's going to get a treat. Within a couple of weeks, he will recognize the command."

Leg-Scoop Learning: The "Down-Stay" Command

How do you teach Fido to stay put when you want him to? Here are Liz Palika's suggestions.

1. When Fido is sitting, scoop his front legs out in front of him, so he's lying down.

2. Hold him there for a second. Then say, "Stay," and move away.

3. If he gets up to move, put him back down by scooping the paws and holding him down for a second.

"With repetition, he'll learn," says Palika.

Mutant Rebel Teenage Canines

Many dogs seem to make progress until about 10 months, when it appears as though they've "lost" all their knowledge. Not to worry: "The dog is going through a normal stage of development, kind of like our teenaged years. He's rebelling more than anything," says trainer Palika. "You will succeed," she adds, "if you show persistence."

Pats and Treats for Petulant Pups

It doesn't hurt to offer a treat every time a job is well done, notes Palika. One way is with physical affection. "Dogs are very social animals, and they *need* to be petted. Like humans, if they don't get a good hug every once in a while, they feel deprived. The best time for a hug is immediately after your dog does something right."

Praise the Dog Who Knows Where to Go

"The easiest way to housebreak a dog is to set a schedule where the puppy can go outside after he wakes up from a nap, after he eats, after play, and on a regular basis sometime in between," says Palika. "When the pup goes outside, make sure you go with him. When he goes to the bathroom, praise him. Let him know it's *not* play time: Don't talk to him except to praise him for going."

FYI

How Far Does Fido Need to Walk?

Taking your dog for a stroll? Fido may head for the closest fire hydrant, but he actually needs a lot more exercise than around-the-block-and-back. According to veterinarian David Alderton, author of *The Dog*, if a dog doesn't settle down immediately after going for its daily walk, he hasn't walked far enough. Here are Dr. Alderton's guidelines to ensure that your pooch gets the right amount of exercise.

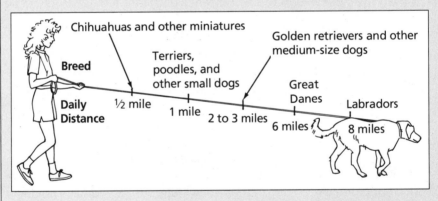

Wondering how much exercise your dog needs daily? Here's a guide.

Even more important than distance is consistency. According to animal behaviorist and veterinarian Myrna Milani, D.V.M., author of four books on animal behavior, it's important that you exercise your dog *every day*.

Advice: Pick an amount of time you can spend with your animal on a *daily* basis and stick with it. "You don't have to go to the park," says Dr. Milani. "You can provide great exercise for your dog by playing fetch or running up and down the stairs to play hide and seek."

Dog-in-a-Box Training

If no one is home during the day, most experts recommend you "crate-train" your pup. Keep the dog in a large box during your working hours, letting him out of the box only when it's time for him to relieve himself. "No dog wants to go in his living area, so he'll hold it in until he's out of the crate," says Dr. Donovan. *Note:* If you crate-train, make sure you let the dog go outside at the same time every day.

More Pep for Pooch

For Pup's Molars, Skip the Mush

Puppies are better off staying away from wet food for the first year, according to Dr. Donovan. "It's so mushy, it can mess up their teeth. As long as they're puppies, they're better off with only dry food."

The Badness of Beef Bones

Steak bones, a popular treat, are among the *worst* things you can give a dog, observes veterinarian Dr. Milani. "Beef bones splinter off and make razor-sharp needles that can get stuck in the animal's throat or damage his insides. And beef bones are about the only thing that will constipate a dog."

A QUICK PUP CHECKUP LIST

Want to give Fido a physical? Here are things to look for.

Eyes. Something's wrong if pupils are not jet black or corneas are foggy.

Stool. Look for a difference in normal color and consistency. (The "ideal" stool looks like a Tootsie Roll.)

Drinking habits. Increased thirst, especially during the night, could be a warning sign of diabetes, kidney failure, or two types of liver disease.

Urination. There's a problem if your dog is suddenly having to urinate in the middle of the night or is straining to urinate.

Abdomen. A swollen abdomen could suggest fluid or tumors.

Diet. If your dog begins eating dirt, that often indicates anemia.

Change in weight. If your pet is losing weight, it's a good sign something is wrong. Even the loss of 3 or 4 pounds in a large dog could be significant. Dr. Donovan suggests that you weigh your dog every three or four months just to keep tabs on his health.

Doggie Dental Care

The best way to make sure Fido's bark is always worse than his bite is to practice the same good dental hygiene as you do: Brush your pooch's teeth.

When your dog is as young as eight weeks, start getting him used to the idea that you're going to brush his teeth, advises Bruce Ilgen, D.V.M., a Pennsylvania veterinarian who specializes in pet dental care. "Stick your hand into his mouth and rub his teeth and gums. Once the dog is accustomed to your handling his mouth, you can start brushing."

The reason? Without brushing, many dogs develop periodontal disease, which can lead to loss of appetite, generalized infections, kidney or liver disease, or behavioral changes.

To keep pooch's chewers in prime shape, you'll need a regular, soft-bristled toothbrush and a specially formulated dog toothpaste available at your veterinarian's office. Don't use human toothpaste: It contains ingredients that can cause gastric problems and foaming in your dog's mouth. And baking soda is not advised either, since it can harm your pet because of its high sodium content.

Apply the toothpaste to the brush, lift the dog's upper lip, and brush teeth *and* gums, rubbing gently in an up-and-down *as well as* a side-to-side motion. Pull down the lower lip and brush the bottom teeth and gums with the same back-and-forth motion. "The whole routine will probably last about 1 minute," says Dr. Ilgen. The purpose isn't to do it for a long time, but to brush regularly. Ideally, you should brush your dog's teeth daily—but even if you can't do it that often, you should brush, at minimum, once a week, according to Dr. Ilgen.

A Marrow Escape

Even if you're careful not to serve an animal any type of bone, most pets will come across them. Rummaging through garbage cans in search of a snack seems to be their favorite hobby.

What should you do if you find the remnants of a bone—and you know the rest is in Fido's stomach?

"Most of the time, if a dog thoroughly chews the bone, his stomach acids should soften it," says Dr. Donovan. "What you should do then is feed him bulky foods in small amounts *very often* for 24 hours. The point is to fill the stomach and keep it wide so it doesn't 'close' on something sharp."

What Dr. Heimlich Didn't Tell You

What if your pet is *choking* on a bone and there's no time to call a vet?

"The first thing you should do is try and reach in the mouth and clear the airway if you can," says Dave Thompson, D.V.M., a veterinarian at the 17,000-patient North Asheville Animal Hospital in North Carolina. "If you can't feel anything in the airway, try the Heimlich Maneuver."

Wait a minute—isn't the Heimlich Maneuver for *people*?

"There's no specific Heimlich for animals," says Dr. Thompson. "Just try and constrict the abdomen so the diaphragm pushes forward and makes the air in the lungs go out through the trachea. Go behind the rib cage, grab the abdomen, and yank it." If you give your pet a good healthy squeeze, the bone in the throat may pop out.

The Heimlich maneuver for dogs: If a dog begins choking, hold him around the abdomen and give a hard squeeze. The rush of air from the lungs should force the object out of his trachea.

Rx for Vomiting—No Water!

When any pet is vomiting, the natural inclination is to give him water. Don't.

"The typical scenario is that the animal will lap up the water, then vomit again," says Dr. Donovan. "The best thing to do is *remove* all food and water whenever an animal vomits."

A New View on Nostrils

Perhaps the biggest fallacy of all is that a cold, wet nose indicates a healthy dog.

Nonsense, says Dr. Donovan. "A lot of sick dogs have cold, wet noses, while a lot of healthy ones have dry, crusty noses. What I suggest is to look for a *change*. If your dog usually has a cold, wet nose and suddenly it becomes crusty, then that could be a sign something is wrong."

Have Ipecac on Hand

Dr. Donovan recommends Ipecac syrup for puppies or kittens, since they're prone to pick up things and swallow them. Ipecac induces vomiting, so it's a quick way to rescue a pet who swallowed the wrong object. But be sure to call the vet before administering Ipecac, so you know the right dose for your pet. When giving Ipecac, tilt your pet's head back and push back the loose "cheek" along the side of the teeth. Then pour in the right dose.

Shortcuts to Kitty Control

Cat Got Your Goat?

If your cat is scratching the furniture, you might think a scratching post is the easy answer. But even if he claws the post to shreds, it's no guarantee he won't try the same moves on your new living room furniture.

"Scratching posts do work—with some cats," says Bruce Ilgen, D.V.M., director of the Detwiler Veterinary Clinic in Reading, Pennsylvania. But how do you teach your cat that the scratching post and not your furniture is *his* area to scratch? Dr. Ilgen suggests that you encourage cats the same way you encourage dogs—with behavior modification techniques. "You pet them and reward them when they're in the right place, and holler at them in the wrong place," says Dr. Ilgen. "More than anything, you discourage them from even *approaching* the inappropriate place, like the furniture."

According to Dr. Ilgen, spraying vinegar on the chair or table legs *won't* keep your cats from scratching the furniture. He says the best way to discourage them is to yell at them when you catch them in the act of scratching.

Beware of the Claws That Catch

Convincing Kitty to visit the vet isn't always so easy—especially when it's time to place him in a carrier. Without some careful feline-restraint techniques, *you* may end up seeing a doctor for cat-scratch injuries.

"If you're trying to get a cat into a carrier, I suggest you try coaxing him in with some food," says Dr. Ilgen. "A few days before the appointment, if possible, get the cat used to the carrier by placing it in your house and putting food in it. Then, before it's time to go, it will be easier to coax the cat inside with some food and then close the door when he's inside."

If your cat is reasonably good-natured, it may be possible to get him into the carrier without all the pre-vet preparation. Just grab him by the paws—hind legs in one hand, front legs in the other—lift him gently, and lower him inside. (You're better off with an assistant to help you close the lid *immediately*.)

Put a Damper on Catfights

"Groowww-rraaooww-hissss" are just everyday hellos between territorial cats, who don't take kindly to strangers on their turf. But don't be alarmed if you see your cat heading for a catfight: Just head for the faucet.

The best way to safely break up a cat fight is to throw water on the participants, according to animal behaviorist Dr. Milani.

(For dogs, by the way, the best breakup tactic is the same: Turn the hose on the warring canines, or douse them with a bucket of water.)

Litter-Box Logistics

Training cats to use a litter box is usually fairly easy. When a new cat comes home, place him in a *full*, clean litter box—and that's it. Maybe he'll need a short time to adjust to his new surroundings, but most cats rarely have accidents after they know where their litter box is.

But a word of warning from Dr. Milani: Once you decide where the box will stay, *keep it there*. Cats don't adapt well to change.

For a Feeling-Good Feline...

Who Says Cats Like Lactose?

Some of the most popular types of foods we serve our pets are some of the most harmful.

Take Kitty's bowl of milk, for example. While we may think of milk as the perfect food for cats, many felines are actually lactose-intolerant. That means they get severe nausea and other reactions, just like lactose-intolerant people. "I suggest you stay away from giving them dairy products because many cats get diarrhea when given a big bowl of milk," says Dr. Donovan.

For Kitty's Sake, Say No to Fish

"The most common cause of male cats being in the hospital is a condition called feline urilagic syndrome that's caused by consuming too much magnesium," says Dr. Donovan. "And seafood cat foods are *loaded* with magnesium."

Dr. Donovan notes that excess magnesium can cause a blockage of the urinary tract. If it's not detected and treated in about 48 hours, the pet can die. "If your cat *will* eat chicken or beef, stay away from seafood if you can," he urges.

Easing Hairball Distress

When your cat is choking on a hairball, don't be alarmed. "There's really nothing to worry about with hairballs," says Dr. Donovan. "No cat has ever died from one."

All cats get hairballs, which are the result of fastidious grooming. As kitty licks her coat, excess hair gathers in the back of her throat, and she swallows it. You can reduce but not eliminate the discomfort by combing Kittypuss frequently to remove excess hair.

"There are also pastes and laxatives available at any pet store," adds Dr. Donovan. "They lubricate the hair so instead of wadding up into a ball in the cat's stomach, it goes through him and winds up in the stool."

One Preventive for Kitty Leukemia

One of the biggest concerns for cat owners is feline leukemia. The virus, which doesn't affect other pets or humans, is extremely common where there are a lot of stray cats.

Feline leukemia is spread from one cat to another through casual contact—grooming, sharing a litter box or water dish—and it's nearly always fatal. Once it gets into the cat's bloodstream, "there is nothing you can do about it," says Dr. Donovan. "But you can *prevent* it with a vaccine that costs about $20."

Is Your Cat Losing Weight?

A common problem among cats is a loss in appetite. Often, a cat that doesn't eat is losing her sense of smell. To check if that's the cause, Dr. Milani suggests serving your cat a "smellier" variety of cat food.

Quality Control—For Lower Magnesium

"A lot of people buy a low-ash cat food thinking that they're protecting their cat," says Dr. Donovan. "The truth is, 'low-ash' doesn't mean low magnesium, and putting them on a low-ash diet often does nothing to control magnesium." His advice? Buy good-quality cat foods, which tend to be lower in magnesium.

In Case of Emergency

What if your pet is badly injured and has severe bleeding or broken bones? Call the vet immediately. Then...

"In most emergency situations you need to protect *yourself* from being bitten," says Dave Thompson, D.V.M., of the North Asheville Animal Hospital in North Carolina. "When an animal is hurting, there is a high probability it will try to bite. My advice is to muzzle the pet as best you can, *especially* if it's a dog." Here's how: Make a single loop in the middle of a tie or stocking. Slide the loop over the nose of your pet and pull it *tight!* Bring the ends down under the jaw, and tie another loop. Finally, pull the ends behind the back of the neck and tie them so the muzzle can't be pawed off.

Once the animal is muzzled, get ready to drive to the vet's. "If the animal is bleeding, take a white sock or a clean rag and wrap the cut area," says Dr. Thompson. "Then apply *soft* pressure to the area."

If your pet has been hit by a car, Dr. Thompson says to keep the fractured or hurt area *up,* so there's no weight on it. "Don't worry about moving the animal as you would a human. Paralysis isn't your main concern at this time; shock is. You have to act fast."

Of course, it's essential to know the phone number, emergency-care procedures, and operating hours of your local veterinarian or humane shelter. "There is nothing sadder than driving 10 miles only to realize the vet isn't open," says Dr. Thompson. "One of the best things a pet owner can do is to have the vet's number posted on the refrigerator."

Planned Pet Parenthood

The Pluses of Spaying

Unless you're a breeder, it's wise to avoid unwanted litters of puppies or kittens by spaying female pets and neutering males. These procedures not only prevent pet overpopulation, they actually lead to *healthier* pets.

"If you spay before a dog's first heat period, you can cut the likelihood of breast cancer from about 10 percent to about 0.1 percent," says Dr. Thompson. "You'll be buying your dog some quality time eight or ten years down the road." Spaying cats also reduces the incidence of breast cancer, but not as drastically, according to Dr. Thompson.

Ward Off Pyometritis

Early spaying can "practically eliminate" a disease called pyometritis—an inflammation of the uterus—that affects dogs four to six weeks after their heat period. "Prevention is important, because pyometritis doesn't respond to antibiotics," according to Dr. Thompson.

So if you're wondering whether to have your dog spayed, consider health benefits as well as population control.

It's Safe to Neuter

Neutering calms "hyper" dogs and cats, and produces no adverse side effects. "A lot of people are still resistant to having their pet neutered because they can remember 15 or 20 years ago when pets commonly died under anesthesia," says Dr. Thompson. "But I can assure you, the chance of that happening today is virtually nil if you pick a good veterinarian."

Putting Fleas to Flight

Is Fido Allergic to Flitting Fleas?

Fleas can be devastating to your pets. "A good percentage of dogs are allergic to fleas," says Dr. Donovan. "They'll literally chew their skin raw to make the itching stop. If left untreated, they get what are called *hot spots*—oozing, infected skin lesions that can be real bad news." If your dog *is* allergic, you can usually tell; he'll keep biting in a triangular spot above the base of his tail. Antiflea action is *essential*.

Flea Control I: Shampoo!

"Controlling fleas is an ongoing process because a single female flea lays anywhere from 600 to 800 eggs in her lifetime, which is only a few months," says Dr. Donovan. "The first part of attack is what everyone knows: Get the animal in the tub with good shampoo."

Unfortunately, if you stop there, the job's only half done. "The moment the animal goes outside, the fleas are back on him again."

Flea Control II: The Big Dip

It's essential to follow a shampoo with a flea dip. "Pour the dip on the animal's coat while he's still in the tub. Let the animal drip-dry for a couple of minutes, then turn him loose so the product dries.

Some dips are good for 10 days, some 20 or 30. But according to Dr. Donovan, you should redip a little before the time period ends—especially in the summer and fall when fleas are most active.

Wintertime...And the Fleas Are Still Busy

"There's a fallacy that flea season ends when first frost comes," says Dr. Donovan. "Once fleas get into the house—and they get into the house as soon as the animal does—there's no end to flea season."

To ban these visitors from your winter hearth, Dr. Donovan suggests treating rugs with "products made especially to get rid of fleas." For most effectiveness, look for products that contain carbaryl.

Thinking of an Electronic Flea Collar?

Don't bother. "No study has shown that electronic flea collars have *any* impact on fleas at all," says Dr. Thompson. "The only reason they are legal is because they are not a drug and therefore don't have to be proven effective."

Do Fleas Flee Collars?

"Flea collars are pretty toxic," warns Dr. Donovan. "They project the pesticide from head to the tail, so everything in that area gets a dose." Yet no study shows they kill fleas *unless* you and your pet happen to live in the Pacific Northwest. (That's the only area where the collars seem effective!)

An Old Brewer's Tale

Feeding your pet brewer's yeast *won't* control fleas, says Dr. Donovan. It sometimes helps *humans* prevent mosquito bites because it affects perspiration. It doesn't work with dogs—they only sweat on their tongues and foot pads.

The Experts

Paul Donovan, V.M.D., is the director of the Alburtis Animal Hospital in Alburtis, Pennsylvania.

Bruce Ilgen, D.V.M., director of the Detwiler Veterinary Clinic located in Reading, Pennsylvania, specializes in pet dental care.

Myrna Milani, D.V.M., a veterinarian and animal behaviorist in Charlestown, New Hampshire, is author of several books including *The Body Language and Emotions of Dogs.*

Liz Palika is a dog obedience trainer in Oceanside, California, and a columnist for *Dog Fancy* magazine.

Dave Thompson, D.V.M., is a veterinarian at the 17,000-patient North Asheville Animal Hospital in Asheville, North Carolina.

CHAPTER 13

Personal Safety and Security

Take Steps
to Protect Yourself

A stitch in time saves nine. An ounce of prevention is worth a pound of cure. Don't lock the barn door after the horse is stolen.

Proverbs became proverbs for a good reason. Those worn words of wisdom addressed an issue that you still deal with today: protecting your life, your loved ones, and the worldly goods that belong to you. To quote another worn phrase, "The best offense is a good defense." Steps that you take ahead of time, when there seems to be no imminent threat, can pay off if and when a real threat appears.

These expert tips on personal safety can help you protect yourself and your family from injury in the home, in the car, and out on the streets. And they'll also help you with *security*—protecting your home and all its contents from the threat of fire, and burglarproofing your property to reduce the risk of theft.

These experts not only have good ideas—they also remind us of the commonsense cautions that sometimes save lives. Good advice is what it boils down to. But a lot is left up to you—because, even the best advice will mean nothing if you don't act on it. A seat belt, a 911 telephone number, a first aid kit, a smoke detector are just tools for security. If you want them to work for you, you have to *use* them.

Guarding Your Goods

Win This Numbers Game

You may daydream about leaving your mark on history, but do make a point of leaving your mark on your personal possessions. The valuables that a thief is likely to carry away include your TV set, CD player, camera, and computer. These and other household items can all be marked with an engraving tool, supplied by your local police department as part of Operation Identification. The price is right: It's free.

The identification number you engrave on the items is placed on file with the local police department, making it easy for you to get property returned if it is stolen and subsequently retrieved, according to Mindy Moore, spokesperson for Brinks Home Security in Carrollton, Texas. She recommends using your driver's license number as the identifying mark.

HOME-SECURITY DOCS

Your home may not be as safe from intruders as you think it is. Your local law enforcement agency can make a "house call" to provide an on-site inspection to point out potential points of entry for a burglar.

Sheriff Walter Heinrich of the Hillsborough County, Florida, Sheriff's Office, set up a crime prevention bureau that offers just such home check-ups for his community. Sheriff Heinrich's prevention specialists recommend that to protect yourself, you look at your home through a burglar's eyes. Here's what a burglar notes.
- Are there loosely secured windows or doors?
- Does tall shrubbery surrounding the front, sides, and back of the house provide convenient concealment?
- Are there dark areas near the windows and doors?

And put away that innocent ladder you left standing by the garage. It can give a burglar the boost he needs for a second-story job!

Ask a Specialist

Ask your police department if it has a security specialist who can visit your home and recommend steps to make your home safer and more thief-resistant, says Moore. A local specialist will have the scoop on the kind of crime that affects your area—and practical advice on how to counter it.

FYI

THE BASICS OF CITY SMARTS

"The criminal is an opportunist," says Gerald S. Arenberg, of Miami, Florida, who is chairman of the Florida Crime Prevention Commisson and executive director of the National Association of Chiefs of Police.

Arenberg's personal safety checklist is based on signals that criminals watch for and take advantage of.

- When going on local errands, plan a route along well-lighted, safe streets. Preferably, walk with a friend or a dog.
- If you're headed out of town, even for a day trip, let someone know where you are going and when you expect to return.
- Avoid going near vacant lots or deserted alleys.
- Walk in the middle of the sidewalk, rather than close to buildings or near the curb, so you'll avoid alleys or parked cars.
- If you believe that someone is following you, head for a well-lighted place where people congregate.
- Carrying a purse? It should be close to your body, the clasp facing you, with your hand on the clasp.
- Carry your keys and cash in pockets, not in your purse.
- If you carry a wallet, keep it in a buttoned, inside jacket pocket.
- Don't carry large sums of money; never flash a roll of bills.
- Don't dress in a manner that calls attention to yourself.
- If a car pulls up alongside you, turn around and go back the way you came. The car will have to make a U-turn to follow you.
- Don't hitchhike; don't pick up hitchhikers.
- When traveling on trains or buses, select an aisle seat near the driver.
- Never travel in an unoccupied subway car.

An Inventory Tells the Story

When you return home and find that valuables are missing, your frantic telephone call to the police will bring the inevitable question, "What goods were taken, and how much were they worth?"

You'll hear the same question later from your insurance agent. You can save yourself a lot of aggravation by preparing a household inventory that indicates purchase prices, serial numbers, and replacement costs. Store the list in your refrigerator's freezer compartment, suggests Moore. ("A burglar will *never* look inside your freezer," she adds.) You should store a second copy of the household inventory in a safe deposit box.

Another way to record vital information about personal possessions is by videotaping. On videotape you can show the object from various angles, helping your insurance agent to determine values of the damaged, stolen, or destroyed goods.

Peek-a-Who?

Home security ranges from flimsy to formidable, but for most of us, some easily installed devices can greatly enhance security.

Thomas P. Kaika, regional sales manager of Yale Security Products in Charlotte, North Carolina, recommends a door-viewer for everyone. This simple device allows you to peek through and see who's outside your door. If the person you see through the viewer is a stranger with no reason to be there, you can always invite the person to call and make an appointment. You don't *have* to open the door!

Bolt-Action Backup

The standard lock in a doorknob may not be sturdy enough to be really effective, according to Wayne Parker, owner of A-1 Key and Safe in St. Petersburg, Florida. "If your residential front door is of wood or metal, buy a dead bolt to add more protection," he advises. While the doorknob lock is only a spring-loaded device, "the dead-bolt lock is stronger and extends farther into the door jamb for home protection," he explains.

The quality of that dead-bolt lock is of prime concern. Beware of dead-bolt locks manufactured in Taiwan, China, or Japan, warns Parker. Their materials are usually thin, the locks are easier to pick, and parts for damaged locks are not available in the United States. He recommends the stronger dead-bolt locks manufactured in the United States or Germany.

For greater home security: a dead-bolt lock.

Automatic Theft Machine?

With automatic teller machines (ATM), "ATM holdup" is a brand new type of crime frequently reported to local police departments.

One tactic: Robbers hide in shrubbery near an ATM, then get the jump on customers who have just made bank withdrawals.

"The basic rule for using an ATM is to be aware of how vulnerable you may be," says John Lorenz, deputy in the Hillsborough County, Florida, Sheriff's Office and a member of the Sheriff's Crime Awareness Team (SCAT).

He adds these safety tips for using an ATM.

- Always pick a well-lighted ATM, one that is away from vegetation. (Better yet, find one in a store that is well lighted and full of people.)
- Don't use the machines at odd hours or late at night.
- Bring a friend.
- Keep your eyes open. If anyone is "just hanging out," hold on to your plastic—and try another ATM.

A Key in the Car Says, "Steal Me!"

Want to lose your car in a hurry? Try leaving your key in the ignition while you make that quick dash into the mini-mart.

According to Jerry Ralph Curry, administrator of the National Highway Traffic Safety Administration (NHTSA) of the U.S. Department of Transportation in Washington, D.C., statistics show that nearly half of all the cars stolen in the United States had keys in the ignition. What better invitation to car thieves?

A simple tip: *Always* take your key with you when you leave your car.

Don't Make Car Heists Easy

Here are some other theftproofing tips from Curry for car owners.

- Don't hide a spare key under the seat, above the sun visor, or in one of those cute magnetic boxes. The thieves know all those places; you simply make their task easier.
- Park at night in well-lighted areas, preferably close to a street corner.
- Never leave your title and registration papers in the car. (The title belongs in a safe deposit box; the registration in your purse or wallet.)
- Report a stolen car immediately. If you delay, the car could be used in the commission of another crime.
- Alarm systems are expensive toys that seldom deter thieves. As a better alternative, consider a $25 cutoff switch, an easily installed device that leaves your car "dead in the water." Rather than spending time looking for the switch, the thief will prefer to steal a less protected car instead.

The Road to Car Safety

Belt Yourself in for Life

When auto seat belts were first introduced, a controversy was born. The belters squared off with the no-belters. Now the verdict is in: The belters were right.

"Buckling up every trip is perhaps the single most effective safety precaution a person can take. It's truly a habit for life," says Curry.

Each year, about 47,000 lives are lost in traffic accidents, and an additional 1,800,000 people are permanently disabled. The NHTSA has concluded that you *double* your chances of surviving a car crash if you're belted in.

Most states and the District of Columbia have laws requiring seat belt use by both adults and children. These laws have proved effective in reducing the numbers of injuries and fatalities in traffic accidents.

Pumping Action for Icy Roads

Common advice: "Pump" the brakes if you want to stop quickly. But that pumping action works *only* if you're trying to stop on clear or rain-wet pavement. If you need to stop on ice or snow, follow this advice for "squeeze braking" from the American Automobile Association (AAA).

- Shift into neutral. (If you have a manual transmission, push in the clutch.)
- Press steadily on the brake, then ease off...but not completely.
- Press again, then hold.

Don't slam on the brakes, as they may lock and you'll skid out of control (unless you have antilock brakes). If you use the squeeze-brake technique, you'll be able to maintain steering control.

Don't Drive under the Influenza

We all know that driving under the influence of alcohol is the *big* reaper—implicated in nearly half of all fatalities.

But a bad cold or a nasty case of flu are bad influences, too. According to the Medical Research Council's Common Cold Unit in Salisbury, England, flu victims have a reaction time that's *worse* than moderate drinkers. Even people with colds flunked a battery of tests for hand/eye coordination.

So if you have a bad case of flu or the serious sniffles, avoid driving. Better to miss a day or two of work than to risk your life on the road.

Highway Menace: Hot-Collared Drivers

Spat with the spouse? Boss got your goat? Try to stay out of the driver's seat for a while.

That's the advice of Ming T. Tsuan, M.D., Ph.D., professor of psychiatry at the Harvard Medical School and chief of psychiatry at the Brockton–East Roxbury Veterans Administration Medical Center in Massachusetts. At least one survey showed that one out of every five drivers killed in auto accidents had some kind of emotional upset sometime during the previous 6 hours.

Fighting Fire with Foresight

Your Phone May Be Zapped!

You're on the telephone when you hear, somewhere in the distance, the clap of thunder. Worse yet, you look out the window and see lightning. Quick, get off the telephone!

Ron Douglas, safety administrator for General Telephone of Florida, in Tampa, offers this advice: Avoid using the telephone when you see lightning. "If you have an urgent call to make, be brief," says Douglas. "Even though the telephone company uses protective measures to prevent abnormal electrical surges from entering your home, there is a remote risk of a dangerous electrical shock from lightning if you use the telephone when there's a nearby electrical storm. Lightning-induced voltages can follow telephone lines into your home, even into your telephone."

Big Bolts in the Boob Tube

Your telephone is not the only thing around the house that attracts lightning. The outdoor TV and FM antennas on your roof also attract those giant bolts of electrical energy.

Going by the National Electrical Code, the antenna must be grounded and suitable antenna-discharge units should be installed on the lead-in wire. Your best bet? Hire a licensed antenna installer or an electrician familiar with lightning protection.

Save these appliances by installing protective devices on electrical service lines. Check to see if your local power company offers a lightning/surge protection service.

Strong, lightning-induced power surges can enter your home and destroy refrigerators, TVs, and radios.

Bigger Ashtrays Are Better

Cigarettes can kill. Medical considerations aside, smouldering cigarette butts can start dangerous home fires, according to Bill Larabel, a property claims consultant for Foremost Insurance Company located in Grand Rapids, Michigan.

Cigarette butts can fall off shallow ashtrays and ignite paper or other materials. "If you must smoke, select a proper ashtray," warns Larabel. "Use one that is 6 or more inches in diameter, with enough depth to fully contain the cigarette."

Larabel has another tip for smokers: "Empty your ashtrays each evening before you go to bed. Be sure that no spark remains in the butts you are discarding, and wait until morning to smoke again."

Avoid an Inferno

Gasoline cans must *always* remain outside the home, says Larabel. When transporting gasoline for lawn mowers, carry the container in the trunk, not in the passenger area of the car. And when you store gasoline in a shed, garage, or workshop, make sure it's not close to any electric motors.

Why the concern? Gasoline is a potential fire-starter when stored improperly. Fumes from gasoline can be ignited relatively easily by any spark, including that provided by the refrigerator kicking on, the hot water heater, or a pilot light.

Watch That Fat

When heating cooking oil, don't turn the burner to high and then walk away, says Butters. Cooking oil can reach a temperature high enough to cause a fire to break out. The best way to avoid grease fires is by staying in the kitchen while foods are cooking. And, of course, turn off cooking appliances when you are finished with them.

Cap That Blaze

More than 100,000 fires start in home kitchens every year, according to the National Fire Protection Association. As a result of these fires, hundreds of people are killed annually, and thousands are injured.

A common cause—overheated fat in a frypan. According to Timothy Butters, director of government relations and public affairs for the International Association of Fire Chiefs in Washington, D.C., the best way to fight these fires is by capping them.

"If flames occur," Butters suggests, "immediately put a lid on the pan. This is far better than putting baking soda on the pan or using a small, handheld fire extinguisher. A cookie sheet will do as well, just so long as all the air is blocked from the pan." (See illustration on page 328.)

Sometimes extinguishers cause a splash of burning fat, which in turn can burn someone standing nearby or can spread the fire even farther, he says.

To put out fire in a kitchen pan, slide a cookie sheet over the top of the pan.

Smokey the Chef Sez...

To keep your kitchen safe from fire, follow these tips from the National Fire Protection Association.

- Remove built-up grease in ovens and on cooktops.
- Make sure that you don't wear loose, long-sleeved clothing while standing over a hot stove.
- Never cook while wearing a tie.
- Don't reach over hot burners to get items you need for cooking. Instead, store the items in cabinets that are *not* over the stove.
- Be wary of steam burns from microwaved food. If you carelessly open a bag of microwaved popcorn, for instance, the rush of hot steam can leave you with painful burns on your face, neck, chest, or hands.

Hate Those Precooked Meals?

Then keep your grocery bags *off* the stove, warns Kenneth L. Cramer, fire chief of the Pinellas Park, Florida, Fire Department and president of the Pinellas County Fire Chiefs Association. The stove is *not* a table, he cautions. If you put grocery bags on the stove, you're playing with fire. "Danger can come not only from the electric burners but also from gas pilot lights."

So do yourself a favor—stow those bags elsewhere.

Be Saved by the Buzzer

There's no insurance that can stop a fire before it happens. Fire can be caused by a lightning strike, an electrical short, or an accidentally activated stove burner, among other things.

All the more reason to have a couple of well-placed smoke detectors. "Installing smoke detectors can save more lives than anything else you do," says David A. Lucht, Ph.D., professor and director of the Center for Firesafety Studies at Worcester Polytechnic Institute, in Worcester, Massachusetts.

Because smoke rises, the detectors should be placed on the ceiling or high up on the wall, he notes. Dr. Lucht recommends a smoke detector bearing the Underwriters Laboratories (UL) seal. It means the national testing organization has certified the safety of the appliance.

Happy Birthday, Smoke Detector

Make sure that your smoke detectors are operational *before* a fire starts, urges William E. Wanless, agent for the Mutual Insurance Agency located in Seminole, Florida. "If your detectors are part of an electrical circuit, check your fuses on a monthly basis," he advises. "If your smoke detectors are battery operated, change the batteries annually, whether or not new batteries are needed."

Typically, a smoke detector runs on a 9-volt battery for a year. When the battery gets low, a chirping sound signals the need for a battery change.

Don't wait for the chirp! "If people test their detectors on a significant day each year, then they will not forget," says Wanless. He suggests making the smoke detector check-and-change on your birthday!

Shower Power to Battle Blazes

If the occupants of your home include the elderly, the disabled, or children, consider installing sprinklers.

The idea of home sprinklers began in rural parts of the country, where fire trucks needed more than 5 minutes to respond, explains Steve A. Muncy, president of the American Fire Sprinkler Association in Dallas, Texas.

The sprinkler system can be installed in one room or throughout the whole house, whichever you prefer. (Cost depends on the size of the rooms that are sprinkler-equipped.) If a fire breaks out, the sprinklers will not only put out the fire but will keep the heat source from spreading to adjoining rooms. This factor is very important in wooden frame structures.

HOME OR WORK—WHICH IS SAFER?

Job-related injuries do occur, but you're more likely to be injured at home than at work. According to a study by the National Crime Survey compiled by the Department of Justice, 58 out of 1,000 adults can expect to experience some type of accidental injury at work. At home, the chances of accidental injury are 79 out of 1,000—about one-third greater.

FASTEN YOUR SEA BELTS

If you spend much time on small boats, you may get casual about such things as life jackets and other basic precautions. But pause to consider: Seventy percent of boating fatalities are caused by falling overboard. And many of those drownings begin with carelessness. The U.S. Coast Guard strongly recommends that all boaters take a course with a local auxiliary unit before they head for the high seas. Among the precautions:

- Don't drink while you're boating. (One-half of all drowning victims have significant levels of alcohol in their blood.)
- Don't overload your boat—and keep the weight low. (Many boats carry labels indicating their weight capacity.)
- Don't stand up in a small boat. (It's easier than you think to fall out!)
- And *do* wear a proper flotation device. If you suddenly get dunked— especially in cold water—a life vest may save your life.

Avoiding Household Mishaps

Beware the Stairs

Home may be where the heart is, but it's also a dangerous place, especially around the stairs. Jan Weyhrich, senior loss control representative for State Farm Insurance Company of Bloomington, Illinois, identifies the stairway as the location of many of these home accidents.

Here are a few things he suggests you can do to protect yourself and your family from not-so-funny pratfalls.

- Make sure stairs are kept clear of small toys.
- Do not use loose throw rugs or mats near the stairs.
- Carpet the stairs with short-napped or looped carpet, or install stair treads.

Skid-Stops on Slippery Stools

Most kitchen floor coverings are of the never-wax or no-wax variety, and it's all too easy to slip on such floors. You may keep your footing, but what about your kitchen stools?

Those long-legged stools can by tippy and slippery, especially if the floor gets wet.

If you have a bar-style stool at a kitchen counter, Weyhrich recommends rubber caps for the legs.

DON'T DIVE BLIND

About 1,000 people are killed or paralyzed in diving accidents every year, and 70 percent of those accidents result from diving into water that's *less than 4 feet deep.*

Watch out for the old "familiar" swimming hole, especially. "A swimming hole that was deep enough to dive into last year may be shallow this year, due to lack of rainfall," according to John F. Ditunno, M.D., project director of the Regional Spinal Cord Injury Center of the Delaware River at Thomas Jefferson University Hospital in Philadelphia. The American Red Cross urges swimmers to slip carefully into the water or walk in slowly any time you try out a new swimming spot. Never dive off the sides of piers or rock jetties: That's an invitation to disaster. And according to the Red Cross, you should never dive head-first into an above-ground pool.

Keep Tykes from Exercise Bikes

Exercise bikes, popular indoor vehicles for weight loss and health gain, should be operated with caution around little kids, according to the U.S. Consumer Product Safety Commission. During a five-year period, nearly 1,200 children had fingers amputated because of contact with exercise bikes.

If you're using a bike around young children, make sure they stay away from wheels, chains, and sprocket assemblies.

Fallproof Tactics

Afraid of slipping on that rug? Skidding on the bathroom floor? Falling in a badly lighted hallway?

You have reason to worry—and take action—especially if there is an elderly person in your household. Studies show that accidental falls kill more people over age 65 than any other injury—and 44 percent of all falls are caused by hazards in and around the house.

Here are some trouble spots to watch out for, as pointed out by Rein Tideiksar, Ph.D., and Arthur D. Kay, M.D., co-directors of the Falls and Immobility Program in the Ritter Department of Geriatrics and Adult Development at Mount Sinai Medical Center in New York City.

- Uneven front steps or sidewalks
- Slippery throw rugs
- Just-out-of-reach shelves or cabinets

- Slippery surfaces in the bathroom
- Poorly lit (or unlit) halls between bedroom and bathroom

Handling Home Emergencies

Kids and Poison Spell Trouble

Don't leave kids alone with any poisonous substance, even for a second.

"You might be killing an insect or polishing a coffee table when the doorbell rings, distracting you for just a second," says toxicologist Sven Normann, Pharm.D., who is clinical and administrative director of the Florida Poison Information Center, and serves on the board of directors for the

---

FYI

STORE KILLER STUFF UP HIGH

There is a high incidence of children's deaths by accidental poisoning—and that's because so many poisonous items are commonly found in the home environment, according to Sven Normann, Pharm.D., toxicologist and clinical director of the Florida Poison Information Center. Prevention? Keep poisons and potential poisons locked up and out of reach of children.

Take a look at the following list of "killers." In your own home, which ones are within easy reach of an unsuspecting toddler?

Poison experts divide dangerous substances into two major categories: common household substances and medications. In the common household substances group are:

- Cleaning products
- Cosmetics (lipsticks, cologne, etc.)
- Insecticides
- Plants (most commonly, diffenbachia and philodendron)

The medications most often involved in accidental poisonings of children include:

- Analgesics (aspirin and aspirin substitutes)
- Cough and cold medicines
- Topical ointments (diaper cream, salves)
- Sleeping medications
- Antibiotics

American Association of Poison Control Centers. "Many accidental poisonings occur in that brief moment when a child is unattended as you answer the doorbell or pick up the telephone," he notes.

If a child is present in the home when you are using polishes or cleaners for some household chore, take the product with you when you go to the door or answer the phone, advises Dr. Normann.

Switch Off for Safety

If someone has been injured by electrical shock, your first instinct may be to rush to the rescue.

Think twice. In many cases, you may be risking your life if there's live electricity involved. "The only way to be completely safe in an electrical-shock situation is to leave the victim alone and call immediately for professional help," according to Neil F. Comins, Ph.D., an electrical engineer, emergency medicine technician, and astronomy professor at the University of Maine at Orono.

But there is one thing you *can* do: Know the location of the master electrical switch in your home. If there's an emergency, turn off the switch, then call for emergency assistance.

FYI

OLDER IS SAFER

"Crime is everywhere," is what we often hear. And it sometimes seems that older people are frequent victims. Is that true?

Statistically, not so, according to the U.S. Bureau of Crime Statistics, which keeps track of the ages of people who fall victim to crimes of violence. Here's the very good news: The older you get, the *lower* your chances of being mugged, stabbed, or otherwise injured in a violent crime.

In a recent year, according to the bureau, about 74 out of every 1,000 youngsters in the 16-to-19 age group were victims of violent crime. In the 35-to-59 age group, the risk of being a victim fell to a third of that—or about 21 in 1,000. And for those over 60? The risk of violent crime is less than 8 in 1,000. In other words, a 60-year-old is about *nine times* less likely to be a victim than a 16-year-old.

Obviously, some things *do* get better as we age.

The Shocking Truth

People in rural areas get struck by lightning more often than their city cousins. (This is not surprising, of course, since they spend more time outdoors.) Based on reports that indicate the location of occurrences during the past 30 years, the majority of deaths and injuries resulting from lightning have occurred in open fields, under trees, or during boating, fishing, and other water-related activities, reports Roger Tanner, chief of computer support and the product generation section with the National Climatic Data Center in Asheville, North Carolina. (He adds that about 40 percent of the reports do not indicate the location of occurrence.)

What to do about it? "If you're caught in the open and there's lightning striking around you, *get as low as possible without lying flat on the ground*," suggests Bill Read, meteorologist in charge with the National Weather Forecast Service in Houston, Texas. "Crouch down, with only your feet on the ground. That allows the lowest exposure. You don't want to lie flat, because when lightning strikes, it travels along the surface of the ground."

And stay away from trees! They may provide shelter from rain but they attract lightning. Also keep clear of wire fences, clotheslines, pipes, or other metallic objects.

Keep Informed

The best protection from weather-related injury is to "be aware of what's expected," suggests Read. NOAA Weather Radio is available on FM bands around 162 on the radio dial across most of the United States.

The Experts

Gerald S. Arenberg is a 30-year veteran of law enforcement, serves as chairman of the Florida Crime Prevention Commission in Miami and is the executive director of the National Association of Chiefs of Police.

Timothy Butters is director of government relations and public affairs for the International Association of Fire Chiefs in Washington, D.C.

Neil F. Comins, Ph.D., is an electrical engineer, emergency medicine technician, and an astronomy professor at the University of Maine at Orono.

Kenneth L. Cramer is the fire chief for the City of Pinellas Park, Florida, and the president of the Pinellas County Fire Chiefs Association.

Jerry Ralph Curry is an administrator for the National Highway Traffic Safety Administration at the U.S. Department of Transportation in Washington, D.C.

John F. Ditunno, M.D., is project director of the Regional Spinal Cord Injury Center of the Delaware Valley at Thomas Jefferson University Hospital in Philadelphia.

Ron Douglas is safety administrator for General Telephone in Tampa, Florida.

Walter Heinrich is sheriff with the Hillsborough County Sheriff's Office in Tampa, Florida.

Thomas P. Kaika is regional sales manager for Yale Security Products, Inc., in Charlotte, North Carolina.

Arthur D. Kay, M.D., is a co-director of the Falls and Immobility Program in the Ritter Department of Geriatrics and Adult Development at Mount Sinai Medical Center in New York City.

Bill Larabel is a claims consultant for Foremost Insurance Company in Grand Rapids, Michigan.

John Lorenz is a deputy in the Hillsborough County Sheriff's Office and a member of the Sheriff's Crime Awareness Team (SCAT) in Tampa, Florida.

David A. Lucht, Ph.D., is director of the Center for Firesafety Studies at Worcester Polytechnic Institute in Worcester, Massachusetts.

Mindy Moore is a spokesperson for Brinks Home Security in Carrollton, Texas.

Steve A. Muncy is president of the American Fire Sprinkler Association in Dallas, Texas.

Sven Normann, Pharm.D., toxicologist and clinical director of the Florida Poison Information Center in Tampa General Hospital in Tampa, Florida, is a director of the American Association of Poison Control Centers.

Wayne Parker is a locksmith and owner of A-1 Key and Safe, Inc., in St. Petersburg, Florida.

Bill Read is meteorologist in charge with the National Weather Forecast Service in Houston, Texas.

Roger Tanner is chief of computer support and the product generation section with the National Climatic Data Center in Asheville, North Carolina.

Rein Tideiksar, Ph.D., is a co-director of the Falls and Immobility Program in the Ritter Department of Geriatrics and Adult Development at Mount Sinai Medical Center in New York City.

Ming T. Tsuan, M.D., Ph.D., is professor of psychiatry at the Harvard Medical School and chief of psychiatry at the Brockton–East Roxbury Veterans Administration Medical Center in Massachusetts.

William E. Wanless is an agent with Mutual Insurance Agency, Inc., in Seminole, Florida.

Jan Weyhrich is senior loss control representative for State Farm Insurance Company in Bloomington, Illinois.

CHAPTER 14

Traveling the U.S.A.

Better Bargains
on Visits and Vistas

Paris, London, Hong Kong, and Rome have their attractions, but more Americans than ever are rediscovering your land and my land—from the Grand Canyon and New Orleans, to California and, yes, even the New York island.

Domestic travel and tourism make up America's third largest industry, trailing only automotive dealerships and food stores. Altogether, U.S. vacation travel is a $350 *billion* industry, a recession-resistant sum of our wanderlust that just figures larger every year. But our spending on travel is by no means one-sided. The 50 states spend about $350 million a year trying to tempt *you* to come see their historic, cultural, and scenic wonders.

Considering all the visits and vistas America has to offer, it's sometimes hard to decide where to begin, especially if you're limited to a precious two or three weeks of vacation time. Of course, this is where the advantage of seniority comes in. If you're retired, the travel season never has to end; you can celebrate the grandeurs of this endlessly curious country from January to December, should you so desire. And not only that, you can find some superb deals in discount travel if you know what to ask for and where to look.

Whether you're planning on months, weeks, or days of travel—or merely setting up business trips—certain questions come up again and again, such as: "How can I save money?" "How can I make my trip safer?" "How can I stay healthy along the way?"

Fortunately, you can find a wealth of published material to help guide you—travel guides and directories, destination descriptions, and the vast acres of literature that tourist-seeking states are willing to send to you absolutely gratis. If you're planning a trip, your local travel agent can be a valuable friend, and there are dozens of clubs—motoring and otherwise—devoted to helping members make the most of vacation times.

"Focused planning" is a key phrase in the travel industry these days. Take a look at a few specialized tours as an example. Does Buddhism fascinate you? There's a tour of Buddhist sites in the United States that any travel agent can arrange. Prefer folklore? Bird-watching? A houseboat holiday? Dog-sledding? Desert adventure? Cathedral-prowling? Arrangements are no more than a phone call away.

Tours with others of like interests can be easily arranged, so you end up with a group whose whims are similar. When it's bedtime, do you prefer posh hotels—or the serenity of an open sky at night? What's your preferred mode of travel? Jet plane? Private car? Tour coach? RV? Bubble-top train car?

The following tips from experts in the field of domestic travel should help answer your pretravel questions—or guide you to the right source. Here are the best of their hints for saving dollars and saving time, plus many great ways to make your trip more comfortable and meaningful.

Happy traveling...

Before You Go

Play the 800-Numbers Game

Before you begin making travel plans, jot down this valuable phone number: 1-800-555-1212. That's the nationwide number for the toll-free information operator.

As travel writer Dorothy Fields of Placerville, California, points out, "In most cases, you can book all the hotels for your trip, airline tickets, rental cars, even many restaurants by using an 800 number."

Since making reservations for an extended trip involves a lot of comparison shopping via telephone, you can reduce that cost to nearly zero via the toll-free route. Many local and state travel information agencies are also hooked into the 800 system.

Take a Tour...Of Your Local Phone Book

When most people pick up the phone book, they either look in the white pages (for residential and business) or the yellow pages (for business listings and paid ads). But in many large cities, the phone book has another, often-overlooked section that holds a bonanza of information for the traveler.

"In a new city, I always look in the front of the phone book to get a 'feel' for that city, even before I begin leafing through my travel guidebook," says Leonard D. Ash, a freelance travel writer in San Diego. "Then, it's a logical next step to the white and yellow pages for the specifics."

The up-front white page section that appears *before* the regular white pages may list local historical landmarks and other points of interest. Also, some phone books have a seasonal calendar of events, along with hours when local museums, galleries, and the like are open.

In the San Diego phone book, for example, are details on the city's famous San Diego Zoo, a map of San Diego airport showing airline locations, a listing of local beaches, and there's even a where-to-find-it guide to downtown Tijuana in neighboring Mexico. "Altogether," says Ash, "it's better than a chamber of commerce booklet."

Bibliotravelfile

Another tip from travel writer Ash: "If you can't find an answer any other place, phone the library. Librarians by nature are research fanatics. Toss an intriguing question their way, and they won't give up until they have an answer.

"I once phoned the library to find out where I could find California golden poppies and what the weather would be the next day. I also asked for some background on the 'Guardian of the Waters' statue in front of the San Diego County building. Within just a few minutes, the librarian had all the answers."

Be Guided True, Not Askew

When choosing a guidebook, be skeptical if you see the firm's logo (its symbol) printed next to its listing in the book.

Mark Orwoll, senior editor at *Travel and Leisure* magazine in New York, tells travelers to make sure the guidebook they use has its *own* listings and ratings of restaurants, accommodations, and local attractions. If the book has logos alongside its ads, he says, that's a clue that it probably takes paid advertising and the listings reflect the advertiser's point of view. While there's nothing wrong with those kinds of listings, it means they're not objective.

Another clue: Beware if the listing refers to the place as *we*—as in "We take good care of our customers." That's another signal that the advertiser is helping to create the editorial opinions in the book.

The Case with the Telltale Tassel

At airport baggage carousels, you'll often see signs warning travelers that suitcases look alike. What they *don't* tell you is how to prevent a mix-up.

To avoid ending up with someone else's pajamas, toothbrush, and paperback novel, tie a brightly colored tassel of yarn to your suitcase, suggests Michael Milan, a San Francisco builder who travels frequently on business.

Halting a Heist Before It Happens

If you label your luggage with a tag that shows your home address, you're offering unnecessary temptation to airport thieves. According to San Diego writer and business flier Martin Hill, some masters of deviousness lurk around airports, copying home addresses from luggage tags. The objective: to raid the home while the traveler's away.

Since most airlines require tagging, what's a foolproof way to thief-proof your luggage?

Hill suggests using a business card that gives only your business address. That satisfies the airline's requirements, but without helping would-be housebreakers.

Rush-Season Traffic in National Parks

Our national parks are literally being loved to death, says Don McQuiston of Del Mar, California, a book designer who has produced more than two dozen books related to the U.S. National Parks system. Because of America's passion for midsummer travel in the great outdoors, campsites are jammed at midseason, and some of the hottest hiking trails resemble rush-hour freeways.

McQuiston points to many advantages of *off-season* travel in fall, winter, and spring. "In many parks, there's gorgeous tree color in fall and wildflowers in spring," he notes. "With fewer people around, more wild animals show themselves. Fall is the time when most animals migrate and can best be seen"—for example, the beautiful sight of the fall migration of Canada geese over Mount Lassen National Park in California.

Winter also has many attractions, whether or not you enjoy winter sports. "You can watch bald eagles feeding on salmon in the Skagit River of North Cascades National Park, Washington, from December to the middle of February," says McQuiston. For winter skiing? "I'd recommend Hidden Valley in Rocky Mountain National Park in Colorado."

And finally, photography is better in the off-season when you don't have summer haze, notes McQuiston. "That's all the more reason for avoiding the people-rush of the summer months."

Off-Season Gambol: Double Your Savings

What *really* determines travel costs?

Often, it's just the season, says Robert W. Seckman, managing director of Travel Agency Services for the American Automobile Association in Heathrow, Florida. As Seckman points out, planning a trip *outside* of the peak season can save money—sometimes, lots of it.

Example: Travelers can save up to 20 percent on a visit to Alaska by going in May or September, as opposed to the summer months. For a family, that one-fifth savings can mount up to many hundreds of dollars. If you're traveling to California or Florida, on the other hand, you'll get the best bargains in early summer.

You'll not only save on accommodations but other expenses as well. "During the off-season," Seckman says, "many airlines and restaurants reduce their prices."

If you can arrange to travel during off-seasons, talk to a knowledgeable travel agent who can tell you how to cut costs at each destination.

The Film's in the Mail

What would a vacation be without the postvacation slide show? While many people look forward to sharing slides and photos after the vacation's over, travel can be tough on film. Extreme heat can damage film that's stored in a sizzling parked car, and even perfume vapors have been known to scar a roll of best-in-a-lifetime shots.

There's a simple way to avoid these problems, notes Dan Guravich of Greenville, Mississippi, a professional nature and travel photographer who has published more than 15 books. "Don't wait until you get home to have the film processed. Buy the kind of transparency film (for slides) that comes with mailers. Chances are, by the time you reach home, your slides will be ready for viewing—all paid for."

When you buy film this way, the cost of the mailer and processing is part of the purchase price. Although pros prefer slides, many mail-order film houses make the same plan available for color print film; some even provide envelopes that are postage-paid. In most cases, the cost of developing is less than it would be if you took your roll into a local camera store.

Cashless Travel May Cost You a Heap

The travel habits of Americans prove that we're fast becoming a cashless society. With the ease and availability of traveler's checks and credit cards, there's little need to carry much cash on the road, notes Kristin Ross, an assistant manager of People's Heritage Bank in Camden, Maine, who specializes in loans and mortgages.

But here's the new risk: If you're using a credit card and taking out big cash advances, you're incurring very high interest. In fact, high interest is the lurking bandit of the modern highways, and it can swipe a huge chunk of your postvacation funds. Accounts like Visa and MasterCard may charge interest in the range of 16 to 20 percent (annual rate) on cash withdrawals. And interest is charged from the day of withdrawal. (For more interesting details, read the fine print on your monthly statement.)

A better idea: Use an ATM (automatic teller machine) card that will be recognized through one of the many inter-bank systems such as Star, CIRRUS, or Plus. The card allows you to draw cash for a minimal flat fee—usually from 50 cents to $1. Teller machines operate 24 hours a day, which is a help to the traveler caught cashless late at night or on weekends. .

If you *have* to draw a cash advance on a credit card, mail a check to your account the same day. It's the best way to stay current on your account, instead of running up big interest costs—and the best way to prevent postvacation regrets.

Tips for the Trip

Carry On the Essentials
Traveling by plane? Your carry-on should hold whatever you can't live without—such as your passport, wallet, and a second pair of eyeglasses—suggests Robert Ermatinger, executive vice president of the Luggage and Leather Goods Manufacturers of America in New York City, and the publisher of *Showcase*, a trade publication among the luggage industry. According to Ermatinger, a carry-on should not be any more than 22 inches high, to fit under an airline seat. He also suggests including a "packing list" of the clothing and valuables you have in your suitcases, just in case your luggage is lost.

Ermatinger says he always travels with the following in his tote: slipper socks, a photocopy of his passport, a bottle of spring water, a razor, and an electronic watch that stores important addresses and phone numbers.

What Any Woman Needs...For 6 Days of Business Travel
Here's a travel list from Patricia A. Beegle, fashion marketing manager of the DuPont Company Fibers Division in Wilmington, Delaware.

For packing economy, she travels with two suits, one gray and one blue with complementary blouses. She also takes a printed dress of a style and fabric that blend with the suits for mix and match. ("This give me six days of business outfits," she says.) For shoes, she takes one pair of charcoal pumps—and two pairs each of gray, blue, and nude panty hose.

Essential Steps to Packing

Robert Ermatinger, the publisher of *Showcase,* a trade publication serving the luggage industry, has come up with some ways to pack that are guaranteed to reduce wrinkling.

Some general rules:

- Always pack a jacket's collar at the hinge of the case to allow the width of the shoulder to remain smooth.
- Full, voluminous skirts, dresses, and other garments should be packed lengthwise. The width of the case should be used for slacks and narrow items.
- Make sure that jackets are buttoned, sleeves are folded over the front of each other, and the trousers are zippered.
- As you pack, try to layer coordinates on top of each other whenever possible.

According to Ermatinger, here's a sure-fire way to layer your clothing.

- Pack heavy objects such as shoes, toilet kit, and hair dryer in the bottom of the suitcase—that is, on the side *opposite* the handle.
- Roll up any wrinkle-resistant items, such as jeans, sweatshirts, robes, and sweaters. Place them along the bottom, beside the heavy objects you packed first, as shown in the illustration.
- Add suits, slacks, and dresses, starting with the heaviest clothing first. As you place each layer in the suitcase, let the ends of the clothing hang over the edge until you put the next layer in place.
- To reduce creases, fold the end of each garment over the edge of the next as you fill up the case. This alternate-overlap method allows you to fill the case evenly.
- With every step, smooth wrinkles from clothes.
- When it's properly packed, your entire, overlapped wardrobe can be lifted from the case as a whole.

As for undergarments, Beegle packs five panties, three bras—all nylon, for hand washing. In go a nylon/spandex leotard that can double as a swimsuit, and for lounging or spare-time sightseeing, two pairs of cotton/Lycra leggings and two versatile sweaters. Last but not least, Beegle takes along two pairs of socks, preferably acrylic for hand washing.

"With a whirlwind itinerary, I can't allow lost luggage," says Beegle. She often carries everything on in a duffel bag, a garment bag, and a briefcase.

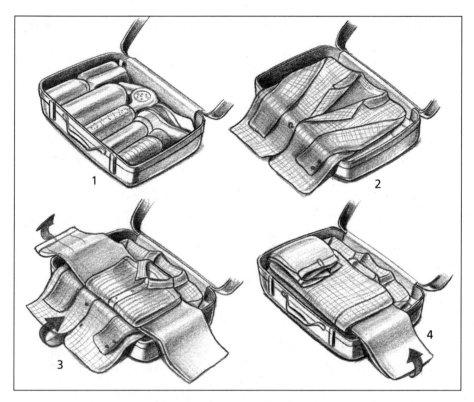

For high-efficiency, low-wrinkle packing, place the heaviest items near the hinged side of the suitcase with rolled-up clothing alongside (1). Then add dresses or suits (2), slacks, and shirts (3). Finish by folding in any clothing that hangs over the edges (4).

A Lesson from Sardines

What causes wrinkles in your clothing?

Often, the wrinkles occur *after* you're packed—when clothing shifts around in the luggage. Ermatinger suggests using tissue paper, rolled T-shirts, underwear, and socks to fill out gaps between garments and pack them tight as sardines.

Ready for a Night on the Town?

Beegle likes to pack a midcalf black skirt in nylon/Lycra that teams up with a black nylon and Lurex shirt—an outfit that rolls up and fits into a space the size of a big coffee mug. This ensemble fits with the gray pumps she wears for day. And sometimes she wears accessories such as dangling earrings, a necklace, or a belt.

Clothes That Go the Distance: Packing for Special Occasions

Headed out of town for a niece's wedding or a gala black-tie affair? Need to get your jet-beaded, tea-length silk gown safely to the Riviera?

Designer Lynda Joy found out about packing for travel after she created intricate beaded accessories and headpieces for "Harlem Nocturne" on Broadway. Here are her tips for traveling with elaborate, often delicate garments and accessories.

- First of all, call the airline ahead of time. Find out about specific space limitations. Find out if they can accommodate oversize boxes or extra-large garment bags.
- Choose a dress that will travel well. "Polyester will fare far better than silk on long journeys," says Joy. Designer Mary McFadden, for example, is noted for developing special crinkled polyesters for evening gowns that travel.
- Ask a professional dry cleaner for a cardboard bust form. Whether you box or hang your dress, be sure to use the form.
- Try to box whatever you can. A dress that's not too long and voluminous might fit easily in a generous-sized box. But don't cramp or crease the garment; if you have to do that, the box is too small.
- Stuff the box and delicate areas of the dress with tissue paper. Use the colorless kind only. To be really safe, use acid-free materials.
- If you choose to hang your outfit in a garment bag, stuff delicate areas with tissue paper, and wrap in dry cleaning plastic.

A Purse in a Case, Just in Case

Carrying precious extras such as jewelry, contact lenses, and medicine? Tuck it all into a small evening purse and put the purse in your briefcase, suggests Beegle.

And, of course, hand carry your briefcase onto the plane.

Flying with Santa

Around holiday time, flights fill up early, advanced booking is necessary, and prices may be high. But if you can fly *on* a holiday—Christmas or Thanksgiving day, for example—you'll rarely have a problem getting a seat. Not only that, you may get a real price break because few flyers choose that day to travel.

FLYING JITTERS?

According to a study by Boeing Aeronautical Company, more than 25 million American adults have a fear of flying. Truman W. Cummings, a retired Pan American captain in Coral Gables, Florida, says "There are many ways to reduce the fear, even eliminate it."

Among his practical tips to combat anxiety:

- *Expect* to feel nervous, excited, and uneasy. "Accept those feelings," says Cummings. "They are really not much different from your reaction to other big events in your life—like getting married, giving birth to a baby, or being stopped by a traffic cop." If you expect and accept the feelings, you'll realize they're perfectly normal for you.

- Concentrate on regular breathing. When you're scared, you probably have a tendency to take short, quick breaths, which only contributes to feelings of light-headedness. "Breathing is the primary antidote for fear," Cummings says.

- Move around. "Stretch, wiggle, shake, and bend as much as possible while preparing for a trip or during the flight," suggests Cummings. The physical motion takes your mind off the "what-if" thoughts that often lead to fear. Even when you're seated and belted, there's still a lot of possible body movement. "Yawn, or smile at a baby," Cummings suggests.

Knowing how many people are afraid of flying, Captain Cummings has developed a course called "Help for the Fearful Flier," which includes a booklet and two audiocassette tapes. It is available from Freedom from Fear of Flying, 2021 Country Club Prado, Coral Gables, FL 33134.

What Was That Fare...Again?

Before you fly, double-check the fare you paid. If the price goes down between reservation time and flight time, you may be owed a refund.

Air fares sometimes change dramatically between the time you buy your ticket and when you board the plane. "I once paid $468 for a nonrefundable round trip ticket from Maine to California," recalls Anne Brown of Rockport, Maine, a frequent airline customer. "The *very next day*, the fare dropped to $338."

Fortunately, Brown found out about the change and brought it to the attention of her travel agent. "I was able to have the ticket rewritten at the lower rate," she says. Cost: One phone call. Total savings: $130!

As a rule, airline and travel agent computers are supposed to catch any such changes. While prepaid tickets cannot be adjusted upward if there's an increase, the customer is supposed to be credited for favorable price changes. "But checking it out yourself at the last minute *certainly* never hurts," says Brown, "and it might save you money."

It's a Bird. It's a Plane. It's...

Super-saver!

Although they are loaded with restrictions and qualifications, super-saver or ultra-saver airfares can save as much as half the cost of a full-priced airline ticket, says Anne Gardner, travel agent for It's a Small World Travel in La Jolla, California. "The business traveler who must book at the last minute in effect subsidizes the pleasure flier who can plan air travel weeks or even months ahead of time."

Some major restrictions do apply to super-saver or ultra-saver tickets, says Gardner. Among them:

- They are nonrefundable and can't be changed once written (except in certain, provable emergencies).
- They must be booked in advance—one week to 21 days or more.
- Round-trip travel, with a Saturday night stay-over, is generally required.
- Maximum length of stay is usually 21 days.
- Only a limited number of seats is available on each flight.
- Cancellations or changes for cause (an emergency situation such as an illness, certifiable by a doctor's letter, or a death in the family, which must also be verified) can cost a penalty of up to 50 percent. However, airlines have the option of charging only a small penalty for changes.

There may be other restrictions as well, so check with your travel agent before you confirm a reservation. If you can meet these requirements, you may be able to book a seat at a fraction of what it costs a business passenger who booked a day or two before the flight. (The person sitting next to you, in fact, may have paid twice as much for his or her seat.)

Kid-Hint #1: Shut-Eye on the Red-Eye

Youngsters can be a problem while flying, especially on long flights, notes San Franciscan Katherine Overend, a veteran flight attendant with American Airlines who often travels by air with her own preschooler, Jack.

One way to outfox kids who get the fidgets is to book an overnight "red-eye-special" flight. If you choose a time when youngsters are usually tucked into bed, they just might keep to their sleep pattern even though they're in the air. If all goes well, you can snooze together in harmony instead of battling the squirmies.

Kid-Hint #2: Play with Clay

"Always try to keep kids busy," says Overend, who has helped divert hundreds of tykes during her career as a flight attendant. "Take along plenty of books, games, puzzles, coloring books...that sort of thing."

"Modeling clay is a terrific time-consumer," she adds. "If clay is playfully tossed at another passenger, it doesn't hurt when it hits."

Kid-Hint #3: The Seat of Contentment

"Keep the kids' feet off the floor; in other words, keep them in their seat as much as possible," says Overend. She notes that once children's feet touch the floor, "it's hard to settle them down again."

The Mailing List for Bargains

If you're willing to gamble on vacations that must be planned at the last minute, the growing family of discount travel clubs may be for you. They're also known as standby, flexible schedule, or short-notice clubs. All of them capitalize on the fact that many airlines and tour groups have space left over at the last minute and are willing to slash prices to fill those places.

Most charge a membership fee. For the fee, you'll get travel information and discount arrangements, along with mailed notices of travel bargains. Some discount travel clubs send out a regular publication: Vacations to Go, a discount club headquartered in Houston, sends its members four issues each year of Vacations magazine, jammed with travel ideas.

Usually, the discount club will confirm your reservation—unlike the airlines' standby system, where you show up at the gate and hope (or pray) for a seat. Once you've booked through a discount club, fares, and other travel charges are normally nonrefundable.

The Tour du Jour

You've arrived in a strange city for the first time. Your guidebook lists its major attractions, but the traffic is daunting. Besides, how can you see the sights if you're stuck behind the wheel of a car, trying to figure out how you ended up headed the wrong way on a one-way street?

One way to outflank the traffic and get an all-city overview is with an in-city bus tour. Not surprisingly, that recommendation comes from Cathy Clonts, director or marketing for Gray Line Worldwide in Dallas, Texas, one of the nation's largest tour operators. Many big-city visitors confirm her reasoning: "It's really the best way for any traveler to introduce himself to a new city, either for business or vacation purposes."

TOUR DE CHOICE

Dozens of kinds of tours are available, but what's the right one for you? With a little advance planning and "reading up," it's not too hard to land the right one, according to Robert E. Whitley, president of the United States Tour Operators Association (USTOA). The homework, he suggests, is just about what you'd do when planning a trip on your own.

Choosing the climate and appropriate clothes for various activities is just as important as picking which company you'll travel with. Also, look very carefully at the price and conditions of the tour agreement, Whitley says. For tour planners, he offers this checklist.

Price. What's included in the tour price and what is not? Airfare? Meals? Accommodations? Sightseeing? Be sure to ask *beforehand.*

Itinerary. Are all or most of the places you want to see included? Read the itinerary thoroughly.

Specialized tours. Rather than a general tour, ask if any focused tours are available that are keyed to your special interests. There are, for instance, tours for students of religious studies, for folklore buffs, and opera lovers. If your tastes run to the outdoors, look for specially planned tours for canoeists, hunters, ski mountaineers, and other aficionados.

Group size. Which is your preference, a smaller, more personalized tour, or a larger group where you share the trip with a variety of people? Think of your own needs and pick a tour accordingly.

Hotel terms. Ask what's meant by commonly used descriptions such as "economy" and "deluxe" class hotels. In European travel, there's a big difference: Economy usually means a shared bathroom and saggy bed, while deluxe often includes enough frills to sate the ego of a starlet. In U.S. travel arrangements, on the other hand, the distinctions may be quite small, and the price differences quite large.

Single supplement. Some tours charge more for single travelers who won't be sharing a room. Check beforehand.

Conditions. This is the "fine print" section of the tour contract, and it may have as many contingencies as an insurance policy or used car contract. *Especially* read the clauses relating to baggage allowances, damage claims, cancellation, and penalty policies. And note the section that explains the legal responsibilities of the tour operator and tour customer.

For further details, you can write for a copy of USTOA's free booklet, "How to Select a Package Tour," USTOA, Suite 12-B, 211 East Fifty-First Street, New York, NY 10022.

Gray Line Tours are routed past the scenic, cultural, and historical high-lights of a particular town, city, or region. Guides knowledgeable about the area point out sights along the way.

If you decide this is the route for you, Clonts suggests that while you're on the tour, take notes about places you would like to explore. Later on, visit those spots on your own. The bonus: When you're taking a bus, there's no chance of getting into a fender-bender while you rubberneck. And you'll pack a full-city tour into a few hours.

A Package Deal on Wheels

Add it up: Getting there, plus lodging, plus dining out. Then weigh the cost against...

A deluxe recreational vehicle (RV) renting for between $80 and $150 a day. Although rates vary with season and location, vehicles in that price range may sleep six or more people, according to Philip L. Ingrassia of the Recreational Vehicle Industry Association (RVIA) in Reston, Virginia. RV rent-als range from about $400 a week (a basic model for a couple or small family) to $1,000-plus a week for a frills-loaded luxury vehicle. As with other rental vehicles, there may be a per-mile charge, so be sure to check. And also ask

---

FYI

RV SPECIALS FOR WHEELCHAIR TRAVELERS

Robert Skummer of Mount Prospect, Illinois, is president of the Handi-capped Travel Club, which helps arrange vacations for the handicapped. "There's no limit, these days, on where you can travel in a wheelchair," says Skummer. There are about ten travel agencies in the United States that specialize in aiding handicapped travelers. The oldest is Flying Wheels in Minnesota (1-800-535-6790).

Although confined to a wheelchair himself, Skummer has taken rides in a hot-air balloon and visited the tombs of Egypt. "All it takes is guts and a little money," he says.

Skummer's small, nonprofit group helps arrange travel for groups of handicapped vacationers. The U.S. transportation is by RV, and the over-nights are in campgrounds rather than hotels or motels.

For further information from the Handicapped Travel Club, write to them at 109 North School Street, Mount Prospect, IL 60056.

how many miles per gallon you can expect to get. (If you're not prepared, you might be unpleasantly surprised at how few miles-per-gallon an RV gets.)

The advantages? A typical RV, notes Ingrassia, has many of the comforts of home, including a full kitchen, living room, and bathroom. So you get lodging and transportation in one complete package. And if you want to cook in rather than eat out (a considerable savings right there), you have a complete kitchen in your rolling home.

Where to park at night?

There are some 20,000 campsites in the United States that accommodate RVs, with costs ranging from $5 to $20 per night. Even in small, remote campgrounds you'll often find hookups for power and water. Some RV resorts offer swimming, tennis, golf, and a varied social calendar.

Rent-a-Car Dealing

Check Ur Policy B 4 U Rent a Car

Before renting any car, you should check your personal car insurance policy first, says travel writer Don Dedera of Phoenix. You may discover that you don't need the optional collision damage (CDW) coverage most rental companies offer. Chances are, your own auto insurance policy offers you the same coverage while driving a rented vehicle as you have on your own car.

Rental CDW can add $8 to $12 per day to the other rental charges. To avoid the extra CDW tab, you'll have to initial that section of the rental agreement, indicating "decline." Be sure to ask, though, whether initialing the contract means accepting or refusing CDW.

Car Rental: Far from the Madding Terminal

Car rental rates vary almost as widely as fares of the deregulated airlines, according to Dedera. He notes that the four "biggies" that usually charge the most—Hertz, National, Budget, and Avis—are generally located *inside* the airport terminal, where rental space is at a premium.

How can you save?

Choose companies located away from the airport, suggests Dedera. Most of the remote rental companies operate vans or buses that frequently roll by the arrival section. Near the baggage area, you'll usually find a bank of phones with toll-free lines to various car rental agencies. If you need to find out whether a car is available, or where to get the bus to the remote rental agency, just pick up the phone.

Money-Saving Rent-a-Car Tips

As Don Dedera has discovered, there are four golden rules for saving when you rent a car.

1. Rent on weekends. It's cheaper.
2. If you plan to rent a car for four or five days, consider booking the weekly rate. It's usually cheaper than paying a daily rate when renting for four or more days. (Some companies let you shift to the cheaper plan when you return the car; but others don't.)
3. Be sure to ask how much free mileage you'll get.
4. If you have to pay for the gas (most unlimited mileage contracts require it), fill up just before returning the car. Rental companies usually charge escalated gas prices for every gallon they have to pour in when they top off the tank.

And here's a fifth tip: To avoid inflated overtime charges, return the car *on time*. Most companies charge hefty extra fees for the hours immediately after the time it's due.

The Lowdown on Lodging

All Beds Are Not Priced Equally

Calling for reservations?

The first question to ask is "What discounts do you honor?" suggests Jerry Marcus, a Miami stockbroker from Coral Gables, Florida, who flies about 50 round trips on business every year. If you belong to a national organization, chances are you'll be eligible for a discount at many hotels. Marcus has found that many hotels don't even ask for proof: All you have to do is ask.

You're probably eligible for discounts if you hold membership in the American Association of Retired Persons (AARP), the American Automobile Association (AAA) and other motor travel clubs, and some fraternal organizations. The Travelodge chain offers a 10 percent discount to AAA members, and between 15 and 20 percent to members of AARP. Another example: The American Hotel in Atlanta, Georgia, offers the 15 to 20 percent AARP discount, plus similar savings to government employees, military personnel, and (because Atlanta is a busy airline hub city) airline employees. And when you ask, "What discounts do you honor?" the reservations clerk may name one that hadn't even occurred to you.

Note: Some hotels honor discounts only if they are made with advance reservations, so *ask* if you are phoning ahead. And since some hotels and motels within a chain are individually owned, discount rates may vary slightly from one to the next.

On Business? Snooze Cheaper

Since major hotels cater largely to businesspeople, corporate or business rates are widespread in the hotel industry.

It doesn't matter how large or small your company is—even self-employed freelance writers have saved money by being smart enough to ask.

A Weekend Bonus

That, in effect, is what you get from many hotel chains that want your business on the weekends. According to business traveler Marcus, major American hotels cater to the business traveler rather than the holiday-seeker—so you may save as much as 20 percent on Friday afternoon after the business-convention crowd has staged its mass exodus.

Most of the big chains like Hilton, Holiday Inn, Marriott, and Sheraton cut their rates on weekends, especially in summer. Ask for details.

Killer Phone Bills

Many hotels levy a monumental charge for both local and long-distance telephone calls, says Greg Finch, a United Airlines pilot with more than 7,500 hours of flying time in domestic and foreign flights. If you make a lot of calls, your debt at checkout time may look like the national deficit.

Advice: Circumvent the hotel switchboard. Direct-dialing long distance with a telephone calling card means savings. Use a pay phone and you'll save even more.

It Costs Nothing to Try...

...for a better price, that is.

If you've never haggled over the price of a hotel room, it may take some practice. But a quick look around the lobby can tell you whether you stand a chance of getting a cut-rate deal.

"It works especially well if you know the best *time* to haggle, and the best time not to," says stockbroker Jerry Marcus, who has whittled down many a room fee. If a hotel lobby looks as deserted as the Alaskan tundra, if it's late in the day, and if it's not a heavily traveled holiday weekend when hotels are booked solid, you're in a good negotiating position.

"An empty room is a nonprofit room," Marcus explains. If the clerk knows you can easily cross the street to a rival hotel, he or she might be able to accommodate your budget. (In fact, it doesn't hurt to mention that "I'm on a budget—and I didn't plan to spend *that* much for a room.") As Marcus points out, it never hurts to try.

Oh, Give Me a Home...Away from Home

At the outskirts of wilderness, by the shores of the pounding sea, or just a hop, skip, and jump away, there may be a vacation hideaway waiting for you. According to Michael F. Thiel, president of Hideaways International of Littleton, Massachusetts, renting a house for a week or two "can become very attractive as a vacation accommodation from the perspectives of both economics and comfort, especially when you're traveling with a family or a group of adults." Vacation home renting, he says, "can take one as far off the beaten track as is desired."

There are vacation homes ranging from the very basic to the very fancy in many destinations. Taking your family to visit Colonial Williamsburg in Virginia? You might rent a four-bedroom, two-story Colonial home only 35 minutes away. The house sleeps eight people, offers a huge, wrap-around porch with a waterfront view, and rents for $1,500 per week from May to October. A company like Hideaways just acts as broker; negotiating details is left to the renter and the owner.

Version Two: Oh, Swap Me a Home...

A variation on the home-rental theme, house-swapping for vacation, is an even cheaper alternative. "House exchange plans" are offered by Hideaways International, Holiday Exchange in Ventura, California, and about half a dozen similar brokerages around the country. Generally, there is a brokerage fee for listing your own home; other than that, your only expense is the cost of travel to the new location.

Of course, you're most likely to make a great swap if your own home is in a desirable location like a mountainside or seaside resort. Hideaways, for instance, offers a tantalizing swap within hobnobbing distance of George Bush in Kennebunkport, Maine—a four-bedroom cottage, "The Westerly," which is a 1927 teahouse with room for ten people.

Thiel and others in the exchange business suggest that swap-property owners begin corresponding far in advance of the planned vacation, so that details won't be overlooked. Often good friendships emerge from the one-for-one exchanges.

Put Your Stake in America

Even if you changed campsites *every day* within the national park system, it would be 79½ years before you staked your tent on every site.

And if you spent those years strolling around national parklands, you'd have to cover about 6,600 acres a day just to see it all.

Whatever the season, camping in national and state parks and on other public land has become one of America's major travel bargains. In the 356

FYI

FOR WOODSPRITES, DUDES, AND TENDERFEET

For vacationers who prefer something besides the sky or canvas over their heads at night, many of the more than 300 national and state parks offer a wide range of accommodations, ranging from the exotic and luxurious to the downright unforgettable. For instance:

- In Platte River State Park in Louisville, Nebraska, you can spend a night in a teepee.
- Cabins, often with room rates as low as $20 a night, are found in many parks. You can take your pick—from wide-verandahed aeries with broad vistas to comfy log bungalows nestled in peaceful valleys.
- On the luxury side, you can put on your spurs and head out to Triangle X Ranch in Grand Teton National Park, Wyoming, a dude ranch offering river trips, riding, and barbecues.

One excellent guide to noncamping lodging in the national and state parks is *The Complete Guide to Cabins and Lodges in America's State and National Parks* by George Zimmerman.

---

national park sites alone, there are 440 developed campgrounds offering 29,000 campsites. And the National Forest system includes more than 191 million acres, with another 4,000 campsites.

In addition, vast acreage administered by the Bureau of Land Management (BLM), mostly in the western United States, is available for trekking and camping. "As examples of what campers will find on BLM land in Oregon," says Bob Schneider of Washington, D.C., BLM's outdoor recreation planner, "there are wild and scenic rivers, and camping areas that offer hunting, fishing, hiking, river running, cave exploring, rock climbing, snowmobiling, and even hang gliding. Fees for camping on public land are far, far below rates you'd pay in motels and hotels."

For Some Homestyle Bliss-and-Breakfast

An idea transported from England, bed-and-breakfasts offer a very personal lodging alternative while traveling.

Winnie Easton, proprietor of the Sign of the Unicorn Guest House bed-and-breakfast in Rockport, Maine, has this recommendation for travelers trying out the B&B route for the first time: "It's best to make a reservation by

---

FYI

UNIVERSITATAS REDUX

The rooms aren't lavish but they're modestly priced—$18 per night on the average. In summertime, hundreds of college and university dorm rooms stand empty, and many revenue-hungry institutions of higher learning rent out these rooms to vacationing travelers.

In addition to lodging, you may get use of other campus facilities along with the rooms, such as swimming pools, the gymnasium, and the cafeteria. A few include breakfast (and sometimes other meals) for a small extra charge.

So if you're traveling in summer, give a call to some universities in the area you plan to visit. As a starting point, check the *U.S. and Worldwide Accommodations Guide* from Campus Travel Service, P.O. Box 5007, Laguna Beach, CA 92652.

---

telephone, speaking at some length with the proprietor personally, asking about the neighborhood, and finding out about the kind of guests he or she normally caters to. It's as if you're meeting a friend for the first time."

There's no "typical" B&B. Some are homes with a few rooms set aside to accommodate guests. Others are medium-size inns, with amenities like those of a full-scale hotel. Room rates vary accordingly.

Because many B&Bs have only a few guest rooms, it's best to book reservations as far in advance as possible. Many owners keep in touch with each other through trade associations. For the cost of a phone call, they'll firm up your itinerary by helping you find another lodging farther down the road.

The true bonus you get at a B&B is charm, a homelike atmosphere, the personal attention of the host, and the chance to meet fellow guests and even launch lasting friendships.

"Y" Not?

One of the oldest forms of budget lodging, a system that set the stage for the many generations of budget hotels, was the good old YMCA/YWCA—still a bargain! Inexpensive rooms at the Y are available in about 60 U.S. cities. In about 25 of these YMCAs, husbands and wives can room together; elsewhere, accommodations are separated by sex. And you don't need Y membership to get a room.

YMCA rates range upward from $8 for singles to $45 and up for doubles. (The higher rates are generally in larger cities.) Rooms are spartan but clean. Only a few have TVs, and not all have private baths. But most YMCA facilities are located downtown, which is an important advantage, and overnighters can generally use the swimming pool and athletic facilities.

Unlike hotels, YMCAs do not advertise for customers. The easiest way to get a room at a Y is to just show up and ask for one: Trying to reserve in advance can be a hassle. If you do want to reserve Y lodging in advance, the best bet is to inquire at your nearest YMCA before beginning your vacation. In pricey cities where hotel rates are soaring to the moon, try the Y.

Unbeatable Eats!

Finding Dining: Clues and Cues

In a strange city, how do you find a good restaurant?

- Look for crowded ones, suggests Mark Orwoll, a senior editor at *Travel and Leisure* magazine in New York City. "It doesn't always hold true," he says, "but in general, the popular restaurants are crowded because they are the better ones."
- *Ask* the people who live in the city, Orwoll adds. His "sources" of dining tips have included cabbies, concierges, clerks in stores, even strangers on the street. Asking the locals, Orwoll says, is a useful way to find new and relatively undiscovered restaurants, especially in smaller towns where guidebooks are of little help.
- "Ask the bartender in a class bar," suggests Leonard Ash, a freelance travel writer from San Diego. "I've never found one to be wrong."

And, of course, before you go in, check the menu posted in the window—or ask the maitre d' for a look—so the tab won't be a shock.

The Heck with Truckstops

It has been repeated so many times it has almost become engraved in American folklore: "If you're looking for a good restaurant, pick a roadside diner where truck drivers gather. The food there is bound to be good."

'Tain't necessarily so, says long-distance trucker Bill Ford of Fallbrook, California. "There are some first-rate truckstop diners," he says, "but there are also some terribly *bad* truckstop diners."

Truckers are on a schedule, he explains, and time is money. They don't choose diners because their food is good; they choose the ones that have large parking lots that will accommodate 18-wheelers. Food-wise, "Sometimes we're lucky, sometimes not," says Ford. Pleasure travelers should be forewarned.

The Joy of Regional Cooking

Regional dining offers two pluses, according to Kay Prokop, former food editor for the San Diego *Tribune*. One is economy. The other is "learning more about a region and its culture through its food."

Prokop always looks for special foods that reflect an area's history and culinary culture. Because those foods are locally produced, they generally cost less than the same food shipped and prepared elsewhere.

Here's a comparison: If you're traveling in Maine, of course you'll sample the state's famous two-clawed American lobster with all the trimmings that might run from $9 to $14. Get the same special at a Los Angeles restaurant, where lobster is flown in from New England, and the same dinner with the same trimmings will fetch *at least* $25 to $30.

Prokop points out that the South is particularly rich in regional food: Look for Creole grits, hush puppies, Hoppin' John (rice and black-eyed peas), and Cajun gumbo, a New Orleans favorite. In the Rockies, you can feast on trout; in the Pacific Northwest, salmon. Boston is famous for its baked beans. South-of-the-border fare dominates restaurant menus from East Texas to Southern California.

Also watch for festivals and fairs featuring the dishes that are identified with that area. With luck, you may get to the annual Garlic Festival in Gilroy, California, or the Maine Lobster Festival in Rockland, Maine.

For Your Main Meal, Munch Lunch

Compare lunch and dinner menus of almost any restaurant, and you'll usually detect a dramatic escalation in price between noon and 6:00 P.M.

Often the menu prices change even though the entrées don't—or at least not much. True, that T-bone steak at dinner may be an ounce or two larger than the lunchtime version of the same steer. But is it *really* worth an extra ten bucks?

Here's a rule of thumb from San Diego editor Kay Prokop: Make lunch your main meal. You can cut costs enormously and still dine well.

Dining in the Air? Ask for the Moon

If you're planning an airline trip, be sure to ask about special menus that suit your dietary needs.

"The country has become extremely diet conscious in recent years," notes Prokop. "Filling the needs of those who want low-fat, low-calorie, low-salt, or vegetarian meals is no problem whatsoever."

United Airlines alone estimates that it prepares more than two million special meals annually. Just give the airline some advance notice of your dietary desires before boarding. Typically, a United low-cal meal contains about 400 calories as opposed to 1,000 calories in regular meals. Kosher meals and special meals for children are also available.

"If you have special needs, don't be embarrassed to ask for a special menu," says Prokop. "Healthy food is an accepted fact of travel life these days."

Note: While you may not have the same success rate on trains, it's worth asking.

Great Deals for Seniors

Lucking Out at 62...And Up

Air travelers at least 62 years old can realize substantial fare savings, notes Anne Gardner, travel agent at It's a Small World Travel located in La Jolla, California. Many airlines offer coupon books good for trips anywhere in their route system, at a cost per flight substantially less than even advanced-booked, restriction-loaded super-saver fares.

For instance: Here's how it works if you're 62-plus, and you want to book with Delta.

- State your birth date. (You'll have to prove it at check-in time.)
- Order a Delta "Young at Heart" four- or eight-coupon book. (As of 1992, the price for the four-coupon book was $568; the eight-coupon book was $984.)
- Each coupon purchases a one-way ticket to most U.S. cities (plus Puerto Rico); two coupons are needed to fly to Hawaii or Alaska. The return ticket costs the same.
- All reservations must be made or changed at least 14 days in advance.

If you're eligible, notes Gardner, this plan has many advantages over the super-saver or ultra-saver. With coupons, you can fly any day of the week. The coupon books are valid up to a year from purchase, and you can get a full refund if you decide to return the booklet without using any coupons.

Delta and most major airlines also offer a 10 percent discount on the ticket of a "Young at Heart" traveler's seat partner, regardless of the traveling companion's age.

The fine print: Each airline has different plans for seniors. If you're considering one of these plans, be sure to check the specific restrictions of the airline you plan to use.

LIVE AND LEARN...ON CAMPUS

If you're over 60, you can combine travel and education in low-budget style, visiting some of the most pleasant campuses in America.

Inspired by similar programs started in Europe, Elderhostel is a network of about 1,000 colleges and universities that offer courses to "senior students." Enroll for a week and you'll live on campus and select courses from a wide variety of offerings in the liberal arts and sciences. Vacationing students live in the dorms, take their meals on campus, and enjoy extracurricular activities. Costs vary but average a bit over $200 a week.

For details, contact Elderhostel, 80 Boylston Street, Suite 400, Boston, MA 02116.

AARP...And the Over-50 Jet Set

"The AARP—the American Association of Retired Persons—arranges discounted fares for its members," says Gardner of It's a Small World Travel. "And you only have to be 50—not 62—to join this organization."

For 62-Plus: Bargains to Bargain With

Anyone over 62 qualifies for a free lifetime Golden Passport from the National Park Service, entitling the holder to free admission to any park site. You also get a 50 percent discount on any park-related charges, including camping fees.

Many hotels offer seniors a standard discount. For example, if you're over 62 and staying at a Best Western, ask about the 20 percent discount. Also ask whether they'll throw in a free subcompact car: Some hotels will actually do that.

Days Inn has a September Days Club that can get you discounts between 15 and 40 percent on local entertainment, trips, and theme park admission. It costs senior citizens $12 a year, and all members of its September Days Club receive a magazine.

Senior Fare-Checking

Despite substantial savings offered senior citizens, there may be nonsenior discounts that are even better, advises Peggy Patten, a travel agent with Camden Travel in Camden, Maine. "Rates, privileges, discounts, and other perks tend to change quickly, sometimes at a moment's notice," shesays. "Before taking advantage of a seniors discount, it's always best to check for a better deal."

50—And Ready to Ramble

If you're over 50, you'll probably want to contact one of the organizations for seniors that can help you find bargains as you travel. With membership in one of these organizations, all you need is some wanderlust and proof of birth date to get some great deals in lodging, tours, transportation, and tickets.

For detailed information, look for *Unbelievably Good Deals and Great Adventures That You Absolutely Can't Get Unless You're over 50* by Joan Rattner Heilman, which offers a wealth of tips and inspiration for travelers who have passed the midcentury mark.

FYI

JOIN UP FOR DISCOUNTS

Here are four senior citizens' organizations with nationwide membership that help seniors get travel bargains and discounts.

- American Association of Retired Persons (AARP) has 28 million members, and a bimonthly magazine, *Modern Maturity.* For its members, AARP offers discounts at major hotel and motel chains, some discounts at resorts, and special deals on auto rentals. It also has a travel service that offers preplanned cruises, tours, and special-event programs. You can get more information from AARP, 1909 K Street NW, Washington, DC 20049.
- Mature Outlook issues a magazine plus a periodic "Travel Alert," listing last-minute international and domestic travel bargains. Members receive 20 percent discounts on room rates and 10 percent on meals at participating Holiday Inns and Crowne Plaza Hotels—also discounts on some rental cars. For further details, write to Mature Outlook, 6001 North Clark Street, Chicago, IL 60660-9977; or call the toll-free number, 1-800-336-6330.
- National Council of Senior Citizens (NCSC) is primarily a lobby for senior citizen legislation, but it also arranges travel discounts. For more information write NCSC, 925 West Fifteenth Street NW, Washington, DC 20005.
- National Alliance of Senior Citizens (NASC) arranges discounts on car rentals and lodgings for its members and has its own automobile club. To find out more about the automomile club and discount offers, write to NASC, 2525 Wilson Boulevard, Arlington, VA 22201.

FYI

BRIDGING THE GENERATION GAP

A unique variation on group and family guided tours is GrandTravel, a program developed by travel agent Helena Koenig of Chevy Chase, Maryland. GrandTravel makes travel arrangements for grandparents and grandchildren traveling together both in the United States and abroad.

"Adults and their grandchildren make wonderful traveling companions," says Debbie Greenberg of GrandTravel, "because they can learn so much from one another."

The plan works this way: The Ticket Counter, GrandTravel's travel agency parent company, arranges tours of about two weeks each, during normal school break periods. Tours take grandparents and kids to places such as the Grand Canyon, New England, Alaska, and the Southwest. In a typical New England tour, youngsters watch maple syrup being processed in Vermont and walk historic routes through downtown Boston.

Grandparents must book transportation to the starting point; GrandTravel makes all other arrangements, such as hotels, tour buses, and site admissions. Motorcoach schedules are suited to young and old alike. The coaches make rest stops every two hours, and tour leaders keep kids occupied with music, games, and talks en route.

"Each trip sets aside times for adults and children to be alone with their own age group," says Greenberg. "But when they are together, the times are very, very good indeed."

Despite the program's name, you don't have to be a grand-person to sign up: "Parents, great uncles, aunts, cousins, and godparents are invited, too," says Greenberg.

For more information, contact GrandTravel, The Ticket Counter, 6900 Wisconsin Avenue, Suite 706, Chevy Chase, MD 20815.

Healthy Traveling

Ulp! A Move against Motion Sickness

Motion sickness is caused by any movement that upsets the balance-control mechanism of the middle ear, says Art Myers, M.D., a San Diego physician with the California Department of Rehabilitation and adjunct professor at the Graduate School of Public Health at San Diego State University. Traveling by car, plane, or boat, you may experience dizziness, headaches, feelings of nausea, or (worst case) vomiting.

Simple preventives are fairly commonsensical: Avoid eating a lot, avoid greasy foods, cut out alcohol, and try to get plenty of fresh air. If you know you're prone to car-sickness, you're probably better off choosing a route with flat, straight roads, although of course that's less interesting from a sightseer's point of view.

For medical prevention, the generic drug scopolamine is quite effective, notes Dr. Myers. Scopolamine, which requires a doctor's prescription, is applied in a medicated, adhesive patch placed behind the ear. Less expensive over-the-counter rivals include Dramamine, Bonine, and Marezine. But all cause drowsiness and other side effects, notes Dr. Myers.

Jet Lag: Leave the Old Time Behind

The late Secretary of State John Foster Dulles once confessed that he made a major diplomatic blunder at a Paris conference because he began negotiating too soon after a long, time-telescoping flight from Washington, D.C. Like thousands of other air travelers, Dulles was a victim of jet lag.

Studies have shown commonsense treatments for jet lag don't require a trip to your pharmacy. Dr. Myers recommends:

- Reset your clock *immediately*. If you have flown from New York to Los Angeles, it's 10:00 P.M. in New York but only 7:00 P.M. in Los Angeles. Resist the temptation to go to bed for a few more hours.
- Soak up sunshine and get plenty of exercise. Both help the recovery process after a tiring trip.
- Relax in a hot, soaking bath. But remember, don't fall asleep until it's bedtime in the *new* time zone!

Sunburn: Ban the Rays

Don't be fooled if it's an overcast day, warns Dr. Myers. You can sunburn almost as quickly under low cloud cover as when Old Sol hangs brightly in the sky.

The obvious prevention for sunburn is to stay out of sunshine, but for those who spend vacations golfing, sailing, hiking, or the like, shunning sun is worse than staying in from recess. Instead, use some of the dozens of sunburn-prevention medications on the market.

"My recommendation is sunscreen with an SPF [sun protection factor] of 15," says Dr. Myers. Sunscreens are available in higher or lower SPFs, he points out, but 15 is a happy medium. Apply and *reapply* it to the skin as directed, especially after swimming.

The Experts

Leonard D. Ash is a freelance travel writer who lives in San Diego, California.

Patricia A. Beegle is fashion marketing manager for the DuPont Company Fibers Division in Wilmington, Delaware, and has also worked for several major New York advertising firms.

Cathy Clonts is director of marketing for GrayLune Worldwide, one of the nation's largest sightseeing and transportation operators, with headquarters in Dallas, Texas.

Truman W. Cummings is a retired Pan American captain who runs Freedom from Fear of Flying, Inc., in Coral Gables, Florida.

Don Dedera, a travel writer, is the publisher at Prickly Pear Press in Phoenix, Arizona.

Winnie Easton is the proprietor of the Sign of the Unicorn bed-and-breakfast in Rockport, Maine. Started in 1975, this B&B is the oldest in the Camden area and welcomes about 6,400 guests annually.

Robert K. Ermatinger is executive vice president of the Luggage and Leather Goods Manufacturers of America in New York City, and publisher of *Showcase*, a trade publication serving the luggage industry.

Dorothy Fields is a travel writer from Placerville, California.

Greg Finch is a United Airlines pilot based in Washington, D.C., who has more than 7,500 hours of flying time in DC8s, DC10s, and Boeing 737s, 757s, and 767s.

Bill Ford is a long-distance truck driver from Fallbrook, California.

Anne Gardner is a travel agent at It's a Small World Travel in La Jolla, California.

Dan Guravich is a professional nature and travel photographer from Greenville, Mississippi, who has published more than 15 books.

Philip L. Ingrassia is a spokesperson for the Recreational Vehicle Industry Association.

Lynda Joy, is the evening wear and bridal designer for Lynda Joy, Inc., in New York City. She has designed for a number of theatrical productions, including costume accessories for the Broadway show "Harlem Nocturne."

Helena Koenig is a travel agent and the founder of GrandTravel in Chevy Chase, Maryland.

Don McQuiston, a book designer and the president of McQuiston and Partner in Del Mar, California, has produced more than two dozen books related to the National Park System.

Jerry Marcus, a former stockbroker from Coral Gables, Florida, flies 40 to 50 round trips per year on business.

Art Myers, M.D., of San Diego, is a physician with the California Department of Rehabilitation and adjunct professor at the Graduate School of Public Health at San Diego State University.

Mark Orwoll is a senior editor at *Travel and Leisure* magazine in New York City.

Katherine Overend is a San Francisco–based flight attendant for American Airlines.

Peggy Patten is a travel agent for Camden Travel in Camden, Maine.

Kay Prokop is the former assistant managing editor, features editor, and food editor for the San Diego *Tribune*.

Kristin Ross is an assistant manager specializing in loans and mortgages at Peoples Heritage Bank in Camden, Maine.

Bob Schneider is an outdoor recreation planner for the Bureau of Land Management of the Department of Interior in Washington, D.C.

Robert W. Seckman is the managing director of Travel Agency Services for the American Automobile Association (AAA) in Heathrow, Florida.

Robert Skummer is president of the Handicapped Travel Club in Mount Prospect, Illinois.

Michael F. Thiel is the president of Hideaways International in Littleton, Massachusetts, and a broker for those who want to rent their homes to vacationers.

Robert E. Whitley is the president of the United States Tour Operators Association, with headquarters in New York City.

CHAPTER 15

Conservation and Recycling

Doing Your Part to Save the Earth

As the twentieth century comes to a close, more people are becoming acutely aware that planet earth is a finite place. Chernobyl, Bhopal, Love Canal, Three Mile Island, *Exxon Valdez*, and the Garbage Barge have become catchwords for environmental disasters. The advances of modern technology are jeopardizing the earth's natural resources, and it isn't clear whether earth or technology is likely to win.

The effects of many kinds of pollution have been devastating on land, on sea, and in the air.

Although industry and government have been blamed for many of the "one-time" catastrophes, society at large can share responsibility. After all, most of us are part-time contributors to environmental problems—helping to deplete the ozone layer, contaminate water, develop land, and dump garbage. Laying blame is easy, but it's definitely *not* easy to change the habits and lifestyles of millions of people who have become accustomed to modern conveniences. Nor is it easy to change habits in business, where so many outdated and environmentally harmful operations are still in practice.

However, inroads are being made. Governments on all levels are beginning to change the laws on waste management, providing incentives and guidance for local businesses and communities. Industries are starting to "think green" and to manufacture products that are "friendly" to the environment. Many companies have learned that it's economically feasible to invest in less-polluting production methods and to make products that are less harmful to the environment. And individuals are becoming increasingly aware of their responsibilities to conserve energy and resources at home and in the workplace. More than ever, we are becoming more environmentally aware as we go shopping. We are learning to reuse, reduce, and recycle.

Well, then, you may be wondering, what can I do that will make a difference?

There are choices to be made. Although a great deal of effort is required to get things started, a change of habit now can make a big difference to those who will be around at the end of the twenty-first century. In this chapter, some experts tell us what habits we can change now to help our future world.

Saving Fuel and Water

Put Heat on a Timer

Most gas- and oil-fired furnaces are designed for a 65° setting. An automatic setback device, like a lamp timer, can raise and lower the heat a number of times during the day or night.

John Lippert, project supervisor of Conservation and Renewable Energy Inquiry and Referral Service (CAREIRS) of the U.S. Department of Energy in Silver Spring, Maryland, suggests a temperature setting of 65° when people are home and moving around.

"You can preset the automatic timer so whenever the last person leaves in the morning, it turns back 5° or 10° (to 60° or 55°). It's never recommended to go below 40° because of freezing problems," Lippert says.

Setback devices can be obtained through a local heating contractor, some for as little as $30.

Tighten Up the House

By patching up holes and making your house more airtight, you can save from 30 to 40 percent of the heat lost from the house.

"Put weatherstripping at the bottom of all the doors and caulk around the window and door frames where they meet the walls," suggests CAREIRS energy expert John Lippert.

One way to test for leaks is by passing a lighted candle over windows and door frames and along baseboards on a windy day. If the flame jumps around, the area needs sealing.

The Sunblock Special: Shut the Shades

When would you guess is the hottest time of the day?

If you say noontime, you're way off the mark. Between 3:00 and 5:00 P.M. is more like it, according to Ronald Fiskum, program manager for the Office of Building and Technology at the U.S. Department of Energy in Washington, D.C.

"Throughout the day, the sun is heating up the earth and buildings, and by 4:00 in the afternoon that heat has reached its peak," says Fiskum. "You're getting reflections and radiation from the buildings as well as from the ground and sun."

So if you're trying to keep out the summertime heat, *don't* raise the blinds in midafternoon. That's when the worst is just about to begin.

Less Humid, Less Hot

On a 90° day you'll probably feel a lot more comfortable if the humidity is low. That's why the Energy Department's Fiskum recommends a dehumidifier for some summertime home cooling.

The dehumidifier runs off a compressor, which cools a coil. "When the coil is colder than the air, water vapor condenses on the coil and drips into a bucket," says Fiskum.

Since the compressor itself is warm, however, Fiskum suggests putting the dehumidifier in a hallway. That way it will dehumidify the air in general without heating up a room that you're in.

Be Efficiently Cool: Hands off the Thermostat

In houses with central air conditioning, thermostats should be kept at a single setting. "You can set it wherever your comfort level might be: 78° is sort of a norm for maximum energy savings," says energy expert Ronald Fiskum.

"Turn your air conditioner to a certain temperature and leave it there. The house will soon take on that temperature. If you shut it off, the house and furniture will reabsorb heat, and the air conditioner has to work overtime to cool them down again."

Don't play with the thermostat unless you're going away for a few days, advises Fiskum. "Then you should shut it off completely to save energy."

Cool Revolutions: Try a Fan

A ceiling fan can make a big difference in heat perception. "When your body heats up, you begin to sweat. Air moving across the surface of your body, even if it's warm air, dries you off a bit and makes you feel cooler," says the DOE's Fiskum.

The best location? "It should be placed in a room that's most frequently used, like the kitchen."

Preheating Proves Powerless

A lot of recipes advise preheating the oven before cooking, but home-owners can actually achieve a 10 percent savings in energy if they do not.

"We studied eight different products including muffins, cake, soufflés, custards, frozen and fresh casseroles, apple pie, and meat loaf," says nutritionist Dianne Odland of the U.S. Department of Agriculture in Hyattsville, Maryland. "Basically we found that preheating the oven is not essential for good product quality in terms of flavor, texture, height, and tenderness."

In the study, egg-rich products such as custards and soufflés took a little longer to cook in nonpreheated ovens. But according to Odland, the extra time still didn't cost as much (energy-wise) as preheating the oven.

Turn Down the Water Temp

Did you know...Heating up water for bathing, washing dishes and clothes, preparing food, and general cleaning absorbs 20 percent of the energy used in the home?

"The conventional water heater temperature of 140° can be turned back to 120° without losing the benefit of sterilization," says John Lippert of the U.S. Department of Energy. But he adds that some types of old-fashioned appliances such as early model dishwashers need water at 140° for detergents to work best.

"First look at detergent directions to see what temperature you need," says Lippert. Then set your water heater to a lower temperature.

Save Energy in the Rooms You Use

In most homes, there are two to four lamps that are on more than any others—for instance, right above the kitchen sink, next to a favorite lounge chair, or over the desk.

Brady Bancroft, a research associate at the Rocky Mountain Institute in Snowmass, Colorado, recommends replacing conventional light bulbs in these areas with compact fluorescents. "They save four times the energy and last ten times longer than incandescents," says Bancroft.

Compact fluorescents cost $15 to $20 each, but you can save up to $40 on electric bills during the life of the bulb. The first place to look for compact fluorescent bulbs is at a local electrical supply store. But if you can't find them there, you can order them from a number of mail-order companies that supply energy-saving products. Three sources are the Energy Store (1-800-288-1938), the Energy Federation (1-800-876-0660), and Seventh Generation (1-800-456-1177).

Techno-Tip

GRAY WATER FOR THIRSTY ROOTS

Every day millions of gallons of water drain out of our bathtubs, showers, and washing machines. This "gray water" then goes into the sewer system. According to Robert Kourik, author of *Gray Water Use in the Landscape,* much of this water is still usable. With proper piping it can go directly to the roots of trees and bushes, says Kourik.

Guidelines for using gray water?

"It should never come in contact with people or with the leafy portions of plants. As long as it stays in the soil and makes contact with the roots, it is not a contaminant," says Kourik.

To avoid damage to plants, only simple soaps should be used in the household. Stay away from bleaches and detergents that contain chlorine or boron.

Gray water gets from the house to the shrubs and bushes via a series of pipes and valves. The water is then distributed to various portions of the garden under 4 inches of mulch or via mini-leach fields. When it rains, or in the winter, the valves are closed and gray water is rerouted to the regular sewer system.

As of 1992, gray water systems were already legal in two California counties. But acceptance has been slow in other parts of the nation. "Health departments are reluctant to approve gray watering due to lack of standards," says Kourik.

Thoughtful Water Saving Is Voluntary

In our water-guzzling everyday life, we usually turn on the water and leave it running until we're through at the sink. As a result, a lot of wasted gallons go down the drain.

Consider the simple act of shaving. If you turn off the water while you shave and turn it on again to rinse the razor, you'll end up conserving water.

Estimated water-savings? 2 to 3 gallons per shave, according to Larry Jones, an environmental scientist for the Delaware Department of Natural Resources and Environmental Control in Dover.

If everyone in the household uses the same technique for brushing teeth and washing dishes, you can save up to 10 gallons per day per household, according to Jones.

The Marvels of Mindless Mechanical Conservation

Install a 2½-gallon-per-minute shower head, or an ultra-low flow toilet that uses 1½ gallons per flush, and those fixtures will use about half as much water as conventional fixtures, according to Jones.

Also look for faucet aerators and shower heads that have "soap-up buttons." Just push the button to turn the water off while you soap up, then on again to rinse off.

The Footprint Lawn-Thirst Test

If you walk across your lawn without leaving footprints, then your grass doesn't need water, says Jones.

Should the grass not bounce back, however, what you want to do is give it a good, long, penetrating drink.

"The grass can survive off a deep watering once a week," says Jones. "If you just coat the surface a little bit every day, the result is shallow root growth."

Soak in the Predawn

The best time to water the lawn is between 5:00 and 9:00 A.M., when the air is cool and water is less likely to evaporate.

For how long?

"It may take only 15 or 20 minutes per spot," advises Jones. However, soils with a lot of clay may take longer to soak than more absorbent sandy soils.

To find out the composition of soils in your area, consult with lawn specialists. "Then ask them how long you need to water to penetrate 6 inches into the soil," he suggests.

Recycling Everyday Items

Save Your Phone Book—For a Cow

More and more phone book publishers are making recovery programs available to their customers. According to Willis Hengy, a representative of the Michigan Directory Company, Southwest Bell sets up drop-off points for old directories when they distribute new ones. When they're shredded, the old directories are used for animal bedding.

The National Yellow Pages Organization advises customers to contact the phone book publisher in their area for instructions on proper disposal methods. The publisher's name is usually found on the cover of the directory, and the phone number is listed under *Advertising*.

THE SCRAP INDUSTRY: A HEAP OF HELP

By recycling used products, the scrap industries in the United States have been able to preserve natural resources such as trees, iron, tin, and zinc. In doing so they also reduce high energy needs of industries that manufacture materials from virgin stock.

According to estimates, each year the scrap industry:

- Processes nine million automobiles—more than the auto industry produces in a year.
- Turns over nearly two million tons of used copper—an amount that would provide copper wiring and plumbing for all the buildings constructed each year in the United States.
- Remanufactures 26 million tons of used paper—enough paper to print the Sunday edition of the *New York Times* for the next 58 years.
- Handles 752,500 tons of used beverage cans—or 36,356 aluminum cans recycled each minute of the year.

Try the WMO—Then the YP

When in doubt about the proper way to discard a particular item, a phone call to the waste management office in your municipality is often the way to start, according to scrap waste expert Evelyn Haught, public relations director for the Institute of Scrap Recycling Industries in Washington, D.C.

After that, use the Yellow Pages, Haught advises. Some Yellow Pages headings: Recycling, Scrap dealers, Junk dealers, and Peddlers. Call first to find out if those companies will take your item.

Think before Tossing: Where Can I Use This?

Remnants of wallpaper, fabric from drapes or upholstery, and carpeting can be used within the home for lining drawers, closets, and dressers, says Caroline Gelb, a researcher for INFORM, a nonprofit environmental research and educational organization in New York City.

"These materials can be especially useful in basements to cover objects that usually get grimy from the burner," says Gelb.

To Be or Not to Be...Recycle on Stage!

Theater groups will take just about anything because they are constantly redesigning sets, changing wardrobes, and using new props.

According to Gelb, the following items are usually needed: eyeglasses, musical instruments, toys, prom dresses, costume jewelry, used furniture, and leftover paint.

So before you clean your attic, check with your local stage company or school drama teachers.

New Uses for Old Drawers

For handy, kitchen-site recycling of old newspapers, you can't do better than an empty utensil drawer.

"I took a large drawer, removed the utensils that were in it, and put small cleats on each side, *inside* the drawer," says David Goldbeck, a writer and kitchen designer in Woodstock, New York, who is the author of *The Smart Kitchen*.

Why the cleats?

"When the drawer is empty, cut off a piece of twine, lay it across the bottom of the drawer, and hook it on the cleats on opposite sides of the drawer." When the drawer is filled with newspapers, unhook the string from the cleats, tie up the bundle, and add the bundle to your paper-recycling pile.

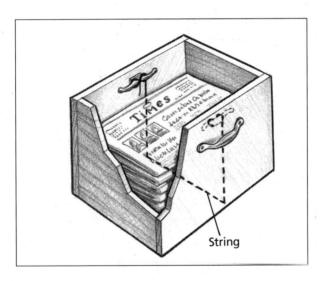

String

A newspaper recycling drawer: Fasten string to cleats and stack news-papers inside. When you're ready to take out a bundle, unfasten the string from the cleats, tie a knot on top of the bundle, and lift the newspapers from the drawer.

Recycle Steel

When you want to discard a large appliance, buy from a company that will take the item that is being replaced, recommends Evelyn Haught of the Institute of Scrap Recycling Industries.

"Large companies like Sears generally will provide the service of removing the old appliance," she says. Generally, these companies have long-term contracts with scrap dealers to take away the scrap steel.

According to Haught, about 60 million tons of scrap iron and steel are processed every year.

Second Life for Piping

Most plumbers are happy to take old pipe off your hands because they get a good return on it from scrap dealers, according to scrap industry spokeswoman Haught.

Similarly, if you have used electrical wire or cables, contact an electrician. He probably makes a regular visit to the scrap dealer.

With Your Help, the Band Plays On

If you're cleaning out your closets and you have discardable items, why not contact the Salvation Army? The number is listed in the white pages—and there are more than 7,000 units around the country.

Each year, the Salvation Army assists about 30 million people in the United States and around the world, according to Colonel Leon Ferraez, national communications director of the Salvation Army National Headquarters in Alexandria, Virginia.

Secrets Revealed

HOW THE JAPANESE DO IT

One of the key concepts of Japan's solid waste program is *respect for the opinions of housewives.*

"It's almost an all-male workforce in Japan, and most women are at home all day managing the house, so they're the ones that are targeted for household waste managment," says Eugene Salerni, coauthor of *Garbage Management in Japan.*

A typical Japanese housewife will separate waste into six categories and either put it out for pickup or take it to a collection area about a block away.

Female professionals help lead Japan's recycling initiative. "They are more sensitive to the problems of housewives, and they enjoy more community acceptance in field surveys," according to Salerni.

Put Your Old Goods to Use

The Salvation Army has more than 9,000 alcohol and drug users in residence. "For them, we need household goods, clothing, books, and magazines," says Salvation Army Colonel Leon Ferraez.

Go for Containers with a Second Life

If you buy liquid or oily foods in paper containers, you're chipping away at a tree or two.

"A recycling symbol and a notice that 'this carton was made from 100 percent recycled paperboard' are usually found on boxes that contain cereal, facial tissues, napkins, cookies, crackers, and cake mixes," notes Rodney Edwards, vice president of the Paperboard Group of the American Paper Institute in New York City.

Edwards points out that "moist, liquid, and oily foods are packed in bleached white paperboard made from 100 percent virgin fiber." For these foods, look for containers made of metal, plastic, or glass that *can* be recycled.

Secrets Revealed

SEALED WITH APPROVAL

Rena M. Shulsky, of Washington, D.C., a typical modern, busy working woman with a career in broadcasting, faced yet another dilemma when shopping in her local supermarket 2½ years ago.

"I was standing in front of detergents, trying to remember what I had read about phosphates—whether they were good or bad—and about what kind of packaging was the best for the environment. Who can remember all these things?"

"I just wished that an organization that I really trusted would do an environmental seal of approval, so I wouldn't have to mount a research project every time I went to the supermarket," says Shulsky.

After conducting some research on her own, Shulsky contacted an environmental consumer-oriented group that she thought would support her idea.

"Their board of directors decided against it, so I started my own organization called Green Seal," says its founder and chairperson.

So...look for the Green Seal label, next time you shop for detergents.

Techno-Tip

THE TRANSFORMATION OF PLASTIC

Product-wise consumers are familiar with the number-and-letter codes and symbols on all plastic containers, bottles, film, and bags. But what do those telltale codes really mean?

The purpose of the Society of the Plastics Industry resin identification code is to help recyclers sort different types of resins for reprocessing.

The table below shows the code used for each material, how that material is used in primary products, and how it's used in recycled products.

Symbol	Material	Primary Product	Recycled Product
1 PETE	Polyethylene terephthalate (PET)	Soft drink bottles, peanut butter jars	Fiberfill for pillows/jackets, carpet fibers, tennis ball containers
2 HDPE	High-density polyethylene	Milk jugs, detergent containers, juice/water bottles	Remade into HDPE bottles, base cups for soda bottles, traffic cones, buckets
3 V	Vinyl/polyvinyl chloride (PVC)	Bottled water containers; cosmetic packaging; cooking oil bottles	Remade into PVC bottles, floor tiles, pipes
4 LDPE	Low-density polyethylene	Wrapping for produce and baked goods, trash bags, lids, toys, disposable diapers	Remade into LDPE; exported to foreign markets
5 PP	Polypropylene	Ketchup and syrup bottles, shampoo bottles, appliances, indoor/outdoor carpet	Recycled from food containers to laundry detergent bottles
6 PS	Polystyrene	Egg cartons, cups, fast food trays, packaging "peanuts," dairy containers	Reused to make new polystyrene products; used as insulator for roofing
7 OTHER	All other resins and layered multimaterials	Containers made of multiplastic resins	Lumber, docks, farm structures, outdoor furniture, benches

Steering Clear of Pollutants

Running an Errand? Think Twice!

In highly populated areas, emissions from automobiles contribute at least 50 percent to ozone problems, and their exhaust accounts for nearly 90 percent of carbon dioxide pollution.

According to Mark Simon, director of alternative fuels for the New York City Department of Environmental Protection, carpooling and combining errands are two ways to significantly reduce the pollution contribution.

"Try not to drive just to pick up a quart of milk," Simon says. "If you do, you'll be making many separate little trips every day."

Do Away with Chlorine Fumes

Instead of chlorine bleach to clean mildew, use borax and hot water, suggests Joy Williams, community assistance director of the Environmental Health Coalition of San Diego.

"Borax, a salt called sodium polyborate, does nearly as good a job," she says, "and it's much less toxic because you're not breathing fumes from the chlorine."

She advises mixing ¼ cup borax to 1 gallon of hot water. "Apply to mildew, without rinsing, for long-lasting residual action," says Williams.

Unclogging Drains—Without Toxic Help'rs

For sink and drain stoppages caused by hair, food, or other solid matter, the Iowa Department of Natural Resources recommends using boiling water, snaking the clog with a metal line, or using a plunger. All are better than toxic chemical alternatives.

A Shop Vac for De-Wasping

For pesticide-free wasp removal, try a shop vacuum, suggests Howard Russell, head of the Insect Diagnostic Laboratory at Michigan State University in East Lansing. The "wet and dry" vaccuum used in many home workshops is a handy de-wasper, he points out.

Suck the wasps out of their nest, then leave the vacuum running while you vacuum up some garden dust—a mild commercial pesticide. Or just let the wasps dehydrate inside the vacuum.

"With ground-nesting wasps, try sticking a hose or boiling water down the hole to drown them out," says Russell.

For the Kids: Look for the Nontoxic Label

Look for The Art and Craft Materials Institute's AP seal (approved product) on child-related art materials such as crayons, chalks, clays, markers, water colors, tempera colors, finger paints, and pastes. Products bearing the AP seal are nontoxic even if inhaled, ingested, or absorbed.

According to executive vice president Deborah M. Fanning, a CP (certified product) seal indicates products that are nontoxic but also meet or exceed performance standards. The HL (health label) seal symbolizes proper toxicological labeling.

The institute, with headquarters in Boston, also certifies art materials used by adults, including acrylic and oil colors, inks, pigments, ceramic clays, glazes, and varnishes.

Choose Applicators That Don't Pollute

The use of aerosol sprays can cause inhalation of fumes, skin irritation, and possible contamination of nearby food products. On a larger scale, gases emitted from these propellants contribute to urban air pollution.

"When shopping, look for pump sprays, screw-top containers, roll-on applicators, or refillable bottles," says safe-substitutes expert Joy Williams of San Diego's Environmental Health Coalition.

Better yet, she advises mixing up your own solution and putting it in a reusable plastic spray bottle.

Secrets Revealed

LEAD ANTS INTO TEMPTATION

Carpenter ants are the biggest household pest problem referred to Michigan State University's Insect Diagnostic Clinic. But you don't need toxic poisons to get rid of them, says director Howard Russell.

The following mixture is a perfect bait for carpenter ants. Just stir together the following ingredients:

- 4 ounces of grape jelly
- 2 tablespoons of canned dog or cat food
- 1 tablespoon of boric acid powder (a mild antiseptic that can be purchased at a pharmacy)

"Put out a teaspoonful at a time on a jar lid or foil, out of reach of children and pets. The ants will take it back to queen and brood, and the colony will eventually die out," says Russell.

Green Cross: The Truth and Nothing But

Consumers should look for *detailed information* about products, says Linda Brown, vice president of Scientific Certification Systems (SCS), in Oakland, California, an independent, nonprofit agency that measures the accuracy of manufacturers' claims on products. If a product is environmentally safe, SCS issues a Green Cross Label:

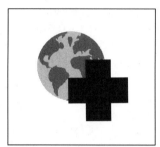

Scientific Certification Systems' Green Cross Seal of Achievement. The symbol is found on more than 400 products that have low environmental impact.

HOBBIES WITH HAZARDS

Hobbies seem fairly harmless—but many of the materials used in the home craft shop can do damage to your health or the environment.

Want some safe substitutes for hazardous substances? Check the list below before you begin your next project.

Art/Craft	Hazardous Material	Safe Substitute
Ceramics	Heavy-metal glazes that contain lead and chromium	Lead-free and talc-free glazes
Painting and refinishing	Solvent-based heavy-metal pigments (such as cadmium, copper, cobalt)	Water-based paint
	Water-based mercury antifungal agents	Mercury-free paint
	Solvents in thinners	Heat gun; sandpaper strippers
Silkscreen printing	Inks, lacquer thinners, washes with Toluene, Xylene, MEK, mineral spirits, Ethanol, and Acetone	Water-based inks

HOBBIES "AU NATUREL"

Some of our favorite hobbies, crafts, and pastimes are completely non-polluting, involving only natural or recycled products. If you want to be good to the environment, the following should be high on your list.

Hobby	Natural and Recycled Products Used
Basketry	Willow branches, cattails, cornhusks
Collages	Fabrics and scraps
Collecting	Antiques and collectibles
Flower arranging	Dried leaves, buds, and flowers
Garden crafts	All forms of dried and preserved greens, vegetables, herbs, and flowers
Needlepoint	Natural threads and fabrics
Origami	Paper
Preserving foods	Fruits and vegetables
Quiltmaking	Cloth scraps
Shell crafts	Seashells
Tie-dying	Dyes made of berries, tea, seaweed
Winemaking	Grapes, plums, flowers
Wreathmaking	Dried herbs, flowers, or vines

Sharing and Reusing

Pass It Along

Do you have leftover household cleaners, paints, and pesticides?

Share them with a family member, friend, or neighbor who can use the remainder of the product, suggests Sharon Rehder, environmental engineer with the New York State Department of Environmental Conservation in Albany. But first, check to make sure they have not been banned or restricted since they were first purchased. The waste management office in your locality should be able to answer that question for you.

Think—Which Group Could Use This?

Old, serviceable musical instruments or cameras can be donated to schools. Sports equipment can go to Little Leagues or after-school recreational programs. And as for magazines—they're wanted by hospitals and nursing homes.

These suggestions come from INFORM's Caroline Gelb.

"It really depends on the community where you live. If yours doesn't need the items you wish to donate, then find those communities, usually big cities, where they are needed," suggests Gelb.

GREEN SEAL BARKS APPROVAL

If a store-bought item has a special seal showing a blue globe and green check—a Green Seal—it means that product and its packaging do the least amount of damage to the environment within its category.

According to Susan Alexander, vice president of communications for Green Seal in Palo Alto, California, this label should be found on products in the following categories: facial and bathroom tissues, light bulbs, motor oil, laundry detergents, and water-saving devices.

The Green Seal project, set up by Rena Shulsky of Washington, D.C. (see page 374), is modeled after Underwriters Laboratories (UL), which sets the standards for product safety.

Cutting Out Waste

Junk Mail: Take the Envelope...Please!

The best way to stop the junk mail you don't want is by using the no-postage-necessary envelope usually found within the junk mail packet.

Cut out your name and address label and send it back in that envelope, along with a note saying "Please take me off your mailing list," says Gelb.

Why Not More Food, Less Packaging?

The smart environmental shopper compares similar products to see how much packaging surrounds them—and then purchases the item with minimal or no packaging.

That's the recommendation of Betsy Rich, program director of the Pennsylvania Resources Council in Media, Pennsylvania.

"Individual servings are overpackaged because you get a small amount of product with a large amount of wrapping around it," Rich observes.

She advises buying one large bag of a product, such as potato chips, frozen vegetables, or cereals; then redistribute the contents of those large packages into a number of small, reusable plastic containers.

"This way only one bag is discarded as opposed to a dozen little bags, a paper box, and the plastic around the box—none of which is recyclable!"

GROUPS THAT GET IT TOGETHER

Getting people in your community to agree on ways to improve the environment isn't always easy, but it *can* be done. Here are some ideas.

- Every Saturday, citizens in Boulder, Colorado, need only look at the nearest stop sign to find out if it's time to recycle. That's where the "Eco-Cycle Pickup" notices are conveniently posted.

  "In 1979 we divided the city into four sections, and each Saturday we'd pick up from a different section," says Eric Lombardi, executive director of Eco-Cycle. The pickups are done with a fleet of old yellow schoolbuses.

- In Oklahoma City, community leaders created a tree-planting program called Putting Down Roots.

  It's a four-way cooperative effort, according to Sydney Dobson, executive director of Oklahoma City Beautiful. The Oklahoma City Planning Department initiated the program; eight local nurseries provide customers with discounts; the Oklahoma City Beautiful organization advises homeowners and businesses on tree selection and care; and a neighborhood alliance keeps all the records. The result: During 1990 and 1991, more than 25,000 trees were planted in Oklahoma City!

- A grade school composting program in Alcott Elementary School in Concord, Massachusetts, produced 7 tons of compost in just one year.

  After lunch, 380 first- to fifth-graders stop at a trolley to distribute leftovers from their trays and lunches into five bins. Meat or fish scraps are picked up three times a week, while other biodegradable food waste and soiled paper is composted in outdoor tumblers and wire bins. Plastic trays and cutlery are recycled. Only the milk cartons and aluminum foil go to the dump.

- Mandatory curbside recycling, a concept before its time in 1981, was quickly embraced by 12,000 pioneers in Woodbury, New Jersey.

  That's because town residents were threatened with a $500 fine if they didn't comply. "Normally we give homeowners one chance," says Woodbury councilman Donald Sanderson. "If upon inspection, they're in violation, we send them a letter and they usually say, 'Well, gee, I forgot' or 'I'm new in town.' "

  That letter is enough: During the program's first ten years of operation, no resident was fined for a second violation. During that decade, Woodbury's recycling program diverted about 52 percent of waste from the garbage bin into the recycling container.

Reservations for Your Leftovers

"Community organizations will take food left over from conferences or big catered parties," says Gelb.

If you're planning an event where you might have leftover food, call an organization *before* the event so leftover foods can be picked up afterward.

Scoop Your Way to Conservation

You can usually get around all kinds of packaging if you join a co-op where products are bought and distributed in bulk. And there's another bonus—savings to the consumer.

"We have 105 different herbs that people just come and help themselves to, 7 different kinds of rice, 13 varieties of beans, and numerous snack items," says Robin Clement, general manager of Felene Whole Foods Co-Op in Media, Pennsylvania.

At Felene Whole Foods, members pay between 32 and 49 percent above cost. Nonmembers pay 64 percent. "A nonworking member would save about $13 off street price if they're spending $70 to $100 here," says Clement.

To find existing co-ops in your area, look in the yellow pages under Consumer's Cooperative Organizations.

Research Life Expectancy before Buying

Toasters, alarm clocks, radios, and cameras are small appliances that are apt to break down. When they do, advises Caroline Gelb, an environmental specialist, the best thing you can do is fix them.

"When people are buying these items in the first place, they should do research to find out what's the most durable brand and how easy it will be to have it repaired." This will save consumers money in the long run, according to Gelb, because "you're not going to have to throw the item away as you would a piece of junk that costs $50 less."

Outdoor Ecology

Leaving a Cleaner Campsite

Campers, mountain-climbers, and backpackers should all be aware of campsite "ethics," says Jackie Johnson Maughan, coauthor of *Hiking the Backcountry: A Do-It-Yourself Guide for the Adventurous Woman.*

"Pack out everything that you bring in," says Maughan. "This includes cigarette butts, tinfoil, bottle tops, eggshells, orange peels, and used sanitary napkins."

THE SPORTING LIFE, LOW-IMPACT STYLE

True, we're all entitled to our bit of fun, but the fact is, some forms of outdoor sports are a bit kinder to the environment than others.

Here's a short list of sports with a high environmental impact, and some low-impact alternatives.

High-Impact Sports	Low-Impact Alternatives
Dirt-biking	Skateboarding, hiking, running, kite-flying
Jet-skiing	Surfboarding
Motorboating	Sailing, rowboating, canoeing, windsurfing
Motorcycle-riding	Bicycling
Snowmobiling	Downhill skiing, tobogganing, snowshoeing, cross-country skiing

The Cold Coals Test

After you've put out a campfire, make sure the coals are cold and the campsite is restored to its original condition.

"When you're breaking camp, make sure you can touch the coals with your bare hands," says Maughan. Then scatter the remains and place needles or leaves over the bare spot.

Dishwashing—Out of the Main Stream

Never bathe or wash dishes in a water source, says Maughan. If you're camping near a lake or stream, go ahead and dip water out of the source, but do your washing elsewhere.

The camping expert recommends using a large pot or washbasin as a sink—and washing with plain hot water. (If you have to use soap, make sure it's biodegradable.) After cleaning, dump the "gray water" far away from any water source.

Don't Dump on the High Seas

Prepare to be fined if you dump sewage or boat waste overboard within 3 miles of the U.S. coast. Jay Tanski, extension specialist for the New York Sea Grant Extension Program in Stony Brook, New York, recommends first and foremost using on-shore restroom facilities to solve the problem of human waste disposal.

The next best thing is to use a marina that has a pump-out station, as marked in local boating guides. The *least* acceptable alternative, according to Tanski, is an on-board sewage treatment system.

Past Performance

SANITARY PRACTICES SPAN 2 MILLION YEARS

As long as there have been people, there has been garbage.

"The first nomads tossed their garbage far away from their huts and moved on when it got too deep," says William Rathje, an archeologist and professor of anthropology at the University of Arizona in Tucson.

This worked out well, he said, until people began to farm.

"The first garbage crisis probably occurred around 6000 B.C. when settlers had to decide what to do with their mounting garbage. Eventually they carried it off to a midden—a dump!—situated downwind, just outside the village," says Rathje.

Anything that was left around the village was usually consumed by the wild pigs. (This led to the domestication of pigs.)

"With the emergence of the first large cities in 3000 B.C. in the Near East, scavengers began to pick up garbage. It was understood that the scavengers had the right to keep and sell anything that they found."

With the Industrial Revolution, garbage took a squalid leap, due to factory discards and the refuse from close workers' quarters. City governments were forced to clean up.

By 1894, a systematized street cleaning and refuse removal system was introduced in New York City by Colonel George E. Waring, Jr.

"Since then, cleanup has become a municipal responsibility," says Rathje.

Little Drops Add Up to a Big Spill

One quarter-teaspoon of spilled oil will create a film covering 2,000 square feet of water, according to a study by the Tri-State Sea Grant Program of New York, New Jersey, and Connecticut.

To prevent oil spills from small boats, Tanski suggests using bilge pillows. Made of an absorbent material, they're put inside the hull to soak up small gas or oil spills. "That way, you prevent any gas or oil from being pumped out with the water in the bilge," says Tanski.

To prevent spills from overfilled gas tanks, Tanski recommends installing a gas gauge.

But running any power boat means more water pollution. So why not take the next step—get a sailboat!

Are You Sure You Need Grass?

If you're tired of watering, mowing, and fertilizing grass—and you don't want to spray for pests—there probably *is* a better way.

It's called xeriscaping.

"The xeriscape alternative is to use paving stones, brick, and mulched beds in combination with ground covers, shrubs, plants, and trees that thrive naturally in the region," says Kathryn Boone, manager of the Native Plant Nursery at the Sanibel Captiva Conservation Foundation in Sanibel, Florida.

Boone suggests contacting an agricultural service, plant society, or botanical garden in your locale to find out which native plants flourish in your area.

Gifts to the Earth

Donating gifts of cash, stocks, bonds, or real estate to nonprofit organizations that preserve endangered plant and animal species can benefit not only the organization but the donor as well, according to Gregory Edwards, planned giving officer of The Nature Conservancy in Arlington, Virginia.

According to Edwards, "The Nature Conservancy has a Planned Giving Program where supporters can make a donation and receive income during their lifetime (see "Planned Giving Strategy" on page 386). After their lifetime, the principal can be used by the Conservancy to help protect critical natural areas. "This type of gift-giving is particularly popular with older donors," says Edwards.

Other organizations that may have similar programs include The Wilderness Society, the Sierra Club, and the National Wildlife Federation.

Wiggling out of the Food Waste Dilemma

Adding food wastes to the compost heap can attract pests such as rodents and flies.

"In Seattle we tell people to either bury food and pet wastes under at least 8 inches of soil or use a worm composter," says Woestendiek.

To make a worm composter:
1. Make a wooden box out of plywood, or use an old drawer with a tight-fitting lid.
2. Fill the composter with shredded leaves or newspaper.
3. Stock it with red worms (purchased from a bait shop).

4. After that, you can add kitchen food waste such as vegetable and bread scraps, coffee grounds, and tea bags.

A 2-by-4-foot worm bin will hold an average of 8 pounds of food scraps a week. Other food wastes such as meat, bones, fish, cheese, or butter should not be put in the worm composter, according to Woestendiek. Instead, these items can go in a garbage disposal or be thrown out.

A sturdy box with a tight-fitting lid becomes a "worm bin." The best worms for composting are red worms, also known as red wrigglers or manure worms.

FYI

PLANNED GIVING STRATEGY

How can you donate money to an earth-helping cause and still receive an income from the donation during your lifetime?

Here's an example provided by The Nature Conservancy, which encourages such contributions through its Planned Giving Program.

Mrs. Bond, age 67, holds ten New York State tax-exempt bonds with a total fair market value of $55,652. She donates these bonds to a life income arrangement. Through this arrangement, she continues to receive the $5,504 in tax-exempt income produced by these bonds each year. In addition, under current tables, she receives an income tax deduction of $18,949 the year she makes the gift. This "shelters" $18,949 of ordinary income from taxation.

Do-It-Yourself Composting Bins

Ordinary wood and wire are the easiest materials to use in making your own compost receptacle, says Carl Woestendiek, project manager for the Backyard Composting Program in the city of Seattle.

For a wire mesh bin, use inexpensive chicken wire. Sturdier, 3-foot-square homemade bins can be constructed of pressure-treated wood and hardware cloth.

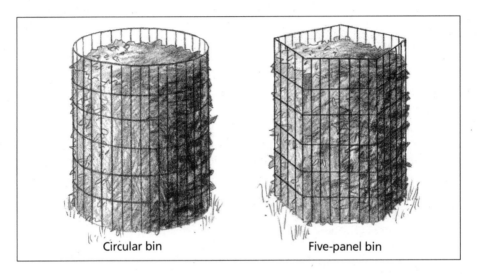

Circular bin   Five-panel bin

With wire mesh composting bins, you can compost moderate amounts of yard wastes such as leaves and grass clippings. Bins can be made of chicken wire or hardware cloth. To speed decomposition, use chopped materials, keep the piles moist, and turn them frequently. Covering the bins with plastic also speeds decomposition.

The Experts

Susan Alexander is vice president of communications for Green Seal, Inc., a nonprofit educational organization in Palo Alto, California. Green Seal issues environmental seals of approval for consumer products that meet strict environmental standards.

Brady Bancroft is a research associate at the Rocky Mountain Institute in Snowmass, Colorado, and an associate at the Solar Technology Institute. The Rocky Mountain Institute fosters the efficient and sustainable use of resources as a path to global security.

Jaime Bemis, author of "Composting Goes to School," is composting advisor for educational facilities in Concord, Massachusetts.

Kathryn Boone is manager of the Native Plant Nursery at the Sanibel Captiva Conservation Foundation in Sanibel, Florida.

Linda Brown is vice president of Scientific Certification Systems, Inc. (SCS), a company that independently evaluates product claims, in Oakland, California.

Robin Clement is general manager of Felene Whole Foods Co-Op in Media, Pennsylvania.

Sydney Dobson is executive director of Oklahoma City Beautiful, Inc., a nonprofit organization supported entirely by private donations and dedicated to improving the image of Oklahoma City.

Gregory Edwards is the planned giving officer of The Nature Conservancy in Arlington, Virginia.

Rodney Edwards is vice president of the Paperboard Group of the American Paper Institute in New York City.

Deborah M. Fanning is executive vice president of The Art and Craft Materials Institute in Boston, a nonprofit trade association of art and craft material manufacturers.

Colonel Leon Ferraez is national communications director with the Salvation Army National Headquarters in Alexandria, Virginia.

Ronald Fiskum is program manager in the Office of Building and Technology in the U.S. Department of Energy in Washington, D.C.

Caroline Gelb is a researcher for INFORM, Inc., a nonprofit environmental research and educational organization in New York City.

David Goldbeck, a writer and kitchen designer in Woodstock, New York, is the author of *The Smart Kitchen*.

Carl Grimm, an architect with Perkins and Will in New York City, is president of the New York Society of Architects.

Evelyn Haught is the public relations director for the Institute of Scrap Recycling Industries in Washington, D.C. The institute represents private recycling industries before Congress and state governments and conducts educational programs.

Willis Hengy is a representative of the Michigan Directory Company in Pigeon, Michigan.

Jackie Johnson Maughan is coauthor (with Ann Puddicombe) of *Hiking the Backcountry: A Do-It-Yourself Guide for the Adventurous Woman*.

Larry Jones is an environmental scientist for the Delaware Department of Natural Resources and Environmental Control in Dover, Delaware.

Robert Kourik is author of *Gray Water Use in the Landscape* and a member of the committee that developed the ordinance for the first legal use of gray water in the nation.

John Lippert is project supervisor of the Conservation and Renewable Energy Inquiry and Referral Service (CAREIRS) of the U.S. Department of Energy in Silver Spring, Maryland.

Eric Lombardi is the executive director of Eco-Cycle, Inc., a nonprofit recycling organization in Boulder, Colorado.

Dianne Odland is a nutritionist with the Human Nutrition Information Service at the U.S. Department of Agriculture in Hyattsville, Maryland.

William Rathje, an archeologist and professor of anthropology at the University of Arizona, Tucson, is the founder and director of the university's Garbage Project, a study of modern household garbage to see what people eat, drink, and recycle.

Sharon Rehder is an environmental engineer with the New York State Department of Environmental Conservation in Albany.

Betsy Rich is program director of the Environmental Shopping Program of the Pennsylvania Resources Council in Media, Pennsylvania.

Howard Russell heads the Insect Diagnostic Laboratory at Michigan State University in East Lansing.

Eugene Salerni, coauthor (with Allen Hershkowitz) of *Garbage Management in Japan*, is a principal in the consulting firm SS&B in Albany, New York.

Donald Sanderson is a city councilman in Woodbury, New Jersey.

Rena M. Shulsky is the founder and chairperson of Green Seal, Inc., in Washington, D.C.

Mark Simon is director of Alternative Fuels for the New York City Department of Environmental Protection.

Jay Tanski is an extension specialist for the New York Sea Grant Extension Program in Stony Brook, New York.

Joy Williams is community assistance director of the Environmental Health Coalition of San Diego, California.

Carl Woestendiek is project manager for the Backyard Composting Program in Seattle, Washington.

INDEX

Note: Page references in **boldface** indicate illustrations.